George Washington Grayson and the Creek Nation 1843–1920

The Civilization of the American Indian Series

George Washington Grayson and the Creek Nation 1843–1920

MARY JANE WARDE

University of Oklahoma Press
Norman

This book is published with the generous assistance of The Kerr Foundation, Inc.

"The Old Council House," by George Reilley Hall, is from the May 13, 1935, issue of the *Oklahoma City Times.* © 1935 Oklahoma Publishing Company, reprinted by permission.

Library of Congress Cataloging-in-Publication Data

Warde, Mary Jane, 1944–
    George Washington Grayson and the Creek nation, 1843–1920 / by
Mary Jane Warde.
       p.   cm. — (The Civilization of the American Indian series;
v. 235)
    Includes bibliographical references and index.
    ISBN 0-8061-3160-8 (cloth: alk. paper)
    1. Grayson, G. W. (George Washington), 1843–1920. 2. Creek
Indians—Biography.   3. Creek Indians—Politics and government.
4. Creek Indians—Cultural assimilation. I. Title. II. Series.
E99.C9G78   1999
976'.6004973'0092—dc21
   [B]   99-23667
                                                  CIP

George Washington Grayson and the Creek Nation, 1843–1920, is Volume 235 in The Civilization of the American Indian Series.

Text design by Gail Carter.

The paper in this book meets the guidelines for permanence and durability of the Committee on Production Guidelines for Book Longevity of the Council on Library Resources, Inc. ∞

1 2 3 4 5 6 7 8 9 10

Contents

Illustrations

PHOTOGRAPHS

MAPS

Preface

George Washington Grayson is a biographer's dream. He lived a very full public and private life, which was amply recorded in his personal papers, territorial newspapers, the Creek National Records, and federal documents relating to the Indian Territory and early Oklahoma. To find so much documentation related to, let alone written by, an American Indian of his day is quite a rare and valuable occurrence.

Even more valuable are Grayson's daily journals covering the critical period in the affairs of the Creek Nation from 1898 to 1917. I had the opportunity to study them briefly and found them extraordinary in their content, perspective, and frankness. They reveal him as a man with human virtues and human flaws; he was an ambitious, sometimes opportunistic, and occasionally vindictive politician who could verbally flay even close friends and associates in his private writings. He was a racist with contempt for both blacks and whites. He was a convivial host and friend who valued his private time with his family and his library. He was a devoted husband in spite of his long absences and a loving father who frustrated and was frustrated by his children. But the journals also validate the persona Grayson projected through his public writings and actions, that of a man proud of his accomplishments and his successful negotiation of the white world, but emotionally and intellectually dedicated to the Creek Nation.

Unfortunately, even though fragments of the journals have been published previously, some of Grayson's heirs are reluctant to make them public. In accordance with their wishes, I have used only excerpts previously quoted in published material.

Grayson as a topic of discussion presents a terminological mine field. The stickiest issue has been how to classify him, a person indisputably Creek in identity, yet among whose ancestors numbered, in three recorded previous generations, at least as many Anglo-Europeans as Indians. Since I first became acquainted with Wash Grayson in 1981, historians, particularly the ethnohistorians who have come to dominate American Indian history, have sought to replace terms historically used to describe Indians if those terms stemmed from ethnocentric or outdated concepts. While this is an admirable goal that seeks to do Indians long-delayed justice, it creates some real problems if one attempts to see and describe the world through the eyes of a historical figure. For example, was Wash Grayson a *Muskogee*—the traditional name—or a *Creek*—the name applied by Euro-Americans? He used the terms interchangeably, as the Muscogee (Creek) Nation does today, and I have done likewise.

More important in this study is the use of the terms *mixed-blood* and *full-blood*. When they first came into contact with Europeans and for several generations afterward, Muskogees had no concept of race. Any child of a Muskogee mother was also Muskogee, sharing her town and clan affiliations. But as will be briefly described in the introductory chapter, descent became increasingly important in the late eighteenth century, when unions between Europeans and Muskogees resulted in children with ties to both nationalities and cultures. While these children were still *este Mvskoke*, "Muskogee people," in Creek country, among Euro-Americans, based on European racial concepts, they were mixed-blood, as opposed to full-blood, Indians. Their dual affiliation was important then and became even more important later, because given their home environments, they were often in a position to understand the cultures of both parents and act as cultural brokers. At the same time, as a subgroup of the Muskogee people they were frequently responsible for the introduction and incorporation of European concepts, lifeways, and technologies into Muskogee culture. By the early nineteenth century, operating from a position of power as cultural brokers, they exerted strong influence over

Lower Creek life and politics, exemplified best, perhaps, by the McIntosh family.

This Muskogee subgroup remained important in Wash Grayson's day. As will be shown, he became a prime example of the subgroup of Indians that Anglo-Americans designated mixed-bloods. Although the terminology was based on a faulty belief that culture could be transmitted genetically, or by "blood," by the time of Grayson's birth in 1843, the terms *mixed-blood* and *full-blood* had real meaning on both sides of the cultural boundary. To deny that they did, to attempt to replace them with the less value-laden term *biracial* or *bicultural* or to disregard an individual's ancestry completely is to ignore some important historical facts and dynamics, along with the broadening scope of Muskogee identity.

Grayson's extant documentation makes clear that he and his Creek contemporaries understood and used the terms *mixed-blood* and *full-blood* deliberately. Although the terms originally referred to Creek people of white and/or black descent, by the late 1800s they had much less to do with blood quantum or ancestry. Grayson stated then that there were three "classes" of Creeks—mixed-bloods, full-bloods, and freedmen. He and his Creek contemporaries used these terms to categorize Creek citizens according to their life-style, political views, and perspective on what was best for the Creek people: Full-bloods clung to the old ways, mixed-bloods were more amenable to innovations, and freedmen were the Creeks' former slaves, reluctantly tolerated as Creek citizens. By then Creeks had developed a concept of race, discriminating between *este hvtke* (white people), *este lvste* (black people), and themselves, *este cate* (red people). Even among the *este cate*, Creeks held that there was a clear difference between the members of the "Five Civilized Tribes"—the Creeks, Choctaws, Chickasaws, Cherokees, and Seminoles—and the "wild Indians."

I have stepped into the mine field, attempting to use the terminology Grayson used and understood in the way that he and his contemporaries used and understood it. Although some may object with good reason to the use of the terms *Five Civilized Tribes, mixed-blood,* and *full-blood* as ethnocentric and inaccurate, the International Council of the Five Civilized Tribes still meets in Oklahoma on a regular basis to discuss issues of mutual importance. And ironically, just when we have begun searching for less sensitive and misleading terms than those referring to "blood" as an indication of Indian identity, tribal membership has come to be established by degree of ancestry. A citizen of the Muscogee (Creek) Nation today must be at least one-quarter Creek. DNA analysis from blood tests has recently come into use as the most accurate means of determining Indian descent.

Some may be offended, with reason, by my including in four quotations the derogatory term *nigger*. This was done to demonstrate Creek (and in one case, Anglo-American) racial prejudice toward American blacks. Particularly after the Civil War such prejudice was an important factor in Creek social and political behavior. To delete or launder these statements would be to overlook an important irony: Grayson condemned racial injustice toward the Indian, but, as will be shown, he and his Creek contemporaries regarded and behaved toward their freedmen citizens with casual scorn. While this word was in his vocabulary, it is not in mine.

Grayson demonstrated similar disdain for Anglo-Americans, frequently speaking of them collectively as "the white man." At other times, Grayson and his Indian contemporaries showed their familiarity with the current racial theories by speaking of Anglo-Americans as "Anglo-Saxons."

As for the less inflammatory concepts of "progress" and "civilization," Grayson knew that his people and other Indians possessed functioning religious, social, economic, and political systems long before the arrival of the Europeans. When he spoke of the Creeks' need to become "civilized" in the late 1800s, he spoke as a Creek nationalist, as this study will show. He had in mind a specific strategy for reaching his goal, a far different goal than that envisioned by the federal government and many "friends of the Indian." If preserving Creek sovereignty meant adapting Creek culture to the ways of the *este hvtke*, so be it—Creeks would be "civilized" on their own terms, walking a path of development that paralleled but did not converge with that of Anglo-Americans.

Lastly, I have generally called Grayson's first language *Muskogee*, as he did, although he sometimes spoke of it as *Creek* or *the Indian*. That language is complex and strange to ears accustomed to English. It is a living language, and to date there is no standard orthography. One often finds variations in spelling and pronunciation, which bother Creeks much less than anyone else. The greatest leap from English to Muskogee is to learn to pronounce *v* as "uh" and *r* as "thl." After that, transforming *c* to "ch," *p* to "b," *k* to "g," and *i* to "ay" is relatively simple. I have chosen to provide English-equivalent pronunciations of names and words for the convenience of the English-speaking reader. It should be noted that plural forms of nouns are rare in Muskogee; the reader will recognize the occasional plural in the *-vlke* ending.

Creeks had equal difficulty pronouncing and spelling English names, so that *Kennard* might also be spelled *Canard* and *Kennaird*. Likewise, the surname of Wash Grayson's Scots ancestor was *Grierson*. By the period of Indian Removal, the name had been modified to *Grayson*, and I have so called family members as they trekked west to the Indian Territory. In the Creek National Records, however, in Muskogee passages it was spelled Kelesen, and the most prominent bearer of the name was "Wasenten Kelesen," George Washington Grayson. In cases in which a name might have had one or more spellings historically, I have included alternate spellings in parentheses.

A segment on the boomer movement (see chapter 5) formed the basis of "Fight for Survival: The Indian Response to the Boomers," published in *The Chronicles of Oklahoma*, 67 (Spring 1989): 30–51. And some of the material on the Civil War was included in "'Holding Our Family Together': The Civil War Experience of the Creek Graysons," published in *Proceedings, War and Reconstruction in the Indian Territory: A History Conference in Observance of the 130th Anniversary of the Fort Smith Council, September 14–17, 1995* by the National Park Service at the Fort Smith Historic Site, the Oklahoma Historical Society, and the Arkansas Historical Association, 1996, and "'Now the Wolf Has Come': The Civilian Civil War in the Indian Territory," published in *The Chronicles of Oklahoma* 71 (Spring 1993): 64–87.

In researching and writing this biography, I owe more than I can ever repay to a number of people. Dr. W. David Baird first introduced me to Wash Grayson. Bill Welge at the Oklahoma Historical Society Archives and Manuscripts Division and John Phillips in Government Documents at the Oklahoma State University library were unfailingly helpful.

Others provided intangible but no less valuable aid. Myra Alexander-Starr and her family introduced me to the community of Creek Baptists. Dorothy Follansbee, Lela Whittaker, Kittye McIntosh Stafford, and

Mildred Fuller Ewens (who remembered strolling through the garden with Grandfather Grayson and Mr. Swanton from the Smithsonian) brought early twentieth-century Eufaula, Oklahoma, alive over lunch on several occasions. Colonel David Grayson ("Tod") Hansard (U.S. Army, retired), Mary Hansard Knight, Harold O. Hoppe, and his family kindly loaned me Grayson family materials. Dr. L. G. Moses took me through the final stages of the first version; Dr. Michael Green read and commented on a revision. My greatest debt I owe to Dr. Clyde Ellis, who was my primary editor, sounding board, and cheerleader. None of them should be held responsible for any errors I may have made.

Introduction

George Washington Grayson was a frontier merchant, livestock dealer, rancher, town builder, amateur linguist, and newspaper publisher. He was also a Muskogee, or Creek, Indian nationalist, dedicated to defending the sovereignty of the Creek Nation. College-educated and trained in traditional Muskogee ways, he understood both the Creek and the Anglo-American worlds. As a diplomat and member of the Creek National Government for nearly sixty years, he acted as a cultural broker, interpreting for the Creeks the language, policies, and demands of Anglo-Americans. Simultaneously, he reminded the federal government of its treaty obligations to the Creek Nation and presented the Creek perspective on federal Indian policies, legislation, and administration. Throughout the last half of the nineteenth century, Grayson urged the Creek people to adopt the educational, economic, religious, and political systems of the Anglo-American majority. This study examines Grayson's Creek identity and intense Creek nationalism, his role as a cultural broker, and his motivation for advocating cultural change.

The study of Grayson's life offers opportunities to explore several areas of current research in addition to Grayson's brand of Creek nationalism. First, to understand the man and his perspective, the biographer must take a fresh look at Creek history. Grayson's life spanned nearly eight decades, and he witnessed or participated in every event affecting the

Creek Nation from the aftermath of Indian Removal through tribal dissolution and the Creeks' transition to U.S. citizenship. His traditional education and political career gave Grayson a strong sense of his people's history and his place in it. Although some periods of Creek history have been reexamined recently by ethnohistorians, the last full treatment was Angie Debo's 1941 classic, *The Road to Disappearance: A History of the Creek Indians.* While this study is not intended to recount Creek history as a whole, the duration of Grayson's involvement in national affairs, well past Debo's stopping point at tribal dissolution, necessitates extensive coverage of Creek history as well as the breaking of new ground.

Second, a biography of Grayson, in the third Anglo-Muskogee generation of his family, offers a case study in ethnicity. Karen I. Blu's *The Lumbee Problem: The Making of an American Indian People* (1980) points out that American Indian communities identify and categorize their members according to their own markers, in a system very different from the "blood quantum" utilized by the federal government in Grayson's day and currently in use among many modern tribal governments. The scope of Indian identity and the means by which a man of Grayson's ancestry and life-style fits into an American Indian community is quite relevant today, when "Indianness," particularly that of members of the historically-designated Five Civilized Tribes, is much debated.

Blu also addresses the means by which the Lumbees adjusted their culture and ethnicity to fit their times. The third opportunity present in a biography of Grayson is, likewise, a case study of cultural change and cultural persistence. James H. Merrell's *The Indians' New World: Catawbas and Their Neighbors from European Contact through the Era of Removal* (1989) describes how the Catawbas managed to survive on their side of the Anglo-Indian frontier through successive renaissances, adapting as much as they needed or wanted of Anglo-European ways in order to retain their tribal identity. Similarly, in *When Indians Became Cowboys: Native Peoples and Cattle Ranching in the American West* (1994), Peter Iverson describes how various tribes repeated a historic pattern by reinterpreting and revising their cultures during the reservation period through the vehicle of cattle ranching. This study will demonstrate that Grayson, a Creek nationalist and a proponent of cultural change that he defined as "progress," encouraged his fellow Creeks—neighbors of the Catawbas in the East as well as in the Indian Territory and enthusiastic ranchers—to use the same survival technique.

Lastly, Grayson stands as a prime example of the cultural broker, who—as Margaret Connell Szasz puts it in *Between Indian and White Worlds: The Cultural Broker* (1994)—occupies a valuable but sometimes dangerous position linking and reconciling two disparate peoples, that "middle ground" described by Richard White in *The Middle Ground: Indians, Empires, and Republics in the Great Lakes Region, 1650–1815* (1991). It was a position that Grayson occupied by choice long after other leaders of his generation stepped aside, leaving individual Creeks to fend for themselves. It was a post in which he often served as an intermediary and a rear guard, the latter a duty with which he was very familiar.

The important thing to remember is that George Washington Grayson—merchant, livestock dealer, rancher, town builder, amateur linguist, and newspaper publisher—was also *Yaha Tustunuggee*, "Wolf Warrior." He earned his war name in his early manhood, while defending the Creek Nation during two years' hard campaigning with the Confederate Second Creek Mounted Volunteers. He valued being a *tvsekiyv*, "one who has received his war name," because it symbolized his lifelong ties and obligations to his Muskogee community. He understood that true patriotism sometimes meant going to war. More often in his experience it meant representing Creek interests at Senate hearings, explaining federal regulations to people who spoke only Muskogee, and being a living example to both Creeks and Anglo-Americans of what he described as the "progressive" Indian.

*George Washington Grayson
and the Creek Nation
1843–1920*

Like true patriots and true men, we battled long and well in the unequal contest finally losing out.

GEORGE WASHINGTON GRAYSON, C. 1912

CHAPTER ONE

Driven up the Red Waters

To be born a Creek in 1843 was to be born to a heritage of pride and bitterness, resilience and adaptability. That was the heritage of George Washington Grayson, "a Muscogee Indian by blood," as he described himself, "born and reared in their midst,"[1] in the Creek Nation, Indian Territory. It was a heritage that included a history he considered distinguished, values he believed noble, and a dynamic culture responsive to the demands of changing times—the foundation of a Creek nationalism that motivated him to serve the Creek people as a cultural broker for nearly six decades.

In the late nineteenth and early twentieth centuries, Grayson experienced events that modified Creek culture at an unprecedented rate, while federal policies propelled his people toward the American mainstream. Perhaps as well as any Creek citizen of his day, Grayson understood the demand for and ramifications of cultural change. Until the 1890s, he sought to encourage the social, economic, and political innovations that might allow his people to maintain their status as a sovereign nation. Thereafter, he attempted to retard and moderate changes he viewed as pernicious. Through it all, he clung tenaciously to his Muskogee heritage and identity.

Those who observed Wash Grayson's physical appearance, affiliations, and life-style sometimes missed his strong identification as a Muskogee

George Washington
Grayson about 1917.
Courtesy Western
History Collections,
University of Oklahoma
Library.

Indian. He acknowledged that he was at least three-quarters Scots and
Scots-Irish by descent. A 1908 Bureau of American Ethnology photograph
showed Grayson at sixty-five: a dignified gentleman with a pale, smallpox-
pitted complexion, a neat white beard, an uncompromising dark gaze
behind gold-framed spectacles, a starched collar, and a Windsor tie.
Penciled on the back of the photograph was the note, "Shows no trace of
Indian blood."[2]

Yet his daughter Eloise, who certainly knew his antecedents, remembered her father as a "full-blood" Creek.[3] This was surely an assessment of
the heart and spirit rather than ancestry, but it accurately reflected
Grayson's sincere commitment to his people. He knew who he was: He
was a Muskogee Indian.

What accounted for that firm sense of Muskogee identity and ardent Creek nationalism in a man outwardly so non-Indian? Initially it was based on his traditional education and acceptance by the Muskogee people as one of their own. Then a set of fortunate circumstances provided him valuable skills at the time the Creek Nation needed them most, giving him a place of honor among them. But his Muskogee identification also rested on an ingrained dislike of Anglo-Americans garnered from history and personal experience.

His respect for his Muskogee heritage was evident in his last days, which he spent striving to preserve Muskogee language and history. About 1917 Grayson began writing a history of the Creeks from their perspective, a project that he said was inspired by "a true and sympathetic interest in a people who, prior to their contamination resulting from association with other races and people, were the true embodiment in its pristine beauty and purity of all that is embraced in the terms patriotism, bravery, integrity and many of the other virtues approved of in other peoples by our present Christian civilization."[4] As Creeks entered the new century as American citizens, he attempted to collect the oral traditions entrusted to the elders, but, he wrote sadly, it was already too late. Most of those who knew the old ways and Muskogee history were already gone. When ill-health forced him to put the work aside, he redirected his energies, opening his home and his knowledge of the Creeks to early anthropologists and ethnologists and facilitating their research into the Muskogee language and culture.[5]

Their composite findings presented a people who perceived themselves as unique, as was common among American Indians. In pre-Columbian times this distinctive identity included even their close neighbors to the north, the Iroquoian Cherokees, and to the west, the Choctaws and Chickasaws, who spoke Muskogee dialects. By about 1800 the Seminoles had drifted away from the main Muskogee population to become their neighbors to the south. Muskogee oral tradition spoke of an origin far to the west and a migration across the Mississippi River to the southeastern United States. Eventually the Muskogee forebears made their home in today's Georgia and Alabama, ranging at times into Tennessee, South Carolina, and Florida. What set them apart among the southeastern tribes was their political organization, which anthropologist Edward H. Spicer judged the most significantly developed among any people north of Mexico, with the possible exception of the Iroquois Confederacy.[6]

Unlike the Iroquois, who were a cooperative grouping of related tribes, the Creeks based their political structure on a system of *tvlwv* (pronounced "duhlwuh"), or ceremonial towns. Four towns constituted the early nucleus of the Creek confederacy—Kusseta, Koweta (Grayson's town), Abeka, and Tuckabachee. Over time, other tribes and tribal remnants gravitated to the Muskogee core and were absorbed into the loose confederation. This process probably accelerated with the sixteenth-century advent of the Europeans and the alien viruses that produced devastating epidemics among native peoples. The confederacy offered refuge and security to tribes decimated by enemies or disease. Eventually the confederacy incorporated Muskogee speakers, such as the Hillabees, Alabamas, and Tuskegees, as well as non–Muskogee speakers—Shawnees, Natchez, Catawbas, and Yuchees. One historian attributed the nineteenth-century Creeks' unusual international outlook to this pattern of tribal adoption.[7]

The concept of a town was complex enough to warrant two Muskogee words: *talofa* denoted the physical location of a village or village cluster while *tvlwv* implied the more important internal political and ceremonial organization of the villagers. The number of *tvlwv* varied as peoples joined and left the confederacy and as large towns subdivided. By 1790 there were about fifty Creek towns; in Grayson's day they still numbered more than forty. Heredity and tradition tied the members of a *tvlwv* together, and membership descended matrilineally. Each town adopted Muskogee as one of its languages and agreed to abide by Muskogee laws and traditions, but it retained its autonomy and identity. All members of a *tvlwv* recognized their particular ceremonial ground—or "square ground" because of its shape—with its contiguous public structures as their focal point. Here the ceremonial fire burned, custodians kept sacred objects, and members carried out social, religious, and political activities.[8]

The town king, or *mekko*, met with his council of advisors and warriors at the square ground each morning. The warriors, or *tvstvnvkkvlke*, served in peacetime as police, enforcing the law and punishing offenders. The polite, grave discussions in council reflected the Muskogee belief that maintaining order and harmony—politically, socially, environmentally, and religiously—was necessary to the welfare of the people. Consensus was important, and opinions deferred to the knowledge and experience that had been handed down through the generations. Courteous speech, including simple conversation, avoided any hint of imposing one's views on another. Leaders, chosen by consensus on the basis of their special abilities, were expected to be noncoercive and were held accountable for their actions. With these expectations guiding their proceedings, the *mekko* and his council allotted communal lands according to need, rendered judgments in disputes, and deliberated matters of local or national concern.[9]

The *mekko* introduced important topics to the council and delivered decisions to the people through the *yvtekv* (pronounced "yuhdekuh"), the speaker or interpreter. The southeastern Indians accorded these speakers status and honor for their skill. Among the most honored was the *horre hoponaya* (pronounced "hothlthlee hobonaya"), or war speaker, who traveled with the *mekko* on diplomatic missions, represented the interests of the people before foreigners, and conducted the actual negotiations. It was in the tradition of the *horre hoponaya*—an office modified and renamed "delegate" in the nineteenth-century Indian Territory—that Wash Grayson most often served the Creeks from the 1870s through the 1910s.[10]

Besides town membership, each Muskogee inherited through the maternal line membership in a clan. Clans extended across town lines, so that Grayson, a member of *Katcv* (pronounced "Kadchuh"), or Tiger clan, found fellow clan members in other *tvlwv* within the confederacy. Clan membership dictated the formality of a person's relationships with others and insured a secondary source of support beyond the extended family circle. Clan rules requiring exogamy defined suitable marriage partners and helped incorporate outsiders into Muskogee society. Clans also carried varying degrees of prestige, the highest being the *Hotvlkvlke* (pronounced "Hodulgulgee"), or Wind clan, which often supplied the leadership in a Creek town. But the Tiger clan, as Grayson informed anthropologist John Swanton, also ranked high. Though the importance of the clans declined somewhat after removal to the Indian Territory, they persisted, especially among traditional Muskogees. Grayson believed that as late as his own childhood in the 1840s, clan membership was often

more important than consanguinity. He was quite conscious of the obligations clan membership imposed and the relationships it supported; nor
did he willingly offend the sensibilities of those who still honored the clan
system. To this day, many Creeks and Seminoles in traditional settings
introduce themselves by clan and town.[11]

Some historians suggest that ultimate leadership over the confederacy
and, indeed, the confederacy itself were creations of the Europeans, who
came into contact with the Muskogees extensively in the seventeenth
century. Before that time confederacy-wide councils of *mekkvlke* and
advisors met periodically, but there was no centralized Muskogee government. When the intercolonial rivalry of Spain, France, and England
encroached on the Muskogee homeland, however, Europeans encouraged
the concept of a unified political structure. They helped elevate a
particular chief with whom they preferred to deal, naming him "king" of
the Muskogees. Over time the Cherokees, Choctaws, and Chickasaws
experienced a similar trend toward centralization of authority, culmin-
ating toward the 1820s in the formation of Anglo-American-style
constitutional republics.[12]

During the eighteenth century English deerskin traders working out
of the colonies of South Carolina and Georgia also exerted a growing
influence on Muskogee life and political organization. It was they who
began to call the Muskogees "Creeks," having given Hecheta (Hichita)
Town on the upper Ocmulgee River the name "Ochese Creek" and then
abbreviated it. The traders also began to distinguish between two group-
ings of Muskogees. From their perspective, the eastern-most towns, lying
along approximately seventy miles of the Chattahoochee River Valley
southward from present Eufaula, Alabama, were the "Lower Creeks."
Koweta emerged as the dominant Lower Creek town. To the west in the
valleys of the upper Alabama River and its tributaries, the Coosa and
Tallapoosa, lay the more populous "Upper Creek" towns with Tuckabachee being the preeminent *tvlwv*. The Lower Creeks were geograph-
ically more accessible to the Charleston and Augusta traders, while the
Upper Creeks maintained additional ties with the French and Spanish.
By the nineteenth century the Lower Creeks had more generally adopted
aspects of the Anglo-European life-style, adding a cultural component to
the dichotomy between the two Creek groups.[13]

Many historians have written of the devastating impact European contacts had on American Indians. The demand for objects of European manufacture transformed Muskogees from sedentary hunter-farmers into a nation of commercial hunters. The men ranged farther from home to find items, particularly slaves and deerskins, with which to purchase trade goods. Slaving expeditions led to frequent conflicts with neighboring tribes, and disorder increased as hunting parties spent long periods away from the authority of *tvlwv* elders. Addiction to the traders' rum increased. Items of European manufacture replaced domestic products, causing the abandonment of ancient skills and crafts. Most importantly, a series of epidemics, common to the Europeans but previously unknown to American Indians, struck the vulnerable southeastern native peoples with severe consequences. A Muskogee population extrapolated at two hundred thousand before the Europeans arrived on the continent had declined to about twenty thousand by the time Europeans actually visited their villages. All this terribly and undeniably disrupted Creek life.[14]

But there was a strong continuity as well, as the basic elements of Muskogee life persisted in spite of the alien impact. The elastic Muskogee confederacy testified to their lack of xenophobia. That they adopted the aspects of Anglo-European culture they found useful or desirable speaks strongly of the dynamic nature of Creek culture. This type of cultural change, described by Merrell with regard to the neighboring Catawbas, was probably replicated by many American native peoples as they came to share a frontier with Europeans.[15] The Muskogees possessed, as Cherokee-Quapaw Louis W. Ballard noted, the Indian's ability to take what could be used from other cultures and, in doing so, make it "Indian."[16]

At the same time proximity to European colonists resulted in Anglo-Muskogee children, as English and Scots traders found it both convenient and profitable to take Creek wives. These women, according to Muskogee custom, provided the traders access to Creek society and trade, as well as making available their deerskin processing skills. By the early nineteenth century, Muskogees named McGillivray, McIntosh, Perryman, Carr, Barnett (Barnard), Kennard (Kennaird, Canard), and Grierson (Grayson) were common. These were the *este hvtke hayv* ("white made people"), or mixed-blood Creeks, but they were accepted without question as *tvlwv* and clan members in that matrilineal society.[17]

Scholars agree that these children, often literate and with some knowledge of their fathers' languages and customs, became cultural brokers between the Europeans and the Muskogees. Perhaps they were building upon a native institution in the southeast by which tribes selected individuals who would learn the language and ways of neighboring peoples. These cultural brokers smoothed intertribal communications and served as advocates for their adopted tribes. In the eighteenth century the Muskogee sons of Charleston and Augusta traders often acted as brokers in commerce and diplomacy, running the trading posts and dealing with a people ever more dependent on European manufactured goods. Illiterate, often non-English-speaking Muskogees, less knowledgeable of European ways, depended on them for interpretation, advice, and written communication. These circumstances allowed Scots trader Lachlan McGillivray's son Alexander, a member of the Wind clan through his Franco-Muskogee mother, to rise to prominence among the Upper Creeks in the late 1700s. Similarly, Anglo-Muskogees William Weatherford and William McIntosh became men to reckon with in the early 1800s.[18]

Indians such as McGillivray, Weatherford, and McIntosh posed a problem for Anglo-Europeans who held strong views about racial differences and the inherent superiority of the white race. Muskogees, on the other hand, discerned no racial differences for several generations after European contact. Any child of a Muskogee mother was *este Mvskoke*, a Muskogee person, inheriting the mother's clan and town affiliation. Muskogee society did not force their Anglo-Muskogee progeny into political or social self-consciousness as outsiders; rather it accepted them and made use of their ability to act as cultural brokers with the white man. This was a very different situation from that faced by the Great Lakes metis, who became a separate people from both their maternal and paternal relatives.[19]

Nor was this group of Muskogees, in spite of their primary occupation as skin brokers, so bound to the trade for a livelihood as were the Great Lakes metis. Although southeastern Indians became reliant on European trade goods and turned to commercial hunting to finance their purchases, they lived in a region benevolent toward agriculture. Muskogees had been sedentary farmers with a communal land use system for centuries, and they did not abandon those agricultural traditions. Instead, by the time of the American Revolution, as the deer herds vanished and the skin trade declined, Muskogees sought new ways to finance the Anglo-American manufactured items on which they now relied. During two decades of tutelage and persuasion by Southern Indian Agent Benjamin Hawkins, Muskogees expanded traditional agricultural pursuits and adapted them to the example of neighboring whites. They turned to livestock raising— acquiring cattle, horses, hogs, chickens, and domestic geese. Traditions concerning slavery and adoption were modified as cotton production using African slave labor increased.[20]

Cultural mutations accompanied economic and agricultural changes, and these were often led by the Muskogee descendants of the Charleston and Augusta traders, particularly among the Lower Creeks. The switch from communal village farms to individual Anglo-European-style planta- tions and the acquisition of livestock and slaves began to create economic division among Muskogees. Traditionally Muskogees valued generosity and honored most the person who shared prosperity with others. However, the children of the traders frequently emulated their fathers in accumulating wealth, which they eventually bequeathed to their children.[21]

An indication of changing Muskogee views about property was that at his death in 1793, Alexander McGillivray left an estate that included sixty slaves, three hundred cattle, and numerous horses. William McIntosh was a plantation and slave owner as well as a rising political star of Koweta Town and the Lower Creeks by 1810. Wealth, kinship connections, and the skills necessary to cultural brokers allowed men such as McGillivray and McIntosh to become very important as the Anglo-European frontier pressed closer to the Muskogee homeland early in the nineteenth century. However, their rise to power caused some resentment among some more traditional Muskogees.[22]

Both of Wash Grayson's parents were members of this Muskogee subgroup. Little is known of his mother's ancestry other than her clan and *tvlwv*, but he traced his paternal ancestry back to the arrival of a great- grandfather in the Creek country just as the skin trade declined. Brothers Robert, James, Thomas, and William Grierson emigrated from Scotland in the early 1770s. Thomas settled among the Lower Creeks of Eufaula Town, married a Muskogee woman, fathered a son, and farmed five hundred acres on Little River near his brother James. A militiaman supporting the rebellious colonies, Thomas died about 1775. James Grierson became a colonel of the Loyalist militia and earned an infamous reputation during the Revolution. Robert Grierson settled among the Upper Creeks of Hillabee Town and married Sinnugee, a woman of the Spanulgee clan. In 1796 their children were Sandy (Alexander), Sarah (wife of Stephen Hawkins, a Muskogee), Watt (Walter), David, Eliza (a wife of William McIntosh), and William. Their youngest daughter, Katy, was the grandmother of Wash Grayson. Muskogees and their black slaves, troubled by the unfamiliar consonants and vowels of the Grierson name, modified it to "Grayson" within a generation or so.[23]

In 1796 newly appointed Southern Indian Agent Hawkins took up his duties in the Creek country. Although Hawkins judged most white men who married Muskogee women as worthless frontier drifters, he soon came to respect Robert Grierson. The industrious Scot was farming thirty acres and producing a variety of foodstuffs. He was also raising cotton and had hired a spinner to teach his womenfolk how to process the two thousand pounds of fiber he harvested annually. He owned three hundred cattle and thirty horses, as well as the forty slaves who worked his cotton fields. Although Grierson was a former Loyalist colonel, he impressed Hawkins as a reliable man and good citizen of the Creek country. Hawkins frequently visited the well-run Grierson home and consulted his host for information and aid with his official duties. More men like Grierson, Hawkins commented, would ease his task of preparing the Muskogees for eventual American citizenship.[24]

But the Red Stick War of 1813–1814 disrupted Grierson's pleasant and productive life in the Creek country. This disturbance was a facet of Tecumseh's attempt to create a new confederacy of the tribes that confronted Anglo-Americans across the frontier, from the Great Lakes to the Gulf Coast. About 1811 this Shawnee chief, son of a Muskogee mother, came to the southeastern tribes recruiting adherents to his confederacy. He also brought the unifying message of traditionalism and renewal proclaimed by The Shawnee Prophet, his brother.

Tecumseh found that the relatively powerful southeastern Indians had little in common with his beleaguered followers in the Old Northwest. In their strength they felt less threatened by the advancing whites. And according to one historian, they had already drifted too far into Anglo-American ways, the primary qualification for their subsequent historic designation, the Five Civilized Tribes.[25]

Only among the Muskogees did Tecumseh find adherents, known subsequently as "Red Sticks." One historian has suggested this faction was composed of those most resistant to change, particularly those who resented the shift in Creek government toward a constitutionalism based on the Anglo-American model, as demonstrated in the newly created National Council. Another has described the Red Sticks as "millenarians" intent on throwing off colonial ties symbolized by Anglo-American goods and ways. They demanded a return to ancient values in order to bring into being a new world.[26]

At any rate, the Red Stick rebellion escalated existing political factionalism into a Creek civil war that spilled over onto neighboring white settlers, most notably in the Fort Mims Massacre of August 30, 1813. News of the massacre electrified the frontier settlements of surrounding states and territories. Federal troops and state militia converged on the Creek country in a campaign that made Andrew Jackson of Tennessee a national hero. Lower Creek warriors led by Chief William McIntosh and Timpoochee Barnard joined white soldiers and Cherokee and Choctaw contingents in suppressing the Red Sticks. In 1813 and 1814 they swept through the Creek country, destroying Red Stick villages and driving fleeing tribespeople toward Tohopeka, known to the whites as Horseshoe Bend, on the Tallapoosa River. But their coming was too late to protect the Grierson family.[27]

As an article of faith the Red Sticks destroyed those things Muskogees had adopted from Anglo-Europeans and threatened to put to death everyone who would not join them. They targeted, among others, the Grierson family of Hillabee Town. Not only had they adopted more of the white man's ways than their neighbors, but Eliza Grierson was a wife of Chief McIntosh.[28] Robert Grierson, according to a letter of August 1813, "had all his negroes (73) and every eatable thing taken from him."[29] His daughter-in-law, a woman usually esteemed, had come to Okmulgee Town to teach the women there how to spin and weave. But the Red Sticks stripped her to her shift and stole her cattle and hogs. Two months later the Hillabees sent the elderly Robert Grierson to General Jackson with offers of peace. In spite of the general's immediate acceptance, a separate force of white troops destroyed the Hillabee villages, probably in reprisal for the Fort Mims Massacre. They killed sixty warriors and took two hundred and fifty prisoners. Surviving Hillabees fled to the Red Stick stronghold at Tohopeka. Aware of the strength of their enemies, the Red Sticks hoped for supernatural intervention and deliverance.[30]

But on March 27, 1814, Jackson's army overwhelmed the log breast-works and killed at least 557 defenders. Seventy survivors, most of them wounded, escaped the slaughter to join their women and children, hidden in a swamp downstream. Among them were brothers, Emathla Hutke and Tulwa Tustunuggee from Hillabee Town. They were the sons of Intakfapke, a Muskogee medicine man, and Mary Benson, a Scots-Irish captive adopted as a child by the Muskogees. Wounded nine times in the fight, Tulwa Tustunuggee survived because his brother carried him off the battleground under cover of darkness and hid him in the swamp. He recovered, but the bullets remained in his body, causing him great pain periodically for the rest of his life. Some time later he married Katy Grierson (Grayson) and shared her life as a well-to-do planter. But he never forgot Horseshoe Bend.[31]

Andrew Jackson's victory broke the back of the Red Stick rebellion, but it brought little good to other Muskogees. Even though Chief McIntosh had led Lower Creek warriors in Jackson's punitive campaign, the Treaty of Fort Jackson of 1814, which ended the war, penalized his Creek allies as well as hostile Red Sticks. The Muskogees ceded 22 million acres of land to the United States and made other major concessions before withdrawing to their remaining homeland in Alabama and Georgia. Federal agents estimated that friendly Creeks suffered property losses of nearly two hundred thousand dollars. Among them were the Griersons, who lost slaves and livestock during the rebellion. Their case was still in litigation decades later, and Congress did not make the final payment on their claims until 1853.[32]

Nor were the Muskogees left in peace in their remaining territory. Nationally the arguments for the removal of all eastern Indians to a reserve beyond the Mississippi River gathered force during the next two decades. That Georgia and Alabama coveted their remaining lands intensified the removal argument among Creeks. Most opposed the sale of any more land and refused removal to the West. Then, in 1824 the Creek National Council resisted all the blandishments of commissioners sent out from Washington to negotiate the sale of the Muskogee homeland in exchange for new lands in the proposed Indian Territory (reduced gradually to today's state of Oklahoma, excluding the Panhandle and old Greer County).[33]

But some southeastern Indians, believing that resistance was futile, were more amenable to removal. Already a colony of Cherokees lived in western Arkansas, the Choctaws had capitulated to eventual removal, and other hard-pressed Indians were migrating westward. Among the Creeks, Chief McIntosh emerged as the leader of the mainly Lower Creek pro-removal faction. McIntosh had used his oratorical ability and his membership in the Wind clan and Koweta *tvlwv* to become *horre hoponaya* for the Lower Creek towns. On his father's side, he was related to several well-placed men in the Georgia state government, including Governor George McIntosh Troup. Whether practicality or venality dictated McIntosh's actions in the ensuing negotiations is still debated, but by 1824 federal and state officials had identified him as the man with whom they could deal.[34]

Following the National Council's rejection of the 1824 negotiations, federal commissioners offered McIntosh a generous bonus for his acquiescence. In spite of a law of the council imposing the death penalty for an unauthorized sale of national land, McIntosh and a handful of Lower Creek followers with relatively little authority signed the Treaty of Indian Springs. It ceded all Muskogee lands in Georgia and the northern two-thirds of Muskogee lands in Alabama, principally territory occupied by the Upper Creeks.

Outraged, the National Council condemned McIntosh to death. On an April night in 1825, a party of some one hundred warriors surrounded his home. They allowed all noncombatants to leave, including McIntosh's sons Chilly, about twenty-one, and Daniel Newnan, about three years of age. The executioners then set fire to the house and shot McIntosh as he tried to escape. Within the next two days Muskogees executed Sam Hawkins, McIntosh's secretary, and some Hillabees also attempted to kill Sam's brother Ben. Both men were sons-in-law of Chief McIntosh and sons of Sarah Grierson Hawkins.[35]

These executions sent a wave of fear through the Creek country, especially among resident whites, even though the council explained that it was merely enforcing its own laws over its own citizens and that no general uprising was imminent. The executions also drew the attention of the John Quincy Adams administration, which rejected the McIntosh treaty before continuing negotiations with the council. Under intense pressure the Muskogees in 1826 and 1827 ceded their lands in Georgia. Parties of Muskogees, including some Lower Creek McIntosh supporters, began emigrating west in 1827 and 1828. Among them, traveling at their own expense up the Arkansas by riverboat and covered wagon, were a number of Anglo-Muskogee families—McIntoshes, Stidhams, Kennards, Harrods (Herods), and Graysons, including Katy and Tulwa Tustunuggee—with Katy's slaves. Those who stayed moved into the Alabama lands still held by the Upper Creeks, compacting the population and perhaps increasing their sense of Muskogee nationhood.[36]

The U.S. Congress and public did not give up on the goal of complete eviction, and the administration of Andrew Jackson was even more adamant that all Indians east of the Mississippi River be removed to the West. Attempting to remain in Alabama, on March 24, 1832, Muskogee representatives reluctantly signed a new treaty by which they agreed to abandon their traditional system of communal landholding and to accept allotment in severalty of their lands. Under the new system Muskogees could either farm individual holdings or take allotments in blocks near others of their *tvlwv* to continue traditional communal life. Either way, the federal government promised to protect them from white intrusion. After twenty sections of land were set aside for the support of Creek orphans, surplus acreage was to be opened for white settlement. The federal government, while not requiring Muskogee emigration to the West, encouraged it and offered incentives and subsistence for those who would go.[37] Included in the treaty was the guarantee: "The Creek country west of the Mississippi shall be solemnly guaranteed to the Creek Indians, nor shall any State or Territory ever have a right to pass laws for the government of such Indians, but they shall be allowed to govern themselves, so far as may be compatible with the general jurisdiction which Congress may think proper to exercise over them."[38]

But the signing of this treaty did not bring the Muskogees peace. A census soon began the unwelcome process of allotment. It showed a total of 14,142 Upper Creeks with 445 slaves; Lower Creeks numbered 8,552 with 457 slaves. Heads of families were to choose their allotments in expectation of receiving title in fee simple in five years, after which they could sell the land. But white intruders did not wait for the completion of the process. They swarmed into the Creek country, stealing stock, defrauding Creeks of their allotments, and generally harassing them. Protests against these conditions brought no relief. Gradually some Muskogees began to see the West as a place of refuge as well as exile. A few others fought back against the harassment, and a new "Creek War" broke out in 1836. Some tribesmen helped federal troops round up resisting Creeks, but beginning in 1836, the army forced both "hostile" Creeks and those who had cooperated to head west on the "Trail of Tears."[39]

According to oral tradition as well as federal government reports, the removal was not orderly. Rather, one survivor recalled, soldiers without warning forced families into overloaded wagons and delivered them to stockades, over which hung an "awful silence." There they awaited deportation for weeks or months. Then, one survivor recalled, "[t]imes became more horrible after the real journey was begun. Many fell by the wayside, too faint with hunger or too weak to keep up with the rest. . . . Death stalked at all hours, but there was no time for proper burying or ceremonies."[40] Another lamented, "I have no more land, I am driven away from home, driven up the red waters, let us all go, let us all die together." Die they did—of illness, of weariness, of despair, and of drowning when the steamboat *Monmouth* sank in the Mississippi River.[41]

In the Indian Territory the newcomers joined the Creek immigrants of 1827–1828, who had settled in the vicinity of Three Forks—the junction of the Grand, Verdigris, and Arkansas Rivers (near present-day Muskogee, Oklahoma). The Creek settlers of 1827–1828 had laid out new farms in the rich river bottoms and set up a government under the leadership of Roley (Roderick) McIntosh, William's younger half-brother.[42] Because the Cherokees also claimed the land on which the Creeks settled, in 1833 the two nations had reached a compromise and reset their boundaries. The Creeks retained the Arkansas River Valley roughly to the mouth of the Cimarron River near modern Tulsa, Oklahoma (see map 1). From

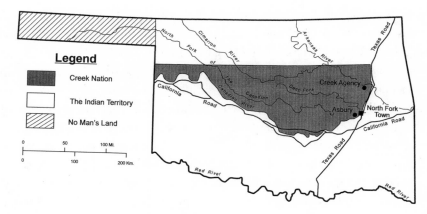

Map 1. The Creek Nation about 1850

there the northern boundary stretched west to the 100th meridian, in those days the Mexican line. To the south the Canadian River divided Creek lands from those of the immigrating Choctaws and Chickasaws. The new homeland was to be theirs in fee simple as long as the Creeks existed as a nation.[43]

The immigrants of 1836 met those of 1827–1828 with mutual hostility and apprehension. The earlier settlers included members of the Lower Creek McIntosh faction; the newcomers were his long-time antagonists and executioners. Circumstances beyond their control forced them to share the assigned Indian Territory lands. While the Lower Creeks generally occupied the Arkansas Valley, the Upper Creeks settled to the west and south, laying out new ceremonial grounds in the valleys of the Canadian River and its North Fork and lighting new *tvlwv* fires on the ashes brought from Alabama.[44]

Times remained extremely hard. The federal government fulfilled inadequately, if at all, its promise to provide subsistence to immigrating Creeks for one year. The immigrants threw up rough shelters and hunted with bows and arrows in the game-rich woodlands, but poverty, malaria, apathy, and other diseases of the body and spirit continued to debilitate and demoralize the nation for some time. Population losses in the next several years were appallingly high. The death rate was such that the Creek population dropped from the 22,694 enumerated in 1832 to only

13,537 in 1859, a decline of at least 40 percent even after twenty-seven years.[45]

Still the Creeks did not resign themselves to extinction. Their three hundred years of contact with Europeans and the even more traumatic, if shorter term, contact with the United States had left them with only a small fraction of their ancient strength. It had modified for better or worse their life-style and political organization. But many basic components of their culture were still quite viable. The dynamic character of Creek culture survived, and the town and clan structure still provided a sense of continuity and identity for the individual. Their agriculture was on a par with that of their white neighbors. Their new landbase was more than adequate for their needs and now included great expanses of natural prairie for grazing their livestock. Christian missionaries, who to this point had made a minimal impact on the Creeks, were eager to offer new hope, support, English education, and reinforcement of many traditional values. Creek experiences had elevated some leaders and suppressed others while factionalizing the tribe, but the old flexible confederacy system absorbed the shocks without crumbling.[46]

This is not to say that the Removal did not leave its legacy of bitterness. Decision making traditionally employed oratory that recalled ancient times, looked to their forefathers for guidance, and reviewed historic events as a means of reaching consensus. All Creeks who heard these deliberations knew who their people were, how powerful and respected they had been, and the calamities that had overtaken them. Around home fires, too, elders told the stories to children and grandchildren, teaching them their people's history along with the values and behavior expected of a Muskogee. This was the earliest education of George Washington Grayson, born in the Creek Nation in the Indian Territory less than a decade after the Removal, when the memories were still fresh, sharp, and painful.[47]

This Creek-style education, Grayson's own experiences, and the knowledge of Indian affairs he acquired during his public life combined to create a man very conscious of his nation's history. Against the positive Muskogee image he absorbed in his youth was juxtaposed a very negative image of the white man drawn from the recent past. He learned early that what he called "the all-absorbing cupidity of the white race" was a constant in Indian-white relationships.[48]

So, although he was a descendant of Mary Benson and Robert Grierson, it was more important to him that he was of the Tiger clan from Koweta Town, that he was an *este Mvskoke*. On this ground the foundation of his Creek nationalism was laid. With many of his Indian contemporaries, in his life he would accept what he found good in Anglo-American culture and use it to his advantage, but he was prepared to resist as long as possible the submersion of his nation's sovereignty and his Creek identity in that alien flood.

CHAPTER TWO

The Grass on the Island

While Creek culture and history laid a foundation for George Washington Grayson's Creek identity and nationalism, favorable circumstances in his youth allowed him to develop the skills and knowledge he would need as a cultural broker. Had he been born five years earlier, he would have found far fewer opportunities to gain the English education that shaped his life and made him so useful as an interpreter of an alien culture. Had he been born five years later, the Civil War might have limited his opportunities. As it was, Grayson was born just as the Creek Nation emerged from the trauma of the Removal. He reached school age as the doors of literacy and politics swung open to a new generation of Creek leaders.

According to his calculations, Grayson was born May 12, 1843 to James and Jennie Wynne Grayson. Their home at the time was on Possum Creek about three or four miles west of North Fork Town (one mile east of present Eufaula, Oklahoma) in the Creek Nation. He was the eldest of the Graysons' six children, the others being Samuel (born in 1849), Pilot (1850), Malone, Louisa Bell (1850), and James, Jr. His parents gave him the English name Washington Grayson, usually shortened to "Wash." He added George during his school days.[1]

Wash Grayson's parents were survivors of the Creek immigration of the late 1820s to the Indian Territory. In the aftermath of the Red Stick War, some of the Upper Creek Griersons had affiliated with the Lower Creek McIntosh faction. Perhaps this was because of the Griersons' harsh treatment at the hands of the Red Sticks in that earlier troubled time. Or perhaps the shift of loyalty resulted from the marriage of Robert Grierson's daughter to Chief William McIntosh and of the chief's daughters to Grierson's grandsons. At any rate, a number of Griersons—or Graysons as they were usually called in the Indian Territory—and their slaves migrated west with the McIntosh faction about 1827.[2]

The eldest son of Katy Grayson and Tulwa Tustunuggee, according to Wash Grayson, was given the name Totka Bahi Hadjo, but he was usually known as James Grayson. James married Jennie (Jane) Wynne, the daughter of John (Jack) Wynne and Percinta Harrod (Herod) of that prominent Koweta Town family. Jennie's parents, among the first Creek settlers at North Fork Town, had brought her to the Indian Territory as an infant. Why the young Graysons chose to live there and not among the Kowetas, who resettled in present-day western Wagoner County, Oklahoma, is unknown. However, it was not unusual by then for Creeks to live apart from their *tvlwv*, particularly in that time of general dislocation. Jennie's parents died while she and her younger sisters—Parthenia (Feenie) and Rebecca—were children. They were left to the care of guardians, who dissipated the sisters' small inheritance, which included one slave. As a consequence, Jennie brought to the marriage little of the material wealth expected of a Creek bride.[3]

But Jennie Grayson was a member of the Tiger clan and the Koweta *tvlwv*, both accorded special importance in the contemporary Muskogee social and political world. According to her son, at the time of her marriage her town affiliation was something of an embarrassment, as perhaps was the fact that she was "nearly white."[4] When her new husband took her to live near his parents in the Choctaw country on Poteau Creek in what is now southeastern Oklahoma, the animosity of some former Hillabee Red Sticks toward the *este hvtke* (pronounced "estee huhdgee"), or white people, and toward the Kowetas, who had defeated them in 1813–1814, made her life unpleasant. Though in later years Wash denied that James's immediate family—particularly Tulwa Tustunuggee—harbored ill feelings toward Jennie, he noted that James was sensitive to his wife's discomfort around the old Red Sticks. He soon took her back to live in the more congenial and familiar community at North Fork Town. But, while Jennie's membership in the Koweta *tvlwv* could have been a liability in the eyes of some in those early days, it became a major factor in her eldest son's rise in Creek politics a generation later.[5]

Katy Grayson and Tulwa Tustunuggee at some point also resettled in the vicinity of North Fork Town, living sometimes on the Choctaw side of the Canadian River and at other times on the Creek side. Besides James, Katy had nine children by Tulwa Tustunuggee. As adults they lived nearby in the matrilocal Muskogee way, creating with the extended families of Katy's older brothers and sisters a sizeable kinship network. Wash recalled that for at least some of the time during his early years, his family lived near enough to his grandparents that he was allowed to go alone through the woods to visit them.[6]

His grandfather made perhaps the greatest impression on the young boy. Tulwa Tustunuggee was, like Katy, half-Muskogee, the son of an adopted Scots-Irish captive. In their youth two of his brothers had spent time with their white relatives in Georgia and afterwards went by the names Dick and Jack Benson, having assumed their mother's surname. They, along with Katy's brother Watt (Walter) Grayson, immigrated to the Indian Territory in the 1830s with the Creek leader Opothle Yahola's party of Upper Creeks. But brothers Emathla Hutke (also called "Hog Meat") and Tulwa Tustunuggee (known to some as "Johnnie Benson"), both survivors of Horseshoe Bend, acknowledged only their Creek names. Unlike Dick and Jack, who customarily spoke English and wore white-style clothing, Tulwa Tustunuggee lived and dressed in the traditional Muskogee way. Both he and James Grayson were dark of skin and very much Creek in appearance.[7]

Tulwa Tustunuggee was also Creek at heart. Whether his attitudes were shaped by genuine Red Stick convictions or only by bitter memories of the Anglo-American attacks on Hillabee Town and Tohopeka, Tulwa Tustunuggee had no time for the white man. Wash Grayson recalled that his grandfather "was one of those when first I knew him who was decidedly unfriendly in his estimation of the professions and character of the white man, and whose stories of his experiences with them may have warped my youthful mind on this subject, which maturer years, information and reflection have failed to remove."[8]

Perhaps it was Tulwa Tustunuggee, taking the place of maternal male relatives, who oversaw Wash's traditional education. Contemporary Catawbas, some of whom settled in present McIntosh County, Oklahoma, within a few miles of the Grayson home, described traditional education as children learning by observing adult activities, eavesdropping on adult conversations, and listening to the elders' stories.[9] Those stories, according to an informant of anthropologist Frank Speck, "were intended to develop the mind, to make children think, to teach them the ways of life."[10] In preliterate societies native children learned how to understand and live in accord with the physical and spiritual worlds through story telling. The Muskogee language that children like Wash Grayson spoke served as the door to the elders' wisdom and knowledge. At the same time, its grammar and nuances helped define their culture, establish relationships with other Muskogees, and set the boundaries between them and non-Muskogees. Along with language, history was an important anchor of identity.[11] It was probably Tulwa Tustunuggee's memories of warfare and the Creeks' eviction from their old homeland that established Wash's first heroes, nurtured his admiration for the Creek warrior tradition, and indelibly colored his first impressions of the *este hvtke.*

A dark-eyed boy with his mother's pale complexion and dark red hair, Wash did not resemble his younger brothers, who inherited their father's dark skin and Muskogee features, but he retained pleasant memories of his youth as part of a large family. Wash greatly admired his mother and enjoyed a close relationship with her until her death in 1875. He remembered his father as stern and reserved, undemonstrative in his love for his children. Although Wash enjoyed the company of his many cousins and younger aunts and uncles, his deepest and most enduring family relationship was with his brother Sam, about six years his junior.[12]

During his childhood at the foot of the low, thickly wooded mountains west of North Fork Town, Wash developed a strong identification with place as well as with the people who inhabited it. Some Creeks of his parents' generation may have yearned for the "old nation," but this western land was home to him. As a child, he learned to love it when it was still primarily wilderness. Looking back later through a haze of Victorian romanticism, he remembered that on "the little farm," his family "lived squarely face to face with nature and nature's denizens." The springtime beauty of quiet woods, clear streams, and busy wildlife "all conspired to instill within our simple natures that love of home, that acquaintance with the true, the beautiful and the good, that affection for the land of our birth that will never give place to any power short of death."[13]

Translated into practical terms, Wash Grayson, in common with most Creek boys, learned a woodsman's skills in that wild frontier country. He learned the lessons so well that as a Confederate soldier he was competent to scout and travel alone for days through rough, unfamiliar terrain. In quieter times he continued to love hunting, going west each fall into the broad band of black jack oaks known as the Cross Timbers on week-long expeditions that included swapping tales around the campfire with his brother Sam and other good companions. Wash also learned a farmer's skills, in earlier days the domain of Muskogee women. Although he lived most of his adult life in town, he always had at least some land of his own under cultivation, and he took a keen interest in weather, crops, and new varieties of plants, from flowering shrubs to pasture grasses.[14]

Remaining within a few miles of North Fork Town, James Grayson relocated his family several times, at least once to the Choctaw side of the Canadian River. The Graysons' movements kept them near James's kin rather than Jennie's. This may have been circumstantial rather than indicating a shift away from traditional Creek matrilocalism and toward Anglo-American patterns. Jennie was an orphan, apparently with few close relatives other than her sisters. In his autobiography Wash referred only to his father's search for suitable land for farming. Again, this reference to his father's, rather than his mother's, farming pursuits may suggest that the decision was partially the result of Jennie's impoverished circumstances at the time of her marriage. Whatever the young Graysons owned was the gift of James's well-to-do mother or the fruit of their shared hard work to create a home and farm. Wash may also have been viewing these events as paralleling his experiences at making a home for his own young family in similar circumstances following the Civil War. At any rate, James's and Jennie's ambition was to give their children a better start in life than had been their lot. If their motives were economic and their means individualistic rather than traditionally Muskogee, they were no different from many of their fellow Creeks who had drifted away from communalism.[15]

That communalism, exemplified in the landholding system of the Creek Nation, gave James and Jennie the right to occupy, farm, and improve as much vacant land as they cared to use. They paid any previous occupant only for improvements. This allowed the Graysons to move from place to place until they found a location that suited their growing family's needs. This right to free use of common land meant that the Graysons, though not so wealthy as many Creeks, provided for their family according to their own resources, abilities, and energies. The system accommodated a wide economic range, from those Creeks content with or limited to communal subsistence farming to those who amassed individual fortunes based on free land use and the means to exploit it.[16]

According to Creek Agency reports for the mid-1840s, the Lower Creeks generally occupied an area approximately eighty miles by fifty in the rich bottom lands of the Arkansas Valley, an area later given political designation as the Arkansas District. Some district families and individuals demonstrated a relatively high degree of adaptation to Anglo-American ways with their large farms and plantations worked by black slaves. The Perrymans, the Lewises, and Jennie's Harrod relations, were known for their wealth. The McIntoshes were said to be worth one hundred fifty thousand dollars, while rumor had it that Benjamin Marshall, a Muskogee of Irish descent, owned as many as one hundred slaves and enjoyed a personal fortune of fifty thousand dollars.[17]

Upper Creeks, usually perceived as more traditionally Muskogee, generally settled to the west of the Arkansas Valley and upstream on the Canadian, North Fork, Deep Fork, and Little Rivers, an area later designated the Canadian District as a political division. Their aggregate towns spread over an area eighty miles by sixty. In the Canadian River bottom in 1843 several *tvlwv* reportedly created a common cornfield eight miles long and three miles wide, evidence that some persisted in communal living in the new homeland. But even among the Upper Creeks and Canadian District residents, there were those who demonstrated adaptation to Anglo-American ways. Opothle Yahola of Tuckabachee Town, a man widely honored as a *yvtekv*, or speaker, owned herds of livestock and numerous slaves. He was reputed to be even wealthier than the leading Arkansas District plantation owners. Moreover, he was the partner of J. W. Taylor of New York—the husband of a Creek woman—in a trading post at Tuckabachee, twelve miles southwest of North Fork Town. Motey Kennard, Jennie Grayson's kinsman, grazed large herds of horses on the substantial farms he worked, the nearer being eight miles north of North Fork Town and the other in the Choctaw Nation.[18]

But while Katy Grayson owned many slaves and much livestock, her son James owned only the man Wilson, her gift to him. Together James Grayson, his slave, and later a hired man cultivated the kind of small farm, colloquially known as a "*sofky* patch," more typical of the Creek Nation at that period.[19]

To a certain extent the Removal had weakened old ties and customs, but Creek oral history maintained that there was a strong continuity of traditions and values in spite of the disruptions. While some, such as James and Jennie Grayson, chose to live as individual farmers, many Creeks had resettled in their ancient town pattern, rekindling new town fires on the ashes brought from Alabama. *Tvlwv* members continued to look after their own, sharing the work and the harvest and performing the old ceremonies. Wash Grayson grew up understanding and appreciating both systems. Even though he never lived among the Kowetas, they knew he was one of them. Likewise, although he had strong kinship ties to the wealthy Anglo-Muskogee Lower Creek families, he had a special regard for the Upper Creeks, particularly the Eufaulas and the Okfuskees, who were his closest neighbors.[20]

Not surprisingly, many adult Creeks remained homesick for Georgia and Alabama. They complained to an Indian Territory missionary that "the summers here are hotter, the winters are colder, the rain is wetter, the crops lighter, the game scarcer, and their people are dieing [*sic*] off faster than ever before was known in the 'old nation.'"[21] Indeed, the death toll continued high in "this rigorous climate," with its unpredictable, sometimes extreme weather. The humid easternmost sections of the Creek country, which Wash knew best, were drained by the Arkansas and Canadian river systems. Usually sluggish, shallow, and easily fordable, in times of heavy rain these rivers could produce a headrise that could wash away homes and crops.[22]

Such was the case in 1845, when Wash was a toddler. After such a flood, receding waters left stagnant pools, from which "noxious effluvia" arose and on which residents blamed their frequent debilitating bouts of bilious and intermittent fevers.[23] Measles, typhoid, cholera, and smallpox periodically ravaged the Indian Territory. By 1857 a census of the Creeks revealed that the population had continued to decline and now stood at 14,880. Two years later the figure had dropped to 13,550.[24]

In spite of the drawbacks, some of the Creek immigrants found the new lands pleasing and saw opportunities to recoup their material losses. Fertile river valleys and wide natural prairies alternated with ranges of low hills and mountains. Forests of oak, hickory, and pecan provided lumber, mast for hogs, and cover for game. Head-high bluestem grass fattened cattle and horses on the open range. The newly settled Creeks suppressed the wildfires that had kept the land free of brush, so that by the mid-1840s some formerly open country became too tree-covered for good pasture. Increased hunting eventually made game scarce, but there were still deer and wolves nearby when Wash was a boy.[25]

Eventually some Creeks moved west into the Cross Timbers, a band of post oak and blackjack oak that belted the Indian Territory from the Red River northeastward to the Kansas border. It served as an informal boundary to the eastern range of the Plains tribes. The Cross Timbers clothed a jumble of red sandstone hills that petroleum geologists decades later recognized as a good indicator of oil deposits. In some spots black outcroppings exposed coal seams. Beyond the Cross Timbers the Creek Nation stretched on to the 100th meridian, but most Creeks left these thousands of square miles of short-grass prairie to the buffalo and the nomadic Plains tribes who followed the herds.[26]

Once the immigrants had brought their new lands into production, Creek agriculture made a resurgence. Quite early, Creek settlers raised more corn than they needed and sold their surplus to contractors at nearby Fort Gibson. By 1843, the year of Wash Grayson's birth, Creek farmers had added peas, sweet potatoes, melons, peaches, rice, and cotton to their traditional crops of corn, beans, squashes, and pumpkins. Two years later they were also growing Irish potatoes, apples, pears, plums, cherries, and oats and were experimenting unsuccessfully with wheat. Livestock, turkeys, ducks, and geese flourished. In 1847 Creeks exported one hundred thousand bushels of corn, mostly to famine-stricken Ireland. Their white neighbors in Arkansas reportedly preferred Creek rice to grain shipped upriver from New Orleans. Stock drovers from Illinois, Indiana, and Missouri bought their hogs and cattle. Observers commented that the Creeks were good farmers if not, according to white standards, very neat ones.[27]

Both Upper and Lower Creeks farmed with African slave labor, although a relative few owned the majority of slaves. Slavery was a practice that predated the arrival of Europeans and Africans in North America, but it had taken on new facets as contact between American Indians and English colonizers increased in the seventeenth century. Quite early, Creeks realized that slaves, especially black slaves, were a valuable commodity for which English frontiersmen paid well in trade goods. Some historians have speculated that when Creeks observed black male slaves doing what they then regarded as women's work in the white plantation owners' fields, their respect for blacks as fellow men declined. Gradually Creeks began to view blacks as property and symbols of wealth, a trend that the shift toward cotton culture in the early nineteenth century reinforced. Although some blacks possessed skills the Creeks valued, especially as artisans, farmers, and interpreters, they were the victims of increasing Creek racism by the mid-1800s. People of mixed black and Creek ancestry, though still accepted through the clan and *tvlwv* system, became less respected.[28]

One could speculate that nuances of Muskogee language may also have had something to do with the declining status of blacks. Polite conversation attempted to avoid any indication of imposing one's will or opinions on another. Even observations of fact addressed to another person were expressed courteously as questions rather than statements. Second person verbs were modified accordingly, and commands were restricted to children and those the speaker considered subservient. The style of address Creeks customarily used toward those to whom they gave orders would help institutionalize and perpetuate perceptions of Creek superiority and black inferiority.

Wash's first contact with blacks was probably through the slave Wilson, whom he evaluated in terms of labor in his autobiography. Wash also spoke of his grandmother Katy's many slaves in the same breath as her livestock.[29] That members of the Grierson family had produced children through relationships with their slaves embarrassed him and remained "a lasting cloud over his family's name."[30] So it appears clear that Wash Grayson was little different from other Creeks of his day who, in common with contemporary Anglo-Americans, came to think of blacks as an inferior race and, along with southern whites, to view them as property rather than people.

Still, by the time of the Civil War Creeks counted far more of their wealth in cattle and horses than in slaves. Unfortunately, the Osages, Pawnees, Wichitas, Caddos, Comanches, Delawares, and other Eastern immigrant tribes coveted their stock and frequently raided the western settlements. The federal transfer of the new homeland in fee simple to the Creek Nation meant little to the Plains tribes that historically traveled, traded, and hunted on the Southern Plains. According to Creek historian James Roane Gregory, Wash's contemporary who grew up on the western frontier, Skidi Pawnee raiders killed their first Creek victim after the Removal on the banks of the Arkansas River near present Muskogee, Oklahoma. The incident was memorable to the Creeks because before the skirmish they had real doubts whether their firearms would be effective against the Skidis' feather-fringed white war shields. They were much relieved to see the damage done by their half-ounce rifle balls, but they were jubilant when an intermarried white man in their party killed a Skidi scout with a lucky shot at seventy-six yards. In any case, because raiders sometimes massacred whole families on scattered frontier farms, the rumor of a major Pawnee invasion in 1845 sent panicky families scurrying to Fort Gibson for protection.[31]

Hostilities with other tribes periodically forced the Creeks to counter with punitive expeditions and ambushes, using the warrior's skills they had learned in the old Creek country. Once Loney Bruner led outnumbered Creeks in a hand-to-hand fight with Wichitas at the base of Concharty Mountain, probably near present-day Haskell, Oklahoma. A band of Creeks from the Yuchee *tvlwv* took on the same enemy on Dick Creek Prairie. In the fall of 1859 Long Tiger, Tiger Bone, and their crippled brother—members of the McIntosh family and Wash's kinsmen—held off a Comanche-Wichita war party on Tiger Creek. Tradition holds that Creek warriors surrounded and annihilated a band of fifty Little Osages near present-day Checotah, Oklahoma, only about twelve miles north of the Graysons' farm. These incidents convinced their neighbors on the Southern Plains that the Creeks had lost none of their warrior skills in their move to the Indian Territory and that it was sometimes better to engage in trade and sit in council with them.[32]

For their part, the Creeks willingly continued their diplomatic tradition while they defended their frontier. Chilly McIntosh capably led an expedition of 150 Creeks against the Pawnees, but he was also instrumental in negotiating in 1831 the final settlement of the bitter thirty-year-old Cherokee-Osage War. In 1844 the Creeks invited the Plains peoples and the Great Lakes tribes to a council at the Great Salt Plains (in modern Alfalfa County, Oklahoma).[33] But federal authorities had mixed feelings about supporting Creek diplomatic activities. Although he had "*no good* reason" to be suspicious and realized the council might be a way of keeping the peace, Creek Agent James Logan felt it would be wise to keep an eye on such meetings.[34]

Unlike the nomadic Plains people, almost all Creeks, including the Grayson family, lived in hewed log houses carefully situated near abundant grass and fresh water. Creek houses consisted typically of two rooms with a dogtrot through the middle and a rock or stick chimney at either end. Walls and chimneys were chinked with clay mixed by foot with grass and water and then applied with a flat paddle. A cellar dug near the chimney kept stored foods from freezing. The dirt or puncheon floors and split-oak shingle roofs were the hallmark of any contemporary American frontier home. The homesite of a single Creek family consisted of a cluster of buildings that might resemble a small village. Besides the house and usual outbuildings—a smoke house, an arbor for refuge from the summer heat, a stable, and a corn crib—there were also a separate kitchen, sleeping houses, and in line with Muskogee tradition, a cabin reserved for women experiencing their menstrual cycles. Willow branch brooms were used to keep the yards scrupulously free of grass and weeds. This discouraged snakes as well as roving spirits.[35]

The difference between the homes of wealthy and poor Creeks often lay in size of the main house and the luxury of its furnishings. Creek Agent Logan noted that the items in Creek households that surprised him most were the "Yankee clocks, an article not in general use among Indians."[36] In a society that took little account of time, these were probably not necessities but marks of wealth.

To some extent dress also distinguished the more traditional from those who had adopted Anglo-American ways, even as, among other things, it came to differentiate the Five Civilized Tribes from those they called the "wild tribes" of the Plains. Small Creek children usually wore "flaps," breech clouts made of skins. As they grew older they graduated to long-tailed shirts and then to clothing much like their parents'. Creek women had been spinning thread and weaving cloth at least since the turn of the century, and spinning wheels and looms were common household items. But by the 1840s many preferred to buy factory-produced, brightly dyed cloth from the traders to sew white-style clothing.[37] Creek women so widely adopted the ankle-length ruffled, ribbon-trimmed cloth dress and apron that the style of that period is considered the "traditional" women's regalia among today's Muskogee people. The Office of Indian Affairs was slow to perceive the transition in clothing styles, for which the Creek chiefs took them to task in 1849. Through their agent they requested that the office substitute "cotton goods of heavy course [sic] quality, fitting for making pantaloons" in place of the "Broad Cloth, strouding, and small blankets" routinely issued to native peoples.[38]

Well-to-do Creek women often wore silks and muslins cut in the latest eastern fashions. Lower Creek men commonly wore white-style hats, vests, pants, and shoes but brightened sober outfits with ruffled calico hunting shirts. The wealthy of both sexes wore gold and silver watches, chains, rings, and other jewelry. Most Upper Creek men refused to wear white-style trousers, which one historian has interpreted as a refusal to submit to white ways.[39] Lieutenant J. W. Abert, passing through the Upper Creeks' western settlements in October 1845 with a group of topographical engineers, noted that Creek men "dressed most tastefully. Handsome shawls were gracefully twisted around their heads. They also wore leggings and moccasins of buckskin, handsome calico shirts, and beautiful pouch[es], with broad belt[s] ornamented with massive bead work."[40] Tulwa Tustunuggee and James Grayson were among those who clung to the old Creek style of dress. Wash recalled that his father always wore a shawl fashioned into a turban. As for himself, he noted that it took him some time to become "civilized" (his adjective) in his dress when he first went away to school in Arkansas.[41]

Travelers through the Creek Nation in the 1840s found it a strange place, an exotic mixture of the familiar and unfamiliar, peopled by Indians who were known as the "civilized tribes," yet still retained many of their traditional customs and clung to their tribal identity. Often the hospitality and courtesy of even formerly hostile Creeks surprised white travelers, who did not know how much Muskogees valued these qualities. Some Creeks spoke or understood English, but even the Lower Creeks often knew only Muskogee or other languages of the old confederacy. James Grayson spoke English well, but Jennie spoke it so poorly that Muskogee was the language of their home and their children's first language. So non-English-speaking Creeks relied on the bilingual, including slaves, to conduct their business with whites and act as cultural brokers. The Creek agent routinely employed an interpreter to ease his communication with his clients. By the late 1840s this interpreter was George Washington Stidham, a literate Anglo-Muskogee of Hecheta Town and a young man on the rise.[42]

White travelers also remarked on the absence of towns, as they understood them, in the Creek Nation. Arkansas District Creeks did not need market towns because they could export their produce and import goods by steamboat or keelboat from several landings along the river, depending on water levels. Canadian District Creeks, living above the head of navigation on the western rivers, conducted commerce at scattered trading posts such as Edwards' Post on Little River, at Shieldsville (near present Okmulgee, Oklahoma), and William F. McIntosh's store at Honey Springs on the Texas Road (roughly today's U.S. Highway 69). A village of sorts grew up near Creek Agency in the vicinity of Three Forks. It enjoyed a parasitic existence and an ephemeral boom whenever an annuity payment was due. At such times cockfights, horse races on Daniel N. McIntosh's oval track, and other types of vice and gambling flourished. These activities gave the village its name, "Sodom."[43]

Otherwise, the only "town" in the Creek Nation, as whites understood the term, was North Fork Town, to which the James Grayson family moved in the mid-1850s. Travelers often described it as a dense settlement with several stores. It straddled the Texas Road on the west side of the north fork of the Canadian River just above its junction with the main, or South,

Canadian. The Graysons lived on the west side of this broad trail, the main route for livestock and wagon traffic across the Indian Territory from southeastern Kansas and southwestern Missouri to the Republic of Texas. The Texas Road entered the Creek Nation from the Cherokee country at Three Forks, angled southwestward across Elk Creek near Honey Springs, forded the North Fork River at North Fork Town, and then crossed the Canadian River to continue through the Choctaw Nation to the Red River. Beyond the Canadian crossing, the Texas Road intersected the California Road, which paralleled the Canadian River all the way to the 100th meridian.[44]

The location of these two main arteries through or near North Fork Town and its convenient central placement in the Indian Territory gave the settlement a commercial and political importance beyond its actual size and population. It was a major stopover for an ever-increasing number of commercial, civilian, and military travelers. When the Graysons moved there, it possessed a post office designated "Micco," several stores, numerous Christian churches, schools, the office of a white physician, possibly the shops of several white craftsmen, and after 1855 a flourishing Masonic lodge with a Creek and white membership.[45]

A maze of horse paths and trails connected North Fork Town and the Creek Agency with outlying settlements, ranches, and plantations. Slaves, freedmen, and licensed whites provided vital blacksmithing, wheel-wrighting, and milling services, but also some Creeks operated white-style businesses. In addition to his store at Honey Springs, William F. McIntosh, son of Chilly McIntosh, maintained a toll bridge on the Texas Road over Elk Creek. Creeks and white men, such as Gray Eagle Scales and Frederick B. Severs, who were under permit of the Creek government, ran trading posts. There being no banking facilities and very little currency in the Indian Territory except at annuity time, most commerce relied on the barter system with "imported" items—sugar, coffee, and ready-made clothing—exchanged for furs, meat, salt, produce, and merchants' scrip.[46]

Some adventurous Creeks made the long journey out to the western half of the nation to meet roving Plains bands and transient eastern immigrants—Kickapoos, Shawnees, Delawares, and Sacs and Foxes. Around distant council fires Creeks traded for furs, horses, mules, and captives—the last three usually Comanche plunder from the Mexican frontier. Agent Philip Raiford was convinced that Creek purchases of plunder—particularly captives to be enslaved or ransomed—perpetuated frontier depredations by making them profitable.[47]

Taken altogether, the life in the Creek Nation that Wash Grayson knew in his youth was rustic, rural, and agricultural—much like that on any other American frontier. The illicit liquor trade remained a perennial problem, but by the mid-1840s, according to Agent Logan, the Creeks had generally overcome the decline into vice, indolence, and drunkenness that followed the social disruption of the Removal. They had adjusted to life in the Indian Territory and seemed well on their way to fitting into the image of the self-sufficient individual farmer that was so long the goal of well-meaning "friends of the Indian." In three respects only, in the agents' opinions, did the Creeks lag behind their Cherokee, Choctaw, and Chickasaw neighbors: The Creek chiefs and government system were not yet so democratic (or accommodating) as the Office of Indian Affairs would have liked, and the Creeks were slow to accept both Christianity and English education.[48]

Although the Choctaws and Cherokees had written constitutions in 1826 and 1827, respectively, providing for elected governments on the Anglo-American model, into the 1850s Creeks adhered to traditional tribal government that white officials considered antiquated. Each of the two districts maintained its own council in the first years after the arrival of the main body of Creeks. The Red Stick War and Removal-era strife exacerbated factionalism between the McIntosh adherents and their enemies to the extent that bloodshed often seemed inevitable. Agent Logan declared that in the late 1830s the two parties rivaled each other in "animosity and bitter hatred . . . jealousy and discord."[49]

About 1840 the factionalism subsided enough to allow the two districts to reconstitute a National Council, but a letter to Agent Logan from the council in 1847 bore the mark of each *tvlwv* representative, with the towns still grouped under Upper or Lower Creek categories. The old dual leadership continued. Roley McIntosh presided as principal chief of the Arkansas District, while the Canadian District acknowledged several chiefs. Meeting at High Spring (Uekiwv Hvlwe), one mile north of present-day Hichita, Oklahoma, midway between the two districts, council members deliberated national issues and enacted laws. Among the issues of the

1840s and 1850s were the distribution of annuity money, Christianity, and educating the nation's children.[50]

Distribution of the $34,500 annuity seemed symptomatic of the problems of Creek government, viewed from the white perspective. The federal government had obligated itself in the Removal treaty to make yearly payments to the Creek Nation in exchange for ceded lands in Alabama and Georgia. Allocation of the annuity payments was handled by numerous chiefs and council members, often one and the same. This method incorporated federal treaty obligations into the old Muskogee system, whereby the *mekko* was responsible for distributing gifts and supplies from the communal granary, taking a tithe as his due.[51]

Agent James Logan did not understand this distribution system. He viewed it as allowing each Creek official to draw fees for his service at the expense of the general populace, while adding to the expense of operating the Creek government. Agent Logan's frustration with Creek officials who operated in traditional ways was evident as he declared: "Generally speaking, they are extremely ignorant, are noted for their superstitious bigotry, for their old customs and ceremonies, and most bitter prejudices against all measures calculated to reform the conditions or enlighten the minds of their people. . . . Their authority," he continued, "is often exerted arbitrarily and their laws are unjust and unnecessarily severe."[52] He and subsequent agents recommended a per capita distribution of the annuities as a democratic reform. They may have believed this would curtail the power of chiefs and council members, whom they viewed as backward, and that placing Creek funds directly into the hands of heads of families might encourage individualism and undermine the tribalism white officials deplored.

Logan also supported the imposition on the Creek nation of a written constitution, a code of laws, and an elected government. Chilly McIntosh had compiled a code of written Creek laws as early as 1817, but the nation had not followed the example of the Choctaws and Cherokees in writing a constitution providing for an elected government. Logan and later agents argued that regular elections would allow discontented Creeks to choose better leaders.[53] A more structured, concentrated government based on a familiar written framework would also be easier for federal agents to deal with and possibly manipulate. Perhaps another outcome would be to provide access to leadership for those Creeks white officials considered progressive—the Ben Marshalls, George W. Stidhams, and Samuel Checotes. At the same time, opposition to further white-supported reform, such as Christian missionary activity and English education, would presumably diminish.

The latter opposition was unusual among the Five Civilized Tribes. The Cherokees, Choctaws, and Chickasaws had demonstrated a keen appreciation for literacy and English education. Sequoyah's syllabary had allowed almost all Cherokees to achieve literacy in their own language within a remarkably short time. The Cherokees and the combined Choctaw-Chickasaw government had functioning public school systems supported with national funds by the 1840s.[54]

Early attempts to establish English education in the Creek Nation, however, floundered in spite of work in the mid-1830s to print educational and religious materials in the Muskogee language. In 1841 Presbyterian minister Robert Loughridge visited the Creek Nation, hoping to persuade the Creek council to allow him to open a mission and school. While touring the Creek country, he found only one school in operation. Supported by the Creek government, it suffered from lack of space and was poorly attended except in the spring and summer. Loughridge did receive permission to establish Koweta Mission near Koweta Town in 1843, but the National Council closely circumscribed his work and evangelism, limiting the staff to four men and their wives.[55]

Through the early 1840s little changed. Agent Logan set up a school among the Lower Creeks with his son-in-law as teacher, but Roley McIntosh and others complained that little real teaching went on there. Another option was to send young Creeks to Choctaw Academy in Kentucky. McIntosh and other chiefs objected to the expense and protested that some of the boys had been sent away to school without the permission of their parents or the chiefs. Nor did the chiefs see positive results from the fifty or more who had attended Choctaw Academy. They declared, "not one ever [returned] capable of transacting any kind of business or was improved in civilization so as to be a fit example for their home acquaintances."[56]

What McIntosh and his supporters wanted was "a manual labor school conducted by literary men. By this plan we would soon have good mechanics among us as well as learned and in our opinion would add greatly to improving that class of people among us directly opposed to learning and civilization."[57] One year later, in 1846, Benjamin Marshall echoed these sentiments, stating, "The inlighted [sic] part of the Creek people is very anxious to have the school go in operation soon as possible but these are infortunately [sic] in the minority and cant [sic] do as they wish and depend upon the government to aid them."[58] These remarks suggest that by the 1840s some Creeks had identified cultural changes they believed would be beneficial for their people but realized their views set them somewhat apart from their fellow Creeks.

The conservative majority to whom Marshall, McIntosh, and the chiefs referred in these letters often included Creeks who either rejected the white man's ways or linked English education to unwelcome Christian missionary activity. While Christianity and traditional Muskogee religion shared some values—honesty, generosity, and hospitality, for example—they differed in some important respects. Muskogees envisioned three worlds. Hesaketumese, the Master of Life, also known as Ohfunkah, "the One Who Rules Over All," presided over the Upper World, which represented order, boundaries, and limits. Upper World creatures were finer, larger, and purer models of those that appeared later on earth. The Under World opposed the Upper World. It was inhabited by ghosts, witches, and monsters, who represented madness, disorder, and change, among other things. Formed later and situated in between was This World, inhabited by three categories of creature—humans, animals, and plants—that were inferior images of those in the Upper World. In This World, people must strive to maintain a balance between the other two worlds by paying strict attention to the rules and ceremonies that had been handed down by their ancestors.[59]

Unlike Christian beliefs, which focused on the next life in which people would be rewarded or punished, Muskogee focus was on the present. In This World Muskogees could hope for a pleasant, prosperous existence if they obeyed the laws and kept the feasts and ceremonies. Failure to do so or wrong doing would bring misfortune on the whole community. When Christian missionaries exhorted the Creeks to turn from their traditional feasts, dances, ball games, and ceremonies, they threatened the stability and welfare of the whole Creek community.[60]

Christian missionaries had worked with some success among the Lower Creeks both before and after they came to the Indian Territory, a period that corresponded with the intense evangelism of the Second Great Awakening. But hostility toward Christianity and missionaries flared following the arrival of the Upper Creeks. The abolitionist sentiments of some missionaries working among a slaveholding people and objectionable behavior by individual missionaries perhaps exacerbated and focused diffuse resentment toward whites. In 1836 Christian missionaries were expelled from the nation with the concurrence of the Lower Creeks and the Office of Indian Affairs.[61]

On his preliminary visit to Tuckabachee Town in 1841, Loughridge commented that although he heard no anti-missionary statements, it was clear that the "imprudence of one of their coloured preachers" had turned some against Christian preachers.[62] The restrictions imposed on Loughridge in his labors at Koweta were the result of anti-missionary sentiment. Another reaction was the National Council's 1843 prohibition against the preaching or practice of Christianity in the Creek Nation. An unfortunate side effect of the anti-missionary feeling was that English education suffered as the missionaries and teachers who conducted schools for Creek children left the nation.[63]

However, not all Creek Christians gave up their faith; some continued to worship secretly. When they were caught, they suffered the prescribed fifty lashes with inch-thick elm or hickory sprouts. Creek rowdies, who some said included Chilly McIntosh, intimidated worshippers and ministers and broke up services with gunfire. But by the mid-1840s even the most adamant acknowledged that the suppression of Christianity had neither stamped out the new religion nor revived the old beliefs. Besides, some anti-Christian leaders had themselves seen "spiritual visions" and secretly converted.[64]

Officially the Creek National Council ended the ban on Christianity in 1848, but an evangelistic campaign was already well underway as missionaries renewed efforts to convert Creeks within the nation or at strategically located revival meetings on the borders.[65] In the summer of 1848 a Baptist camp meeting on the North Fork River lasted four days. Of the fifteen hundred persons present for Sunday services, twenty-three joined the church, including "the most talented and popular chief in the nation," Chilly McIntosh.[66] "He joined before preaching on Sabbath morning. He spoke loud enough in giving in his christian experience, to be heard by the whole assembly," missionary Americus L. Hay exulted. "He spoke of his conviction and sorrow for sin. . . . He made known that his remaining days would be devoted to the service of God."[67]

That year the Baptists, or Uewvaksumkvlke (water divers), who worked mostly among the Graysons' Upper Creek neighbors in the Canadian District, reported that they had one white, four Creek, and three black preachers in the Creek Nation as well as seven churches serving 550 members. Methodists, the Ohkalvlke (pourers), who served converts in both districts, reported 592 members. Presbyterians, the Ohfeskvlke or Uewvohfeska (water sprinklers), made fewer but ultimately more influential converts among the Lower Creeks of the Arkansas District. All the denominations rejoiced in the conversion and training of Creek men.[68] James McHenry, who had been a Red Stick leader under the name "High Head Jim", Joseph Islands, James Perryman, Samuel Checote, Chilly McIntosh, his son William F. McIntosh—"young, thoughtful, . . . devotedly pious," English-educated, and bilingual—would now preach to their own people.[69] It was probably during this period that Jennie Grayson was immersed in Baptizing Creek, which joined the North Fork River just upstream from North Fork Town. But even though she remained a devout Baptist throughout her life, her husband never affiliated himself with a Christian church. Rather James Grayson remained, according to his son, "somewhat opposed to them."[70]

These new Creek Christians did not see themselves as radically departing from Muskogee culture by converting to the new religion. First, they reasoned that their people had always known Hesaketvmese; Jesus simply revealed Him more clearly and made Him accessible as a personal savior. Then, as illustrated among Creek Baptists such as Jennie Grayson, they put their own mark on Christianity. The church ground began physically and socially replacing the *tvlwv* ceremonial ground, or square ground, as the focal point of the new communities of believers. The church building always faced east, recalling the customary siting of Creek public buildings. Clustered around it were the arbors and camp houses that sheltered extended families during protracted camp meetings. Nearby was the cemetery with its distinctive grave houses. Within the church building custom dictated that the men sat on the left, the women on the right of the aisle. The church offered new leadership roles for men as ministers and deacons, symbolized by the staffs they carried, and older women were also asked to lead prayers and hymns, a departure from most Anglo-American denominations that denied women a public role. Some songs were the familiar English hymns translated into Muskogee, but new hymns were Creek in melody, lyrics, language, and style. Ministers preached in the rising and falling rhythms of the Muskogee language. When the congregation prayed, all might pray aloud simultaneously, offering individual petitions. From its new beginning in the 1840s, Muskogee Christianity became a basic component of Muskogee culture, acting as a unifying agent and reinforcing Creek identity.[71]

The return of the missionaries during that period revitalized the movement to establish and support literacy and English education in the Creek Nation. Chiefs and council members, most of whom could not sign their names, realized that they needed literate, English-speaking men who could act as cultural brokers, presenting Creek views to the president, Congress, and the Office of Indian Affairs. At the same time, they would explain to the Creek people policies made in far-off Washington. Even the intransigent traditionalist Opothle Yahola of Tuckabachee Town was quoted as telling the Creek National Council that, although he had always opposed the white man's religion, he did not oppose his education. The white man's culture, he said, was a river. The Creek Nation was an island in that river, and education was grass growing on the island. Without the grass the island would soon be washed away. The Creeks must educate their children so that they might stand between their people and trouble. Opothle Yahola's words carried weight. If the Creeks needed further persuasion, they had before them the examples of the Cherokees and the Choctaws, whom they admired for setting aside part of their annuity payments to support their national school systems.[72]

Consequently in 1847 the Creek National Council agreed to build a boarding school in each district, supported jointly with Christian denominations. The Presbyterians opened Tullahassee Mission (in present Wagoner County, Oklahoma) for the Arkansas District in 1850. The Methodists chose North Fork Town in the Canadian District as the site of Asbury Manual Labor School. Besides access to good building stone and sawed lumber from the Choctaw-Chickasaw country, this location offered a setting among a generally English-speaking, church-going population. Conversely, it was some distance from the nearest *tvlwv* square ground, at which ceremonial dances and ball games might distract the students. Even these two new boarding schools failed to meet the rising demand for English education for Creek boys and girls, and neighborhood day schools proliferated.[73] With these developments and with the pride Creek parents began to show in their children's acquisition of literacy, Agent Logan reported confidently, "the rising generation of the Creeks will indeed be a different people."[74]

This rising generation included young Wash Grayson, who reached school age as the new educational opportunities materialized in the North Fork Town vicinity. While James and Jennie Grayson provided their children a home much like that of their Canadian District neighbors, they perhaps stressed one goal more—the Graysons, neither of whom could read or write, were determined that their children should have the advantages of literacy and an English education.[75] James was ambitious for his children, that they might earn their living in a less arduous way than farming and that they might also "attain to positions of honor and trust in the public affairs" of the Creek Nation. Jennie's ambition was simpler—she wanted them to be able to read the Bible she could not read herself.[76]

Consequently, as neighborhood schools opened in the Creek Nation, the Graysons enrolled Wash and later Sam. The boys had the added advantage of their grandmother Katy's interest in educating her youngest daughters, the twins Caroline and Adaline. Because Katy and Tulwa Tustunuggee lived on the Choctaw side of the Canadian River, Katy had cabins built just outside North Fork Town. Here she installed her daughters with a slave woman to look after them; here also James Grayson sent his eldest sons to stay during school sessions before the whole family moved to the settlement.[77]

Baptist missionary Americus L. Hay operated that neighborhood school in the belief that "ignorance . . . is an open door for fraud, both civil and religious."[78] In October 1849, about the time Wash first attended classes, Hay reported that he and his wife were finishing their third twenty-two-week school session. Their average attendance was thirty students, of whom twenty were boarders. The boys learned farming, and Mrs. Hay instructed the girls in housekeeping and sewing. Academic subjects included reading, writing, spelling, arithmetic, and geography. Fourteen of Hay's students had learned to read, but according to Wash Grayson, he was not among their number. He believed he actually learned very little either in Hay's school or the second school he attended, possibly Methodist, run by a Mr. Adkins.[79]

Asbury Manual Labor School, in which Wash and Sam Grayson enrolled about 1856, probably at about ages thirteen and six, respectively, provided the real foundation of their English education. The thirty-acre site, one and one-half miles north of North Fork Town, combined good farm land and timber with the convenience of access. The brick and stone building, completed in 1850, stood 110 by 34 feet. Two stories high with a basement, it contained twenty-one rooms and was one of the grandest structures in the Creek Nation. In addition to the main building, on the campus were a good log house, smokehouse, kitchen, stable, and orchard. A few years later a two-story frame building was added. When the first stage of construction ended, the cost totaled $9,165, of which the Creek Nation contributed $5,000. During the next several years Asbury achieved a good measure of success, although the staff made far fewer intellectual and practical contributions to the Creek people than did Dr. and Mrs. William S. Robertson at Tullahassee Mission.[80]

Teachers identified several problems that interfered with the Creek student's ability to learn. First was the child's familiarity with English. (Wash had the advantage of his schoolmates as his father was bilingual.) Disease was another. Periodic epidemics of measles and similar sicknesses swept through the crowded boarding schools with devastating, sometimes lethal, effect, occasionally forcing the suspension of classes. With good reason, Creek parents were fearful of such epidemics and wanted their children home before summer, the "sickly season," set in. They frequently came to remove their children in time for them to attend the annual Green Corn Ceremony in July, whether or not the school year was over.[81]

In fact, absenteeism was a chronic problem for all the schools. One administrator complained, "Indians let their children have their own way entirely, so every person at all acquainted with them must know."[82] Indian parents "would as leave put their hands in the fire as to flog or compel [the child] to go to school against his will."[83] James Grayson was apparently an exception. He left his sons at Asbury with the promise that they would be allowed a visit home after the first three weeks, but he would not condone truancy. Getting an education was too important, and he would not permit his sons to squander their opportunity. Homesick or not, Wash and Sam resigned themselves to sticking it out until the official end of the session.[84]

As an adult, Wash Grayson had a well-earned reputation among Indian Territory citizens and outsiders as a scholar, but he judged himself only an average student during his Asbury career. Nor did Superintendent Thomas B. Ruble list him among his exemplary pupils. But Sam was a quick learner, as Wash noted proudly. As Asbury students, the boys were expected to absorb spelling, reading, writing, mental and written arithmetic, English grammar, physiology, natural philosophy, and algebra. On Sundays they attended Bible study and classes in vocal and instrumental music.[85]

In addition, students acquired the mechanical and agricultural skills the chiefs had hoped for by providing labor on the school farm. Seventy-five acres produced corn, oats, millet, potatoes, and turnips, while school employees experimented successfully with Chinese sugar cane. In the fall of 1858, the last year Wash Grayson attended Asbury, Superintendent Ruble reported that "[d]uring the fall and winter the boys helped to gather the crops, chop wood, make fires, etc.; in the spring they assist in repairing fences, cleaning up the grounds for cultivation, and do most of the hoeing in the fields and garden. Besides this, they grind nearly all the meal we use on steel mills; for this we pay them, as an inducement, ten cents per bushel."[86] Girls cleaned their rooms, washed, ironed, sewed, and helped in the dining room. Separation from extended families along with the physical and mental requirements imposed on Creek students used to a less structured and demanding way of life probably accounted for some of their reluctance to remain for the full term. However, Ruble believed that he was enlightening the minds of a people "just emerging from the rubbish of ages."[87]

In retrospect Wash Grayson was not so convinced of the benefits of an Asbury education. His and Sam's primary accomplishment in their first two years, he believed, was to become much more proficient in Muskogee, as most of the eighty students spoke it much more readily than English. Few of his teachers made a real impression on him until W. C. Munson, a dedicated and effective educator, joined the faculty. Still, sixty years later Grayson gave Asbury credit for having laid the groundwork for his achievements as an adult. He was proud that the "slow, plodding learner" eventually surpassed most of his classmates.[88]

After perhaps three years at Asbury, Wash Grayson was about sixteen and eager to leave school and begin his life as an adult. By then he had probably experienced his naming ceremony, the rite that demonstrated new expectations of him as a member of the Creek community. Ordinarily parents gave a Creek infant an informal name used among his family and friends. Females kept the same name all their lives, but males in their mid-teens received a new name at the Green Corn Ceremony. As he left childhood behind, Wash accepted the responsibilities of the adult Creek male: providing for his family and participating in ceremonial and political life of the community. This might include war and the stickball game known as the "little brother of war" because it demanded a warrior's aggressiveness, conditioning, endurance, and self-control.[89]

The Green Corn Festival, which Creeks called *pvsketv* (pronounced "buhsketuh") and whites corrupted to *busk*, occurred in July, when the staple crop of Indian people became edible in the year's growing cycle. It was the most sacred of Creek ceremonies, and members of a *tvlwv* were subject to fine if they did not attend. This was a season of renewal and forgiveness; singing, dancing, moral lectures, thanksgiving, and feasting highlighted the ceremonies. Jennie Grayson and her children were expected to celebrate it with the Kowetas. After cleaning and refurbishing their square ground, town members prepared themselves physically and spiritually to eat the first of the year's corn crop. The men drank *vsse passv* (pronounced "uhsee bassuh"), or the black drink, a strong herbal purgative that induced vomiting, symbolically cleansing the physical and spiritual being. The Kowetas served the black drink in the large conch shells they had brought from Alabama and had used from time immemorial.[90]

For the young man taking the black drink for the first time, the festival was especially significant. The elders called him out to confer his adult name, drawing the syllables out in a prolonged shout. The name usually recalled some incident significant to him. As he grew older, proved himself, and earned promotion through the ranks of Creek society, a new name or title might be added in recognition of those accomplishments. Chief Roley McIntosh conferred the name "Yaha" (Yvhv, or Wolf) on young Wash Grayson. The name referred to an early morning hunt on which he went seeking a deer but killed a wolf. From that time, Creeks knew him by his English name as well as his Muskogee name. He was both "Wash Grayson" and "Yaha."[91]

Perhaps as a part of this new maturity, Wash became restless, bored with school, and eager for more from life than Asbury could offer. Ironically, that meant continuing his schooling elsewhere. Since 1854 the Creek Nation, according to stipulations of the Removal treaty, had used a total of four thousand dollars in tribal funds to maintain about fifteen young Creeks in institutions of higher education "in the States." The first four who entered Arkansas College at Fayetteville acquitted themselves well enough so that about 1858 the Creek government prepared to name more students to study there at the nation's expense.[92]

James and Jennie Grayson did not expect their son to receive any consideration for the appointment. They believed the young men selected would be the sons of the most influential citizens of the nation, those with the most "pull," as Wash termed it. Even when rumors suggested that a boy from Asbury would fill the last vacancy, the Graysons still did not expect it to be one of their sons. They were surprised as well as gratified to be notified that Wash had been chosen.[93]

As much as they valued the opportunity the appointment offered, they recognized the dangers attached to it. The opportunity for further English education suited their long-held ambitions and beliefs about what would create the best future for their children. At the same time, they found it hard to think of sending their son, who had never been further than a few miles from home, all the way to "the States" to study. He would be among people who were not only strangers but alien in many ways.[94]

Moreover, another latent danger existed. Many young men who went away to study learned white ways too well. They came home with different ideas, a different perspective on the world, and perhaps a different life-style. In 1845 Agent Logan reported the sad experience of an agency employee. This young man came back from an eastern school planning to use his new education and skills for the benefit of his people. But when he approached the chiefs with his ideas, they scoffed, "You advise us? You are a white man! You cannot talk Indian. If you desire to be one, pull off your fine clothes; put on a hunting shirt and leggins [*sic*]; go to the busk and drink the physik [black drink]; and then talk like one and we will listen to you." The young man took the only job open to him, that of agency interpreter. In his frustration and alienation, he became an alcoholic and died in a drunken brawl. What good, Logan asked bitterly, had his education accomplished?[95]

When Agent Logan reported this incident, the Creek National Council was still reacting to the Removal. Unlike the Cherokees, who made a place for literate, English-educated young men and women in the national government and school system, the Creek governmental structure as yet had little use for them. But more than a decade later, as the Graysons considered the appointment, the Creek political climate and structure were changing. They could hope that when Wash came home from Arkansas College, he would find a place for his English education.[96]

James and Jennie Grayson went through the soul-searching universal to parents. In the end they decided they could not deprive their son of this unexpected opportunity, whatever the cost. Besides, Wash was eager to go, to see something of the "outer world." They accepted the appointment, a benefit their grateful son always believed came not because of his academic promise but because he, as much as the other appointees, had "pull": Jennie Grayson was kin to newly elected Principal Chief Motey Kennard.[97]

The trip to Fayetteville was eye-opening for Wash. James escorted his son to the college to see him settled. Valentine N. McAnally, only a month older than Wash and the son of James's sister Tility, went along for the adventure. The three rode northeast by horse for several days, crossing the Cherokee Nation toward Arkansas. The high point of the trip was their night's lodging at Rose Cottage, the gracious plantation home of Cherokee Principal Chief John Ross at Park Hill, near Tahlequah, the Cherokee capital. Used to simpler surroundings, they found Rose Cottage beautiful but oppressively luxurious with its carpets, plush upholstery, and ornate furniture. But Chief Ross, who kept open house for travelers, was affable and kept James talking far into the night.[98]

On their arrival in Fayetteville, the Grayson party excited as much curiosity among the residents as that town did in them. With about nine hundred inhabitants, it boasted at least four times the population of the North Fork Town settlement. A more sophisticated Wash Grayson was amused to recall how they craned their necks to see the upper floors of its two-story buildings while bystanders stared at James Grayson's Creek-style turban. Inquiry led them to the ten tree-covered acres of the Arkansas College campus.[99]

Arkansas College, founded by minister Robert Graham, was affiliated with the Christian Church when Wash arrived in 1859. It stressed the "great and moral principles of the Bible" and required attendance at the church of the student's choice. Its faculty offered courses in mathematics, languages, and moral and intellectual philosophy but insisted that "Science, not Religion, [was] the special subject of instruction."[100] President Graham personally welcomed the Graysons, accepted Wash's enrollment, and suggested a suitable boarding house for him. Then after one night's stay, James Grayson, his emotions barely under control, left his son to make his own way in this alien white world.[101]

As an old man Wash still remembered the strangeness and loneliness of those days at Arkansas College. White boys did not speak or dress or play in the same ways his Creek friends did. Not one of them spoke Muskogee. Though he stood out at home among the Creeks with his pale skin and dark red hair, his own eyes were used to brown skin, black hair, and dark eyes. All his life he admitted to irrational distaste for blond features such as those of some of his new classmates. At the same time, with the acute self-consciousness of the adolescent, he was uncomfortably aware that they thought he was peculiar. He was afraid he would embarrass himself by doing or saying the wrong thing. True, other Creek boys were there at the same time, but they were William McIntosh and Eli Jacobs, sons of prominent and wealthy Arkansas District families. As such they were far enough above him socially to prevent his feeling at ease with them for some time.[102]

Defensively he adopted a pose of aloofness behind which he studied the behavior of his schoolmates. This must have been a particularly hard period for him, for Creeks were a gregarious people. Wash had grown up surrounded by family and was sociable by nature. But only when he was sure that he could conduct himself acceptably did he begin to enter fully into school and extracurricular activities. It was also at this time that he developed his taste for fastidious and fashionable dress. After one purchase of clothing chosen more for the hard wear of the Creek frontier than for style, he wrote that he "became more civilized and more careful of my apparel and personal appearance, and thereafter had my clothing cut and sewed by the city tailor, and in the prevailing style."[103]

The Indian boys at Arkansas College lived under the careful scrutiny of the Creek agent as well as President Graham. They boarded just off the campus in the homes of Fayetteville families who served as their tutors in white culture and behavior. Wash Grayson's hosts were the Joe Lewis family.[104] The Creek boys' trustees allowed them to buy clothing, books, and school supplies from the firm of Stirman and Dickson, but Graham controlled all their purchases to guard against "habits of expense and dissoluteness."[105]

Looking back, Wash Grayson described Arkansas College as "a small and weak school." Yet the two years he spent there were profitable in several ways. He acquired ease in white society, and Fayetteville's "best families" welcomed him into their homes, in which he "enjoyed the amenities and hospitality of the refined."[106] In his studies he was a mediocre student except in Latin, in which he excelled somewhat to his surprise, never having encountered the language before. In fact, he discovered that he had a talent for languages, giving rise to his life-long interest in linguistics. That first year he converted to Christianity and was immersed by William Baxter, interim president of the college.[107] While this last development may have been the result of genuine conviction, it probably owed something to the desire to fit in and to the influence of his mother and teachers. Finally, in developing ease of movement in Fayetteville's society, Wash learned the skills he would need to navigate through Anglo-American society as a cultural broker.

Wash's successes justified the Creek Nation's faith in him and so gratified his parents that they had little hesitation about sending him back to Fayetteville to begin a second year of study in the fall of 1860. But his return home at the end of that second year brought his formal education to an end. His father was in failing health and now needed him to help support the family. Tensions between the Northern and Southern states were threatening to escalate into civil war. So his returning to Fayetteville in 1861 was out of the question.[108]

When Wash came home from school the last time, the Indian Territory had reached a remarkable state of prosperity and stability, considering the conditions under which the Five Civilized Tribes colonized it. Relations among those tribes, their Indian neighbors, and the federal government were reasonably cordial. Lawlessness was at a minimum, and factionalism was at least in remission. Each of the Five Civilized Tribes except the Seminoles had an elected constitutional government and a national school system.

Some aspects of this comfortable state of affairs had not come easily to the Creeks, especially their relationship with the Seminoles. The federal government had attempted to settle the two nations together in the Creek country during the Removal, but the amalgamation proved unsatisfactory. As a minority within the greater Creek Nation, the Seminoles feared the loss of their national identity, slave property, and sovereignty. They resisted the merger until 1856, when the two nations signed a treaty carving out for the Seminoles a strip of land between the North and South Canadian rivers in the southwestern Creek domain. By this cession the Creeks received $1 million and the Seminoles their independence.[109]

Another development was the further evolution of the Creek government toward the republican ideal held up by the agents. About 1858 the Creeks wrote a constitution and a code of civil, criminal, and slave laws. The constitution called for the election of a principal and second chief from each of the two districts, with the chief of Arkansas District having precedence. The constitution was, according to Angie Debo, "artificial" in that it ignored the *tvlwv* structure and traditional political forms. It never became operational.[110] In 1858 Roley McIntosh, who had exercised nearly complete control over the Lower Creeks since the execution of his half-brother, stepped down, as did the elderly Tuckabachee Mekko, "a staunch friend of his people, a maker of treaties, and a good man."[111] In their places, the Canadian District chose Echo Hacho (Harjo) as principal chief and Sands, or Oktahasas Hacho (Oktarharsars Harjo) as second chief. Arkansas District elected Motey Kennard principal chief and Jacob Derrisaw second chief. It was Kennard, a seven-foot-tall Baptist deacon and Jennie's kinsman, whom the Graysons credited with securing the school appointment for Wash.[112]

To ensure that the laws of the Creek Nation were enforced these men commanded the lighthorse, a troop of Creek mounted police. In general the Creek Nation was an orderly and law-abiding place except for the illicit liquor trade. Once the federal government abandoned Fort Gibson in 1857, stopping the trade became more difficult.[113] At the same time, a "vicious little town" grew up near the site of the fort.[114]

Most disturbing were those occasions when the federal government delivered annuities or supplemental payments of national funds. In 1857 treaty obligations totaling four hundred thousand dollars were divided per capita and distributed at the Creek Agency and at Chilly McIntosh's place on the North Fork. Part of these payments were made to Creeks who had immigrated at their own expense, including the families of Katy Grayson and Jennie Wynne Grayson. At such times Creeks en masse abandoned their plows and looms to gather at the distribution sites, pay off debts to the traders, visit, and receive their shares of the national wealth.[115]

These occasions never failed to upset their agent and the missionaries, either because they regarded the distribution of these funds as somehow unearned, demoralizing, and destabilizing or because of the carnival atmosphere that accompanied them. At the payment of August 1859, Southern Superintendent Elias Rector reported that "spirituous liquors were freely vended in the neighborhood, and on the ground; and, though a law prohibiting gaming was enacted and passed, 'faro' was openly dealt, and other thieving games played by the gamblers, who had resorted thither from Arkansas and elsewhere, as well as by the resident professors."[116]

Except for these lapses, the Creeks lived peaceably and industriously. Public opinion supported the laws, and an active temperance movement among the Christian converts and missionaries created a "cold water army" to aid the lighthorse in suppressing the liquor traffic. The Creek chiefs and people treated their agents courteously, becoming obstinate only when asked to cooperate with federal officials in taking a census and the possible survey of their lands in 1859. Their memories of the last such undertaking were all too clear.[117]

During Wash Grayson's youth, then, the Creek people demonstrated their resilience by rebuilding and stabilizing their lives in the ways they understood while incorporating the aspects of white culture they found useful. To outsiders the Creek Nation seemed well on its way toward adopting the forms of agriculture, education, religion, and government that white officials and missionaries regarded as "progressive" and "civilized." Theoretically these changes were preparing them for eventual assimilation into the larger Anglo-American society. But Creeks accomplished these changes for their own purposes and on their own terms, whether it was creating a school system or converting to Christianity. They moved warily, with an eye to the past as well as the future, refusing to sacrifice their identity or sovereignty.

Young Wash Grayson, representing the rising generation of Creeks for whom so many held high hopes, only knew that he found the Creek Nation to which he returned quiet to the point of boredom. There were friends and relations around him again, there was work to be done to help support his family, and there were barbecues, fishkillings, and camp meetings for entertainment. But these were no longer enough. His two years in Arkansas had acquainted him with a little more of the world and broadened his perspective considerably. He missed the bustle of Fayetteville and yearned for more excitement than North Fork Town could provide. The year 1861, however, was about to initiate changes that would satisfy his restlessness, lend definition to his Creek nationalism, and open new doors in his future.[118]

CHAPTER THREE

The Spirit of Our Fathers

Although conditions in North Fork Town and the Creek Nation in 1861 seemed placid to young Wash Grayson, they masked a growing national anxiety. Within months of his returning home, the Creek Nation was caught up in the tragedy of the Civil War, and the Grayson family was uprooted and driven into exile once more. The war devastated the Indian Territory and propelled the Indian nations toward the end of their sovereignty. But for Wash Grayson, it offered an opportunity to prove himself a man and demonstrate his abilities according to Muskogee standards. At the same time, the war years allowed him to observe for himself the interaction between the Creek Nation and its neighbors, Indian as well as white.

He was well placed to witness events of that critical year and at eighteen was legally of age to participate in them. On his return from Fayetteville in the spring of 1861, he found James Grayson in declining health, but the severity of his father's illness varied. It was possible for Wash to leave the family farm to clerk at Smith's general store and then at S. S. Sanger's in North Fork Town. He had access to American newspapers and heard the informal discussions of Creek affairs that took place in these gathering spots, so he was undoubtedly aware of rising tensions among his fellow Creeks.[1]

Some of this tension stemmed from questions currently dividing the Northern and Southern states. Although Creeks occupied a distant frontier, they were aware from the constant traffic through their country and from territorial and neighboring state newspapers that states' rights, slavery, and the threat of Southern secession were critical issues. And as these issues grew in prominence, Creeks hardened their own racial attitudes, bringing their slave laws into line with those of the Southern states. They, too, feared the loss of their slave property should Republican Abraham Lincoln win the presidency in 1860.[2]

But slavery was only one issue that concerned the Creeks. Equally alarming, perhaps more so, was the prospect that the federal government might once more dispossess them. Even though the Removal treaty guaranteed the Creeks sovereignty and possession of their Indian Territory lands, they knew that white Americans coveted those lands. In his 1858 report, a public document, Southern Indian Superintendent Rector paid lip service to Indian rights and title, but then trumpeted praise for "the rich alluvial valleys . . . vast extents of the most beautiful and fertile limestone prairies; ranges of mountains abounding in minerals; lovely valleys in between; incalculable wealth of coal, limestone, and marble; salt springs, water power; everything in short that is needed to make a great and flourishing State, a great grain-producing, stock raising, vinegrowing country."[3]

True, he conceded, the Indian nations held this land in fee simple; but that *really* (his emphasis) implied only a usufruct right as far as the individual tribal citizen was concerned. Necessity, the supreme law of nations, he reasoned, must soon force the federal government to allot Indian land in severalty, give the Indian the right to sell or lease his allotment to non-Indians, and grant him United States citizenship. That end being both inevitable and desirable, Rector concluded, "how insignificant their petty nationalities and half independencies, and quasi-ownership of the soil which they cannot alienate?"[4] It probably came as no surprise to the Creeks that in 1859 the Commissioner of Indian Affairs proposed that they allow their lands to be surveyed and allotted in severalty.[5]

Sincerely dedicated to Creek welfare, missionary Loughridge protested passionately, "If the desire is to destroy the Indians in the most complete and expeditious manner, this is the way to do it." If allotment took place and whites were allowed to move into the Indian Territory, he warned, one only had to look into pre-Removal history to know that "soon, very soon, we [would] see the great body of the Creeks wandering about, like other Indians in many parts of the State, without lands, without homes, or any means of support." Loughridge urged the federal government to honor its treaty obligations to protect their land, educate the rising generation, and allow them to mature as an "enlightened Christian nation."[6]

Principal Chiefs Motey Kennard and Echo Hacho agreed with Loughridge, for they politely but definitely refused to submit to allotment. Having tried the plan before in 1832 in the old Creek nation, they reminded their agent that the results were "evils and evils continually. . . . The misery and punishment endured by our people growing out of sectionalization . . . is fresh upon our minds. Hence there is no consideration that can induce us to try the experiment again."[7]

But the idea reemerged in the presidential campaign of 1860. Republican William Seward declared, "The Indian Territory . . . south of Kansas must be vacated by the Indians."[8] This may have been only campaign rhetoric, but coming so soon after the commissioner's proposition, Seward's statement must have compounded Indian fears concerning their lands and their future as well as their slaves.

While fear of federal intentions propelled the Creeks out of the Union, common concerns, economic ties, and heritage drew them toward a Confederate alliance. The Confederacy appreciated that the Indian Territory had much to offer should war follow secession. Its resources of grain, meat, salt, lead, and horses could supply and transport armies, while many of its men were skilled, experienced guerrilla fighters. The Texas and California roads, intersecting south of North Fork Town across the Canadian River, carried a heavy volume of commercial, civilian, and military traffic. The Indian Territory was a natural buffer or, conversely, an invasion route between secessionist and loyal states. Both the Confederacy and the Union recognized these conditions, but only the South took positive steps to secure the allegiance of its one hundred thousand inhabitants.[9]

Between February and June 1861 representatives of the Confederacy attended a series of councils at North Fork Town with the Creeks and their

Indian neighbors. These emissaries stressed the common concerns and values that bound the Indian Territory and the Confederacy, while they underscored the unreliability of the Union, which they described as irrevocably fractured. They persuaded a number of influential Creeks— Chilly McIntosh, his half-brother Daniel N. McIntosh, Benjamin Marshall, Chief Motey Kennard, Tuckabachee Mekko, Timothy Barnett, Samuel Checote, and G. W. Stidham—that their best interests lay with the Confederacy. However, according to one Creek observer, other "principally full-blood Indians of no education and not of much wealth outside of immense herds of cattle," resisted Confederate overtures.[10] With nothing yet resolved, the leaders opposed to the new alliance journeyed to the western frontier to confer with the Plains tribes. In their absence the "Southern" faction cooperated in creating the Grand Council, the first step toward a pro-Confederate, unified Indian government for the territory.[11]

During this critical period, the federal government inadvertently drove the Indian nations further into the arms of the Confederacy. First it evacuated its troops from Forts Cobb, Arbuckle, and Washita, leaving the western frontier open to Plains raiders and white intruders.[12] Then nervous federal officials withheld the 1861 annuity payments to keep them from falling into the hands of "armed rebels and banditti."[13] In the best of times those funds were needed to operate Creek schools and maintain the government. But early 1861 saw especially hard times in the Creek Nation, as a shortage of corn left only one family in ten, according to one witness, with enough to eat. Without the annuities the Creek government would be hard pressed to offer desperate families relief.[14]

Withdrawing protection and withholding the annuities violated the Removal treaty while undermining the federal government's credibility. Nor were there communications from Washington advising the Indian nations what its policies would be during the secession crisis. On the other hand, Albert Pike, an Arkansas politician and poet widely respected by Indians as a brother Mason, brought the Indian nations a liberal proposal from Richmond. The Confederacy promised the Creeks that it would assume the treaty obligations of the United States, including paying the $71,960 annuity, protecting Creek lands and slave property, and allowing the Creeks and Seminoles a joint delegate to the Confederate Congress.[15]

In fine summer weather during early July, while Pike camped just off the Texas Road in the woods outside the settlement, more than one thousand Creeks responded to Chief Kennard's call for a council near North Fork Town. The deliberations took place in the shade of a brush arbor on the west bank of Baptizing Creek at the north foot of Chintz Mountain (presently Foley's Mountain on the west edge of Eufaula, Oklahoma). The site, a broad prairie with abundant grass, water, and space for the large encampment and livestock, was about four miles west of North Fork Town. It had been the scene of many a Baptist camp meeting. Wash's great-uncle Watt Grayson, who lived about five miles from the settlement, ordered his slaves to drive a herd of cattle in for butchering and barbecuing. S. S. Sanger, William H. Rogers, and fellow merchants Eliason and Adkins provided groceries to feed the gathering at the expense of the Creek Nation.[16]

Ordinarily such councils strove for consensus, democratically providing a courteous hearing to all who wished to speak. This time, though, an unusually intense and acrimonious debate took place between supporters and opponents of the proposed Creek-Confederate alliance. Representing the opposition leaders still absent on the Plains, Opothle Yahola, a bitter antagonist of the McIntoshes, argued eloquently and stubbornly that signing the proposed Confederate treaty violated the one already extant between the Creek Nation and the United States. Sands, Locha Hacho (Lochar Harjo), and Cotchochee supported him. Finally, seeing that he could not dissuade the pro-Southern faction, Opothle Yahola followed Muskogee tradition in cases in which consensus was impossible and withdrew with his followers to the western frontier. The McIntoshes, Stidham, and Chief Kennard then signed the Confederate alliance for the Creeks.[17]

It is likely Wash Grayson had a ringside seat for these events. He was related to several of the pro-Confederate leaders and probably knew Opothle Yahola, a neighbor of the James Grayson family when they had lived near Brush Hill in the vicinity of North Fork Town. (Even though Wash eventually identified with the Confederate Creeks, in later years he spoke admiringly of the Creek elder's stand in support of the old treaty, calling him, "a wise and patriotic counselor."[18]) As a clerk for S. S. Sanger, purveyor of foodstuffs to the council, Wash had good reason to be at the campground. Nor is it likely that he would have missed participating in what was to him and his fellow Creeks a great event. Years later, the Creek-Confederate Treaty resided in his personal library, acquired perhaps from his future father-in-law, G. W. Stidham.[19]

The consequences of the council came so quickly that within four months of the Confederate attack on Fort Sumter, the Civil War set Creek against Creek. Opothle Yahola's withdrawal from the council at North Fork Town signaled the revival of bitter Removal-era factionalism, followed by open warfare.

Historians continue to debate whether that factionalism was political, cultural, or both. Many have generalized that the pro-Confederate Creeks were the old Lower Creek McIntosh faction composed of the more acculturated mixed-bloods, while the neutralists, later designated Loyal or Unionist Creeks, were the traditionalist full-bloods of the Upper Creek faction.[20] One has termed the factions "change-oriented planters" versus "fundamentalist conservative subsistence farmers," stating that the division was regional within the Creek Nation.[21] Recently some ethnohistorians have suggested that African slavery, viewed by traditionalists as an unwelcome adaptation of a foreign culture, became as divisive among Indian Territory residents as among Anglo-Americans, and thus was a prime factor in their participation in the Civil War.[22] Muskogee tradition offers yet another explanation: Tuckabachee *tvlwv*, to which Opothle Yahola belonged, originated in the sky, whereas Koweta *tvlwv*, to which the McIntoshes belonged, appeared from the crust of the earth. Thus, their enmity was generations old, and the Civil War simply rekindled it.[23]

None of these theories adequately explains how Creeks chose sides in the Civil War crisis. Among the Loyal Creeks were wealthy slaveholders, implying that some were no longer traditional subsistence farmers. Opothle Yahola of Tuckabachee Town, though often represented as the quintessential Upper Creek traditionalist, owned numerous slaves and had been a merchant in partnership with a white noncitizen. According to some accounts, he was much Anglo-Muskogee by descent as the Graysons and the McIntoshes. Moreover, Opothle Yahola and Tucka-bachee Mekko took opposing sides, illustrating perhaps that the division cut across even *tvlwv* lines. Future Creek Chiefs Joseph M. and Legus C. Perryman and future Yuchee Creek Chief Samuel W. Brown, all from wealthy slaveholding, Anglo-Muskogee families, became Union soldiers. Oral history holds that Una McIntosh, brother of the executed chief William, enlisted with his slaves in the Union Army, while some Creeks of black descent fought as Confederate soldiers. Grayson family members likewise joined both factions. Simpson Grayson sold his slaves and joined Opothle Yahola's faction. James's sister, Tility Grayson McAnally, "went North" while her son Valentine became a Creek Confederate trooper.[24] All of this suggests the complexity of choosing sides in the Creek Nation of 1861.

By the summer of 1861 neutrality was fast disappearing as a viable option in the Creek Nation. Opothle Yahola had gathered around him like-minded Creeks, Seminoles, Wichitas, Delawares, Shawnees, Kickapoos, Quapaws, Chickasaws, Cherokees, and Comanches. They declared they wanted no part of a "white man's war" and intended to keep faith with the federal government.[25] Opothle Yahola and Sands appealed to President Lincoln, the "Great Father," to uphold his treaties with the Creeks: "You said that in our new homes we should be defended from all interference from any people and that no white people in the whole world should ever molest us unless they came from the sky but the land should be ours as long as grass grew or waters run, and should we be injured by anybody you would come with your soldiers & punish them, but now the wolf has come, men who are strangers tread our soil, our children are frightened & the mothers cannot sleep for fear." The old speaker pleaded, "Keep off the intruder and make our homes again happy as they used to be."[26]

But the Great Father was busy with more pressing concerns. He failed to reassure Creeks of his protection, and a great migration began within the Indian Territory. Federal employees, missionaries, and white non-citizens living in the Indian nations under permit left for the relative safety of "the States." Even though Opothle Yahola, a major slaveholder, stood less for abolition and the Union than for what seemed to him to be Creek interests, runaway slaves and freedmen sought refuge in his camp on the upper Deep Fork of the Canadian River. Likewise anticipating hostilities, some pro-Confederate Indians moved their children, herds, and slaves to the greater security of the Red River Valley. The exodus of these groups depopulated and transformed the prosperous, peaceful western countryside into an eerie desert in which corn and sweet potatoes lay unharvested in the fields, untended cows lowed, lonely dogs howled, and roosters crowed in abandoned yards.[27]

By fall Opothle Yahola's following numbered seven or eight thousand, and his presence on the western frontier worried Confederate leaders in the Indian Territory. Slaveholders believed his camp enticed runaway slaves. More ominous was the possibility that he would join General John C. Fremont's Union army in Missouri. Their combined forces might then sweep down on the Arkansas River Valley settlements. To prevent these eventualities, the Confederate leaders planned an expedition designed to suppress Opothle Yahola and break up his following. By this time they had at their disposal regiments from the Five Civilized Tribes as well as token forces from the other Confederate-allied tribes of the territory. Choctaws and Chickasaws almost unanimously joined the Confederate alliance, and Seminoles and Cherokees, in common with the Creeks, divided almost equally into Confederate and Unionist factions. The Confederacy combined its allies under the Department of Indian Territory, Brigadier General Albert Pike commanding. Eventually these troops were designated the Indian Brigade and placed under the command of Cherokee Colonel (later Brigadier General) Stand Watie.[28]

In November 1861 several Confederate Indian and Texas units, in addition to Creeks commanded by Colonel Daniel N. McIntosh and Lieutenant Colonel Chilly McIntosh, set off after Opothle Yahola's Loyalists. At first his people left a broad trail as they drove their stock and packhorses toward the Kansas border. Three times his painted warriors fought off the pursuing Confederates but each time at greater cost. Finally the desperate Loyal Creeks dropped their belongings and abandoned those too old, too young, too sick, or too weak to keep up. Their dead lay unburied beside a trail marked with the blood of the wounded and the tracks of those struggling barefoot through early snow. At the end of that unusually harsh December, they burned the prairie behind them to erase their trail and scattered. The Confederate troops, their own supplies and ammunition gone, gave up the pursuit, allowing the survivors to slip away into Kansas.[29]

The remnant, "a famishing, freezing multitude," took refuge near the headwaters of the Verdigris River.[30] Their temporary agent reported that they arrived with nothing except the clothes on their backs: "Families who in their country had been wealthy, and who could count their cattle by the thousands and horses by hundreds, and owned large numbers of slaves . . . were without even the necessaries of life."[31] Kansas authorities were not prepared to deal with a refugee problem of that magnitude, so that bitter winter the exiles starved and froze while waiting for Congress to authorize spending the unpaid Creek annuities for their relief. Opothle Yahola, before his death in exile, bitterly advised federal officials to show the rebel (Confederate) Creek women and children no mercy: the best way to get rid of a bad breed of dog was to kill the bitch.[32]

With the war less than a year old, former missionary J. S. Murrow wrote in January 1862, "The western portions of this Indian Territory are all ruined and laid waste. All improvements are burned, stock all driven off or killed, and the entire western settlements deserted. 'Tis *sad*, and made my heart ache as I beheld settlements and farms, where a few months ago families lived in plenty and pleasure, now deserted and ruined—nothing but the rock chimneys left. It seems as if the good and wise God is purposing to destroy this Indian race entirely."[33]

Such devastation became the hallmark of the Civil War in the Indian Territory. Each side pledged itself initially to protect civilian life and property and to limit attacks to military targets, but they soon abandoned such lofty aims. Livestock, foodcrops, groceries, and structures were civilian property, but they were also necessities to armies on the farthest ends of the Union and Confederate supply lines. Men and women also forfeited their personal inclinations under the demands of the times, and those who preferred to remain peaceably at home had that option taken from them.

But until the middle of 1863 the family of Jennie Grayson, widowed in about 1860, and most Confederate Creeks escaped the worst of the violence. Once the excitement over Opothle Yahola's pursuit subsided, life was fairly peaceful. The fighting was far away in the eastern Cherokee Nation, where Federal troops tried unsuccessfully to restore control to the Unionist followers of Principal Chief Ross. Still, some Creeks anticipated a possible Union invasion and began a leisurely migration southward. The well-to-do sent their children to school in states they believed relatively safe from Northern invasion. They moved their portable goods, including their slaves, to the safety of the Red River Valley. Some, such as George W. Stidham and Jennie's kinsman, Chief Kennard, secured their property there and then returned to North Fork Town to await developments. But the McIntoshes, Lewises, and Marshalls who remained in self-imposed exile formed a Southern Creek government with Stidham temporarily chosen principal chief.[34]

Wash Grayson and his family were not a part of this early migration. Jennie chose to remain at home near North Fork Town, working the farm with her three teenaged sons and three younger children. That he was needed at home and other factors kept Wash from following his inclination to join the 1,375 Creek men already enlisted in the Confederate regiment by the fall of 1861.[35]

Writing about those dark times forty years later, Wash did not find it necessary to explain why he chose to support the Confederate Creek faction. At first glance, his Southern affiliation was obvious. He was the son and grandson of slaveholders, if slavery was the issue. Also, the Grayson family had allied itself with the McIntosh faction through marriage as well as cultural and political inclination, and in that matrilineal society his mother's Lower Creek kinsmen were leaders of the Confederate faction. Somewhat complicating the issue was the Graysons' Upper Creek background—especially traditionalist Tulwa Tustunuggee's— if the Upper Creeks, as some historians suppose, generally followed Opothle Yahola. An important clue lies in Wash's statement that when he eventually enlisted in a Confederate Creek regiment he joined his "old neighbors of long acquaintance" in the Canadian District, the Upper Creek Okfuskees and Eufaulas.[36]

A related, more compelling motive for his yearning to fight lay in his understanding of that Creek community's expectations of him. Wash had grown up among traditionalists, and he had already received his ceremonial name, Yaha (Wolf), during the Green Corn Ceremony. At eighteen he stood on the threshold of manhood and was ready to accept a Muskogee man's responsibilities to provide for his family and participate in the ceremonial life, politics, and wars of his community. Wash had learned at his elders' knees to honor the Creek warrior tradition. He knew the acquisition of war names and titles denoting personal courage and achievement in his people's battles validated a man's place in the

Muskogee social structure. Young men like Wash ardently desired these honors and public recognition, especially from their elders.[37]

In the changing times of the mid-1800s, warfare was severely curtailed, limited to defending the western frontier against sporadic Plains Indian raids. Although English education and agricultural and commercial enterprises offered young men new avenues for advancement, opportunities to prove oneself as a warrior and a leader of men in battle, the traditional means of achieving status, were increasingly rare. To have missed this opportunity and failed to meet the expectations of his community would have been devastating to an ambitious—and bored—young man.

At the time, Wash excused his remaining at home as his fulfillment of the eldest son's responsibility to care for his mother and his younger siblings. He also justified his initial refusal to enlist by pointing out that according to their treaty with the Confederacy, Creek troops were to remain in the Indian Territory, far from the real fighting. Nor was the Creek Nation threatened now that Opothle Yahola was in exile in Kansas. That being the case, he did not see the point of hurrying to enlist only to sit idle in camp.[38]

But he was uncomfortably conscious that others did not see his remaining at home in the same practical light. He could ride and shoot, and he was certainly able-bodied enough to fight. Six feet tall and weighing 170 pounds, his once-red hair toned down to brown and worn flowing to his shoulders, he resembled other young Creek men of his day, who loved to make a great show by galloping their ponies into town and swaggering into the stores. Wash's elders murmured that because of his English education, he more than most should be taking his place in one of the Confederate Creek units. In an international army that spoke at least three Muskogee dialects and a number of related and unrelated languages, an officer whose fluency in English, the lingua franca, allowed him to read, write, and interpret orders was highly valuable. In other words, he could begin repaying the Creek Nation for his English education by serving as an interpreter as well as a warrior.[39]

But Wash delayed enlisting. As late as April 1862, he visited William H. Rogers's general store in North Fork Town to buy staples, cloth, articles of clothing, and sundry items. Other customers included his kinsmen

Chilly McIntosh and Chief Kennard, Stidham, ardently pro-Confederate Baptist missionary and family friend H. F. Buckner, and James M. C. Smith, quartermaster of the Confederate Creek regiments. They probably pressured him to enlist, and he heard talk that a lieutenancy in one the of the regiments could be created for him. Still he refused to sign up.[40]

It was a galling situation. Wash knew that community opinion of him as a man was sagging. He longed to follow his cousin Valentine into the regiment and share the excitement of the moment, while he chafed at the knowledge that others suspected him of cowardice. He soothed his frustration during those months with the somewhat adolescent promise that when he enlisted he would do so as a private. He would serve in that lowly capacity, he promised himself, until he had demonstrated that his personal courage as well as his English education entitled him to an officer's rank and the respect of his peers. He would show his critics, he said, "the stuff I was made of, even if it cost my life to make the exhibition."[41]

Eventually Wash did enlist, but his vagueness later about the date of his enlistment suggested he remained sensitive to the criticism leveled at him. It was perhaps as early as May 1862, but it could have been a year later that he joined the Second Creek Mounted Volunteers as a private in Company K. True to his vow, he remained in the ranks for some months before consenting to be promoted to regimental adjutant. He must have lived up to expectations then, because the inspector who audited his records in October 1863 remarked that the books and files in his care were in good order—probably a pleasant surprise given the usually haphazard or nonexistent state of paperwork in the Indian regiments.[42]

Wash mused many years later that he accepted the promotion because the additional increase in pay would be useful to his mother. Wartime shortages by 1863 had caused prices of even common items to skyrocket, as hostilities disrupted the trade routes into the Indian Territory. Denim cloth that sold for fifty cents per yard before the war and which Wash bought for seventy-five cents in January 1862 cost seven dollars one year later. Brown and bleached domestic cloth was similarly inflated in price. Common ready-made shirts and pants brought nine dollars each, whereas Wash had paid only five dollars for two coats early in 1862. The poorest quality homemade shoes cost twelve dollars a pair. Tobacco brought five dollars per plug. Flour was expensive, if it could be obtained at all, and even corn meal was in short supply once the noncitizen millers left the territory for the States. For the time being there were vegetables and meat enough, but such imported items as coffee and sugar were luxuries. As an officer, Wash could not only expect to send more money home but also to receive a larger share of any goods captured from the enemy.[43]

As a member of the regiment he was among friends, kin, and clan. Like Wash, his commander, Colonel Chilly McIntosh, was a Koweta and a descendant of Robert Grierson. He was also married to one of the Benson relatives. Lieutenant Colonel Pink Hawkins, Major Timothy Barnett, and Captain Goliah (Goliath) Herrod were relatives by blood or marriage. Wash's cousin Valentine N. McAnally, who had accompanied him to Fayetteville three years earlier, was there, as was Captain David Yargee, another Arkansas College student. Lieutenant Colonel Samuel Checote, Lieutenant Pleasant Porter, First Sergeant Moty Tiger, and Lieutenant Jackson Lewis became life-long friends and associates.[44]

Lewis, like Wash, was a member of Company K. Part Hetcheta and a member of Eufaula Town, he was about a decade older than Wash and a survivor of the Trail of Tears. Wash later remarked that Jackson Lewis was one of the few people he ever knew who understood the ancient mysteries and possessed the powers of the Creek medicine men. While officially serving first as sergeant of Company K and then as second lieutenant, he was the company medical officer, caring for both the physical and spiritual well-being of the men. Wash had the greatest respect for him. Their friendship grew when Wash at some point returned to the company as its lieutenant, then as its captain and Lewis's immediate senior officer.[45]

Wash Grayson's war was quite different from that of the usual Civil War soldier. Few formal battles were fought in the Indian Territory; nor did engagements ordinarily involve great numbers of troops. On paper, the entire Indian Brigade consisted of only about eight hundred men, with about two hundred of them officially in the Second Creek Mounted Regiment. Lack of Union activity in or near the territory and shortages of food, supplies, and fodder for the horses frequently led the Confederate commanders to furlough most of the troops. In the informal Indian fashion individuals also drifted away home periodically for their own reasons until word came that they were needed. Then they returned to their camps and their Indian officers, who were much less perturbed by this seeming dereliction of duty than white officers.[46]

Confederate Brigadier General William H. Steele wrote sourly in February 1864, "An experience of twelve months in the command of Indian country has convinced me that, with a few exceptions, the Indians are wholly unreliable as troops of the line."[47] Steele had no time for either the Indian troops or the officers who commanded them, whether they were Indian or "Indianized white men" such as Colonel Douglas H. Cooper, formerly the Choctaw agent.[48] In fact, few white officers either understood or appreciated the Indian troops. This was partially a racial judgment, but it also demonstrated a lack of understanding of Indian ways.

One who did understand was Brigadier General Pike, negotiator of the Creek-Confederate Treaty of 1861. He reminded his senior officers that the Indian troops received little or no equipment, arms, uniforms, blankets, or tents from Confederate quartermasters. Supplies meant for the Indian troops were often diverted to white soldiers before they ever reached the territory. Bitterly he complained that the mules drawing his baggage train were "scarecrows . . . [but] considered good enough for the Indian service."[49] Frequently pay for the Indian troops was also months behind, forcing him at one point to spend twenty thousand dollars of his own money to insure their loyalty. But even he recognized the short-comings of the Indian troops and particularly their officers, who cared little for the forms and reports white officers considered a necessity of military organization. He also thought of the Indian troops as undisciplined, needing the bracing of white troops in a fight.[50]

Indian soldiers contributed to their own unmilitary image. Because the promised Confederate uniforms rarely if ever arrived, Indian troops dressed in civilian clothing or whatever they could "yamp," or confiscate. Wash recalled that his men usually "presented a very motley appearance" and "were never very presentable."[51] By the winter of 1864 his only protection from the cold weather was a small Mexican blanket. Routinely Watie's Indian Brigade troops stripped prisoners of any item of clothing they could use; Wash's men usually gave the prisoners their castoffs in exchange.[52]

One of Wash's favorite recollections involved his cousin Valentine McAnally's hat. It was standard Confederate issue, made of unbleached (and from the smell, unwashed) sheep's wool, conical in design once hard

wear and weather reduced it to its unblocked shape. To make it conform
to Creek notions of style, Valentine attached to the crown a hawk's feather
(a traditional Muskogee war symbol), which he had shaved down so as to
make the limber shaft sway and bob over his head. But when the
opportunity came, Valentine readily traded his hat for one belonging to
a tall, gangling white prisoner. Wash considered the white man's woe-
begone face, topped off by the jaunty, plumed Confederate Indian hat,
one of the most ludicrous sights he ever saw.[53]

Less amusing was the chronic shortage of weapons. Creek troops used
whatever they had or could capture. Members of Company K were
equipped with sometimes unreliable flintlock rifles, while Wash was proud
to own a cap and ball pistol. His commander, Colonel Chilly McIntosh,
complained in June 1862 that his men had received only a scanty ration
of sixty pounds of gunpowder. They needed one hundred guns and the
services of a blacksmith but would take what they could get. A month later
Pike complained that the Indian soldiers had only about thirty-five
percussion caps each.[54]

Likewise, these mounted troops provided their own horses. Having
grown up on the Creek frontier, Wash was an experienced rider and
regarded his horse Rover as a friend and companion as well as military
equipment. More than once he credited Rover with saving his life. On
one occasion Wash was with a foraging party gathering corn in a fenced
field. Unexpectedly, Federal cavalry descended on them, cutting off
escape through the single gate. Unable to break through the stout fence
around the corn field, Wash jumped Rover over the rails, expecting to
land on solid ground on the other side. Both were surprised to find that
tall brush and grass hid the drop-off to a deep, water-filled ravine. Instead
of striking firm ground, horse and rider tobogganed helplessly down the
steep slope and landed saddle-deep in a creek. From there they easily
reached dry ground and the safety of a haw thicket where, Wash recalled,
they both ate their fill of the ripe fruit and "meditated on the funny things
. . . incident to a warrior in time of general belligerency."[55]

This was only one of several times Wash was cut off from the main body
of the Indian Brigade yet safely made his way back. Brigadier General Pike
understood, if most white officers did not, that Indian troops were at their
best if free to fight the individualistic style of warfare they knew best.

Unwilling to stand in ranks on open ground and face massed enemy or artillery fire, they were skilled guerrilla fighters and scouts. Small groups and lone men traveled easily through the rough country they knew so well, slipped up to darkened windows, and picked up needed food, clothing, and information from friends and relatives.[56] By the end of the war even white Confederate officers gave the Indian Brigade grudging respect as raiders, while federal officials fumed that Watie's "700 ragamuffins" stole, drove off, carried away, or destroyed at will anything beyond the range of then Union-occupied Fort Gibson's cannon.[57]

The war in the Indian Territory, then, had less in common with the formalized conflict of the eastern theaters than with traditional Indian warfare. Creek troops, as they had from time immemorial, put on their paint before battle. Wash remembered vividly how Jackson Lewis in his role as their spiritual advisor painted their cheeks and chests red for the warpath and black for death. Then, devout Baptist that he was, he made the sign of the cross over them. Once the battle was over he had them cleanse body and spirit by bathing in a creek, drinking water, and regurgitating it. Company K kept a special article of war medicine, which they believed gave them strength and protection in battle. Wash refused to rub it over his body and clothing as they did, not because he discounted its supernatural power but because he wanted to show that he possessed enough courage to face the enemy without it.[58]

True to Muskogee warrior tradition, Wash was preoccupied throughout his Civil War experience with demonstrating his personal courage and upholding the honor of the Creeks under his command. This was due in part to traditional Muskogee expectations of what was proper in a young man and a leader of men, but it was also a means of erasing any stigma attached to his late enlistment. As an officer he was aware of white disdain for Indian troops, and this created a certain tension within him. While he knew the value of his men and their type of warfare, he felt compelled to make them measure up to Anglo-American expectations. Company K frustrated him by failing to understand the need to drill and fight in formation as white soldiers did, but they never disappointed him when the battle was hand to hand.[59]

Eventually he was also satisfied that he had refuted any doubts as to his own personal courage, at least among his fellow Creeks in Company K.

Around a campfire one evening Jackson Munawe, a descendant of a famous warrior, stated casually that if their former company commander had lacked courage in leading them into battle they had nothing to complain of now. That quiet comment was his assurance that Wash had met their expectations. In their eyes Wash Grayson had earned the honor and status of a *tvstvnvkke*, the rank awarded to those who had led men in battle. For the rest of his life, Creeks would know him both as "Captain G. W. Grayson" and "Yaha Tustunuggee," (Wolf Warrior). Looking back on his youthful exploits with the maturity of six decades, he still took great pride in having carried on the tradition of the Creek warrior. But he was also forced to admit that at the time he simply was not wise enough to be frightened.[60]

Wash Grayson's initiation as a warrior occurred as the relative calm in the Creek Nation ended in the spring of 1863. Through the winter of 1862 the Federals failed to curtail Confederate control of most of the Indian Territory except the eastern Cherokee Nation. There in the preceding summer they had returned Chief Ross and his Unionist adherents to control, but Ross's old enemy Stand Watie eluded them. Now principal chief of the Confederate Cherokee faction and commander of the Confederate Indian troops, Watie executed vindictive raids against Ross's adherents as well as Federal units. Unwilling to retreat further south and too weak to retake the Cherokee Nation, Watie's Indian Brigade set up winter quarters on the lower Canadian River. Confederate Creek troops were garrisoned at Fort Gibson, abandoned back in 1857, where they passed the early winter months fairly quietly and comfortably.[61]

Stephen Foreman, a Cherokee Presbyterian minister, visited the camp that December and found the Creeks "short on bread stuffs, but [with] beef a plenty. In some instances they [were] destitute of shoes and clothing." A more appalling condition to the pious Foreman was the riotous living that went on in the camps, especially near Fort Gibson. There he discovered dancing and drinking at "twenty dollars *a bottle!*" [his emphasis]. Horse racing, he fulminated, was the besetting sin. "All go to horse races, as far as I know, without any exception, Baptists, Methodists, and Presbyterians. Col. McIntosh, once a Baptist preacher, is the leader in horseracing now." Foreman concluded righteously, "Had the Federals come today many a one of the Regiment would have been killed or taken prisoner, and it would have been well enough, for it seems to me that this

Regiment needs some heavy affliction to teach them their duty in guarding against the approaches of the enemy." The backsliding Colonel McIntosh refused to listen to Foreman's moral or military advice, and his faction rebuffed a Federal offer of terms in order to allow Opothle Yahola's people to return home.[62]

Then on January 10 the weather turned bitter as rain changed to four or five inches of snow. "The soldiers must suffer a great deal in weather such as this, because it is impossible to keep the feet dry for the snow and slop around the fire," Foreman commiserated. "They nearly all have good tents to screen them from the snow and rain overhead, but cannot protect their feet."[63] The next day an additional five inches fell with a cold wind following. Twenty horses died from starvation. Wash might have shared the troops' misery, but it is likely that he spent the winter on furlough at home with Jennie and the family.[64]

Spring brought a sharp escalation of the war in the Indian Territory. In April 1863 Federal Colonel William A. Phillips reoccupied Fort Gibson as the first step toward extending Union control into the Cherokee, Creek, and Choctaw Nations. As a wave of alarm swept the Creek country, Confederate forces congregated just north of North Fork Town on the Texas Road and set up a depot at Honey Springs (near today's Rentiesville, Oklahoma). Creek soldiers who had scattered during the winter hurried back to duty. On April 22, Cherokee, Creek, and Texas troops gathered to listen to addresses from their leaders. Chief Kennard encouraged the Creek troops in their own language to fight with honor and dedication to their cause and through an interpreter thanked the Texas troops for their aid. Colonel Watie spoke to the troops in Cherokee with Foreman translating.[65]

This seemed to mark the official opening of the spring campaign. For the next several weeks Watie's men harassed Fort Gibson and its long supply line to Fort Scott, Kansas. Though they failed on July 1 and 2 to intercept a large Federal supply train at the First Battle of Cabin Creek, they slowly accumulated supplies and waited for reinforcements and artillery from Fort Smith, Arkansas. Their aim was to retake the fort (see map 2).[66]

The Federals in the Indian Territory likewise grew stronger with the arrival of Major General James G. Blunt and reinforcements from Kansas. Aware that the six thousand Confederates in the Creek Nation already

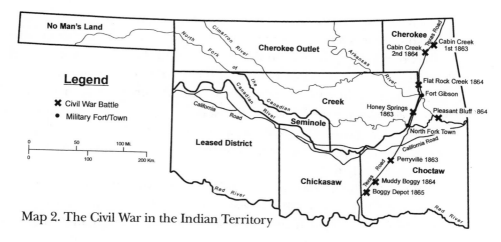

Map 2. The Civil War in the Indian Territory

outnumbered him two to one, Blunt decided to attack them before the reinforcements from Arkansas raised the odds to three to one. On the night of July 15 he left Fort Gibson, putting his force, now including Opothle Yahola's refugees and freedmen enlisted in the Union Army, across the rain-swollen Arkansas River. By midmorning the next day Federal troops were moving south down the Texas Road toward North Fork Town. That evening and at daybreak on July 17 they skirmished with Confederate scouts and found the main body of Brigadier General Douglas H. Cooper's troops about five miles north of Honey Springs. Where Elk Creek made an elm- and oak-lined S-curve along the north side of Pumpkin Ridge, the Texas Road dropped down over a low, wooded sandstone bluff. It traversed a narrow floodplain and crossed the creek at a stone-piered wooden toll bridge before angling south to Honey Springs. Cooper had drawn his troops and artillery up along the bluff and astride the road north of the bridge. Though Blunt was outnumbered, he could put twelve cannon in the field to Cooper's four.[67]

Wash Grayson was stationed with the Second Creek Mounted Volunteers on the extreme left of the Confederate line. Crouching in the dense undergrowth of Elk Creek bottom that rainy morning, they could see little through the brush and mist but could hear the war cries of their fellow troops, the pop of small arms, and the roar of artillery. Determined and eager, they waited for orders to enter the fight, which commenced about ten o'clock. Colonel Chilly McIntosh had addressed them earlier:

"When you first saw the light, it was said of you 'a man child is born.' You must prove today whether or not this saying of you was true. The sun that hangs over our heads has no death, no end of days. It will continue indefinitely to rise and to set; but with you it is different. Man must die sometime, and since he must die, he can find no nobler death than that which overtakes him while fighting for his home, his fires and his country." Because this was his first real engagement and because of his determination to prove his courage, Wash considered his colonel's war-talk particularly striking.[68]

Consequently, he was dismayed and frustrated when the Creeks never entered the fight; rather, they received orders to retreat without firing a shot. In the four-hour battle, the Confederates withstood an artillery barrage and initially returned heavy fire before losing one of their four cannon. Then in the confusion they misunderstood shouted Federal orders to one misplaced company of Unionist Creeks to fall back. Thinking the whole Federal line was retreating, they surged forward into the deadly fire of desperate, determined black Union soldiers, former slaves who knew they could expect no quarter. Cooper, seeing the heavy losses his men were taking as they were pushed down off the bluff, ordered a withdrawal southward across Elk Creek Bridge. They were to hold it while the Honey Springs depot beyond was evacuated. This they did in good order. Though Cooper saved most of his troops, artillery, and baggage train, he ordered the stores of foodstuffs burned as his men retreated. Even then, Federals arrived soon enough to put out the fire and save much of the valuable contents, compounding their coup.[69]

Officially, the Confederate commanders blamed the defeat on the poor quality Mexican gunpowder supplied to their troops. Unlike that imported from Europe, powder manufactured for the dry climate of Mexico had no protective coating of graphite. It absorbed moisture from damp air, a morale-lowering fact that became apparent in early skirmishing the evening before the battle. A heavy thunderstorm had rolled through early on the morning of the battle, leaving high humidity that turned the powder into a useless paste. But Wash Grayson, knowing that Cooper never even ordered his Creek regiments into the attack, agreed with Watie that the loss at Honey Springs was due to Cooper's mismanagement of his Indian troops.[70]

The Battle of Honey Springs was the turning point of the Civil War in the Indian Territory, for Blunt used the momentum of the victory to drive on into the Creek and Choctaw Nations via the Texas Road. He was unable to end all Confederate resistance, but neither could the Confederates force the Union troops out again. Eventually the Federals retook Fort Smith and the Arkansas River Valley, effectively cutting the Indian Territory off from substantial Confederate support. The last two years of the war settled into the type of guerrilla raiding and harassment of Union troops and supply lines that Watie's Indian Brigade did so well. For the Confederate Creeks who had remained in their homes, Honey Springs was also a turning point, escalating their nervousness into panic and setting off a prolonged exodus that they called "the Stampede." When it was over, the Creek Nation lay virtually deserted.[71]

Wash's fellow Confederate Creeks understood clearly the implications of the defeat at Honey Springs. When their troops began withdrawing down the Texas Road, remaining civilians, including Confederate Cherokees who had been refugees in the Creek country, wavered between running or staying. The more fearful expected mayhem and pillage if the Federals loosed Unionist Indians and former slaves on them, while the more hopeful doubted that civilians had much to fear from Federal troops led by competent officers. Some threw necessities into wagons and fled westward toward Little River, trying to find a passable ford across the flooding Canadian River. Others went only a short distance and halted to see what would happen next. Rumor had it that the Federals were as badly cut up as the Confederates in the late battle and in no condition to fight.[72]

After the battle Wash Grayson rode with the two Creek regiments some eight to ten miles north up the Texas Road to keep an eye on the enemy. On Sunday, July 19, they returned through North Fork Town, having scouted as far as Briartown, a small settlement to the east on the Canadian River. They brought word that Confederate reinforcements were due momentarily and predicted Cooper would soon reverse the Honey Springs defeat. But three days later when Cooper did indeed meet Blunt at Prairie Springs, he suffered a second loss. Even so, Blunt did not immediately follow up his victories with an occupation of the Creek Nation. Rather, he waited several weeks for reinforcements before he moved deeper into the Indian nations.[73]

This left Creek soldiers and their families in a state of agitation and uncertainty, exacerbated by news of Lee's defeat at far-off Gettysburg and rumors of the surrender of Vicksburg. In the Creek camps frequent alarms probably heightened Wash's worry about his unprotected family. Warnings from pickets set the troops scrambling to load wagons, catch and saddle horses, and check weapons. Then, when no attack materialized, they settled back into a brittle calm. Harried officers, minister Foreman reported disapprovingly, tried to calm their nerves with whiskey. Even after the promised reinforcements arrived, talk was of retreat rather than attack. Other rumors, though, said Watie had taken a stand—that the Cherokee, Choctaw, and Creek regiments would retreat no further, but would hold their present line.[74]

Watie did agree by the middle of August that Southern families should move into the Red River Valley for safety. He was discouraged, more so than at any time in the past, and he placed no confidence in Confederate promises of aid for the Indian allies. Watie communicated his pessimism to Creek Chief Kennard in a letter charging that incompetent white Confederate officers had frittered away the strength of the Indian troops while an inferior Union force despoiled the Cherokee Nation.[75]

The task of saving themselves would be costly to the Indians, but he concluded, "If we possess the spirit of our fathers, and are resolved never to be enslaved by an inferior race, and trodden under the feet of an ignorant and insolent foe, we, the Creeks, Choctaws, Chickasaws, Seminoles, and Cherokees, never can be conquered by the Kansas jayhawkers, renegade Indians, and runaway negroes." Watie reminded the other principal chiefs that if the Cherokee Nation fell, the Creek Nation would go next, followed in turn by the remaining Indian nations.[76]

Less confident and resolute, remaining Southern Creek and Cherokee families waited nervously. Stephen Foreman wrote from North Fork Town on August 23, "We are still here but how much longer we shall remain unmolested it is difficult to tell, as almost every body feels unsafe on account of the various rumors afloat that our forces will certainly fall back, if the Feds advance on us. There was much riding about today by the Creek soldiers and others, yet no one could account for it only that something was [up] more than usual."[77]

It was about this time that Jennie Grayson and her family decided to leave the Creek Nation. On a quick trip home Wash found them debating whether or not to join the Stampede of their relatives and neighbors. Jennie wanted to assure the safety of her older sons, the most likely of her children to be swept up by either army. She favored sending them south with their grandparents and Uncle Watt Grayson's family, but she preferred to remain at home with the smaller children and hope they would not be harmed. Wash had to agree with her. "The idea of loading into one small ox wagon a few supplies and groceries," he recalled, "that would last but a very few weeks at most, and starting out with a mother and four helpless children appeared to be going right into a state of starvation and ruin."[78] His little brother Malone cried that when the Yankees came and killed him it would hurt and he was afraid to stay.[79]

In the end, though, it was Sam, now about fourteen, who settled the argument. He believed the entire family should go south. Wash conceded eventually, realizing that Sam was approaching manhood by Muskogee standards and was willing to assume responsibility for the others once he rejoined his regiment. Consequently, the Graysons hastily loaded a few belongings into their oxcart and set off to join their relatives on the south side of the Canadian River.[80]

In retrospect Sam's judgment was wise, for when the Federals finally swept into the Creek Nation late in August, events justified the Confederate Indian civilians' worst fears for their lives and possessions. Federal officers in some instances not only allowed but also encouraged their men to loot and vandalize the property of Confederate Creeks and Cherokees. After rounding up remaining Creek slaves and delivering them to the relative safety of Fort Gibson, they enlisted the able-bodied men in Union regiments. Other freedmen joined the ever-growing throng of Unionist refugees clustered around the fort. Confederate Creek civilians felt lucky if they escaped with a few belongings and their lives.[81]

As the Stampede moved southward, refugees found plenty of vacated cabins in which to shelter. Untended gardens offered turnips, pumpkins, sweet potatoes, and late corn; abandoned hogs supplied fresh meat.[82] But while there was food enough for now, many Indian refugees had little else. Foreman, writing from exile at Chickasaw Governor Winchester Colbert's place in September 1863, described their plight: "A great many of the Creeks have also passed, on their way to some better camping place where water and grass are more abundant. Many of them are in a very destitute condition. All they are with now is a pony, one [or] two pot vessels, and a few old dirty bed clothes and wearing apparel. If they ever had any more it is left behind at the mercy of their enemies. But many who passed I was acquainted with and knew to be in good circumstances having an abundance of everything, now their all is put into one or two small wagons."[83] Among these refugees were the Graysons, who eventually settled into exile in the Chickasaw Nation in the Red River Valley.[84]

Wash Grayson inadvertently joined the Stampede as well. After seeing his family off, he searched for his regiment, only to find it scattered as other soldiers looked to the safe removal of their families. That being the case, he set off after Jennie and the children, expecting to find them just across the Canadian River at his grandmother Katy's plantation. But they had already gone, and he failed to catch up with them. With another straggler he moved southward in the wake of the retreat. Although close enough to hear artillery rumbling through the mountains, he missed the next engagement of the Indian Brigade, which occurred as Federal forces pushed down the Texas Road into the Choctaw Nation to burn the Confederate depot at Perryville.[85]

The resulting dispersal of the Confederate units sent the Creek regiments westward, while the reinforcements they had so hoped for in July retreated into Arkansas. The Federals followed, taking Fort Smith and thus gaining control of the Arkansas River supply route into the Indian Territory by September 1863. The Confederate line of defense along the Arkansas River, which had allowed Southern Creeks to remain safely in their home country, sagged further south. The Unionist half of the Creek people had gone into exile in Kansas in 1861. Now the Confederate half fled as well, leaving the Creek Nation virtually abandoned for the last two years of the war.[86]

Wash Grayson's war, then, was a backwater of the greater conflict, but it was no less exciting and certainly no less violent than the fighting in the East. Watie's Indian Brigade constantly harassed Federal supply lines into Fort Gibson and at the same time they protected northern Texas and their own exiled families from Federal invasion. This was a point that Major

General Samuel Bell Maxey of Texas, the new commander of the district, comprehended clearly. The defeats of the last few months had somewhat demoralized the Indian troops, he wrote in August 1863, but they were still willing to fight if the Confederacy gave them and their dependents proper support. This being the case, Maxey strove to keep their families fed, clothed, and sheltered in order to keep men like Wash Grayson in the field.[87]

Crops were abundant the first two years of the war, but the winter of 1863 was the fiercest since 1832. Forage for cattle and horses was sparse all over the Indian Territory. Recently arrived refugees and soldiers alike knew the pinch of hunger. Their Chickasaw hosts, who had at first welcomed them with typical Indian hospitality, began to resent the sacrifice of their livestock to feed so many foreigners. To keep the peace and loyalty of the tribes, Maxey encouraged the refugees to grow their own food and fiber. He also set up a commissary, which provided flour, beef, and soap to nearly 14,000 refugees, of whom as many as 4,823 were Creeks encamped along the lower Washita River.[88]

With their dependents reasonably secure, the Creek troops followed Watie on guerrilla raids limited only by the scarcity of forage for their horses. A successful venture, both for Watie's Indian Brigade and for Wash Grayson personally, took place the following summer on June 15, 1864. Having taken Fort Smith, the Federals expected to use the Arkansas River to supply the Fort Gibson garrison and its dependent refugees. When the river rose temporarily, they sent the small steamer *J. R. Williams* upstream with a cargo of flour, bacon, textiles, boots, and assorted much-needed goods valued at one hundred twenty thousand dollars. The nature and timing of the shipment not being much of a secret, Colonel Watie planned to attack the steamer at Pleasant Bluff, about five miles below the mouth of the Canadian River.[89]

According to Wash Grayson, Watie sent him on ahead with a detachment of three hundred men and three small cannon. At Pleasant Bluff the river curved to the south, and Wash ordered the artillery pieces camouflaged in the brush on the high ground overlooking the channel. He stationed his men nearby and waited several days for Colonel Watie to come. This being the first time he had commanded more men than his own company, he was excited and eager to do well. Wash greatly admired Watie, and he was pleased and proud that when the colonel came he approved of his preparations and changed nothing.[90]

It must be noted that official accounts of the incident did not mention Wash Grayson at all. Rather, Watie's report said only that Lieutenant Henry Forrester commanded the battery. One can only speculate as to why the discrepancy exists. Perhaps Watie gave credit to Forrester rather than Wash because of the crucial role the artillery pieces played and the fact that the white officer was an artilleryman. Some might also have questioned Watie's giving command of three hundred men to a very young, relatively inexperienced junior officer. It may have been that in this instance Wash Grayson's fluency in English and Muskogee gave him the advantage over more experienced and higher-ranking Indian or white officers. Or it may have been that the actual orders originated elsewhere and that it was the bilingual Wash Grayson who relayed them to the troops and saw them carried out, thus placing him in command, in his own mind, at least. Later events would demonstrate that he was not hesitant to award himself credit if he felt it was due. At any rate, in all other details his account of the incident exactly matched those of the official reports.[91]

When the steamer came, the field pieces quickly disabled it, and the crew let it drift ashore on the sandbank on the north side of the river. The handful of Federal guards quickly abandoned the boat and hurried away for help. Watie's men overwhelmed the remaining crew and towed the steamer to their side of the river, where they stripped it and set it afire and adrift. Well before they finished packing the cargo off to the Confederate camps the next morning, scouts reported a Federal column on its way from the salt works at the mouth of the Illinois River about ten miles upstream. With too small a force to fend off the Federal column, Watie decided to burn the remaining goods and retreat to avoid capture.[92]

Before he left, he ordered Lieutenant Grayson to remain behind with a small guard from Company K. They were to keep watch until sundown and warn the rest of the brigade if the Federals arrived. Otherwise, they were to rejoin the regiment after nightfall. Wash was pleased with the assignment because it demonstrated confidence in him and his Creeks. He was furious when he found that his men, like many of the other Creek and Seminole troops, had loaded down their horses with plundered supplies and were hurrying back to camp. Wash, not wanting to admit to

Watie that he had lost control of his company, had no choice except to let them go, but privately he was determined to carry out his orders. As the main column vanished, he took his place on a nearby hill as the solitary and very nervous rear guard. There he remained, watching the sun creep down to the horizon at a glacial pace, until darkness fell and he could follow the column with the honor of the Creeks at least partly intact.[93]

Although the capture of the *J. R. Williams* was not a complete victory for Watie's Indian Brigade, it lent encouragement to the Confederate cause in the Indian Territory and demonstrated to the Federals that they must continue supplying Fort Gibson overland from Fort Scott, Kansas. For Wash Grayson and the Creeks in Watie's command, this meant continued opportunities to strike the enemy in the way they knew best. So in September 1864, when Watie and General Richard M. Gano of the Fifth Texas Cavalry planned an expedition against the Fort Gibson supply route, Wash, ever eager to prove his warrior's courage, went along.[94]

On September 16 the expedition crossed the Verdigris River above Fort Gibson and moved down toward the prairies intersected by Flat Rock Creek.[95] There a party from the fort, including thirty-seven black Union soldiers, were busily cutting hay. The Federal officer in charge, Captain Edgar A. Barker, wrongly informed that only two hundred Confederates were on the way, decided the odds were about even and he should stay and fight. He had time to get his troops into a defensive position in a ravine and then, too late, learned that the Confederate column consisted of ten times as many troops. They came down on his party from five directions, and after a half-hour or so Captain Barker realized that his position would soon be overrun. They all knew that black troops could expect no quarter from Confederate Indians, so he mounted as many as possible and charged the spot at which the attack seemed weakest. Black soldiers who were left behind hunkered down in the tall grass and shallow backwaters of nearby Grand River.[96]

Soon the Confederate troops were flushing them out like quail and shooting them down without mercy. Wash Grayson, in common with many Creeks of his day, had little regard for blacks, disdaining them generally as inferiors. And in his eyes these men were worse: they were rebellious slaves in Union uniforms. Even so, he wrote later, the slaughter at Flat Rock Creek dismayed him. "I confess this was sickening to me, but the men were like wild beasts and I was powerless to stop them from this unnecessary butchery," he recalled. Somewhat ambiguously in later years he stated that he was able to save one white prisoner by telling his men, "it was negroes that we were killing now and not white men." Whether his use of the plural "we" was meant to be generic or included himself as a participant in the massacre remains unclear.[97]

That night the Confederates camped nearby, savoring their victory. They had burned three thousand tons of hay and the haymaking equipment. They had killed forty Federal soldiers (only four blacks escaped), and another sixty-six were missing in action. They had captured the Union camp with its assorted loot and a number of horses and mules—all within a few miles of Fort Gibson. Still, the hayfield fight was only a diversion from their main goal, a supply train approaching Fort Gibson from Fort Scott, Kansas.[98]

The coming of this train of three hundred wagons was no more a secret than was the presence of the Confederate force sent to intercept it. On September 18 Major Henry Hopkins, the commander of the train, hurried the wagons to Cabin Creek, the site of an earlier attack (First Battle of Cabin Creek, July 2, 1863), where there was a log stockade behind a number of hay ricks. Hopkins placed his wagons in an arc opening onto the stockade and deployed his six hundred troops within it. After midnight Gano and Watie arrived within striking distance of the stockade, conferred, and decided to attack immediately. The two Creek regiments were on the extreme left end of the Confederate line as they felt their way through the darkness toward the stockade. Once in position, they were close enough to exchange insults and potshots with the defenders while waiting for enough light to see. In the darkness Company K passed their medicine bundle around in preparation for the coming fight. At daybreak their initial attack forced the Federal troops facing them to give way. As the Federals retreated, the Indian troops seized the abandoned wagons.[99]

Morning allowed both sides to reevaluate the situation. The Confederates brought their two pieces of artillery up and sent the Seminole and Texas troops charging forward. Their attack nearly succeeded before being repulsed. The Creek troops, meanwhile, maintained such heavy fire that Wash, standing in front of his company, exhorting them in Muskogee and directing their aim, was in danger of being shot accidentally as clouds of smoke and mist periodically covered him. Still resenting the doubts about his courage, he refused to heed his cousin Valentine's warning to move back behind the line even after his voice failed from hours of shouting orders.[100]

Eventually the Creeks and Seminoles exhausted their ammunition and hurried to the rear for fresh supplies. Their return to the firing line was the pressure needed to break the Federal resistance. In the series of assaults on the Union lines, Company K mixed in with Texas troops. Unable to regroup his scattered company, Wash surged forward with the Texans in the final assault on the stockade. Ever after, he and Lieutenant Pleasant Porter claimed the honor of being the first Creeks over the barricades at the Second Battle of Cabin Creek.[101]

With the Federal defense broken, Confederate troops swarmed into the stockade to seize their prize. Wash noted that all he got in the looting was a valise containing little of value. However, the 130 wagons they captured, along with 750 mules, contained uniforms, blankets, liquor (which never left the battlefield), clothing, shoes, and food—about $1.5 million worth of vital supplies. Within an hour Watie and Gano headed the captured wagons homeward, deftly slipping past a weak Federal attempt to stop them.[102]

Even so, it was not an easy trip back as they forced the cumbersome wagons over the rocky, hilly terrain and streams of the Cherokee Nation. Near Tulsey Town (present-day Tulsa, Oklahoma) they forded the shallow Arkansas River at the spot thereafter known as Gano's Crossing and turned southward. Excited but exhausted, the Confederate troops pushed on without pause to avoid being overtaken. Wash noted that from the time he left camp at the beginning of the expedition he did not unsaddle his horse, and he slept many miles in the saddle. Word of their coming went ahead, and Creek reinforcements hurried to meet them. Near the old Grayson homeplace at North Fork Town, General Cooper personally welcomed them back.[103]

The successful raid was a great morale booster in Confederate Indian Territory. The supplies helped keep the men in the field for several months longer, while the blankets warmed their cold families through the coming winter. Coffee, sugar, rice, flour, and tea stretched their meager rations. Bolts of calico, candles, and cans of pineapple and oysters shared out among the officers and their wives added to the general celebration. For one young Cherokee refugee in the Choctaw Nation, the capture of the "million dollar wagon train" meant a new pair of shoes for which she was very grateful, even if they were of different sizes. For the hungry, sick, and war-weary Unionist refugees penned up at Fort Gibson, however, the raid only underscored the misery and helplessness of their condition.[104]

Neither one such success nor the resolution of the Confederate Congress saluting Gano and Watie changed the ultimate course of the war. As the winter of 1864 faded quietly into the spring of 1865, Major General Maxey did his best to convince allied leaders of the Five Civilized Tribes that the Confederacy had survived the losses of New Orleans, Vicksburg, Port Hudson, Savannah, and the entire Mississippi Valley and would continue to resist subjugation.[105]

They understood, however, that the Confederacy was beyond protecting them. Once again they must face the United States government from a posture of defeat. Still, they did not give up hope or the will to fight. As planting time came in 1865, Creek Colonel Timothy Barnett wrote to now Brigadier General Watie, "The men are all busily engaged in making little patches to plant something in, but are ready to go into camp when called upon—although there is great suffering among their families for something to eat."[106]

Wash Grayson was not among those who rode out that spring, but it was not because he had lost faith in his Indian leaders, particularly Watie. Looking back, he wrote, "Let me say . . . whatever else the Indians of the old Indian Territory may lose in the shock and crash of time, be it property, land or name, let it be provided . . . in stone and story that the name of General Stand Watie may never fade away. Let his memory and fame stand forth proud monuments to the virtues of patriotism and devotion to duty as exemplified in his life, as long as grass grows and flowers bloom."[107] Rather, Wash became a casualty of war. In his quest to prove himself, he accompanied any raiding party that left the Creek camp near North Fork Town until December 1864. Shortly afterward the mild fall weather broke, and the Creek regiments moved on south to the vicinity of Wapanucka Creek in the Choctaw Nation for the winter. There, having passed through two years of raiding and four major engagements unscathed except for a powder burn, Wash came down with smallpox.[108]

Epidemics periodically ravaged the crowded camps of soldiers and refugees on both sides during the war years, adding to the general misery and high death rate. The symptoms were all too familiar. There was no room for Wash in the overcrowded military hospital at Boggy Depot, so his men took him, delirious, to Wapanucka (Rock) Academy, a Chickasaw Nation school now being used as a military hospital. Fortunately his Aunt Feenie found him there and looked after him until his mother could ride the forty miles from her refugee's cabin on Glass's Creek.[109]

A month passed for Wash in a nightmare of pain, high fever, and skin eruptions that turned him from a 170-pound man into a 100-pound scarecrow. His long, flowing hair fell out in clumps. At the depth of his illness everyone, including Wash, gave up hope of his survival. He discussed his burial with Jennie and prepared to die but passed the crisis within hours and, to his surprise, began a slow recovery. Before he regained his strength news came of the surrender of Confederate forces in the East. The war was finally ending.[110]

The Civil War cost the Graysons and the Creek Nation dearly. The family lost old Tulwa Tustunuggee, who was buried in the Red River Valley near the grave of the youngest of Jennie's children, James Jr. The surviving Graysons faced return to a country that was completely devastated. Soldiers of both armies routinely burned houses and outbuildings to prevent their use by the enemy. On his last raid Wash and his men had set fire to the remaining buildings of the settlement near Creek Agency even though the place was deserted and no one disputed their presence. Creek public buildings and schools were looted, vandalized, and misused. Livestock, the pre-war wealth of the Creek Nation, had disappeared, eaten by hungry refugees and soldiers or lost to predators, human and animal. What remained of this national wealth was stripped in the last year of the war in an organized operation that saw stolen Creek beef sold to Kansas farmers or Unionist Creeks as refugee rations. One Creek noted wryly that all that remained to his people at the end of the war was the land, and that was because, of all Creek property, only the land was immovable.[111]

Even here the Creeks were victimized, with loyalty to the Confederacy or the Union mattering little in the end. The federal government, ignoring the fact that about half the Creek Nation had staunchly stood by their treaties with the Union, suffered much for their loyalty, and fought in Union uniform, took the opportunity to punish the Confederate Creeks at the same time it satisfied the land hunger of white Americans. The Reconstruction Treaty forced on the Creek Nation in 1866 compelled them to cede the western half of their lands—three and a quarter million acres—for thirty cents per acre. Although the Creeks retained residual rights, the federal government took an option on this area for the future resettlement of other Indian tribes who obstructed the westering white frontier.[112]

This price, according to one of the attorneys who handled the transaction, was generous, because Secretary of the Interior William Harlow believed no Indian land was worth more than the fifteen cents per acre the Seminoles had received for their domain under the same circumstances. Nevertheless, the federal government then forced the Seminoles to buy an additional two hundred and fifty thousand acres of Creek land at fifty cents per acre for a new, much reduced national domain.[113]

Nor was the remaining Creek domain safe. The Reconstruction Treaty, similar to those signed by all the Five Civilized Tribes, forced the Creeks to free their slaves and accept them as citizens. They agreed in principle to the future creation of a unified government for the territory. The treaty also granted Creek lands as rights-of-way for one east-west and one north-south railroad through the Indian Territory. These grants, immediately awarded to eager railroad corporations, could reach maximum profitability only when the Creek national title was extinguished, Creek land was allotted in severalty, and any surplus opened for homesteading. Herein lay the germ of the final destruction of Creek sovereignty.[114]

To the material devastation must be added loss of life and faith. Censuses taken just before and at the end of the war showed a decline in the Creek population of about 24 percent, the highest death rate among the Five Civilized Tribes. If this was ever a "white man's war," it quickly became a war of Creek against Creek and Indian against Indian, certainly no less fratricidal than the Civil War in the East. The old fears and hatreds, revived in 1861 and nurtured through four years of total war, had to be subdued again.[115]

Wash Grayson and other Confederate Creeks went to the old Creek council ground at High Spring in November 1865 to effect a reconciliation with the Loyal faction, a meeting the Unionists failed to attend. And one of his first actions on his return to the Creek Nation was to ride across the Arkansas River to the camps of the Unionist Creeks to visit Simpson Grayson, his Aunt Tility, and his other kinsmen who had "gone North."[116]

Although Wash had given his allegiance to the losing side in the conflict, he made important personal gains. For two years, he had associated with the prominent men of his nation, the ex-Confederates who would dominate Creek affairs in the post-war period. By their standards he had upheld the Muskogee warrior tradition. They knew him now as a warrior, a leader of men, skilled in dealing with the white man. Scanty rations, miserable living conditions, and hard fights won and lost in the brotherhood of the Confederate Creek regiments had strengthened old ties and reinforced his Muskogee identity.

Wash Grayson's Civil War also fortified his Creek nationalism. His knowledge of the white man was no longer limited to the elders' stories, to travelers passing through North Fork Town, or to the citizens of Fayetteville, Arkansas. Broader firsthand experience had brought a clearer idea of how little white men esteemed Indians, their property, and their rights—adding another line of demarcation between the *este hvtke* and the Creeks with whom Wash Grayson identified. Finally, the war added a new dimension to his Creek nationalism, a sense of common cause with other Indian nations, nurtured in the Indian Brigade. Stand Watie, its commander and a man Wash admired greatly, had pointed this out in the aftermath of Honey Springs: The Five Civilized Tribes must stand together or they would fall one after the other, "trodden under the feet of an ignorant and insolent foe."[117]

CHAPTER FOUR

Indian Capital and
Indian Brains

For Confederate veteran Wash Grayson the closing years of the 1860s and the decade of the 1870s were a time of rebuilding and wary optimism. While the Creek people struggled to regain their pre-war prosperity and stability, he married, founded a family, and started several business enterprises. He also entered Creek national politics, identifying himself with the "progressive" faction and seeking to explain and exemplify its agenda to the Anglo-American public and more traditional Creeks.

Grayson's role in the economic and political development of the Creek Nation in the last half of the nineteenth century illustrated the concept, execution, and goal of Creek progressivism. Not to be confused with turn-of-the-century Anglo-American progressivism in spite of some similarities, Creek progressivism as exemplified by Wash Grayson was the conscious, selective adoption of contemporary Anglo-American economic, political, and institutional patterns. It was not based on any Creek desire to become Anglo-American. It was a nationalistic, defensive measure to strengthen and assure the survival of the Creek Nation against an aggressive, often hostile, Anglo-America.

Creek progressives such as Wash Grayson—literate, aware of the broader world beyond the Indian Territory, and often of Anglo-American descent—had compelling reasons to work toward the survival of the Creek

Nation. They were advantageously placed to profit individually from the exploitation of communally held national resources. Their activism was rewarded in that they often became the Creek Nation's economic, political, and social leaders.

Conversely, there was little for them on the other side of their nation's boundaries. Even though they had the tools to succeed as U.S. citizens—usually some English education, energy, ambition, and intelligence—they would have faced Anglo-American racism and second-class citizenship. They could look to Creek history for examples of this treatment among those who had elected to remain in Alabama in the 1830s or to the current treatment of freedmen. Most importantly, though, they were Muskogees, identifying with *tvlwv*, clans, and the Creek Methodist, Baptist, or Presbyterian congregations that were now the alternate Creek religious and social institutions. Their social and economic welfare as well as their heritage was tied to the survival of the Creek Nation, and they believed that Creek national survival could be best achieved through selective cultural change.

In the years immediately following the Civil War, survival on any terms was questionable. Life in the Indian Territory was very difficult, a repetition of the resettlement after the Removal. In spite of war-weariness and homesickness, Indian exiles returned slowly and cautiously to their old homes. Veterans of both armies knew the devastation they had left behind them during four years of ruthless warfare. They had made bitter enemies among their own people. How would they deal with each other now that the war was over? How would the victorious federal government treat them? What remained of their old lives? How would they live until they could harvest crops again?[1]

The Indian Brigade disbanded in the summer of 1865 as former soldiers drifted away to look for family and friends. After weeks of recuperation Wash Grayson, emaciated and permanently scarred by smallpox, rode back to the old homeplace near North Fork Town with his teenaged brothers, Sam and Pilot. They were among the fortunate few Creeks who found a home still standing. They planned to make it habitable that summer before returning to the Red River Valley refugee camps to escort their mother, Malone, and Louisa home. By day they worked furiously clearing brush from the overgrown fields, putting up fences, planting a crop, and repairing the house. By night they slept lightly, aware that prowling wolves and panthers, which had reappeared with the abandonment of the countryside, were not the only predators around. The Creek Nation, its government and law enforcement machinery in disarray, provided a favorable habitat for all kinds of desperate characters, some of them squatting uncomfortably close to the Grayson farm. Eventually the three young men accomplished enough to bring the rest of the family home in the spring of 1866.[2]

Other Creeks also returned in the next several months, but not necessarily to their pre-war residences. Former Creek slaves, now freedmen, expected to receive federal allotments on the rich bottomlands wealthy Creeks once farmed in the Three Forks area. Many, including "States" freedmen—those originally from outside the territory—congregated there, the nucleus of the new town of Muskogee. The Creek Agency, which had reopened just west of town (and was replaced in 1874 by the Union Agency to the Five Civilized Tribes), contributed to the economic base. However, with the exception of the Perryman family, who resettled on the upper Arkansas River, most Anglo-Creek residents of the antebellum years abandoned this part of the Arkansas District to the freedmen. They moved on to the vicinity of North Fork Town, displacing some returning Canadian District Upper Creeks, who resettled still further west. So the Graysons' new neighbors included Wash's kinsmen, Daniel N. and Chilly McIntosh (Wash's former commander), who relocated on Chilly's Prairie near present-day Fame, Oklahoma.[3]

Wash Grayson's stay on the farm with Jennie and his brothers and sister was fairly short. Although he was philosophically drawn to agriculture, he was less inclined toward the physical work of farming. Rather, he returned to his pre-war occupation, clerking in various general stores in North Fork Town as the old settlement revived. He was a salesman for the firm of Butler and Cox when George W. Stidham bought the enterprise, beginning an association that had a profound affect on Grayson's life and career.[4]

Born in the old Creek Nation in 1817, Stidham was the son of Delilah Hardage, an Anglo-Creek of Hecheta Town, and John Stidham of Alabama, also known as "Hopaycute," who died when his son was twelve. In 1835 young Stidham emigrated with his widowed mother to the Indian

Territory. Though he spoke only Muskogee until he was eighteen and always thought more clearly in that language, Stidham was literate, self-educated, and articulate in both languages. His fluency in English won him the position of interpreter to the Creek agent and perhaps contributed to his increasing political influence in the 1850s. He went on to hold several Creek national offices in both the legislative and judicial branches. A prosperous farmer owning many slaves before the war, he was also a merchant with trading posts at the Creek Agency and Shieldsville. In 1855 he helped establish the Creek Nation's first Masonic lodge at North Fork Town. Stidham was a cultural broker, often interpreting during Creek-federal negotiations and making at least fifteen visits, beginning in 1850, to Washington, D.C., as a Creek delegate or spokesman. Stidham's dark Muskogee features and erect, nattily dressed figure were a familiar sight in federal offices. Stidham represented Hecheta Town on the Creek National Council for several terms and was serving as a supreme court justice in the new constitutional government when he employed Wash Grayson.[5]

The war had dealt harshly with Stidham, one of the pro-Confederate leaders and a signer of the Creek-Confederate Treaty of 1861. When hostilities began he had moved his family and about forty of his more valuable slaves to Hopkins County, Texas, where he purchased six thousand acres near present-day Texarkana. Unfortunately he lost the deeds to the land in the course of the war, his farms and trading posts were destroyed, and emancipation freed his slaves. Even so, he returned to the Creek Nation with enough twenty-dollar gold pieces to freight several wagonloads of stock to his new North Fork Town general store.[6]

Stidham's beautiful daughter Georgianna, known to family and friends as "Annie," soon caught the attention of his young clerk. Wash Grayson had been engaged briefly to Molsie James, daughter of a wealthy and prominent Chickasaw, at the end of the war and before the family returned to the Creek Nation. Responsibility for his family and his lack of prospects caused him to break the engagement, although Grayson commented later that genuine love was lacking in the relationship. That was never the case with him and Annie Stidham.[7]

Born in 1849 at Sodom, Annie was the child of Stidham's fourth wife, Ariadna Carr, one of the beautiful twin daughters of Irish-Creek Paddy

Carr. At six Annie's parents sent her to the neighborhood school, and at eight she made the two-day wagon journey to boarding school at Van Buren, Arkansas. The next year she transferred to Mrs. Smith's Female Seminary at Fayetteville. A bright, popular child, she studied music and German and enjoyed school.[8]

The easy life ended with the Stidham family's exile in Texas in 1861 when Annie was twelve. As refugees, they felt fortunate to have the shelter of a weatherproof, mud-chinked log cabin. Stidham tanned leather and pegged together their shoes, while Annie, in common with other refugee women, knit stockings, spun and wove cloth, and braided cornshucks and wheatstraw into hats. On their return to the Creek Nation, she and her sister cooked for the family and laboriously ground all their cornmeal by hand until the gristmills reopened. Stidham still had cash, but Annie later recalled that this did not matter because there were no stores and "there was nothing in the country at all to be bought for love nor money."[9]

Stidham's new store at North Fork Town and the farm he put into production gradually restored their prosperity. Although the war had limited Annie's formal education as it had Wash Grayson's, she continued to read and study. Travels with her father on his official visits to Washington added polish to her natural dignity. Annie was a guest at the last White House reception given by President Andrew Johnson and stood in a sea of umbrellas to witness Ulysses S. Grant's inauguration in March 1869. By that time nineteen-year-old Annie and twenty-six-year-old Wash Grayson were engaged to be married, and she returned eagerly to the B.I.T.—"beautiful Indian Territory."[10]

Marriage to Annie Stidham offered a number of benefits to an ambitious young man. Her father was an established and influential member of the Creek government. A Creek nationalist, he was also a leader of the progressive faction with whom Grayson identified. Stidham was recovering financially and could perhaps help the young couple begin their life together. Related to several prominent Creek and Cherokee families, Annie further knit Grayson into the Anglo-Indian elite of the territory. Although at sixteen Wash Grayson had felt too diffident and awkward to move in such circles, at twenty-six he had gained the maturity and self-confidence to propose to Annie. Besides, the war had been a great leveler.[11]

While there were positive, practical aspects to such a marriage, these were less important to Wash than was Annie herself. Theirs was a genuine love match, based on respect as well as attraction and reinforced by their common experiences and perspectives. She referred to him as her "Brave Warrior"[12] and took great pride and pleasure in his successes. He admired the "quiet, unobtrusive and uncomplaining" assistance she gave her stepmother Sarah in caring for the Stidham home and younger children. Forty years later he still considered her "the most handsome young lady I have ever seen" and "the greatest woman in all the world." Wash professed a "never-dying attachment and love"[13] for Annie in a fifty-one-year marriage that endured his extended absences. They could even laugh when they remembered that it had been her childhood home he had set ablaze on that last raid on the Creek Agency. In a simple ceremony at the Stidham cabin Thomas B. Ruble, his old teacher at Asbury Manual Labor School, performed their marriage on July 29, 1869—the only date besides his birth that Grayson recorded in his autobiography. "We could not put on any style," Annie remembered, because the times were still so hard. "But we were as happy as if we had been married in a mansion."[14]

Times remained hard for a number of years. The young Graysons stayed a while in North Fork Town, looking after Stidham's business while he made yet another official trip to Washington. On his return they moved to Jennie Grayson's farm until a local property became available. Like James and Jennie Grayson a generation before, Wash and Annie took advantage of the communal landholding system of the Creek Nation to begin farming. There being no banking facilities in the Creek Nation, Wash borrowed five hundred dollars from his great-uncle Watt Grayson to buy cattle, hogs, a double log cabin, and the improvements on about twenty acres. The cabin was their home until they could build a new house nearby.

Because lumber was still expensive and scarce, Wash cut trees and hauled them to Daniel N. McIntosh's new sawmill for planing. The new house, two rooms with a long porch on the east side and a detached kitchen, boasted a wallpapered ceiling and a chimney of finished stones—the best home, Wash noted proudly, for miles around. There the first of their nine children, daughters Orlena (Lena, 1870), Mabel (1872), and Annette (1874), were born.[15]

A Creek log home of the post–Civil War period. Courtesy Archives and Manuscripts Division of the Oklahoma Historical Society.

Wash's great-uncle Watt ("Uncle Watt") Grayson also furnished the capital for the business enterprise that became Grayson Brothers Mercantile. The idea germinated after Sam Grayson persuaded his older brother to join him as a salesman in Gray Eagle Scales's general store in town. In the summer of 1875, the two borrowed enough money to buy out the elderly Scales. With Watt's son Edmond they went into business and later hired as clerks their brother Pilot, home after finishing his education in 1878, and Charles Gibson, an Anglo-Creek Union veteran. In January 1878 Edmond was killed by a lighthorseman in a drunken brawl, so that ownership of the business devolved on Sam and Wash.[16]

Charles Gibson later recalled that the Creek Nation general store of the 1870s was a fairly simple and primitive operation. A fourteen-foot-square log building carrying two hundred dollars' worth of stock was considered a big establishment.[17] Grayson Brothers Mercantile was typical of the time and place, but by 1876 the proprietors advertised seed, harnesses, farm machinery, and groceries in addition to "Traveler's supplies, Prints, Hosiery, Boots, Shoes, Hats, Caps, and all the etceteras requisite to a First Class Western Business House."[18]

Although founded in North Fork Town, Grayson Brothers became one of the first businesses in the new town of Eufaula. In the early 1870s the Missouri, Kansas, and Texas Railroad, familiarly known as the "Katy," extended its line across the Creek Nation along the route of the Texas Road. Railroad officials designated several stops on the line, and new Anglo-American-style market towns—Wagoner, Gibson Station (Fort Gibson), Muskogee, Oktaha, Checotah, Bond Switch (Onapa), and Eufaula—grew up at these sites. The track passed about one mile west of North Fork Town on the higher ground above the river valley. The Grayson brothers, G. W. Stidham, Gray Eagle Scales, D. B. Whitlow, and Joseph McDermott Coody—all local merchants—contributed one thousand dollars to subsidize a depot. They named it Eufaula in remembrance of the old eastern homeland (see map 3).[19]

Railroads were a mixed blessing to the Indian Territory. They brought the benefits of easy access to markets in and out of the Indian nations. Sam and Wash Grayson frequently traveled to Kansas City, St. Louis, Chicago, and Ft. Worth to restock their general store. Using this cheap form of transportation also expanded the possibilities of exploiting Creek natural resources, particularly the coal seams evident further west in the Cross Timbers.[20]

Unfortunately, railroad construction also brought an influx of noncitizens to the territory, both those under permit of the Creek Nation and unlicensed "intruders." The newcomers might be legitimate railroad laborers or crewmen, but the railroaders also attracted the intruder merchants, gamblers, prostitutes, and bootleggers who catered to them. The railroad lines had little compunction about violating the limits of their rights-of-way, illegally appropriating Creek timber for building materials, and discriminating against Indian Territory shippers by charging them higher rates than neighboring Kansans paid. Moreover, they constantly lobbied Congress for the opening of the Indian Territory, the dissolution of the Indian governments, and the allotment of Indian land in order to maximize their investments in construction and to claim grants of public land under the Railway Act. Passed in 1862, that act

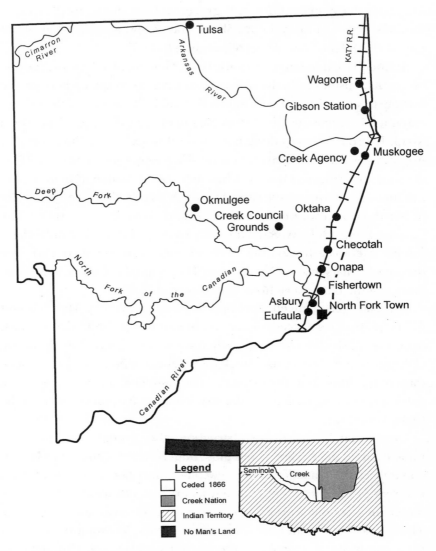

Map 3. The Creek Nation about 1880

subsidized national railroad expansion through generous grants of public land adjacent to the tracks.

As a businessman and a knowledgeable Creek citizen, Wash Grayson understood the ramifications of the coming of the railroad, yet his contribution of two hundred dollars toward securing a depot for Eufaula demonstrated that he hoped the intangible and financial profits of this new technology would outweigh the risks. In this he was little different from other Indian Territory businessmen, who quickly came to rely on the railroads crossing their country.[21] Consequently, he and Sam were among the North Fork Town businessmen who relocated along either side of the track in the pattern typical of the railroad town. Businessman W. F. Crabtree put up the first building; merchant D. B. Whitlow opened the first trading house.[22] William Bertram, a white intruder of dubious reputation, established the Eufaula House—"a sort of hotel"—a bakery, and a harness shop near the depot.[23] In 1874 and 1875 the Grayson brothers, Stidham, and W. B. Crabtree shifted their trading establishments up to the new site. The hillside was still cloaked in blackjack oak and persimmon trees, among which the businessmen cleared building lots. Stidham, Grayson recalled, once shot a buck from the door of his half-finished store.[24]

Within a very few years the new town took on a more permanent aspect. Stidham and the Grayson brothers hired William Gage Fryer, a white contractor, to replace their original frame structures with native stone commercial buildings. W. F. Crabtree and Stidham installed cotton gins and a grist mill. Within three years Eufaula boasted a wagonmaker and three carpenters, two physicians' offices, a transplanted twenty-year-old Masonic lodge with forty members, and twelve Creek Baptist churches within a twelve-mile radius. Only one mile from the new depot Asbury Manual Labor School, severely damaged during the war, reopened. For convenience the businessmen also moved their residences to Eufaula. Soon the little town occupied several acres at the base of Chintz Mountain. But as Eufaula flourished, North Fork Town died, leaving only a few stone foundations among the weeds.[25]

Proud of their enterprise, Eufaula's city fathers looked forward to continued growth with typical nineteenth-century booster enthusiasm. Their town, they noted, lay midway on the thousand-mile stretch of track from St. Louis to Galveston. In time they hoped projected railroad lines would connect them more directly with the Atlantic and Pacific coasts. Meanwhile, Eufaula served as the market center for a substantial hinterland rich in furs, timber, minerals, and farmland. Merchants in outlying settlements used the town and its stockyards as a supply and shipping point. White immigrants constantly rolled through, their wagon wheels screeching, on their way to distant homesteads. Texas cattle herds so large they sometimes took two days to pass moved north up the broad Texas Road toward midwestern packing houses. Immigrants and cowboys alike stopped off in Eufaula to buy supplies in Creek-owned businesses.[26]

Wash Grayson, no less than the other city fathers, looked beyond the present reality to predict great things for their new town. Even though its three hundred inhabitants made it the largest town in the area, such amenities as bathtubs and flower beds were still scarce. In wet weather mud was hub deep in the wide, unpaved thoroughfare; in dry weather clouds of dust swirled in the wind. Shootings on the street were not uncommon. Eufaula in no way resembled the traditional Creek *tvlwv* but was quite typical of the contemporary white-style market town. Nevertheless, its residents through the late 1800s continued to think of it is an "Indian town," an indication of expanding Creek concepts of place and purpose.[27]

Grayson, too, planned to move his family to Eufaula, but circumstances forced them into the new house on Jefferson Avenue before they were quite ready. The preceding year had been very difficult. The spring of 1875 followed a winter so hard the plow horses died, forcing Creeks to break the ground with hoes for spring planting. Then grasshoppers and chinch bugs devoured the new growth. Uncle Watt Grayson, who was known as much for his generosity as his hoard of gold coins, distributed corn to all who asked, while Grayson Brothers freighted in bushels of potatoes to feed hungry Creeks.[28]

In October a spell of hot weather ushered in such a deadly round of sickness that people prayed for a norther. Jennie Grayson, who now lived with Wash and Annie, as was her habit diligently nursed the sick of the neighborhood. Her patients included her kinsman Chilly McIntosh and his wife Leah, who died two weeks apart. Exhausted, Jennie caught the sickness along with Annette, the Graysons' youngest child. The toddler died only a few days before Jennie, to whom Wash was devoted. Early in March 1876 the first Grayson son, Walter Clarence, was born. One week later while Annie was still recovering from his birth, fire destroyed the Grayson home, forcing the family to move into Eufaula.[29]

The new Wash Grayson residence stood on the north side of Jefferson Avenue across the street from his brother Sam's home. Wash's one-story frame house was modest compared to some of the later merchants' homes in Eufaula. Besides the main house, there was a detached kitchen, a guesthouse, and a small building containing Wash's library. At the rear stood a stable and henhouse near a large kitchen garden. Interested in horticulture generally, Wash enjoyed overseeing its cultivation and gave much time and thought to planting trees, shrubs, and flowers, so that something bloomed at every season of the year.[30]

West of the Grayson homes and near the railroad track was the Grayson schoolhouse. The one-room frame building served as a subscription school for the town's children and as a church and community center when necessary. Each morning its students came to Wash's house to draw a bucket of drinking water from his well. Only six of Wash and Annie's nine children lived to attend the school. Daisy (born 1879) and Anna (1891) died before their second birthdays. Lena, Mabel, Walter, Eloise (1880), Washington (called "Washie," 1883), and Tsianina (called "Dovie," 1885) survived into adolescence. At the turn of the century Eloise and Tsianina and their husbands built substantial houses (both are still standing) on either side of Wash and Annie's home.[31]

Meanwhile, in his business life, Wash Grayson prospered. In 1877 the Grayson brothers expanded their store building. Cotton production became increasingly important to the Eufaula area after the war, and by 1878 the Grayson brothers had added a mule-powered cotton gin. On a good day it turned out three or four bales, generally valued at about sixty dollars each. As of January 1, 1878 Eufaula merchants had shipped out 352 bales. Grayson Brothers alone had shipped 144 bales by the end of February. Their business thrived to the extent that by January 1880 they had replaced their gin mules with a twenty-horse-power engine.[32]

They also went into the livestock business, the natural outgrowth of merchandizing in the Creek Nation. Stockraising, of course, had been a primary part of the Creek economy since the decline of the deer skin trade late in the eighteenth century. It had influenced the dispersal of Creek families to individual farms for adequate grazing, particularly during the resettlement after the Removal. Even though most Creek cattle had been lost during the last two years of the Civil War, the herds were

The Grayson Brothers Store in Eufaula. Courtesy Western History Collections, University of Oklahoma Library.

replenished within a few years. Unfortunately, there was little market for beef at first, so cattle were worth only a few dollars a head. In those days cash was still scarce in the territory; merchants such as the Grayson brothers did most of their trade on credit, the integrity of most Creeks making them good risks. Payment of debts, if not in merchants' scrip or Creek national warrants, might be in furs, skins, corn, produce, or livestock. Because shipping the one or two steers or hogs taken in trade was not economical, Creek Nation merchants began holding livestock in fenced pastures on the communal lands. When enough animals accumulated, the merchants conducted a roundup, drove their animals to a depot such as Eufaula, and shipped them out by rail. It was only a step from this expediency to dealing in livestock, especially after the great age of the range cattle industry arrived with eastern urbanization and the expansion of the railroad onto the Great Plains.[33]

By the mid-1870s the Grayson brothers routinely exported livestock by rail. In March 1878 Sam shipped sixty hogs, driven in from Little River.

In June Grayson Brothers shipped out sixty-three head of cattle. The next month they shipped two cars of livestock. Most of these animals went to packing houses in St. Louis or beyond. Under these circumstances, Creeks such as Wash and Sam Grayson became cattlemen and joined the Seminole and Muskogee Live Stock Association to regulate and protect their new enterprise.

Meanwhile, Creek cowboys added to Muskogee material culture the accoutrements and clothing—broad-brimmed hats, chaps, and high-heeled boots—associated with the range cattle industry of the American West. It was a cultural change many native peoples in the West adopted as a reasonable alternative to traditional ways when the Anglo-American frontier disrupted the old patterns of life.[34]

Eventually Wash Grayson went into ranching partnerships with other Creek citizens, including his father-in-law. Most prominent among his partners was Joseph M. Perryman, a future principal chief of the Creek Nation, but his longest association was with Hugh Henry. An Anglo-Creek of the Alligator Clan and Hillabee Town, Henry was born in Texas in 1848. Like Grayson, he was a Confederate veteran, but he had also been a cowboy and buffalo hunter in his colorful past. Something of a maverick himself, he had often trailed herds up the Texas Road from San Antonio to St. Louis and had a reputation as a tough man. About 1878 he became a partner in Grayson Brothers' livestock operation, fencing a large pasture on Coal Creek near present Henryetta, Oklahoma—named for Hugh Henry. It was rough, hilly country, and Wash and Sam went there most autumns to hunt and check on the roundup. Large-scale coal mining in the area about 1890 ruined the ranching, but Henry estimated that by then he had sent to market thirty-six thousand cattle and hundreds of horses, many wearing Wash Grayson's brand, a shield crossed by a horizontal bar.[35]

Ranching was not Grayson's only agricultural interest. He also kept land under cultivation near present-day Fame, Oklahoma, but employed a tenant farmer to work it. In fact, Grayson in the 1870s saw agriculture as far more than a traditional part of the Creek economic base. At the time, Creek farming was undergoing some technological change. Many Creek farmers continued subsistence agriculture on small *sofky* patches. However, enough Creeks were modernizing and expanding their farming activities that G. W. Stidham found it profitable to stock technologically advanced and expensive reapers, mowers, seeders, and cultivators in his Eufaula general store.[36]

In addition to increased profits, Wash Grayson believed there were intangible benefits to modernized farming. First, it would demonstrate that Creeks were a settled agricultural people, unlike the nomadic Plains tribes Anglo-Americans considered uncivilized and whom they threatened to evict from their homelands. Secondly, it would show that Creeks were moving toward the Anglo-American ideal being pressed on American Indians generally, that of the self-sufficient farmer wisely and efficiently using the land, a transition Grayson described as "progress." Further, he believed that modernizing agriculture could provide a means to reform Creek politics. In a speech delivered at a barbecue at Joseph M. Perryman's in July 1879, Grayson, elaborating on these ideas and sounding remarkably Jeffersonian, described agriculture as providing an honorable, moral, and disciplined way of life. Unfortunately, he stated, while many Creeks were farmers, few were good farmers.[37]

Recalling that ancient Muskogees used social gatherings for educational purposes, Grayson advocated the formation of farmers' associations, with regular meetings where they could discuss the best farming techniques. Using these meetings for self-education and as a power base, they could then demand Creek National Council support for prizes and premiums at agricultural fairs and exhibits. They could even exert enough political influence to replace reactionary council members who did not know potatoes from turnips and were equally ignorant of handling national finances. In a conclusion reminiscent of contemporary Farmers Alliance meetings in neighboring Kansas and Texas, Grayson declared, "We have had enough of law and political scheming, and what we now want is men who are willing to work for the direct benefit of the poor, the weak, the widows and the orphans."[38] Grayson was tying good government to efficient agriculture as part of the positive image the Creek Nation must project to protect its sovereignty and landbase. At the same time, he was recalling traditional Muskogee communalism and concern for unfortunate members of the community.

A number of Creeks and Cherokees apparently agreed with Grayson that agricultural fairs and exhibits could benefit their nations. By the late

1870s the Indian International Fair held annually at Muskogee had become an institution. The fair, usually in September or October, drew members of the Five Civilized Tribes as well as a growing number of Plains Indians from the western frontier. Fair-goers could enjoy informative and uplifting exhibits as well as bootlegged liquor and games of chance. Sympathetic Creeks and Cherokees routinely rescued newly impoverished visitors from the Plains and loaned them horses and money to get home. This influx of fair-goers eventually led the Cherokee and Creek nations, not always on the best of terms in those days, to cooperate in policing the event.[39]

The fair symbolized the transformation of Indians that many Anglo-American "friends of the Indian" and federal officials hoped to see. In 1880 Union Agent John Q. Tufts described it as so valuable an activity that the federal government should subsidize attendance for the Plains Indians. He noted, "Here the wild Indians meet other tribes of the Territory—they mingle with, and learn the habits, manners, customs, and laws of their more civilized brethren, and adopt them—and observe the different grades of civilization, besides they observe all the various kinds of grains, vegetables, fruits, and domestic animals raised by the other tribes, and are stimulated and encouraged to go and do likewise. I know of no greater civilizer than their annual meeting at the Indian International Fair."[40]

Historian Angie Debo, noting that officers of the Indian Agricultural Society and Fair Association were white noncitizens or mixed-blood Creeks and Cherokees, whom she does not consider true Indians, describes the annual fairs as a "white man's project" serving mainly the Muskogee town boosters.[41] Undoubtedly, the influx of fair-goers gratified Muskogee businessmen, the majority of whom were non-Indians. Perhaps this was why, in spite of his belief that agricultural exhibits could be an instrument of Creek progress, Wash Grayson did not deeply involve himself in the supporting organization. Another reason may have been that he collected only one vote in February 1881, when he was a candidate for vice president of the Creek Nation chapter of the Indian Agricultural Society and Fair Association. At any rate, he directed much more energy into a tool of progress that he viewed as even more important, the *Indian Journal* newspaper.[42]

Unlike the Cherokees, Choctaws, and Chickasaws, who had published newspapers before the Civil War, the Creeks had no printed news source other than the Tullahassee Mission student newspaper, *Our Monthly*, until Cherokee William Potter Ross began publication of the *Indian Journal* at Muskogee in 1876. A disastrous fire that Christmas Eve threatened to put the infant enterprise out of business. Then in late April 1877, a joint stock company of twenty-one stockholders—including Creek businessmen David Benson, James McHenry, Joseph M. Perryman, N. B. Moore, John R. Moore, David M. Hodge, Ward Coachman, G. W. Stidham, James McDermott Coody, W. F. Crabtree, D. B. Whitlow, William Fisher, David Carr, and Pleasant Porter—was formed to purchase and move the paper to Eufaula. Only two white men were associated with the *Indian Journal.* Stockholder Frederick B. Severs, a teacher, merchant, and rancher in the Creek Nation for three decades, had been formally adopted as a Creek citizen following his service in the Confederate Creek regiments. Ross, who did not wish to relocate to Eufaula, was replaced as editor by Myron P. Roberts, a U.S. citizen. Sam Grayson acted as treasurer for the stock company, and a committee composed of Stidham, W. F. Crabtree, and Wash Grayson supervised publication.[43]

The *Indian Journal*, perhaps more clearly than any other public voice in the Creek Nation, spoke for the Creek nationalists who believed that some adaptation of Anglo-American ways was necessary to protect Creek sovereignty. Wash Grayson's enduring relationship with the journal was evidence that it reflected his opinions. From the initial issue the supervising committee, of which he was a member, insisted that the *Journal* was an Indian institution, concerned less with making a profit than with protecting Indian interests. Their motto, "We seek to enlighten," may have seemed somewhat hackneyed to Anglo-American journalists, but it stated a real, dual purpose. The 1870s were a time of bloody, headline-grabbing Indian-white conflict in the West, and many whites, the committee believed, thought of the inhabitants of the Indian Territory in terms of "wigwams, robes, feathers, and vermillion." Too often this misperception led to such iniquitous inaccuracies, even in Congress, as "there are no good Indians but dead ones." The *Indian Journal* stockholders believed that if Indians were to defend their rights and lands, they must dispel "this cloud of ignorance" and present the Indian majority of the territory as the law-abiding, settled, agricultural people they really were.[44]

At the same time, the stockholders hoped to inform and educate the Indian public on current issues to enable them to fend off attacks on their sovereignty. Toward all the Indian nations the committee stressed impartiality and unity, the latter an increasingly important theme in the post–Civil War relations among the Five Civilized Tribes. They hoped their readers would not regard the paper as Creek, even though it was chartered by the Creek Nation and served as its official organ. Rather, they strove to "understand the actual interests of the whole Indian people of the Territory."[45]

Six months after the newspaper moved to Eufaula, Principal Chief Ward Coachman ratified the stated purposes of the *Journal* when he declared, "It is absolutely necessary for the Indian race in order to protect their interests, and make known their rights, to have some medium through which to express themselves to the thinking and reading portion of the citizens of the United States."[46] He proposed that the Creek National Council use the journal to publish its laws and that it subsidize subscriptions for each of the tribal towns. Unfortunately, this last measure proved ineffective because many copies were never delivered. Even delivered papers were useless to illiterate Creeks.[47]

Over the next three decades stockholders and editors came and went, and the *Journal* moved back and forth between Eufaula and Muskogee. For a time it even passed out of Creek hands. By 1878 the newspaper was floundering financially and the stockholders were losing enthusiasm. Editor Roberts bought the enterprise and continued publication until his death.[48] The paper remained in white hands until early 1887, when Wash Grayson again led a company of stockholders in purchasing the Indian Journal Printing Company (see chapter 5).

In spite of these vicissitudes, Wash Grayson believed in the mission and the function of the *Indian Journal.* According to one editor, Captain Grayson was "to the Journal what the balance wheel [was] to machinery."[49] Sometimes his name was on the masthead as associate editor; for many years he was the president of the Indian Journal Printing Company, which did job printing for the public and the Creek national government.

Whatever his capacity, people in the Creek Nation knew the *Journal* reflected his views even though its editors insisted their printed opinions were their own.[50]

In content the paper was very similar to contemporary small-town newspapers serving a primarily rural readership. It carried national and international news with many items reprinted from major eastern periodicals. There were serials, sermons, and agricultural advice. A personal column detailed the social events of Eufaula and surrounding communities. Illustrated advertisements showed ladies the latest eastern fashions and directed farmers to merchants selling seed and hardware. In addition, the *Journal* carried news about Indians: the theft of horses on the Kiowa-Comanche-Apache Reservation, Creek Baptist missionary work at Wichita Agency, the visit of Spotted Tail's band of Lakotas to the Creek capital.[51]

Because many Creeks were literate only in Muskogee, the *Journal* published articles in Muskogee and English. For some months Wash Grayson contributed the "Creek Corner," a column in Muskogee, and for several years advertisements for Grayson Brothers and public announcements appeared in both languages. Linguist and missionary Anne Eliza Worcester Robertson's translated hymns were printed for the benefit of Creek Christians. Baptist missionary H. F. Buckner contributed in serial form his "Thirty Years among the Indians." Creeks James Roane Gregory, a poet and historian, Charles Gibson, a social commentator, and Alexander Posey, a poet and humorist contributed regular columns. Posey, whose columns were syndicated, wrote under the pen names "Chinnubbee Harjo" and "Fus Fixico." Each October the *Journal* published the proceedings of the Creek National Council and the annual addresses of the principal chiefs of the Five Civilized Tribes. Dispatches and reports from their delegates in Washington informed readers about the various Indian-related bills Congress considered each session.[52]

Debo, noting that the *Journal* emphasized the social and economic activities of the townspeople and the mixed-blood Creeks, rarely mentioning the affairs of full-blood Creeks living in the backcountry, dismisses the journal as "at its best . . . a foreign institution."[53] Wash Grayson and the Indian Journal Printing Company stockholders saw it quite differently: The *Indian Journal* may have been an innovation to

Muskogee culture, but it was a Creek-owned vehicle reflecting the current interests, concerns, and viewpoints of a substantial Creek faction. Had there been Creeks with editorial and printing skills available to run the paper, the stockholders probably would have employed them rather than the succession of white editors. As it was, not until 1902 did Alexander Posey, a Creek Bacone College graduate, purchase the *Journal* and become editor.[54]

The white editors who preceded Posey understood clearly the nationalistic purpose and progressive position of the *Indian Journal* stockholders. Editor Leo E. Bennett in 1887 reminded subscribers that the *Journal* was the property of Indian citizens who believed Indians knew best what was best for Indians. Their goal was to make the newspaper "an effective instrument for the defense" of territorial interests. This included support for education, the "sole salvation" of the Indian people, including reading, writing, and spelling, along with the "knowledge of farming, fruit growing, stock raising, and the mechanic and all other useful arts, domestic or otherwise, which go to build up intelligent communities."[55] Fourteen years after its inception, the *Indian Journal* still professed to be "a paper published in the interest of the Indians."[56] Creek Columnist Charles Gibson, who often identified with the traditionalists, noted twenty-seven years after its founding that the newspaper "reflected public sentiment in the territory when Eufaula was an Indian village and when this country was truly the land of the red man."[57]

As far as its publishers, editors, and stockholders were concerned, then, the *Indian Journal* performed its dual purpose. On one level, while its columns boosted Eufaula by reporting on agricultural production, commerce, and development, listing the programs of school graduations, and describing encampments of the Muskogee Baptist Association, it was reflecting facets of contemporary Creek life. On a second, more important level, it was demonstrating the progress, as defined by Grayson and his fellow stockholders, that had occurred in the Creek Nation. Consequently, it testified to the white American public that Creeks were proud, intelligent, energetic, and dynamic people—far removed from "wigwams, robes, feathers, and vermillion." They were the equals of their white neighbors and as capable of self-government. As such, their rights and their nationhood must be respected.

If Grayson had not believed so strongly in the benefits of the *Indian Journal*, he would not have invested so much of his time, energy, and resources in it, because it was never a financially profitable venture. That probably accounted for the frequent turnover in stockholders and their attrition by the 1890s. But Wash Grayson relinquished his stock in the *Journal* only when Grayson Brothers' faced bankruptcy at the end of the century. In February 1890 he told a fellow stockholder, "We have had a hard time and indeed it is not much easier now." Yet he was optimistic, concluding, "I feel a double interest in this enterprise because it is being run by Indian capital and Indian brains."[58]

While his business enterprises consumed much of Grayson's time in the post-war years, his involvement in Creek national affairs, especially in the 1870s, was equally demanding. James Grayson had hoped that his sons would someday attain positions of honor and trust in their national government. Wash and Sam certainly fulfilled that ambition. Sam held several important national posts, but Wash achieved more and stayed deeply involved in Creek politics his entire adult life.[59]

Reestablishing their national government was one of the first concerns of both factions of the Creek people as they returned to their country after the Civil War. In February 1867, their old council house at High Spring having been destroyed, they met in a grove of blackjack oaks on the south side of the Deep Fork River near Red Stick Landing. Wash Grayson served as secretary to the convention, where the Creeks agreed to reunite and form a government under a new constitution and a single principal chief. Beneath the new government structure the traditional Muskogee framework could be discerned. Although the constitution divided the nation into six administrative districts, the basic unit was still the *tvlwv*. Each *tvlwv* elected a member to the upper House of Kings and representatives to the lower House of Warriors according to population, reflecting traditional political and military ranking.[60]

One historian has described the new constitutional system with its executive, legislative, and judicial branches as remaining tenuous because of continuing *tvlwv* autonomy and the subjugation of national identity to individual loyalty to *tvlwv* and clan. He also theorizes that the ancient separation of the *tvlwv* into red (war) and white (peace) divisions with specific responsibilities continued, with most national officials elected from the white towns. If this was indeed the case, it was not written into the constitution or otherwise documented; nor did Grayson ever mention it in his voluminous writings about Creek history and politics.[61]

Two political parties reflecting the Creek people's recent experience in the Civil War contested the first election. Samuel Checote, formerly principal chief of the Confederate Creeks in exile, led a Lower Creek former Confederate party supporting the constitutional government and national reconciliation. It called for fewer officials, administrative efficiency, better defined administrative duties and set salaries, more schools, and continuing change. In opposition was the conservative, primarily Upper Creek party led by Sands, Opothle Yahola's successor as leader of the Loyal Creeks. This party called for traditional ways of government and religion. Checote was elected, but Sands's conservative faction remained suspicious of the new voting method of casting written ballots rather than lining up behind a candidate and were hostile to the constitutional government.[62]

The new constitution recognized forty-four tribal towns, with Creek freedmen divided among three exclusively black *tvlwv*. On the first Tuesday of each October, the National Council convened to consider and pass legislation. A judge from each of the six judicial districts, among them G. W. Stidham and Walter Grayson, made up the Supreme Court. A lighthorse company, modeled on those of the neighboring Cherokee and Choctaw nations but recalling the peacetime police duties of the *tvstvnvkkvlke*, bore responsibility for keeping the peace and enforcing Creek law.[63]

The former Confederate faction oversaw the creation of this national government. One could speculate that this was because they had maintained some cohesion through their military units and in their refugee camps. Or perhaps the renovations were simply more comprehensible to them. Either way, they generally had the support of white officials who preferred to deal with a constitutional government.[64]

In 1867 the Creeks also needed a national capitol building. The blackjack grove was too far from supply points and at least thirty-five miles from the nearest post office. Moreover, the Creek population had shifted westward in the post-war years. The council chose a new site more centrally located than High Spring, and at the suggestion of Hotulke Emathla

(Edward Bullette) called it by the historically significant name, "Okmulgee." William S. Brown, Yuchee chief, merchant, and rancher, contracted to build the new council house. He directed groups of Creek workmen who felled trees, squared the logs, hauled them to the site (now Capitol Square in Okmulgee, Oklahoma), raised the walls, and split clapboards for the roof. The completed capitol was a large two-story building with a dogtrot below, a gallery above, and rock chimneys at either end. It served the nation for the next ten years.[65]

Wash Grayson soon found a place in this new constitutional government and its capitol. Newly elected Principal Chief Samuel Checote had served as a colonel in the Confederate Creek regiments and was, like Grayson, a member of the Tiger clan. These factors probably contributed to Grayson's appointment as secretary to the council that reconciled the factions and produced the constitution. Because several of the national officials did not speak English or were illiterate, the position of secretary was important, involving interpretation of language, terminology, and concepts. In occupying the position, Grayson moved forward in his role as a cultural broker at the same time that he began his political career. He received no pay for his services to the war-bankrupt Creek government, but the officials promised him a salary when finances permitted. In the meantime, they claimed his time and labor on the grounds that the nation had financed his English education. Grayson served in this capacity, alternating with Pleasant Porter and Joseph M. Perryman, for about two years before being elected national treasurer in October 1869.[66]

The position of national treasurer was no sinecure. The federal government resumed annuity payments in 1867, but congressional authorization for their disbursement through the yearly Indian Appropriations Act took low priority, some years failing to pass before the summer adjournment. Yet from this primary source of revenue the Creek treasurer had to pay out the salaries of national employees and officials as well as the expenses of running the government. He also issued and recorded the permits required of all noncitizen residents—including businessmen, physicians, mechanics, laborers, and tenants. For this service he eventually received a salary and a percentage of the permit fees.[67]

As treasurer Grayson disbursed national money through warrants authorized by the Creek National Council. In the absence of any Creek currency and because of the scarcity of federal money in the impoverished Indian Territory, these warrants circulated as a substitute. Usually sellers accepted them at a fraction of their face value, relative to the current indebtedness of the nation and the imminence of the next federal payment.[68]

Periodically the federal government delivered special payments as well, frequently as much as forty years overdue. On these occasions, Creek claimants and their heirs converged on the site of the payment in a holiday mood. Army troopers escorted wagons bearing heavy boxes of silver coin from Fort Smith to the agency. The Creek or after 1874 the Union Agent then distributed it through the Creek national treasurer. Sometimes individuals received only a few dollars, particularly the heirs of a claimant who might divide his share of long overdue compensation. But always awaiting the Creek recipients as they stepped away from the treasurer's table were the local merchants, sitting at tables of their own, collecting on debts owed.[69]

Wash Grayson found the job of national treasurer sometimes dangerous as well as onerous. Shortly after he assumed the office, the agent summoned him to accept payment of $100,000, the first installment on the $1,836,830 the federal government allowed the Loyal Creeks for their property losses during the Civil War. Grayson went alone to the Creek Agency near the settlement of Muskogee to collect it. He was well aware of hostile and speculative stares as he rode through a milling crowd near the double-log cabin that served then as the agent's headquarters. In spite of the reconciliation of 1867, serious issues (which will be discussed in chapter 5) still divided the nation. The rebellious Sands faction was threatening violence against the constitutional government. Grayson feared they would waylay him on his return with the cash to Okmulgee.[70]

Colonel Timothy Barnett, a kinsman and Confederate veteran now associated with Sands, confirmed Grayson's fears. He privately advised Grayson to hire bodyguards, leave during the coming night, and take the payment the forty-odd miles to Okmulgee by some back road. Grayson quietly followed Barnett's advice as he spotted Johnson Kennard, a lighthorseman, in the crowd and asked for his escort back to Okmulgee. After dark the two rode casually out of Muskogee and, once out of sight of the settlement, spurred their mounts across the prairie until they felt it was safe to rest. Leaving Kennard on guard, Grayson bedded down at the base of a tree with his head pillowed on his money-laden saddle bags. The night passed uninterrupted. By noon next day they were safely in Okmulgee handing over the funds to Chief Checote.[71]

Many years later Grayson pondered his utter faith in Lighthorseman Johnson Kennard. It never occurred to him that the man might steal the money himself. He concluded, "indeed there was still much of that old fashioned honesty and high respect for personal honor in those days that fully justified me in doing then with an ordinary unchristian Indian officer that which I would not now do with the ordinary christian sunday school superintendent of the white race. Times and people certainly have changed."[72]

As national treasurer, Grayson had every reason to fear for his and his family's safety. The Creek Nation never rid itself of the drifters and desperados of the war years; nor did the federal government fulfill its treaty obligations to keep out intruders. Indians and freedmen alike turned to outlawry in the atmosphere of violence and instability that existed while the Creek government struggled to cope with post-war factionalism. The Indian nations' lighthorsemen and court systems tried to control troublesome elements, but given persistent jurisdictional problems, lawbreakers had only to slip over the border into a neighboring nation to elude pursuing officers.[73]

As a result Indian, white, and black outlaws infested the Indian nations, and violent death was common. The James, Starr, and Dalton gangs made their headquarters a short distance east of Eufaula at Younger's Bend on the Canadian River. The Younger's Bend hangout was operated by Belle Starr, an intermarried Cherokee. Members of the gangs often bought supplies in town. Questioned as to why they usually left the Eufaula merchants alone, one outlaw reportedly replied that there were nine extra fine shots in town. Besides, the kind of money they kept in Eufaula was too heavy to carry off. The notorious Belle Starr also frequented the town. Wearing two large pistols buckled around her waist, she could sometimes be found playing piano at the Ingram Hotel. Daniel Evans, one of the gang that invaded Uncle Watt Grayson's home, tortured the old man and his wife, and robbed him of thirty-two thousand dollars in gold in November 1873, confessed his guilt in the case before his hanging in 1875.

He identified Belle, who he claimed had been dressed as a man, and Jim Reed, her first husband, as the other culprits. But Grayson family tradition holds that Belle was too friendly with the Wash Grayson family to have been a part of that crime.[74]

Understandably, Grayson had some qualms about keeping national funds in his home, especially while the family still lived in the countryside. One frigid winter night he and Annie woke to the sound of quiet hoof-beats approaching their door over ice-crusted snow. His mind went instantly to the several thousand dollars of Creek funds stowed in his old saddle bags. Quickly he slid out of bed, got his pistol, and raked ashes over the fire to hide his movements, while the thumping and scraping against the walls sounded very much as if someone were trying to break in. Much to his relief, he realized a few tense minutes later that the "thieves" were cattle licking the salt-laden clay chinking of the cabin walls. The false alarm remained a favorite family story.[75]

Most of Grayson's fear of robbery ended when the family moved into town. Ironically, it was in town that he was the victim of a burglary sometime later, probably in the summer of 1877. One night someone entered the Grayson Brothers store and took $1,276.75 from the small iron safe the council had given him and in which he kept national funds and documents. Grayson at once reported the theft. Meeting in October, the council took issue with his listing the loss under "disbursements" and resolved that he was responsible for repaying the money. For many months Grayson denied any negligence and refused to repay the loss.[76]

What probably infuriated and distressed him even more was that he suspected, but had no proof, that his cousin Robert Sewell was the thief. Sewell was the son of his Aunt Feenie, who had helped nurse him through smallpox in the last year of the war. Grayson could only suggest privately to Principal Chief Ward Coachman that Sewell be watched and arrested if proof were found. A year later, in August 1878, Grayson finally conceded responsibility for the stolen funds but did not have the cash to pay it. The matter slipped until some years later when Albert Pike McKellop, a Creek political rival, persuaded the Creek Supreme Court to allow him to bring suit against Grayson for recovery. The Supreme Court upheld Grayson's defense, but the incident, McKellop's suit, and the aspersions cast on Wash's competence still rankled years later. Apparently Sewell's guilt in this case was never proved, but he was serving time in a Montana prison in 1902.[77]

Even without such incidents, dealing with Creek finances was no easy matter. While the businessmen in the Creek government understood the management of money and national credit, many of the less sophisticated did not. Creek officials of both types casually signed warrants and trusted the untrustworthy, especially the growing number of white opportunists in the nation. As a result, Creek finances were usually chaotic and the government chronically in debt.[78] Just before he thankfully finished his second term as treasurer, Grayson commented, "[M]any of the members [of the Council] are good enough men otherwise, but have no more ideas of government than the Bedouins of the plains of Arabia."[79]

Wash Grayson's frustration with those he regarded as reactionary was never enough to make him abandon Creek politics. In fact, at the same time he was serving as national treasurer, he was also filling two other public posts. In December 1875 the Creek National Council designated Wash, his brother Sam, Joseph M. Perryman, and Wash's brother-in-law Charles S. Smith as the Board of Education of the Creek Nation. They examined applicants for teachers' certificates in higher education in the fields of arithmetic, English composition and grammar, United States history, natural philosophy, geography, and penmanship. They also kept tabs on Creek students sent to study in the States, as Wash had been in the late 1850s. A few years later Wash informed touring U.S. senators that the Creek Nation routinely sent youths to study in Tuskegee, Alabama, in Tennessee, at the Horticultural Seminary at Louisville, Kentucky, and at Western Central College in Ohio. It was not the Creeks' purpose to train them for professions; rather, he said, "the idea is to give them a good education, so as to fit them for business."[80]

More important to Grayson was his appointment as a Creek representative to the Okmulgee Convention. This duty provided him important firsthand experience in working in international diplomacy and Indian-federal relations, and it honed his skills as a cultural broker. For Indian Territory citizens generally, the convention also fostered Indian nationalism while it underlined Indian unity as a potent weapon in fending off federal attacks on Indian sovereignty.[81]

The convention was in accord with the Muskogee tradition of diplomacy, which underpinned the old Creek Confederacy and long predated their first contacts with Europeans. Resettled in the Indian Territory, Creeks continued to confer with representatives of other tribes, frequently traveling far to the western frontier to smoke the pipe of peace, exchange gifts and messages of good will, and extend advice to those less experienced than they in dealing with the white man. They took a fraternal, if somewhat superior, attitude toward peoples they considered "wild Indians," who often admired what the Creeks had achieved. In fact, in 1855 some bands of the Comanches, the nomadic lords of the Southern Plains, asked the Creeks to intercede for them with the federal government, that they might learn as the Creeks had how to build houses and farm the land.[82]

At the beginning of the Civil War, the pro-Confederate Creeks had helped create the Grand Council, a confederation of Indian nations in the territory. Even in exile in the Red River Valley, the Confederate Creeks attended the meetings of the Grand Council, and at war's end an intertribal conference at Camp Napoleon on the Washita River (near present Verden, Oklahoma) sought to expand this confederation. There representatives of the Five Civilized Tribes and of the Caddos, Osages, Comanches, Lipans, Kiowas, Arapahos, and Cheyennes agreed to pursue peaceful solutions to their mutual problems and to unite against further white aggression.[83]

Although the Indian nations' purpose directly opposed the federal government's, their unification effort coincided with federal post-war plans for the Indian Territory. One of the stipulations forced on all the former Confederate Indian allies in the 1866–1867 Reconstruction treaties was acceptance in principle of a unified Indian territorial government. Congress even appropriated money to pay tribal delegates to attend a territorial convention. But if the federal government saw these conferences as a way ultimately to undermine the sovereignty of the individual Indian nations, its vision was quite different from that of the Indian participants. The Five Civilized Tribes were well aware of the growing influence of the railroad corporations in Washington, the agitation for the opening of the Indian Territory to white settlement, and the number of territorial bills with that aim introduced at each session of Congress.

Although wary and reluctant to attend the federally supervised convention, they hoped to protect their interests and control the damage a federally imposed territorial government might inflict.[84]

Under these circumstances, Wash Grayson was one of eleven Creek delegates chosen to attend the General Council convening in 1870 at their own capitol at Okmulgee. Nine were Anglo-Creeks associated with the progressive faction, but the delegation also included the traditionalist leader Sands. Among them were old hands such as G. W. Stidham, Cotchochee, and Timothy Barnett as well as the younger generation—Pleasant Porter; Joseph M., Legus, and Sanford Perryman; John R. Moore; David M. Hodge; and Wash Grayson. This was not Grayson's first diplomatic experience. In the summer of 1867 he had acted as clerk when the Creek National Council, Seminole Chief John Jumper, and Caddo representatives made an agreement at Okmulgee through interpreter Jesse Chisholm. Still, the appointment to the General Council delegation carried much more prestige and responsibility. It pleasantly surprised Grayson, and it testified to his growing political stature.[85]

The meeting at the end of September 1870 was the first of the series of intertribal assemblies known as the Okmulgee Convention. Office of Indian Affairs Central Superintendent Enoch Hoag presided over delegations of Creeks, Cherokees, Seminoles, Ottawas, Eastern Shawnees, Quapaws, Senecas, Wyandottes, Confederated Peorias, Sacs and Foxes, Weas, Osages, and Absentee Shawnees. The suspicious Choctaws refused to attend, and only one Chickasaw came. Nevertheless, the forty delegates included some of the most prominent men in the Indian Territory—Cherokees William Potter Ross, Riley Keys, and Moses Alberty along with Chief Keokuk of the Sacs and Foxes. Stand Watie, who had in 1863 warned the other principal chiefs of the Five Civilized Tribes that they must stand together or fall separately, was a Cherokee representative.[86]

Getting down to business, the delegates created seven committees charged with issues or tasks ranging from international relations to agriculture and education. Wash Grayson's assignment was to the committee governing transaction of business during General Council sessions. Perhaps the work of the committee on relations with the United States was the most indicative of the Indian perspective and aim for this council. The delegates ordered that committee to draw up a memorial to President

U. S. Grant, calling on him to uphold the treaties of 1866–1867, prevent Congress from creating any territorial government except that of the General Council, prevent any attempt to extinguish Indian title to lands in the territory, and deny access to the territory to any railroad other than those already chartered. The General Council resolved to transmit its actions to the Plains tribes and invite them to send delegates to the next session.[87]

Because several of the committees needed time to prepare their assigned reports, the General Council adjourned until December 1870. Generally the same delegates attended, but the Chickasaws and Choctaws came this time to avoid being forced in the future to accept commitments made in their absence. Sands reported no response to the Absentee Shawnees' transmission of their invitation to the Plains tribes. One of the council's first actions was to assign ten men, one of them Grayson, to devise a permanent organization for the conventions. Eventually he resigned as Creek delegate to serve as permanent secretary to the Okmulgee Convention.[88]

The major product of the December session was the Okmulgee Constitution. It created a federal union, patterned after that of the United States, with an elected governor, a bicameral legislature, and a court system. It was to go into effect once two-thirds of the voters of the Indian Territory ratified it. The Creeks approved the constitution at once, and the Choctaws and several of the smaller tribes eventually ratified it. But the Cherokees and Chickasaws rejected it, the latter on the grounds that it favored the more populous tribes. As the constitution passed through the federal bureaucracy, various officials tried to amend it to give the federal government more control over the proposed territorial government. These changes combined with an outcry in the white press against continued Indian self-government assured the constitution's defeat. A revised version introduced in 1875 received only Creek support.[89]

Historian Ohland Morton wrote in 1931 that Indian Territory voters in 1870–1871, particularly among the Five Civilized Tribes, were divided into three factions: a radical minority who wanted the territory opened to white settlement, an ultra-conservative minority who wanted no change at all, and the majority who favored passage of the Okmulgee Constitution. William McLoughlin's recent study of post-Removal Cherokee politics supports Morton's conclusion. He theorizes that the majority full-blood Cherokees—nationalistic and staunchly opposed to the few mixed-bloods who supported allotment in severalty, territorialization, and U.S. citizenship to protect their private property—supported the confederation effort. Full-blood Cherokees saw it as a way to strengthen national sovereignty and Indian unity. However, the Cherokee National Council failed to ratify the Okmulgee Constitution, fearing congressional modification of the document to establish a centralized, white-dominated territorial government that would erode the Indian nations' sovereignty. The Creeks' immediate ratification of the original document suggests that the Muskogee majority also supported it for defensive, nationalistic reasons. Debo speculates they likewise feared federally imposed territorialization but hoped to guard their interests from within the new Indian. union.[90] McLoughlin summarizes the Indians' creation of the Okmulgee Constitution as ultimately conservative with relation to national sovereignty and the closely related issue of communal landholding. Both Debo's and McLoughlin's views correlate well with Wash Grayson's brand of progressive nationalism.

In spite of their rejection of the Okmulgee Constitution, Indians of the territory made valuable gains from the conventions. Delegates from the less sophisticated tribes were given a preview of the future and an introduction to new ways of conducting tribal and intertribal affairs. The committee reports on territorial agriculture and education gave all the delegates useful information on their current status and pointed them toward future goals while emphasizing the benefits of adopting selected aspects of white culture. The delegates learned to use a new forum from which to deliver to Congress and the white public strong memorials regarding such issues as railroad land grants, the Cherokee Tobacco Case, and pending legislation to end treaty making with tribes as sovereign nations. Lastly, the sessions highlighted the common threat and their common cause, fostering Indian nationalism. A growing sense of Indian unity and identity was strengthened and given immediacy against the backdrop of Anglo-American encroachment. By 1871 the new Indian unity included the beleaguered and belligerent Plains tribes. That year the Cheyennes, Arapahos, Comanches, and Kiowas sent representatives to confer with the delegates of the General Council at the Creek capital.[91]

Delegates of thirty-three tribes, attending the Okmulgee Convention in 1875, posed in front of the Creek Capitol. Photo by John K. Hillers. Courtesy C. W. Kirk Collection, Archives and Manuscripts Division of the Oklahoma Historical Society.

By 1875 the federal government recognized the nationalistic tone of the sessions and grew pessimistic about achieving its ends through the Okmulgee Convention. In the spring of 1878 an inquiry as to whether Congress should fund another session elicited a negative response from Union Agent S. W. Marston. Little good would come, he stated, of sessions devoted to how best to oppose imposition of territorial government and American citizenship on the Indians. Instead, he predicted, the delegates would only use the sessions to strengthen the ties that bound them and encourage the more primitive to imitate the example of the more civilized.[92]

Nevertheless, the tribes of the territory continued to meet regularly at their own expense for the next two decades. From the first meeting in 1870, they published the journals of their sessions, and they realized the impact of their eloquent and politically astute protests on the small but growing number of "friends of the Indian" among the Anglo-American public. At the 1875 session the delegates agreed to go a step further and publish their own territorial newspaper dedicated to Indian rights. It was this newspaper, originally published at Muskogee, that was reborn in 1877 as the *Indian Journal*.[93]

Wash Grayson remained at the forefront of the Okmulgee Convention movement, overseeing its business affairs for ten years as permanent secretary while periodically doubling as a Creek delegate.[94] Often the multilingual nature of the conventions demanded that he serve as an interpreter. These roles contributed to his reputation in the territory, particularly among the less sophisticated Indians. He understood their ways and could communicate their perspective to the federal government. In retrospect Grayson noted, "My complexion and person having so much the appearance of the white man, that I could speak the Indian as I did appeared striking to the wild Indians who attended these councils." Somewhat condescendingly, he continued, "The fact that I was Indian and spoke the language and was also secretary of this great Indian body appointed by the Secretary of the Interior at Washington, impressed the simple representatives of some of those tribes with the belief that I must be a person of very considerable importance and fully entitled to their confidence. Whenever I met any of them either in Washington or elsewhere as I often did years afterwards, they would in perfect confidence state to me their business and ask my advice.[95]

Recognition of Grayson's acumen and abilities extended beyond the territory. A description of the Creek Okmulgee Convention delegates that appeared in the *St. Louis Globe* and several Western newspapers in 1873 gushed that Secretary Grayson was "emphatically the financial man of the Creek Nation—perfectly honest, competent to discharge any duty, he stands very high in the estimation of the people. Capt. Grayson possesses that . . . ability which knowing the right dares to defend it; perfectly regardless of fear, he works for the interest of his people untiringly, but not unrewarded. No man is more popular in the Nation."[96]

There was even a hint that Grayson's popularity might take him much higher. In July 1875 the *Vindicator* of Atoka, Choctaw Nation, reported, "Capt. G. W. Grayson is a candidate for principal chief of the Creeks. Crazy

Turtle [Locha Hacho], who can't run fast, is one of his competitors, while Samuel Checota [Checote], of third term aspirations, is another."[97] The humorous tone of the lines and their authorship by H. F. Buckner, minister and family friend of the Graysons, suggested that the writer was joking rather than making a serious observation about political events. In any event, the chieftaincy eluded Grayson for another forty years.

In the meantime, while his energetic pursuit of business opportunities and his English education set him among the elite of the Indian Territory, it also set him somewhat apart from the traditionalist Creeks. Grayson recognized the disparity as he said, "[F]ortune and circumstances have placed me in some respects in advance of some of my fellow country-men."[98] Even then his "advancement" did not alienate him from them. He still identified himself with the members of Koweta *tvlwv*, the Tiger clan, and West Eufaula Indian Baptist Church. They in turn continued to accept Wash Grayson as one of their own. It must also be noted that in his "advancement" he remained in the company of other Creeks, like-minded constitutionalist leaders and progressive nationalists such as the twenty-one Indian Journal Printing Company stockholders.

Late nineteenth-century developments in the Creek Nation were open to contrasting interpretations. Some critics saw entrepreneurs like Wash and Sam Grayson as driven by self-interest, using the communally held landbase of the Creek Nation for their own benefit. Nor can it be denied that a few individuals, including the Grayson brothers, exploited national resources for individual profit. Other observers, Anglo-Americans who could envision no finer model than their own, saw the founding of a town such as Eufaula and Creek use of modern transportation, agricultural, and communications technology as positive steps. Conversion to Christianity, the creation of a constitutional government, and graduation of Creek children from national schools must lead toward eventual assimilation into the American mainstream.

Paradoxically, for Grayson and other Creek nationalists these "progressive" steps were ultimately conservative. They intended to keep what the Creeks still had—their landbase, their sovereignty, and their Muskogee identity. They did not believe that the cultural changes they supported made them less Muskogee. They believed they were on a course that paralleled rather than converged with Anglo-American development.

They recognized that they would forfeit some honored traditions and acquire greater degrees of some white characteristics, particularly individualism, materialism, and acquisitiveness. But none of these were particularly new to Muskogee culture, as their enthusiastic participation in the deerskin trade of the seventeenth and eighteenth centuries demonstrated. Moreover, the Creek people were gaining new defensive strengths, particularly literacy. Opothle Yahola had understood in 1850 that the Creeks needed educated men such as Wash Grayson to stand between them and trouble. Charles Gibson, who had been Grayson's clerk at the time, echoed the same sentiment forty years later as he advised students at Carlisle Indian School, "Don't forget this: the hand of nearly every man on this our native land is against us Red people, and there is no way to stay the hand of our enemy only to take the education that is offered to us to fight back with."[99]

Grayson, then, saw himself not as alienated from his fellow Creeks but as one of their vanguard. His English education, business skills, experience with the Okmulgee Convention, and wide acquaintance with other Indian Territory citizens had prepared him to defend the Creek Nation as a politician, diplomat, and cultural broker just as he had defended it as a warrior. And by the late 1870s it was quite clear that the legal and political assault on Indian sovereignty was gathering force both on the borders of the territory and in the chambers of Congress.

CHAPTER FIVE

All That Is Left
for Our Children

For Wash Grayson the decade of the 1880s was a time of sharp contrast. On the one hand, it brought success in his business ventures, a growing family, and a happy home. But as a Creek nationalist, he was alarmed that the decade also brought persistent turmoil within the Creek government and two major territorial crises. In dealing with them he honed his skills as a cultural broker and strengthened his reputation as a capable representative of his nation. As he did so, Grayson identified politically and philosophically with the progressive Creek nationalists. But although he supported their attempts to preserve Creek sovereignty, by the end of the decade he questioned both their leadership and their wisdom.[1]

Grayson served two terms as national treasurer and then in 1883 was elected a member of the lower chamber of the Creek National Council, the House of Warriors, or *Tvstvnvkkvlke*. Even though Grayson never lived among the Kowetas, whose ceremonial ground was in the northern part of the nation, they were his *tvlwv* and constituency, electing him to successive terms in the 1880s and 1890s. By the time of his first election, he was already established as a diplomat through his work in the Okmulgee Convention. Eventually that contributed to his concurrent election by the Creek National Council as a delegate to the Indian international councils and to Washington. His experience and position placed him in the front ranks of defense during the first crisis, the "boomer" demand for the opening of the Indian Territory to non-Indian settlement.[2]

With the Indian majority Grayson opposed any change in the status of the Indian Territory, but he knew that the pressure to open it to homesteaders was growing in the late 1870s. The demand for formal territorialization, the dissolution of the Indian national governments, the substitution of allotment in severalty for the traditional communal landholding system, and opening the territory to non-Indian settlement was gaining strength in Congress. The powerful railroad lobby was pressing hard for these changes as a means of gaining the generous subsidies of public lands—currently Indian lands—that were available under federal charter. The further economic development of the territory that they anticipated with non-Indian settlement would allow them further expansion and greatly increase their profits.[3] Joining their chorus, the press and the public in neighboring states condemned the Indian Territory as a barrier to the progress of the whole region. One speaker called it "a grand fenced zoological garden" for savages too lazy to work.[4] This, of course, was the faulty image Grayson and his fellow stockholders in the Indian Journal Printing Company believed they must disprove.

Ironically, it was a fellow Indian citizen who provided justification for a large-scale homesteader invasion of the heart of the Indian Territory. Elias C. Boudinot, a Cherokee lobbyist for the railroads, boldly advocated allotment in severalty and opening the territory to non-Indian settlement.[5] Incensed, Grayson labeled this nephew of his old commander Stand Watie, "the Benedict Arnold of the Indian race."[6] Boudinot, Grayson, and Choctaw Governor Allen Wright addressed a banquet audience at Fort Scott, Kansas, in July 1878. Grayson and Wright rebutted Boudinot's arguments as well as his claim to speak as a representative of the Indian Territory. Not even 1 percent of its Indian citizens, they declared, supported his radical position.[7]

Undeterred, six months later Boudinot published an article in the *Chicago Times* that identified 14 million acres in central Indian Territory as available for homesteading. This area lay west of the current Creek Nation and included the lands forcibly ceded by them and the Seminoles in their Reconstruction treaties. Set aside at that time for the future

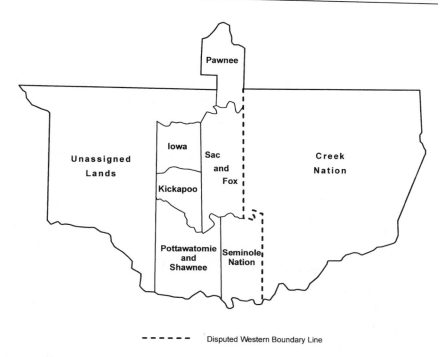

------ Disputed Western Boundary Line

Map 4. The Creek Nation and the Unassigned Lands

settlement of other Indians or freedmen, it had not been utilized for that purpose. Boudinot reasoned that these "Unassigned Lands" were public domain and therefore eligible for homesteading. His article received widespread attention in neighboring states, and several "boomer" colonies quickly organized to homestead the Unassigned Lands they called "Oklahoma"[8] (see map 4).

The visit of Secretary of the Interior Carl Schurz to Muskogee in October 1879 intensified the alarm the boomers inspired among territorial citizens. Schurz, newly appointed to his post, addressed an audience that included Tawacone, Kickapoo, Ottawa, Quapaw, Caddo, Apache, Waco, Keechie, Osage, Comanche, and Five Civilized Tribes people. Hinting that the federal government might not be able to stem the tide of non-Indian settlement, Schurz advised them to give up communal landholding for individual title in fee simple and to prepare for the arrival of homesteaders. This was not a new idea to the Five Civilized Tribes, who maintained direct communications with Washington, but it left other Indians in the audience thunderstruck. Though they showed little public reaction to Schurz's remarks, among themselves they spoke freely of their shock and dismay. Would the federal government fail to keep faith with their treaties? Was this the behavior of a "better civilization," the *Indian Journal* asked.[9]

The incursion of noncitizen intruders into the Indian Territory and the federal government's failure to evict them had been a constant concern to the Five Civilized Tribes, but the boomer threat, combined with Schurz's message, lifted the problem to a critical stage. The Five Civilized Tribes began closing ranks in response. Cherokee Principal Chief Dennis Wolfe Bushyhead warned Creek Principal Chief Checote, "Intrusion on an extended scale which should endanger one of our Nations would endanger all; and due vigilance is required at the hands of each head of the Nations to curb and check intrusion when it begins, so as to prevent extension." Bushyhead asked for an exchange of information and cooperation among their national delegates in Washington.[10] Recognizing the menace to their sovereignty and landbase, the leaders of the Five Civilized Tribes called an international council at Eufaula for March 1880. There Chief Checote reminded representatives of several tribes, "The land which we now possess is all that is left for our children."[11]

This was the first in a series of international councils at Eufaula during 1880. Wash Grayson attended the May session as a newly appointed Creek delegate. While the council conferred, the leaders of the Five Civilized Tribes warned the Indians on the westernmost reservations to keep watch for intruders and reminded the federal government of its treaty obligations to protect their borders. This danger to them all reinforced a trend that had begun during the Civil War: Conscious of intensifying Anglo-American aggressiveness, territorial tribespeople were developing a new Indian identity and defensive unity that transcended tribal boundaries. Under the boomer threat, their international correspondence and public statements emphasized the need to maintain common defense of their mutual interests.[12] The western tribes understood the danger and the need as clearly as did the Five Civilized Tribes. To a Creek appeal for international accord during the boomer crisis, Chief We-qua-ho-ka of the

Sac and Fox people responded, "We always depend on you. Anything you will do we will agree with you. P.S. We are brothers we must be one mind."[13]

In the next few months the crisis crystallized around the person of David L. Payne. The most famous of the boomers, Payne was a peculiar combination of hero and huckster, a charismatic martyr to his followers and a petty but persistent lawbreaker to federal authorities. Historians differ as to what motivated Payne to form his Oklahoma Colony and repeatedly invade the Indian Territory, but the Indians had little doubt. The *Indian Journal* looked no further into such ventures than the Katy Railroad.[14] The editor of the *Cherokee Advocate* declared less specifically, "He is but the tool in the hands of others, who see in the scheme a chance for a big steal."[15]

Payne, accepting his friend Boudinot's premise that the Unassigned Lands were public domain, attracted an army of would-be settlers, who took up stations along the Kansas border to await the opening of the Indian Territory for homesteading. Payne knew that the punishment for the first act of intrusion was simply expulsion from the territory. The second offense would draw a one thousand dollar fine as well. Intending to put the issue of non-Indian exclusion before the courts, Payne invaded the Indian Territory in April 1880, was arrested as an intruder and expelled, and returned in July to be arrested for the second time. Subsequently, federal troops delivered him to Fort Smith, Arkansas, for trial. Federal Judge Isaac C. Parker was scheduled to hear the case in March 1881.[16]

Following these events, the International Council of the Five Civilized Tribes reconvened at Eufaula in October 1880, with the principal chiefs of the Choctaws, Cherokees, and Chickasaws present. Again Wash Grayson was among the Creek delegates. The council easily discerned Payne's strategy to challenge the exclusive nature of the Indian Territory. He was, they believed, only a front man for the railroad interests, which would spare no expense in assuring his courtroom defense. Should the federal court find in his favor, they were convinced the barriers against noncitizen settlement would fall.[17] Above all else, they stressed the need for Indian unity. Grayson signed for the Creeks the joint proclamation that called on "all true Indians to rally with us in our common defense."[18]

The council then created a Committee of Prosecution, which included some of the most experienced and able representatives of the Five

Civilized Tribes. Thomas Cloud, a Seminole, had negotiated with the Plains tribes before the Civil War and had been his nation's delegate to Washington in 1878. James Thompson had been a Choctaw delegate to the Okmulgee Convention and was a long-time national official. DeWitt Clinton Duncan was a survivor of the Cherokee Trail of Tears, a Dartmouth graduate, a writer under the pen name "Too-qua-stee," and an experienced lawyer. Benjamin F. Overton had little formal education but had already served two terms as Chickasaw governor and would serve two more. A conservative and a Chickasaw nationalist, he had greeted the 1876 Custer massacre with a call for Indian unification for self-preservation. The youngest of the five-man committee was the Creek member, Wash Grayson. To meet its expenses, the International Council assessed each nation according to its ability to pay.[19] On December 15 the committee assembled to discuss the situation. Grayson spoke for them all when he described the coming trial as "a crisis in our affairs of a very grave character."[20]

Because a great deal of highly inflammatory publicity was appearing in territorial and state newspapers, they decided their first move was to assess the boomer threat for themselves. On December 17 Grayson and three committeemen boarded the train, traveling incognito to Caldwell, Kansas, a border town near which the boomers had set up winter quarters. The boomers soon correctly identified the visitors as representatives of the Indian nations; even so, they welcomed the four into their camps.[21]

Grayson was not impressed with what he saw there. Instead of the several hundred eager settlers newspaper accounts had led them to expect, Grayson counted about seventy-five "hungry, half-clad backwoods white men, than whom a more worthless horde [could] hardly be found in all the balance of christendem [sic]."[22] Duncan agreed with his assessment. He described them as "the most degraded and ignorant specimens of human society—deluded and shamefully imposed upon by Payne and other leaders."[23] These potential settlers owned about thirty-two "pretty good lumber wagons with shabby teams," and there were no women or children among them.[24]

Grayson and Duncan summed up Payne as a man who spent his time in the local saloons and other "places of dissipation" drumming up support and rallying the faltering. His boomers were "evidently the dregs of the white population of Kansas and adjoining States." Obviously, such people lacked the numbers, resources, and equipment necessary to force the opening of the territory. From such as these, the committee concluded, Indians had little to fear.[25] Still, the committee perceived a real danger in "a wicked superior intelligence" that "might if possible so warp the structure of statutes and treaties as to ostensibly favor this Oklahoma movement." Should even one intruder succeed in bending the law, Grayson cautioned, "it would [be] sufficient to legalize the overwhelming of our entire Territory by just such a population as those."[26]

At the boomer camp Grayson and his party presented the view of Indian Territory citizens that federal law and treaties with the Indian nations prohibited homesteading in the Unassigned Lands, but they failed to discourage the would-be homesteaders. Frustrated, Grayson stormed, "We are doing all we can to prevent the opening of the country, and you had just as well go home, for we have bought, and can buy, your Congressmen like so many sheep and cattle." The committee departed with one final threat: They would raise an army of five thousand to drive out the boomers should the federal government allow the colonists to enter the Unassigned Lands.[27]

That threat titillated border newspapers for several weeks. Indian warfare was no light matter on the Kansas frontier. Kansans recalled with horror the death and destruction left by Dull Knife's Northern Cheyennes as they made their escape from an Indian Territory reservation only two years earlier. Some editors reminded their readers that the Indian Territory was home to as many as eighteen thousand Civil War veterans, many of them skilled guerrilla fighters. Once across the Kansas border, one editor shrilled, they would find little to stop them if they wanted to go all the way to Topeka![28] Adding to the commotion, the *Indian Journal* reported in July that three hundred Indians were organizing, stockpiling weapons, and planning to drive out the intruders if federal troops failed to stop the invasion. Scouting parties were even then combing the Cimarron and Canadian River valleys, looking for intruders. "On every hand," editor Myron P. Roberts declared, "a determination is expressed to fight for their rights."[29]

In spite of rumor, heated speculation, and Grayson's well-publicized threat, Indian Territory leaders had no intention of taking the warpath against the boomers. Six months after the confrontation near Caldwell, Grayson publicly dismissed talk of armed resistance as editorial bombast.[30] Nor, in spite of his bluster, could the usually financially strapped Indian governments afford to outbid the railroad lobby for congressional loyalties. In threatening to raise an army against the invasion, Grayson probably either lost his temper in the face of boomer stubbornness or was playing on the popular imagination to achieve by fear what he could not achieve by reason.

Rather, the Indians' response to Payne's boomer threat demonstrated their familiarity with the Anglo-American legal system and reliance on it. They placed their trust in the federal court system, federal legislation, and their treaties with the federal government to uphold their rights. The same day the Committee of Prosecution confronted the boomers, they issued a press release in which they played down the danger from Payne's followers. The real fight, they knew, would take place in the courtroom in Fort Smith.[31]

While the Indian national delegates in Washington did all they could to influence federal officials there, Grayson and Duncan countered pro-boomer publicity with their own to calm Indian fears and rally Anglo-American public opinion in support of Indian rights. As journalists from the Associated Press spotted a developing story on the Kansas–Indian Territory border, news of the Committee of Prosecution's confrontation with the boomers, complete with Grayson's angry warning, appeared in the *New York Times* within twenty-four hours. The boomer-Indian conflict quickly became national news with editors from Chicago, New York, and Philadelphia championing one side or the other.[32] Cherokee Chief Bushyhead spoke for Indians generally when he hoped that the great mass of the American public did not side with the boomers, who represented, he said, the "infamous Cortez and Pizarro element of freebooters and robbers, as contra-distinguished from the honest Anglo-Saxon Race who control and dictate the policy to the nation."[33]

Grayson also hoped that Judge Parker's court would favor his cause even though its seat was Fort Smith, Arkansas, a town, he noted, "by no means too friendly to Indians."[34] But Judge Parker apparently did all he could to assure a fair, informed decision. During the months before the trial he and the federal prosecutor solicited the Indians' views on the various treaties and land cessions involved in the case and asked their help with the prosecution. In response, the members of the Committee of Prosecution went to Fort Smith to confer with Parker and the federal prosecutor.[35] Benjamin F. Overton believed their presence there would "produce a good effect among the whites who are ever ready to gobble up our lands. It will show them," the Chickasaw believed, "that we are united and determined to meet them on every point that they may make in that direction."[36]

Grayson and the other committee members were in the courtroom when the trial commenced on March 7, 1881. Duncan, a lawyer with several years' practice in the Midwest, aided the federal prosecutor while Boudinot and three attorneys—one of them James M. Baker, president of the St. Louis and San Francisco Railroad—defended Payne. Judge Parker heard the arguments and then, because of the importance of the issue, deferred his decision until the May court session. In the meantime he visited St. Louis, base of several railroad corporations, which aroused suspicion in the minds of Grayson and others who were convinced Payne was the tool of the railroads. Consequently, the Indians maintained their own pressure to assure a decision in their favor.[37]

In the end, though, Parker decided in support of Indian rights. He reasoned that neither Payne nor any other non-Indian could legally homestead Oklahoma. The federal government had forced the Creeks and Seminoles to cede the lands in question as a home for future Indian settlement, he wrote, but they retained residual rights. It was still Indian land whether or not it had been "assigned." The boomers were non-Indians, and having no permits issued by one of the Indian nations, must be considered intruders in the Indian Territory, liable to arrest, expulsion, and fine—at least until the laws changed.[38]

The Committee of Prosecution and all Indian nationalists were elated at Parker's ruling. Grayson, in his final report to the Creek National Council, thriftily returned the unspent portion of the Creek prosecution fund and concluded, "It is pleasant to know . . . that in this decision of the United States Court, the Indians have become possessed of one of the strongest levers yet placed within their grasp for compelling a just recognition of their rights and the integrity of our whole Indian Territory."[39]

Grayson was proud of his role in the Payne affair. Although he had failed to dissuade the boomers from their goal of homesteading the territory, he had presented the Indians' perceptions of their treaties and federal law to the federal court, laid the Indians' case before the American public, and kept Indian Territory citizens calm and informed. Not only had the Committee of Prosecution won this particular fight, it had done so in the white man's own courtroom.

Grayson's pleasure was short-lived, however, for even as he was writing his report on the successful outcome of this crisis, another was developing within the Creek Nation. While the Creeks successfully maintained unity with their neighbors to avert the potential disaster of a boomer victory, they found it difficult to achieve time-honored consensus and harmony among their own people.

Few aspects of Creek life received more credence from Anglo-American observers, including twentieth-century historians, as proof of their acculturation than the creation of a constitutional government in 1867. However, as Wash Grayson reminded readers of the *Indian Journal*, Creeks had governed themselves satisfactorily for centuries under their old customs. When the white man arrived, Grayson continued, he arrogantly concluded that "the Indian's policy and religion were defective and inadequate." The Creeks, Grayson believed, were "lashed" into accepting new ways. A realist, he believed they could have done nothing else and acknowledged that many had "long since learned to adopt, love and respect many of the principles of government and religion that have been so industriously and persistently taught them by . . . diplomatic and Christian missionaries."[40]

But some Muskogees disagreed with Grayson's assessment, as evidenced by two decades of resentment and rebellion toward the constitutional government. Debo theorizes that progressive Creek nationalists such as Grayson adopted constitutional government as the most effective way of protecting their lands while squelching the white man's schemes to destroy their independence. In doing so, however, they excluded the traditionalists, who did not understand or accept the new system. In consequence, while some traditionalists might agree with the progressives on the benefits of English education, Christianity, and expanded agriculture, they objected to the new constitutional government. This dissatisfaction combined with traditional hostilities, Civil War bitterness, and the aspirations of Creek freedmen to destabilize Creek government at least until 1883.[41]

Duane Champagne's more recent study views the constitutional government as being more or less cosmetic, with substantial political force surviving in the *tvlwv*, their traditional social/religious influence still intact. Local authority, according to this work, centered in the *tvlwv* chiefs and councilors and superseded national authority. The *tvlwv* chiefs were not willing to trade status for a streamlined, centralized government, nor were they willing to yield control over the distribution of national funds to the national treasurer. So *tvlwv*-based traditionalists, although frequently elected to the Creek National Council, contested every national election, precipitating one political confrontation after another. But it was the constitutionalists, best representing Anglo-American ideals, who benefited from the support and recognition of the federal government.[42]

Wash Grayson would probably have seen some merits in both explanations. He was a nationalist who supported constitutional government as a means of preserving Creek sovereignty, and he was often frustrated with recalcitrant council members who had "no more idea of [constitutional] government than the Bedouins of the plains of Arabia."[43]

A representative of his *tvlwv* in the House of Warriors, he knew that Creek constitutional government was somewhat cosmetic, its three-branched structure resting on a foundation of Muskogee tradition. Democratic practices and a courteous public hearing for one's opinion had always been central to establishing consensus in Muskogee government. Consensus was still important in making national decisions, while history remained a primary reference in the process. Even after the most contentious of elections for the position of *mekko thlocco*, or principal chief, an attempt was made to reestablish consensus by appointing defeated candidates to positions of honor. The old ways were evident in a response Principal Chief Ward Coachman made in 1878 when asked if he had an executive council. "Well," he replied, "there is no system to provide it, but I generally make it a rule to call upon the prominent men of the nation to come and consult upon matters that come up affecting the nation. I always bring men to the council and consult them before I make a decision upon any question."[44] These prominent men, according to one witness, included Yatekah Hacho, William Fisher, minister William McCombs, and Wash Grayson.[45]

In other aspects as well, Muskogee constitutional government continued traditional ways. Representation by *tvlwv* in the Creek National Council was in accord with the historical Muskogee confederacy organization. Each *tvlwv* was allowed a representative to the upper House of Kings and another to the lower House of Warriors. In the lower house, each *tvlwv* was allowed an additional representative for each group of two hundred town members. The bicameral division of the National Council recalled traditional stratification as much as it imitated the pattern of the U.S. Congress. The centuries-old Muskogee diplomatic tradition was also preserved in selecting council members as delegates to Washington, D.C., the international councils, and conferences around Plains Indian campfires.[46] As in other areas of life, Creeks grafted Anglo-American forms and customs onto the old ways of politics. By the 1870s Creeks were old hands at caucusing, writing party platforms, stumping for their candidates, dispensing patronage, and delivering Fourth of July oratory at political barbecues. Widespread participation in national politics strengthened Creek nationhood, but maintaining unity in Creek government was another matter.[47]

The crisis that followed the Payne conviction was the latest eruption in a series that extended back almost to the adoption of the Creek Constitution of 1867. Recall that in that year the progressive Constitutional Party supported Samuel Checote, the Methodist minister and former Confederate colonel, in his successful bid for the chieftaincy. He chose Mekko Hutke, an Upper Creek, as his running mate in an attempt to attract traditionalist support. Their opponent was Sands, an Upper Creek traditionalist and current leader of the Loyalist faction that had followed Opothle Yahola to Kansas. According to one account, this traditionalist faction was called colloquially the Cold Country People because they had "gone north" during the Civil War. Checote's Constitutional Party were known as the Hot Country People, equated in the minds of some Creeks with the old McIntosh faction, many of whom had taken refuge in the Red River Valley.[48]

In 1867 Checote was declared the winner and took office. But suspicious of the new method of casting written ballots used in this election, the traditionalists, who believed they also had the support of the three new freedmen *tvlwv* and hence the numerical advantage, refused to recognize the legitimacy of Checote's government. Near the Nuyaka square ground they set up a shadow government, refusing to attend national council meetings at Okmulgee and thus refusing to participate in the discourse needed to reestablish consensus.[49]

From 1867 to 1871 Checote's administration oversaw the creation of the machinery of constitutional government. It was at this time that Wash Grayson officially entered Creek politics when Checote drafted him to serve as his clerk, a function that made the most of his literacy and command of English and Muskogee. Among the governmental machinery installed at that time was the court system. This consisted of six judicial districts, each with a judge, a prosecuting attorney, and a lighthorse company consisting of a captain and four privates, assuming the traditional peacekeeping role of the *tvstvnvkkvlke*.[50]

Meanwhile, Sands and his traditionalist followers prepared to preempt the 1871 election. When the Creek National Council met in regular session that October, they went to Okmulgee early, hoping to force a return to the old election method of physically lining up voters behind the favored candidate. Even so, Checote was declared the winner over the traditionalist candidate Cotchochee after federal officials oversaw the tallying of the votes. Calm soon returned with council members from both parties swearing to uphold the Creek Constitution.[51]

Within a few weeks, however, tensions rose again. Each side blamed the other for continuing hostility and accusations of election fraud. Sands specifically named Union McIntosh, Wash Grayson's father-in-law G. W. Stidham, Sanford Perryman, Timothy Barnett, James McHenry, and James M. C. Smith as "endeavoring to destroy our peace."[52] Checote, though, charged that it was outsiders who disturbed the nation. To Central Superintendent Hoag he complained that white intruders such as Charles F. Wheaton and Dr. J. B. G. Dixon constantly agitated among the traditionalists. In his opinion, Creek troubles were "encouraged by the enemies of the President's peace policy toward the Indian in order to give strength to the various territorial Bills now before Congress and to further the ends of *Rail Road Monopolies* [Checote's emphasis] in the great desin [*sic*] in extinguishing the Indian title to the lands."[53]

Tensions ran so high in the summer of 1872 that federal Special Commissioner Andrew C. Williams investigated the election returns. The delay in releasing the results of his investigation for nearly a year negated any immediate pacifying effect. Not until the summer of 1873 were Wheaton and Dixon ordered out of the nation and the commission report released. New Creek Agent E. R. Roberts informed Superintendent Hoag that he thought the whole affair would be settled if the federal government would openly support the Constitutional Party. Eventually the federal government did indeed throw its support to the Checote administration and let it be known that it would not recognize any Creek government except that elected by constitutional means. Traditionalist rebellion subsided then, and representatives of all but one dissident *tvlwv* sent representatives to the Creek National Council, providing an opportunity to reestablish consensus. Meanwhile, during these first two Checote administrations, Wash Grayson moved up in the Constitutional Party and government to national treasurer and secretary to the Okmulgee Convention.[54]

Political instability continued through the 1870s and early 1880s, but it is difficult to produce a reliable explanation for the constantly shifting political alignments. There were a number of contributing factors. First, in the late 1860s hostility between the wartime factions was still strong. The Loyal Creeks remained an identifiable group, bound together by their common experience, surviving wartime leaders, and their large unsettled claim for compensation against the federal government. In the first elections of the constitutional period, they clearly supported Sands and Cotchochee, opposing the Constitutional Party led by former Confederates. But the Loyal Creek faction had never been any more homogenous than the Confederate Creek faction. One can speculate that the passing of time and of aging leaders and the reestablishment of family, clan, *tvlwv*, and church ties gradually eroded each group's cohesion, leaving them less political factions than, in the case of the Loyal Creeks, interest groups.

Two examples of drift away from Civil War loyalties at the individual level stood out. First is Timothy Barnett, who was married to Wash Grayson's relative Mary Benson. Barnett had been a colonel in the Confederate regiments, Grayson's commander in battle, and a close personal friend. After the war Barnett reestablished himself as a wealthy, hospitable rancher in the Wewoka District.[55] But according to Grayson, for some reason Barnett "elected to cast his political lot with those who had been our enemy and were now in active opposition to us." Grayson noted that he "could not help entertaining an attitude of unfriendliness and never sought his company." The feeling was mutual. However, it was Barnett, who was "in the confidence of these northern Indians," who warned Grayson during his stint as national treasurer of the likelihood that they would rob him of the federal payment he was to deliver from Muskogee to Okmulgee.[56]

Barnett's polygamous marriage to Mary Benson and another woman in the Greenleaf settlement was a breach of Christian morality and a return to traditional ways that Grayson disapproved of. Eventually it contributed to Barnett's downfall. In 1873 Barnett and some companions sought out and shot a man who paid too much attention to his wife at Greenleaf. On July 4, 1873, Judge Nocus Yahola sent twenty-one light-horsemen to arrest him. After initial resistance, Barnett allowed himself to be arrested and led away. But about two hundred yards from his house the lighthorsemen suddenly gunned him down, firing some thirty rounds into his back. Although word of the killing spread widely, no one was ever tried for his death. The circumstances and motive for the death of Timothy Barnett will probably never be known, but the incident sheds some light on the layered nature of contemporary Creek politics. Barnett's death required deliberation, cooperation, organization, and the tacit approval, even if after the fact, of Principal Chief Checote's government. This implies an alternative political operation beneath the constitutional surface. The accusations of the white opportunists, who battened on the Loyal Creeks in hopes of exploiting their compensation claim, provided clues to its character. According to them, a clique of former Confederate officers—with Checote at its head—monopolized Creek national offices, excluded Loyal Creek children from the schools, and generally appropriated power. There was probably some truth to this charge, which painted in its most sinister colors, could be expected to play well in federal offices under Reconstruction-era Republican administrations. The motive for Barnett's execution, if it was carried out by this former Confederate faction, could have been his defection to the "northern Indians," but it might also have been retribution—even clan revenge—for his own bloodletting.[57]

Traditionalists may have also engaged in covert activities to counteract conditions they perceived as pernicious. According to Barnett's son and daughter-in-law, his executioners were "Pin Indians," who were jealous of his wealth and "intelligence," a word often interpreted in that context as "progressivism," which had its own connotations.[58] The term *Pin Indians* was originally applied to the Cherokee Keetoowah Society, a secret full-blood traditionalist faction organized within Cherokee Baptist congregations in the pre-Civil War period. According to McLoughlin, their antagonism toward the acculturated mixed-blood Cherokee slaveholders was a factor in their pro-Union partisan violence during the Civil War.[59]

If the Barnett family was correct that the executioners were Pin Indians, they may have been a Creek version of the Cherokee traditionalist movement, which had infiltrated the Creek judicial system and lighthorse. Creek Agent Roberts apparently thought so, for he wrote that a secret organization much like that of the Cherokee Pins was suspected of killing Barnett, and "the 1/2 breeds who compose the officers of the Nation are afraid to do anything. They will not even talk about it openly, speak low and cautious, and give no decided opinion, for they fear they will be next."[60]

The second example of drift away from the old Loyalist-Confederate division was Principal Chief Samuel Checote himself. As will be discussed below, in 1883 Checote, a former Confederate colonel and progressive leader during the creation of the constitutional government, would throw his support in a disputed election to the candidate representing his old wartime enemies, the Loyal Creek claimants, and traditionalist Creeks.

Another factor in shifting political alignments during the 1870s and 1880s was difference of opinion as to the best course for the Creek people. This debate was exacerbated in the mid-1870s by the accelerating economic development of the Creek Nation. As described earlier, Wash and Sam Grayson and other enterprising Creeks during that period established commercial enterprises, large farms, and sprawling ranches. Related to this development was the need for additional labor. With the post-war abolition of slavery the labor supply had dwindled, and under the communal landholding system, Creek citizens had little incentive to hire themselves out to others. The solution for entrepreneurs was to buy annual permits allowing them to employ noncitizen laborers as clerks, craftsmen, tenant farmers, and cowboys. It was risky introducing so many aliens to the Creek Nation, and more traditional Creeks resented their presence and influence. Issues of social and economic change such as immigration, the permit laws, and the developing range cattle industry deepened the division between the traditionalists and the progressives and led to coalitions of those with vested interests to protect.[61]

More often than not, the most visible of those progressives were men such as Wash and Sam Grayson, G. W. Stidham, D. N. and Chilly McIntosh, Pleasant Porter, N. B. Moore, and Joseph and Legus Perryman—all of mixed descent. While these men remained firmly Creek in identity, gradually they came to represent a specific contingent of mixed-bloods within the broader Creek community. The terms *este hvtke hayv* (white-made person) and *este hvtke lane* (white-brown person), referring to mixed-blood Creeks, were common parlance before the Civil War. But according to Wash Grayson, they gradually came in the 1870s and 1880s to have a political significance that overlaid the general understanding and use of the terms.[62]

McLoughlin identifies a full-blood/mixed-blood dichotomy in the neighboring Cherokee Nation, summarizing it as an argument about who were the better Cherokees—the full-bloods who clung to traditional ways or the mixed-bloods who vigorously strove to protect their nation's economic interests and political sovereignty through the adaptation of Anglo-American ways. The latter, according to McLoughlin, became "red nationalists," who measured themselves against a white standard, attempting to prove they could do anything the white man could do.[63]

In many ways this analysis of the Cherokees may be applied to the Creeks. Yet among the Creeks there was not so much a mixed-blood/full-blood dichotomy as a broad spectrum along which individuals might shift, being traditional in some ways while having adapted in others to Anglo-American ways. *Mixed-blood* and *full-blood* in the Creek context continued to refer to descent but came also to indicate life-style and vision of the best future for the Creek Nation. In the political arena, Ward Coachman of Alabama Town, a mixed-blood by descent and a former Confederate, labeled himself a full-blood and the candidate of the traditionalist faction. Spahecha (Isparhechar), a Lower Creek of full-blood descent, until 1877 received a number of appointments within the constitutional bureaucracy and associated himself with the former-Confederate leaders of mixed descent, men such as Wash Grayson.[64]

By the last decades of the century, Wash Grayson identified three classes of Creek citizens—mixed-bloods, full-bloods, and freedmen—basing his classification on life-style, world view, and politics more than descent. Like most Creeks, he had little use for the freedmen, whom Creeks were compelled to admit to citizenship by their Reconstruction Treaty but who remained somewhat peripheral to the Creek community if not to Creek politics. At the same time, he could also speak patronizingly of full-blood traditionalists, whom he regarded as worthy but misguided. In clinging to the old ways, in his opinion, they weakened the Creek Nation that he and other "mixed-blood" nationalists sought to preserve.

To summarize, by the last quarter of the century Creek society and culture were increasingly fluid. Correspondingly, Creeks moved politically from party to party as different issues surfaced to claim their attention and support. Churches, international councils, delegations, and newspapers offered new forums for political discussion in addition to traditional *tvlwv* and national councils. The one point on which the Creek Nation was unanimous was continuing Creek nationhood. The problem was achieving consensus as to the most effective means of maintaining it.

By the second half of the 1870s, the immediate post-war political alignment had become blurred. Sands died soon after the 1871 election, and Locha Hacho (Lochar Harjo) succeeded him as leader of the traditionalist Creeks. He defeated Checote by a margin of two to one in the 1875 race for principal chief, as the arrival of the railroad spurred economic development and increased the number of noncitizens in the nation. His tenure was short-lived, however. Locha Hacho offended many by keeping as a counselor the notorious Dr. Dixon, that "obnoxious white man and intruder" expelled from the nation three years earlier.[65] In 1876 Locha Hacho was impeached for high crimes and misdemeanors ranging from illegally signing a promissory note obligating the nation financially to ignoring acts of the Creek National Council, specifically dismissing legally elected officials and refusing to deport Dixon. Locha Hacho was tried in the House of Kings and found guilty by a vote of twenty-eight to twelve. Second Chief Ward Coachman (1876–1879), who was semiliterate but fluent in the Muskogee, Alabama, and English languages, succeeded him. However, the impeachment of one of their own had revived traditionalist opposition, which again established a dissident government at the Nuyaka square ground.[66]

Gradually traditionalists drifted into two factions. The smaller ultra-conservative faction supported first Locha Hacho and, after his death, Spahecha. This faction called for a return to traditional social, religious, and political ways. The larger Muskogee Party included Creek freedmen and Upper Creeks, many of them former Loyalists, who accepted the constitutional government. But it also included old associates and former Confederate comrades of Wash Grayson—D. N. McIntosh, William McCombs, John R. Moore, and, temporarily, James McHenry, the *liketv ohliketv*, or president of the House of Kings.[67]

In 1877, as the boomer movement escalated, the Muskogee Party's primary concern was that lobbyists might prevail on the federal government to open the territory to non-Indian settlement. As the election of 1879 approached, their platform called for Creek unity, honest elections, support of education, adherence to the treaties and federal laws, friendship with other tribes, and development of industry and Creek resources "by a wise and liberal policy towards labor." That year they nominated the incumbent Ward Coachman, with Pohose Emathla as their candidate for second chief.[68]

The primary opposition to the two traditionalist factions was the familiar but renamed "National" Constitutional Party, which Wash Grayson supported. Its platform advocated republican government, equal justice for all, enforcement of the law, national unity, and insistence that the federal government abide by the treaties and respect Creek land tenure. Adherents of the party were particularly disturbed by the fiscal policies of the Coachman administration. They charged that the national debt had doubled in the last four years, causing Creek warrants to depreciate badly. They also referred darkly to the illegal removal of some national officers and their replacement by Coachman's cronies. They unanimously nominated Samuel Checote for principal chief, with Taylor Postoak for second chief. Checote defeated Coachman in 1879 and was inaugurated as principal chief for the third time.[69]

Through the national political turmoil of the 1870s, Wash Grayson remained a progressive Creek nationalist, supporting Principal Chief Checote. His frustration with Creek finances stemming from his terms as national treasurer likely reinforced his connection with the National Constitutional Party, which included the plank favoring fiscal responsibility. It was probably the reason for his campaign speech at a political barbecue in 1879 stating that some of the council members had "no more ideas of government than the Bedouins of the plains of Arabia."[70] However, he did not become a major player in Creek politics until the early 1880s, when his *tvlwv* first elected him to the House of Warriors. Thus, he was in a better position to sway events when a constitutional crisis occurred during Checote's third term.

At the time, Grayson was serving concurrently as a delegate of the Creek Nation. Having long since recognized that they could expect little from the Creek or Union agents, who were political appointees reflecting the Anglo-American patronage system and agenda, the Five Civilized Tribes routinely sent their own citizens to Washington to represent their interests before Congress and the Office of Indian Affairs. Called delegates by their Indian governments, they functioned in the case of the Creeks in the tradition of the *horre hoponaya*, serving as lobbyists and liaisons with the federal government. Creek traditionalists sometimes protested that they were an unnecessary expense to the nation and worked to the benefit of the progressives, but Indian nationalists such as Wash Grayson knew the value of first-hand information from and communication with *Tvlwv Hvtke*, or "White Town" as the Creeks called the federal capital. He had learned that lesson during the Payne crisis, and it was reinforced during the next crisis, the Green Peach War.[71]

Accounts of this latest and most serious constitutional crisis differed as to exact cause, but trouble escalated as Spahecha tried to take over the Creek government during Checote's third term. A Union veteran, devout Methodist, former member of the House of Warriors, and previously judge of the Okmulgee District, Spahecha was alienated from the constitutional government, a contemporary said, when he was accused of exceeding his authority, impeached by the national council, and removed from office over his vehement protests. Spahecha, a tall, dignified man with great presence, then moved to the vicinity of ultraconservative Nuyaka Town, transferring his considerable leadership abilities to the cause of his new neighbors. Soon he was leading their protests against suspected irregularities in the election of 1879.[72]

By then Samuel Checote had alienated even some of his own party by tinkering with the district judgeships, particularly in deposing Judge Thomas Kenard, a Grayson relative, and the prosecuting attorney of Okmulgee District. In 1881 Wash Grayson, George Stidham, William McCombs, and Roley McIntosh passed along word of strong public dissatisfaction in the district over the removal of Judge Kenard on charges that had no basis "outside of party difference." Recalling similar actions by Checote, they warned Checote that in forcing out elected officials in order to appoint replacements of his choosing he was undermining respect for constitutional government and proper administration of the law. They advised him to reinstate Kenard.[73]

Late that same year, Checote attempted to prosecute Spahecha on criminal charges involving incest, another gambit that Grayson and Stidham viewed as a case of party politics, and they again warned him it was unwise. Spahecha responded by arming his traditionalist followers, who showed their allegiance by tying corn shuck badges to their hats. According to the Constitutionalists, Spahecha's insurgents included not only traditionalist Creeks but also noncitizen freedmen headed by the notorious Dick Glass, some Seminoles, a few Cherokees, and other intruders. Checote called out the militia to aid his lighthorse in keeping control as small-scale clashes and bushwhacking disturbed the peace of early summer 1882. Hungry Creek militiamen, who hurriedly left home with little more than their rifles and horses, helped themselves to unripe peaches from an orchard near present-day Taft, Oklahoma, jokingly giving the rebellion its name, the Green Peach War.[74]

Initial skirmishes between the two factions led Union Agent Tufts to request troops from the Fort Gibson garrison. The presence of a small detachment temporarily quieted the nation, and Tufts suggested each side send five representatives to negotiate their differences. Instead, in late summer Spahecha and his followers scattered. One contingent under Sleeping Rabbit encamped across the Cherokee border near Greenleaf, where according to Chief Checote, a number of ex-patriot, disaffected Creeks lived. The other group, under Tuckabachee Hacho (Harjo), a nephew of Opothle Yahola, hovered near the western Creek border. More insurgents were believed to have collected at Nuyaka square ground. On December 22 rebel freedmen and a Constitutional detachment exchanged fire on Pecan Creek near present-day Taft. Only then did Agent Tufts realize the seriousness of the situation and call for additional troops from Fort Gibson.[75]

Under a cold, full moon on Christmas Eve, 1882, Spahecha's insurgents poured back across the border, heading for Okmulgee with the intent of capturing the Creek capital. Alarm spread through the nation. Only days before about forty of Spahecha's men, armed and wearing war paint, had ridden boldly through Muskogee looking for the Checote adherents who had killed their man Jim Easy. Now new rumors circulated that National Constitutional Party leaders were targeted for assassination, making an overthrow of the government and more bloodshed seem likely. Creeks who remembered the early days of the Civil War hurriedly packed their belongings, preparing again for exile in refugee camps. In Eufaula, husbands hustled their wives and children onto the train and sent them to the safety of Muskogee or the Choctaw Nation.[76]

Checote quickly mobilized the militia and placed it under the command of "General" Pleasant Porter, recalled from delegate duty in Washington. His troops collected at Okmulgee, while Spahecha's men gathered about fifteen miles west at Nuyaka. At Battle Creek near present-day Okemah, then McDermott's Ranch, approximately three hundred insurgents under Tuckabachee Hacho fought a running battle with an equal number of Porter's Constitutionalist militia. It was popularly held that there were heavy casualties on both sides, but only seven militiamen were officially reported killed. Both sides withdrew but remained armed, belligerent, and ready for another fight.[77]

In the midst of the crisis, the federal government informed Checote that Congress had finally appropriated $338,912 from funds and interest held in trust for the Creek orphans of 1832. About one-third of the money remained in St. Louis at the subtreasury, but on January 22 the balance— six kegs of silver weighing 1,875 pounds and $175,000 in paper currency— arrived in Muskogee under military guard for transfer to the Creek Council House at Okmulgee. The Creek government had kept a roll of the original 578 Creek orphans to whom the money was fifty years overdue. Only about 20 were still living, but several survivors and many heirs were known to be with the Spahecha faction.[78]

Union Agent Tufts convinced Checote that the occasion of the payment would afford a good opportunity to parley with Spahecha and his followers. Perhaps they would even send their five representatives to negotiate a peace. Wash Grayson was asked to accompany Tufts, Pleasant Porter, and white merchant Clarence W. Turner to Nuyaka to discuss the payment with the insurgents. Under a flag of truce they rode west about twenty cold, snowy miles to the rebel encampment and persuaded the heirs to go with them to Okmulgee for the week-long payment. On the long overdue Creek Orphan Claim both sides were in agreement, and distribution of the money took place with no problems. Checote spoke with Spahecha and Hotulke Fixico, asking that they appoint their five representatives and begin negotiations, but the conversation proved fruitless. The insurgents claimed they could not negotiate without the consent of absent leaders such as Tuckabachee Hacho. They traded for supplies in Okmulgee and returned with their followers to Nuyaka. Checote then called a caucus of the National Constitutional Party in preparation for taking a hard line of his own. Grayson, who assigned great importance to maintaining constitutional government, seconded Checote's action.[79]

In early February Agent Tufts advised his superiors that the rebellion was an internal Creek affair best handled by Checote and Porter. Meanwhile Porter, with Roley McIntosh and James Larney as his lieutenants, organized a Constitutional army of seven hundred (one hundred and fifty of whom were unarmed) into units of forty men each according to *tvlwv* membership. On February 11 Porter marched on the Nuyaka insurgents. Although he induced three dissident *tvlwv* to desert Spahecha and join his army, the rest fled west with their families through the Sac and Fox country, with Porter in pursuit about a day behind. A three-day norther pelted both pursued and pursuers with rain, sleet, and snow, leaving the road hub deep in mud and barely passable. Porter caught up with Spahecha in the Sac and Fox Reservation, where Spahecha had persuaded that tribe, the Kickapoos, and their agent to intervene. This check, two rain-swollen creeks, and the bitter weather forced Porter to turn back, convinced he had driven most of the insurgents from Creek soil and dispersed the rest. Spahecha went on to the Kiowa-Comanche-Apache Reservation where he took refuge with the followers of the Comanche leader Asahabbe (Isahabit). As spring approached, it was rumored that Asahabbe and his warriors would join Spahecha's insurgent army to clean out the Checote government once the Comanche ponies had fattened on the new grass.[80]

Through early 1883, as these events unfolded and while Congress was in session, Wash Grayson and Legus C. Perryman were in Washington as delegates of the Creek Nation. Grayson may have left the federal capital just long enough to accompany the orphan payment to the nation, confer with Checote, and check on his family before returning to his post. Chief Checote constantly kept him and Perryman informed of events at home in letters that laid out the chief's official position: The Creek national government was simply enforcing its own laws in calling out the militia to suppress Spahecha and his dissidents. Checote urged Grayson and Perryman to present this view to the Commissioner of Indian Affairs and entreat that office to help resolve the conflict that, with the participation of some Seminole and Cherokee citizens, was assuming international proportions. Checote found particularly irritating the number of intruders—Indians, freedmen, and whites—that Spahecha attracted. Some "foreign" traders licensed by the Creek Nation, according to Checote, were giving Spahecha arms and encouraging his defiance of the constitutional government. Checote asked Grayson and Perryman to remind the Commissioner of Indian Affairs that the Union agent had repeatedly ignored his requests for their deportation from the Creek Nation.[81]

To bring peace back to the nation and to prevent further friction with their neighbors, Checote ordered Grayson and Perryman that spring to request federal military support, in Wash's words, "to teach these malcontented Creeks the necessity for obedience of the recognized laws of the nation." With his seven-year-old son Walter Clarence along, Grayson lobbied at the War Department until he persuaded Secretary Robert Todd Lincoln, "a stickler for the conventionalities of the ways of official business in Washington commonly called *red tape*," to send federal troops to arrest Spahecha on the Kiowa-Comanche-Apache Reservation.[82]

While Grayson and Perryman lobbied at the Office of Indian Affairs, they kept an eye on Daniel Childers, one of Spahecha's henchmen and an adopted Creek with a reputation for violence. Israel G. Vore, a widely respected adopted Cherokee and former Indian Brigade officer, wrote from the Union Agency to warn Grayson about Childers, whom he labeled the "Mulatta King . . . whose veins contains [sic] not one drop of Indian blood but white & negro." Vore reported that on the day Childers left Muskogee for Washington, he had bought four pistols, given them to freedmen, and told them to go join Spahecha. At that moment, Vore wrote, a watch was being maintained over the express office and depot to intercept any shipments of arms Childers might have purchased. Vore believed Childers had fallen under the influence of former Union Colonel William A. Phillips, "one of the most insignificant of God's creatures, who is devoid of all manly principles and who has been a pensioner on the Cherokee Nation since the late war, and who is despised by most of that people and causes more trouble than he does good."[83]

Phillips's radical agenda for the territory was perhaps evident in Childers's mission to Washington. When the latter arrived in the capital to present the insurgents' grievances, he horrified Grayson and Perryman by tendering to federal officials a quid pro quo proposal: insurgent acceptance of allotment in severalty in return for a share of all Creek interests, both landed and monetary. This was so "grave and dangerous" an initiative that Grayson believed "Creeks both north and south" would repudiate Spahecha and his lieutenants.[84] But before anything could come of this potentially disastrous scheme, federal troops took Spahecha and Tuckabachee Hacho into custody near the Wichita Agency and escorted them and their followers to Fort Gibson, where they arrived in July 1883.[85]

Through that summer, Wash Grayson and James Larney, who had replaced Perryman in Washington as a delegate, tried to persuade the Commissioner of Indian Affairs to resolve the conflict without doing further damage to Creek sovereignty. Grayson and Larney insisted in an open letter to the commissioner that Spahecha was nothing more than a disappointed office-seeker using the discontent of a few full-bloods and freedmen to attempt the overthrow of the duly elected constitutional government. They charged that the tardiness of federal officials in dealing with this crisis demonstrated a lack of concern for the constitutionalism Anglo-Americans insisted the Creeks adopt in place of their traditional government.[86]

Later Spahecha placed his own interpretation on Grayson's activities, stating that during the contest Mr. Grayson had told the Indian Office it was being much too lenient and should show the Indians who was master. At any rate, once Spahecha was safely under arrest, Checote was anxious to have him remanded to the custody of the Creek Nation and federal troops removed from Creek soil. The chief ordered Grayson and Larney to press these points, taking them all the way to President Chester Arthur if necessary.[87]

The federal government eventually did take action, and in August 1883 Chairman Clinton B. Fiske and Secretary Eliphelet Whittlesey of the Board of Indian Commissioners arrived at Fort Gibson to arbitrate the dispute between the Creek factions. Wash Grayson was a member of the ten-man National Constitutional Party delegation that negotiated peace with Spahecha and his supporters. The settlement and amnesty they agreed on finally ended political violence if not political disagreement in the Creek Nation. By lending its support to the progressive Creek nationalists, the federal government further consolidated that group's dominance over Creek affairs. For Wash Grayson there was also personal satisfaction; for the second time in two years he had served the nation as a cultural broker, this time successfully representing his government in Washington, D.C.[88]

Unfortunately, the following September brought another disputed national election. Spahecha and Checote vied for the position of principal chief against Joseph M. Perryman, a Union veteran, Eufaula businessman, and candidate of the Muskogee Party. The Creek National Council selected a committee, with George Stidham as chair and Wash Grayson as clerk, to count the votes in October prior to the convening of the council. The committee, after dismissing returns from three *tvlwv* as irregular, unanimously found Perryman the winner over Checote with Spahecha a poor third.[89]

Neither defeated candidate was inclined to accept his loss. Spahecha protested the election results, taking his complaints to Colonel E. B. Townsend, a special agent of the Office of Indian Affairs who happened to be in Okmulgee. In spite of his assurances that the office would support Perryman as duly elected, Spahecha remained disgruntled. For his part, Checote found a legal technicality on which to contest the election, while he tried to force through legislation giving the president of the House of Kings power to call a new election for principal chief. By late November

Checote and his "Pin party" had joined forces with Spahecha in attempting to derail the election. Infighting between Townsend and a colleague from the Office of Indian Affairs, who gave Spahecha encouragement, further complicated the situation. Perhaps fearing a renewal of violence, Pleasant Porter asked Wash Grayson to explain matters to Union Agent Tufts, to ask him to observe—and thus officially acknowledge—Perryman's installation as principal chief on December 5, 1883.[90]

Following the inauguration, the Creek National Council elected delegates to Washington, choosing for 1884 defeated candidates Spahecha and Checote along with David M. Hodge. Checote stepped down though, nominating Wash Grayson as his replacement. In the meantime, Checote's new alliance with Spahecha, although it confounded many Creeks, apparently achieved its immediate goal. When the National Council reconvened after the first of the year, it recounted the election returns and declared Spahecha the winner, inaugurating him, too, as principal chief.[91]

Wash Grayson, charged with representing Creek interests to the federal government, recognized the ominous implications of this new political crisis. A Checote supporter since 1867, he with other progressive nationalists found their old chief's defection to Spahecha unpalatable. Grayson attributed it to promised patronage rather than any substantial issue or agenda. He had helped count the votes and believed Spahecha had *not* won legitimately. Moreover, Spahecha represented, in Grayson's opinion, a reactionary perspective. Serving with Grayson in the new delegation was David M. Hodge, a Loyal Creek who shared some of Wash's views about the value of Christianity and English education, but who seemed to him to shift positions otherwise with every passing breeze. Trying to work with these men and to resolve the matter from Washington, Grayson was torn by conflicting loyalties: his personal ties to his old Confederate commander and political mentor, his duty to the National Council that had elected him a delegate, and his dedication to the sovereignty of the Creek Nation, now being undermined by political turmoil.[92]

For several weeks Secretary of the Interior Henry M. Teller delayed delivering an opinion on the disputed election. Grayson, who had come to favor Perryman, grew concerned that the other delegates were giving Teller the wrong impression of the mixed-blood businessman, depicting him as "a white man, and fifty years ahead of the people over whom he was claiming to have been elected chief." Grayson knew that Anglo-Americans often failed to perceive the strong Indian identity of mixed-bloods such as himself and Perryman because they did not fit the prevailing image of the "real Indian," the traditionalist full-blood. To dispel any erroneous impression the secretary might hold of Perryman, Grayson telegraphed the newly elected chief to come to Washington. A few days later in Teller's office, Grayson introduced his candidate, hoping the new chief's appearance and demeanor would meet with the secretary's expectations. Perryman, Grayson noted, was "very dark complexioned, quite as much so as a full-blood Indian, and a man of limited education but of great good common sense."[93] Teller eventually ruled in his favor. Although the secretary justified his decision by explaining that Perryman's election represented the majority opinion in the Creek Nation, Grayson preferred to attribute the favorable decision to his own successful management and brokerage.[94]

Perryman's election further consolidated the progressive nationalists' hold over the leadership of the Creek Nation and placed Grayson very near the center of power. Joseph M. Perryman was a member of a prominent Lower Creek family, a product of the Tullahassee Mission school, a rancher, a businessman, and a large-scale cotton farmer. Grayson and Perryman later collaborated in business as well as in politics and were sometimes neighbors in Eufaula. More importantly, Perryman shared Grayson's progressive Creek nationalism. Congratulating him later that year on securing for the Creeks an exhibition reservation at the New Orleans World's Fair, Perryman noted that this type of display could rectify Anglo-Americans' false impressions of Indians. The exhibit would allow citizens of the territory to "bring themselves to the notice of the world that Indians are capable of receiving a higher grade of civilization."[95]

Grayson, however, did not consider his part in securing Perryman's election an unalloyed victory. He believed the progressive nationalist faction represented the aspirations and salvation of the Creek people, and true, that faction had triumphed. But on two occasions now he had been required to relay to the federal government a call for aid in settling Creek internal disputes. Such problems and pleas undermined the principle of self-government Creek progressive nationalists so strongly advocated while it conveyed the very image Grayson strove to disprove through his private and public life, that of a people too primitive to manage their own affairs. Calling for federal intervention set a dangerous precedent, a point on which he stood in agreement with Spahecha and the Cherokee delegates, who closely observed and commented on Creek affairs.[96]

Still, Grayson's effectiveness in facilitating communication between the Creek Nation and the federal government won him several more elections as a Creek delegate. He went to Washington each year from 1882 to 1888.[97] Matters with which he dealt included the Loyal Creek claims, the Creek-Seminole boundary dispute, problems with the railroad corporations, complications associated with the booming range cattle industry, and federal treaty obligations to the Creek Nation. When Grayson's old alma mater, Asbury Manual Labor School, burned in 1888, on behalf of the Creek Nation he petitioned the federal government for money to rebuild; Eufaula Boarding School was constructed on the hillside on the south edge of Eufaula. Intrusion remained a perennial problem, and Grayson worked hard to stanch it. Generally his instructions directed him to oppose any change in relations between the United States and the Creek Nation, specifically allotment in severalty, the creation of any kind of territorial government without Indian consent, and the homesteading of "Oklahoma."[98] His charge was to guard "the integrity of the Indian territory with the view to holding the same indefinitely as the home of the Indian."[99]

While there were probably many benefits to being a delegate, it could also be a tedious and demanding duty. Grayson attended sessions of Congress and its various committees, kept abreast of the printed news, wrote letters to the newspapers, cultivated contacts with Anglo-American Indian rights groups, studied pending legislation, read past decisions on Indian affairs, and wrote memorials incorporating those decisions whenever a congressional bill threatened Creek interests. By 1888 the delegates of the Five Civilized Tribes had developed a unified strategy and modus operandi. Two blocks from the Capitol on Pennsylvania Avenue was a small hotel with a front parlor they designated, with Indian humor, "the Wigwam." On the mantle lay an ornate calumet carved from Minnesota pipestone, recalling traditional diplomacy. Every Wednesday night they gathered there to smoke cigars and discuss religion, literature, and politics. Often these were work sessions, during which the delegates considered the latest congressional measures affecting Indians. They decided which of them would appear before each congressional committee, designed plans of defense, and determined the best lines of argument to support their common national interests.[100]

The delegates of the Five Civilized Tribes also conferred with representatives of other tribes visiting Washington. In April 1888 Cherokee delegate W. P. Boudinot described for his constituents a general council held recently at the Wigwam. Almost every Indian visitor in the capital had come. There were Iroquois, Senecas, and Stockbridges from the Northeast; Cherokees from North Carolina; and Chippewas from Minnesota, the last decked out in beads, buckskins, and feathers. These tribesmen joined Indian Territory Chickasaws, Creeks, and Cherokees for a partly social, partly political evening during which the progressive Indian nationalists presented their agenda as the best means of tribal survival.[101]

Presiding over the occasion was Chickasaw delegate George W. Harkins, who offered the visitors "a good talk and sound advice." A nonagenarian Chippewa spoke of "the condition of the race before it was bothered with the iron axes of the white man." That reference to history established and the wisdom of their ancestors recalled, they listened attentively while Wash Grayson spoke for the progressive "young" generation and Spahecha presented the views of the "old" traditionalists. Boudinot summarized the evening: "[T]he Creeks, Chickasaws, and Cherokees gave their combined advice to all red men to fall into the ranks of progressive humanity as the surest way to hold their own—or what is left of their own. They illustrated their meaning by giving an account of their schools and the attention their tribes are paying to education wholly at their own cost. These tribes of the Indian Territory . . . are nothing if they are not practical and progressive, and it is to be hoped that some solid good may result from the conference of the delegations."[102]

Such conferences were only one of many duties Wash Grayson fulfilled as a delegate. The Creek National Council routinely attempted to maintain consensus by naming delegates from the various factions, including the Loyal Creeks, whose claim against the federal government for property lost in the Civil War was still pending. Consequently, the Creek delegation frequently included members who spoke little English or were unfamiliar with the workings of the federal bureaucracy. At those times Grayson, more experienced and bilingual, interpreted culture as well as language. Such was the case in 1888 when the other delegate was Spahecha, who was illiterate and spoke little English at the time. (He apparently became more fluent after he married a white laundress he met on one of his several trips to Washington.) Once at odds on constitutional issues, the two men had put their differences behind them. Besides, they were both Tiger clan. An observer noted that they were now close friends, and Grayson always accompanied Spahecha to interpret for him.[103]

The cross-country rail journeys and the long, long weeks away from home must have been even more uncomfortable for those less familiar with the white world than Wash Grayson. He sympathized strongly with Koweta Mekko (Coweta Micco), an esteemed chief from Grayson's own *tvlwv*, who sickened and died in that alien city in "a little second class hotel." He was buried far from home in Washington's Congressional Cemetery with only the other delegates to see him laid to rest.[104]

But the second-class hotels and boarding houses were not for Wash Grayson. He stayed at the National Hotel or the prestigious Willard. He also took these opportunities to expose his children and later his grandchildren to life in the Anglo-American capital. As Walter Clarence, Washie, and the girls grew older, they often accompanied him on his official visits.[105]

So did Annie. More than just an adjunct to his life, Annie Grayson was his intellectual equal and partner. As proudly Creek as he, Annie, Wash wrote, "entertained a loyal affection for our people, and . . . [was] patriotic to a fault."[106] For her, visits to the city included sightseeing, the theater, White House receptions, escorting the children to the annual Easter egg hunt, and social occasions with the families of federal bureaucrats.[107] But because Annie was as dedicated as her husband to Indian rights, she regularly attended hearings related to Indian affairs and listened with particular sympathy when those involved were less adept at Washington politics than the Creeks. She understood just as well as Wash the powerful forces threatening to overwhelm tribespeople she called "those dear red brethren."[108]

While in Washington, Grayson also took the opportunity to press his own claim successfully as an heir of his great-uncle Watt Grayson. In the mid-1880s, he represented family members trying to recover the thirty-two thousand dollars stolen from the old man in 1873. Their claim was based on the federal government's treaty obligation to protect Indian citizens from criminal intruders.[109] As an Indian, Wash Grayson's competency to enter into contracts was automatically suspect and required Office of Indian Affairs approval. However, the attorneys involved testified, "Mr. George W. Grayson does not stand in need of any such protection. He is amply able to protect himself. He understands this claim and its proseeds [sic] as well as we do. He is as competent to write a contract as we are, and it would not be difficult to prove that in this matter he has made as good and shrewd a contract as we have."[110] When Grayson entered into a contract with attorney J. B. Luce in 1886, Supreme Court Justice Arthur MacArthur witnessed the document.[111]

Gradually Grayson built up a wide acquaintance and a reputation in the Indian Territory as an able man experienced in dealing with the white man. In 1888 Lone Wolf, a Kiowa, and Tabananica (Tabenanaca), a Comanche of considerable notoriety as a raider, came to Washington unescorted to protest the Dawes (General Allotment) Act. With no interpreter, they were unable to communicate adequately with federal officials. They appealed to Grayson, who knew Lone Wolf from the international councils. He came to their rescue by telegraphing Superintendent Richard H. Pratt at Carlisle Indian School in Pennsylvania to send two of his students—a Kiowa and a Comanche—to Washington to interpret.[112]

Other Indians, recognizing that they had common cause with the Five Civilized Tribes, regarded them as elder brothers in their experience with white ways. Moses Keokuk, venerable chief of the Sac and Fox tribe, frequently wrote Grayson during his diplomatic missions, asking that he include his people in any measures he took to protect Creek interests. The Seminoles also relied on Grayson and the Creek delegates to represent them and explain what was really happening in Washington. On one occasion an elderly Kickapoo rode more than one hundred miles from his central Indian Territory reservation to Eufaula bearing an official envelope containing a completely incomprehensible letter. Grayson's Muskogee and English being of little use communicating with the Kickapoo, he was forced to send the man home with no real clue as to his need.[113] More amusing was the occasion on which the Caddos inquired whether he knew a "Frogmountain or Jackmartin" who wished to serve as their attorney. Grayson wrote back that he did, indeed, know former Governor James W. Throckmorton of Texas and could recommend his services.[114]

Grayson enjoyed the recognition that came with his elections as a delegate, and it probably went some way toward alleviating the frustration and foreboding he felt as he viewed at first hand the slow erosion of Indian sovereignty during the late 1880s. If Grayson truly believed in 1881 that the Payne decision left "no loophole . . . through which . . . any white or colored citizen of the United States [could] enter and occupy any portion of the Indian Territory," he was proved mistaken quite soon.[115]

Weakened temporarily by Judge Parker's ruling and Payne's sudden death in 1884, the boomer movement rallied under new leadership. Meanwhile, editorial and congressional assaults on the territory continued. Eastern humanitarians added to Indian unease by advocating allotment of communal lands in severalty as the panacea for the "Indian problem." These issues—allotment and the opening of Oklahoma for settlement—represented the Indians' greatest fear, that they would be submerged beneath an "alien flood."[116]

In common with the great majority of Indian Territory citizens, Grayson abhorred the idea of allotment and all its ramifications. He clung to the communal landholding system and regarded the Anglo-European alternative—individual landholding—as one that "had pauperized thousands of people."[117] Choctaw Governor Isaac L. Garvin expressed the same sentiments in his inaugural address of 1878, stating, "Under the traditional system of land held in common we have neither paupers nor tramps."[118] Grayson's father-in-law George W. Stidham expanded upon this theme: In contrast to the Anglo-American system, he wrote, "We have [no tramps], we have our own farms, no taxes to pay; our papers are not filled with advertisements of lands for sale on account of delinquencies."[119]

But the people of the Indian Territory were aware that many whites—friends and enemies alike—were devoted to the idea of allotment as a means of ending tribalism and preparing the Indian for United States citizenship. In 1878 the U.S. Senate Committee on Territories, headed by John J. Patterson, had visited Muskogee, Okmulgee, and Eufaula. Before it arrived in the Creek Nation, the contending political factions put aside their differences to present a consensus to the investigators. Creeks of all ethnic mixtures and political persuasions explained the workings of the Creek government. Wash Grayson as national treasurer and a prominent businessman was one of many called to testify before the committee.[120]

The investigators asked him the questions they asked all the Creek witnesses: Were the Creeks advancing? Grayson confirmed that they were, particularly in agriculture. Did any Creek favor allotment? Grayson, as had every other Creek witness, responded, "I do not know a single man."[121] Seven hundred and five Creek citizens then signed a petition that called on the federal government not to extend over them an alien political and social system which would "entail the degradation and destruction of the masses of our people."[122] Yet when the committee returned to Washington, it reported favorably on the prospect of allotting the communal lands.[123]

Knowing that Congress often demonstrated such deafness toward the Indian's opinion, Grayson grew ever more pessimistic during the early 1880s, but with other Creek nationalists he tenaciously adhered to the principles of self-government and communal landholding. He knew from his official visits to the East that the greatest pressure on the Indian nations originated with the railroad corporations. He reported that they had hired the best legal talent in New York City to lobby for an end to the communal system, which they presented as a humane expedient meant to aid individual Indians. But Grayson was convinced that their true purpose was to secure large land grants for their clients by abolishing the Indian governments that held patents to the land.[124]

In the spring of 1885 the threat appeared closer to home. R. M. Roberts, editor of the *Indian Journal* while it was out of Creek ownership, suggested that it might be time to end the isolation of the Indian inherent in the reservation system by opening the territory through allotment and non-Indian settlement. Grayson refuted this editorial in an article on "The Indian Question." Quoting the former superintendent of the census, Grayson reiterated the Creek nationalists' argument opposing allotment: Assigning the ignorant and ill-prepared tribesman an individual share of communal land laid him open to fraud and poverty. Dispossessed, these Indians became "shifting sores upon the public body," forced into begging, stealing, and prostitution to support life. Grayson predicted an outbreak of violence and crime if whites were allowed to settle among the Indians. This would then provide a justification for those Texans, Missourians, and Kansans who called for law and order imposed by a regular territorial government in place of the Indian national governments.[125]

Grayson advised Indians to expect the worst, for past "Indian management" (that is, federal policy) had been all bad, and "Indian rights" had little meaning. He concluded bitterly, "No wonder Indians are hard to Christianize, for while teaching them to do to others as they would have others do to them, the white man has been practicing on them the philosophy of Pizarro and his priests, DeSoto, Hood, and the rest. If this be the teachings of a Christian civilization, then, shades of Tecumseh and Osceola, hold back your hands a little while and the Indian will gladly die the death of a pagan, and with them and you risk their chances before that other tribunal where it is said all wrongs are righted."[126]

When Grayson returned to Washington for the congressional session that began in January 1886, the fight against allotment was moving into a critical phase. Congress was considering the Dawes (General Allotment) Bill, which proposed to allot to each Indian 160 acres of tribal lands. The expected surplus, once each tribal member received a share of the reservation, would be open for homesteading. The intent was to end both tribalism and the protective isolation of the reservation while meeting the Anglo-American public's demand for access to Indian land. Grayson and the other delegates turned to the new National Indian Defense Association for support in opposing the bill. Among its members were the former governor of Pennsylvania and Dr. Blundell, President Grover Cleveland's minister. The latter incurred public criticism when he went before a Senate committee to speak out against allotment, but the Creek and Seminole delegates called on him to express their appreciation of his efforts.[127]

Delegates Grayson, Koweta Mekko, and Ward Coachman also cooperated with Moses Keokuk and William Hurr of the Sacs and Foxes, and G. W. Harkins and H. F. Murray of the Chickasaws to publicize Indian Territory citizens' views in the eastern press. In June 1886 they wrote a much reprinted open letter protesting allotment. They claimed that based on traditional landholding their people had built prosperous communities free of "paupers, poorhouses, strikers, nihilists, and other evils" afflicting

Anglo-American society. The Indian writers recommended that if the real concern was for the landless would-be settler, then land monopolies in the West held by railroad corporations and foreign syndicates should be broken up first. Indians, they said, wanted only to be left alone to work out their own salvation. "We are willing and eager to appropriate all the desirable results of civilization," they wrote, "but we do not wish to be robbed of the best of our lands under false pretenses and then have a government of men put over us who would rob us of the remainder in a very short space of time."[128]

Meanwhile, the Indian International Council, the lineal descendant of the Okmulgee Convention, convened at Eufaula and attempted once again to create an Indian territorial government. As before, it found too many difficulties in the way. Instead, the council adopted a "Compact Between the Several Tribes of the Indian Territory" with a provision stating that the respective nations "solemnly pledge ourselves to each other that no nation party to this Compact shall without the consent of all the other parties cede or in any other manner alienate to the United States any part of this present Territory."[129]

But in July disturbing news filtered back to the Indian Territory. It was rumored that, with the allotment bill apparently close to passage, the Creek delegates, in direct contravention of the compact, had broken ranks with the other Indian representatives. Now they were said to be secretly suggesting they would be willing to sell their remaining interest in the Unassigned Lands—for the right price.[130]

Grayson publicly denied the rumor as a "pitiful incarnation of mendacity and pusillanimity" perpetrated by the *St. Louis Globe-Democrat.* That newspaper, he believed, meant to sow distrust among the Indian nations. This instance reminded him, he said, of the stick ball game he had attended during the summer. As the players bloodied each other in their eagerness to get at the ball, one complained to a Creek elder that he was being hit unnecessarily. The elder replied that the player should remember that the action was always fiercest near the ball. Grayson shrugged off criticism: "Whenever I am struck, it is perhaps a sign that the Creeks are 'nearest the ball' and trying to do their whole duty."[131]

In January 1887 he was back in Washington continuing the fight. With Pleasant Porter and the other delegates, he called on President Cleveland to protest, among other things, the allotment bill. Cleveland told them he would try to see their rights were protected, but he signed the Dawes Act a few weeks later and fulfilled one of the Indians' greatest fears. The Five Civilized Tribes and the Osages were among the very few tribes exempted. These Indian nations understood the interplay of Congress, the Indian rights groups, and Anglo-American public opinion and business interests. They used their knowledge to oppose this and other damaging policies effectively. More importantly, unlike most tribes, they held their lands in fee simple and had greater control over their disposition. Still they understood that they might not always be exempted from allotment in severalty.[132]

It was during this critical year that a Creek joint-stock company again purchased the *Indian Journal* and returned it to Eufaula. The stockholders elected Wash Grayson president; William E. Gentry, a Creek rancher, vice-president; and Kate Shaw, a recent school graduate, secretary-treasurer. As before, in English and Muskogee the *Journal* announced itself an Indian newspaper dedicated to Indian rights. Significantly, its editorial policy opposed allotment, the greatest threat on the Creek horizon, and supported the international councils, which represented Indian unity and the best common defense of Indian sovereignty. Otherwise, it followed the progressive nationalist agenda in that it supported education, agriculture, and the domestic arts.[133]

The process of allotting the reservations of tribes included under the Dawes Act was necessarily slow because it involved surveying the lands, assessing improvements, making up census rolls, adjudicating claims of tribal membership, and assigning each Indian an allotment as fairly as possible. Tribespeople affected continued to protest and hope that something might yet be done. As they had so often in the past, some turned to the Creeks and the International Council for mutual support and as a vehicle for opposition. Grayson attended the session that met at Eufaula in June 1887 at which delegates of twenty tribes voiced their frustration in the face of federal intransigence.[134]

Grayson asked the delegates to listen to the experiences of Chief Jake of the Caddos. When the chief visited the Commissioner of Indian Affairs to protest against allotment, that official had violated Indian standards of respect by angrily poking his finger in the elder's face and accusing him of saying only what the intermarried whites and mixed-bloods told him to say. At the request of the western tribes, Grayson wrote a resolution that called on the federal government to postpone imposing the Dawes Act on a "powerless and protesting people" until its validity could be tested in the federal courts.[135] But when the commissioner received the resolution, he dismissed it and the International Council as a meddling, trouble-making tool of the Five Civilized Tribes to whom the allotment policy did not even apply.[136]

The Creeks had hardly adjusted to the reality of the Dawes Act before the demands to open the Unassigned Lands escalated. The following year, 1888, marked the crumbling of international unity and the end of Creek resistance to any change in territorial status. Perhaps Grayson felt the shifting undercurrents as early as January 1888, for that month he wrote an article for the *Indian Journal* in which he called for an end to international bickering and recrimination. He signed it not as G. W. Grayson but by his Creek name, Yvhv Tvstvnvkke (Yaha Tustunuggee).[137] This was unusual and perhaps was meant to remind his readers of his and their Indian identity. At about the same time he and his fellow delegate Spahecha presented a protest to House Bill 1277, yet another attempt at territorialization and the opening of the Indian Territory to non-Indian settlement. Such actions, he repeated, would do "irreparable harm to our less-civilized brothers" and loose a "*human cyclone*" [Grayson's emphasis] on "a quiet and confiding people."[138]

But Grayson was by now out of step with some of the progressive nationalists, for by late 1888 a sentiment favoring some final settlement with the federal government over Creek claims to the Unassigned Lands was growing. The new direction apparently grew out of a perennial problem in Creek government—finances. Never very strong in this area, the Creek Nation found its situation increasingly desperate as a result of the Green Peach War, for the government had agreed to compensate citizens of both factions for property losses. Through 1885 and 1886 the claims mounted, and so did pressure on the Creek government to pay off the national debt of one hundred thousand dollars.[139]

As the election of 1887 approached, the debt and federal overtures in regard to the Unassigned Lands found their way into party platforms. That summer the new Independent Party was formed. It deplored senseless strife between the Pin (Union) and Muskogee Parties and sought a new accord. Alarmed by the size of the national debt, the Independents called for a reduction in the number of council members and the number lighthorsemen. They also insisted that the Creek people "should relinquish no interest in any landed estate, but endeavor to strengthen and confirm their rights and title thereto." In convention the Independents nominated John R. Moore for principal chief with James Fife, a former Creek Supreme Court justice, as candidate for second chief.[140] The Muskogee Party nominated incumbent Joseph M. Perryman with Hotulke Fixico as candidate for second chief. Making no real departures, their platform called for support of education, religion, and industry and wise legislation that would reduce the national debt.[141]

The Union Party, led by Spahecha, targeted among other issues the national finances, calling for strict economy and the increase of revenues. They opposed the sale of the Oklahoma lands and demanded that the federal government respect the Reconstruction Treaty of 1866. Soon after the platform was drawn up, Spahecha repudiated it and called a new convention. Legus C. Perryman stepped into the vacancy this created and won the party's nomination for principal chief, with Hotulke Emathla as candidate for second chief.[142]

Perryman won the chieftaincy, but despite calls on all sides for strict economy he presided over a burgeoning national debt. That was the reason for his announcement at the October 1888 session of the Creek National Council of a major change in policy: For the right price he favored selling residual national interests in the Unassigned Lands. His government argued that the Creek Nation had ceded its western lands in 1866 for thirty cents an acre as a future home for other Indians. The nation would be willing to surrender its residual claim if the federal government agreed to supplement the price to $1.25 per acre. The choice of delegates for 1888–1889 was especially critical, given these circumstances. It was suggested the council could do no better than to send Wash Grayson, G. W. Stidham, Spahecha, Hotulke Emathla, and Pleasant Porter to negotiate the final settlement.[143]

But for the first time in several years Grayson was not a member of the Creek delegation. Since spring his daughter Mabel, then about seventeen, had been ill, probably with tuberculosis contracted at boarding school. In

August Mabel's deteriorating condition curtailed Grayson's diplomatic activities. His father-in-law, G. W. Stidham, still vigorous and shrewd at seventy, substituted for him in Washington until the congressional summer recess. Grayson was present for at least part of that critical National Council session, as always representing Koweta *tvlwv* in the House of Warriors. Then Mabel, his favorite child, died on October 16 while the council was still meeting, and he returned home for her funeral.[144] Another reason for his absence may have been his opposition to Perryman's new policy. The Creeks kept no record of debates in their council; but subsequent letters from Pleasant Porter to Grayson counted him among the opposition. "I am sorry you are skeptic [*sic*]," Porter wrote.[145]

The delegation to Washington that fall included Porter, David M. Hodge, Spahecha, and Efa Emathla. Spahecha, of course, possessed a great deal of ability, but his lack of fluent English forced him to rely on an interpreter. Efa Emathla died of pneumonia on December 19, soon after the delegates' arrival. Hodge was a good interpreter and an experienced delegate but, in Grayson's opinion, was prone to vacillation. The real work of the delegation fell to Porter, who readily accepted the accolades later bestowed on him for its success.[146]

Porter, perhaps not so confident as he appeared, corresponded often with Grayson during those winter months, listing the benefits of the proposed sale and soliciting his support as a Creek leader and as a newspaper publisher. Porter argued in this private correspondence that if the Creeks did not sell their interest while they had the chance, the federal government might yet move western tribes into the Unassigned Lands and end any chance of the Creeks' realizing its additional value. Relinquishing their interest immediately might gain them as much as $3 million, which the Creek government badly needed.[147] The agreement signed January 19 indeed awarded the Creeks $2,280,857, a sum Porter believed would solve the Creeks' financial difficulties and allow them to educate every child in the nation.[148]

Chief Legus Perryman seconded Porter's views in his annual address of 1889. "Never before, in all the history of our country," he wrote, "have our prospects for the future been brighter than now. We have the means now within our reach of making our nation the most prosperous, our people the most contented and happy of any nation in the world." By one stroke of the pen, he went on, the nation had gained "the princely fortune" of $100,000 per annum, which, added to other income, would allow the government $180,000 for yearly expenditures. Subtracting the $80,000 of annual government expenses should still leave a handsome reserve. The alternative, he repeated, was losing the Oklahoma lands and any proceeds from them.[149]

The delegates immediately forwarded the agreement to the council, which had been called into special session to consider it on January 29. Porter cajoled Grayson for his support, "You are one of its most intelligent members and leaders. I have but to say, do your duty to your country and people." He repeated an invitation for Grayson to join them in Washington and concluded with a postscript: "Explain the matter to our mutual friends. Esparhechar [Spahecha] sends his best wishes to you. The old man has acted nobly he has a very high opinion of you and believes implicitly in you standing by our work."[150]

As soon as the council ratified the agreement, Grayson telegraphed the news to Porter.[151] Triumphantly Porter replied that this was a new beginning for more equity and justice in federal treatment of the Indian. The Creeks were now in the van, leading the other Indians to "higher successes." Porter once again appealed to Grayson, "If I were in the newspaper business, I would throw off all respect to the prejudices of the past. And lead the public thought to a higher conciption [sic] of their future destiny."[152]

But other Indians had doubts as to where the Creeks were leading them. As late as November 1 the *Indian Arrow* of Vinita, Cherokee Nation, stoutly denied that the Creek delegates would "endanger the interests and safety" of all the Five Civilized Tribes by ceding the Unassigned Lands.[153] The Choctaws' *Atoka Independent* also regarded a possible Creek cession before the fact as unthinkable, "a blot upon the Nation that years could not wipe away," and doubted that "men of such sound reasoning and unquestionable experience in Indian affairs as the Creek delegates, Gen. Porter and G. W. Grayson"[154] would be a party to such a policy. The strongest condemnation after the fact came from the *Indian Chieftain*, which accused, "We made a compact with the Creek nation years ago. They have broken it by selling Oklahoma without consulting us."[155]

More important, though, was the immediate result of the sale. The Seminoles quickly emulated the Creeks in selling to the federal government their own interest in the Unassigned Lands. A presidential proclamation threw this area, the heart of the Indian Territory, open for homesteading by means of a land run on April 22, 1889. Towns and farms mushroomed on the prairie overnight, and the Organic Act of 1890 allowed homesteaders to create Oklahoma Territory. Even that did not appease the land hungry for long. Other openings of former Indian reservations occurred in 1891, 1892, 1893, 1895, 1901, and 1906. One after another, these newly homesteaded tracts were annexed to Oklahoma Territory. With the Oklahoma Cession the Creeks had permitted the first true breech in the defenses of the Indian Territory. In so doing, they made the hold of all the Five Civilized Tribes on their lands and future even more tenuous.[156]

Although it is clear that Wash Grayson opposed allotment and foresaw nothing but ruin for many Indians under that policy, existing documents do not reveal his exact views on the Oklahoma Cession. Pleasant Porter's letters to him during and immediately after the negotiations strongly suggest that Grayson believed it was unwise. Support of the cession would have required a complete reversal of the principles and policies he had advocated and actively pursued as a delegate during the preceding decade. Nothing in his private or public statements suggested this was the case, nor was he a man who altered his convictions easily.

Rather, his absence from Washington until after the cession passed the Creek National Council indicates that he wished to distance himself from the negotiations. He was by no means in seclusion during these critical three months. He went on his annual hunting expedition to the Cross Timbers, made a business trip to Texas, attended federal court in Fort Smith, and got on with his affairs—none of which demanded his exclusive presence. Porter's repeated invitations to join the delegates in Washington suggest that he refused to take part in the negotiations. Political considerations may have carried weight in his decision. Grayson had now held three elective offices in the Creek government and hoped to hold others (as his subsequent actions demonstrated). He may have decided to let Pleasant Porter receive whatever accolades or acrimony the cession was sure to draw. Or he may simply have found the cession so distasteful he would not involve himself in it until it was an accomplished fact. Only after the cession was ratified at Okmulgee and returned to Congress in late February did he join the other Creek delegates in Washington. His goal then was to prevent the next step, the opening of Oklahoma for homesteading, but Congress refused to listen to this last-ditch appeal.[157]

For two decades Wash Grayson had served as a cultural broker for the Creek Nation, explaining the Creek perspective on events and legislation to the federal government, other Indian nations, and his own people, while helping the Creek people understand external affairs. Politically and philosophically, he had identified himself as a progressive nationalist, one of those he viewed as the vanguard of the nation in their defensive, selective adoption of Anglo-American culture. He had optimistically helped found a town, published a newspaper, built a business, encouraged public education, and supported constitutional government—all directed ultimately toward protecting Creek nationhood and sovereignty. He had confidently worked with the progressive nationalists of the other Indian nations, sure that in them lay the salvation of Indian people. But by the late 1880s his high hopes had turned to pessimism and his faith to skepticism.

It became apparent that not all Creek progressive nationalists marched at the same speed or even in the same direction. First Samuel Checote, Grayson's political mentor, forfeited his support when he appeared to sacrifice principles for patronage. In 1888 Pleasant Porter and Legus Perryman engineered a complete reversal of Creek policy, effecting an outcome Grayson had fought fiercely for ten years to avoid. They favored the Oklahoma Cession as a way out of Creek financial difficulties. They justified breaking the defensive unity of the Five Civilized Tribes on the ground that the boomers, the railroad corporations, and neighboring states were demanding access to the Indian Territory. Change was inevitable, and they must accommodate it or risk losing everything.

Wash Grayson agreed that change was necessary, but he was convinced that what seemed a practical solution to a national problem placed Indian control of the whole territory at risk. In ceding the Oklahoma lands the Creeks had undermined Indian unity as well as their own ability to defend their sovereignty. He also knew, though, that the fight was not over. It was time for him to take his place once again as the rear guard.

CHAPTER SIX

Save What We May out of the Approaching Wreck

The Oklahoma Cession was a watershed for the Creek Nation. The Creek people still held their land in common, but their tenure as a nation was in jeopardy. They still governed themselves, but outside forces threatened their sovereignty. The period from 1889 to 1906 on the national level corresponded with a similar phase in Wash Grayson's life. His political career seemingly came to a dead end, and his business ventures collapsed in bankruptcy. By 1906, as Creeks lost control over their future, Grayson bitterly realized that neither his progressive nationalist agenda nor calling on the United States to uphold its treaty obligations was enough to salvage Creek sovereignty. In his role as a cultural broker, he could no longer lead nor could he stop change imposed on the Creeks; he could only try to ameliorate its.effects.

The year 1889 was especially critical for Wash Grayson. On the negative side were his grief for the child closest to his heart and his misgivings as to the Oklahoma Cession. On the positive side was the opportunity to fill a federal office and perhaps influence Indian relations from within the federal bureaucracy. Union Agent Robert L. Owen, a Virginia-born Cherokee citizen, relative newcomer, and ambitious Democratic appointee, resigned as expected when President Benjamin Harrison began filling posts in his new Republican administration. Indian Territory residents speculated that candidates for the vacancy included Leo E. Bennett of Muskogee and Wash Grayson of Eufaula.[1]

Grayson wanted this appointment enough to solicit the support of Colonel M. M. Parker, an Omaha, Nebraska, real estate agent head-quartered in Washington, D.C. In a letter to him in April 1889, Grayson wrote, "Businessmen of Texas and the Indian Territory are proposing my name to the President for the position." He added that he had the endorsement of General Fiske of the Board of Indian Commissioners and a Dr. Morehouse of New York.[2] Parker responded by recommending Grayson to the Commissioner of Indian Affairs as a man of integrity.[3]

That Grayson had the support of "businessmen of Texas" may have raised eyebrows at the Office of Indian Affairs, for that state's range cattle industry was currently much involved in territorial affairs and the exploitation of Indian resources. Texas was also a strongly Democratic state, which may have weighed against rather than for Grayson with a Republican administration. One could also wonder about his connection with an Omaha real estate man with headquarters in Washington. At any rate, the post of Union Agent went to Leo E. Bennett, perhaps a personal as well as a political blow to Grayson.[4]

Bennett, a white immigrant from Kansas City, was some years younger than Grayson. Trained as a newspaperman and a physician, he came to the Indian Territory in 1881, locating in Eufaula in 1883. There the personable newcomer married Lonie, Annie Grayson's younger sister. When the Indian Journal Printing Company was reconstituted four years later, they hired Bennett as editor of the *Indian Journal.* This made him a business associate of the Grayson brothers as well as family. But Bennett and the Creek stockholders could not see eye to eye, and in a few months the ambitious young editor left Eufaula to resettle in the booming town of Muskogee. There in 1888 he founded the *Muskogee Phoenix,* filling the vacancy left by the departure of the *Indian Journal* for Eufaula a year earlier. The *Phoenix* became the *Journal'*s only competitor in the Creek Nation, and Bennett also had his eye on the clientele of the *Journal'*s job printing operation.[5]

That Bennett espoused white boomer attitudes toward the future of the territory did not endear him to the Graysons. Nor did they approve of his relationship with his widowed sister-in-law, Anna Trainor Stidham. The Graysons never severed their family ties with Lonie's children, even after Anna married Bennett following Lonie's death, and that marriage, combined with other factors, such as Grayson's disappointment at losing the Union Agency position, probably added to the hostility that eventually developed between the two men.[6]

As early as the Creek National Council session of October 1888 Bennett attempted to siphon off some of the Indian Journal Printing Company's business. For several years the company had held a charter from the Creek Nation and served as its official organ. At that session, the company asked for passage of a bill granting it an annual appropriation of twelve hundred dollars as printer for the national government. The next day Bennett submitted a bill asking that the contract go to the lowest bidder below a cap of six hundred dollars. Both bills went to the Judiciary Committee and then to the council. There, according to Bennett, his enemies in the House of Warriors, of which Grayson was a long-time member and often speaker pro tem, "slyly pocketed"[7] his bill. On October 16 the council passed the twelve hundred dollar appropriation for the Indian Journal Printing Company, but Chief Legus C. Perryman vetoed it on information that Bennett's bid amounted to less than half the amount asked by the Indian Journal Printing Company. An attempt to override the chief's veto failed, gaining only 72 votes out of 114 after a hot debate.[8]

Grayson must have known about these maneuvers but may not have personally engineered them. He was present during the opening round but was probably absent after October 16, the day his daughter died. It is unlikely he was there for the debate on the veto, but other *Indian Journal* stockholders probably were. In today's terms, Grayson's overlapping business and political affairs constituted a conflict of interest, but until that time no one seems to have raised the issue. Until the advent of the *Muskogee Phoenix* there were no other printing companies in the Creek Nation to compete for national patronage. If, as Bennett suggested, the appropriation asked seemed exorbitant compared to his, there had to date been no standard of comparison in the nation. The stockholders could also defend their bid by noting that the *Journal* was rarely profitable and that, as an Indian-owned enterprise, its symbolic value to the Creek Nation was beyond price.[9]

But Bennett was as quick with criticism as with competition. When the *Indian Journal* derided Bennett's low bid as evidence his printers would supply "shoddy goods" and claimed it was therefore not worth the council's consideration, the *Phoenix* countered that the Indian Journal Printing Company proposal was "the most high-handed and brazen attempt to impose upon one's own kindred that has lately come to our notice." Moreover, little except shoddy goods could be expected from "the poorest excuse for a paper that circulates in this country."[10] Charge and countercharge enlivened several weekly issues, which probably did not hurt the circulation of either paper.[11]

None of this, of course, warmed the relationship between Grayson and Bennett. But the stockholders took seriously charges that the *Indian Journal* had declined from its former standards and principles, for in January 1889 a new editor, Albert A. Wortham, replaced Samuel Benton Callahan, a rising progressive Creek politician.[12] A few days later the Cherokee *Indian Arrow* noted with approval that the *Indian Journal* under new management "presents . . . editorial matter far from that of the 'boomer' kind."[13] Some months later, Wash Grayson's name appeared on the masthead as associate editor and president of the printing company.[14]

By August 1889 Bennett was serving as Union Agent at the same time his newspaper joined a chorus of speculation and accusation aimed at Wash Grayson and former Creek Principal Chief Joseph M. Perryman. The commotion was a result of current territorial concern with the range cattle industry, which flourished from the late 1860s through the next two decades. Texas cattlemen, trailing herds across the territory to Kansas railheads, realized that the Indian Territory had abundant grazing land and water as well as a climate that was ideal for fattening cattle. As cattle ranching became a corporate industry complete with syndicates of foreign and domestic investors by the 1880s, cattle companies with expanding herds began leasing pastures on tribal reservations in the territory. Among the most visible were the Cheyenne-Arapaho Live Stock Association, which published its own newspaper, and the Cherokee Strip Live Stock Association, which in the early 1880s leased the entire Cherokee Outlet on the Creek Nation's northern boundary. Indian businessmen such as the Grayson brothers ventured enthusiastically into large-scale stock raising, forming their own Seminole and Muskogee Live Stock Association. Even with setbacks due to overexpansion and bad weather in the late 1880s, the range cattle industry remained an important part of the economy of the Five Civilized Tribes. But its critics both inside and outside the territory were highly vocal. The possibility of federal expulsion of the non-Indian cattlemen from the territory loomed large by 1889.[15]

Early that spring Grayson and Perryman traveled out to the western half of the Indian Territory in the company of Congressman James B. Weaver of Iowa, a strong supporter of the movement to open it to white settlement. The two Creeks ostensibly planned to visit old acquaintances on the Wichita-Caddo Reservation. Correctly, Grayson and Perryman first called on Agent W. D. Myers at Wichita Agency to present a letter of introduction from outgoing Union Agent Owen.[16] Owen endorsed them somewhat ambiguously as "reputable gentlemen of good standing among their own people, whose interests they are likely to represent faithfully and well."[17] According to Myers, Grayson and Perryman told him that they wished to advise his charges in light of the pending visit of the Dawes Commission charged with preparing the tribes for allotment. Myers gave Wash Grayson and the dark-skinned but bearded Perryman, whom he mistook for white men, permission to approach the aggregation of tribes assigned to his agency.[18]

A few days later Myers was irate when he realized his mistake. Even more infuriating was the rumor that Grayson and Perryman had escorted four of the Wichita headmen to Texas to sign grazing contracts. This could conceivably draw unwanted attention to his reservation at a time during which the practice of allowing Indian tribes to lease their grazing lands to outsiders was coming under growing criticism. And some of the Indians involved belatedly questioned exactly what it was they had signed. Two of them, Sergeant Tom and Arleecher, the latter part Cherokee, added to the agent's embarrassment when they wrote to Cherokee friends about the matter, and it reached territorial newspapers. In mid-May Myers communicated his concerns to the Commissioner of Indian Affairs, and by July hints of a Grayson-Perryman swindle appeared in the territorial press. The *Muskogee Phoenix*, while professing not to credit rumors without proof, insinuated that there was basis for suspicion when it noted that such contracts with credulous Indians for legal counsel often stipulated fees of as much as 25 percent.[19]

Grayson's version of this event made it seem much more innocuous. He explained that he had been acquainted with some of the Wichita and Caddo chiefs for years, often acted on their behalf in Washington, and had a standing invitation to visit their reservation. He knew that unlike the Creeks, who held their land in fee simple, the Wichitas and Caddos had no clear title to their reservation. With drastic changes threatening the Indian Territory, they feared the pending allotment of their lands or, worse yet, another removal. Their latest contract for legal advice had expired, Grayson explained, and they had appealed to him to come to their village near Anadarko to discuss what they should do.[20] Somewhat patronizingly, Grayson noted that the Wichitas and Caddos offered him and Perryman "genuine aboriginal hospitality."[21]

The two tribes wished to establish a true value for their lands, so they designated four men to sign contracts designating agents who would, for a fee, represent them. According to rumor, it was these four men Grayson and Perryman were said to have escorted to Texas without Agent Myers's permission.[22] Writing of the incident about 1912, Grayson considered it something of a coup that they successfully negotiated a contract for the lease of "hundreds of thousands of acres"[23] of Wichita-Caddo grasslands. He did not, however, mention then or later the Texas excursion or another contract, which according to Myers, hired him, former Governor Samuel J. Crawford of Kansas—a leading boomer—and Congressman Weaver to act for the Caddos, Wichitas, and Affiliated Bands at Wichita Agency.[24]

Reconciling these accounts remains difficult because much of the evidence is hearsay and can no longer be documented. The Office of Indian Affairs may have stopped a Grayson-Crawford-Weaver contract in August 1889. Whether the contract was itself objectionable or because of the rumor and speculation, nothing came of it. Nor has this or any other contract survived to shed light on the incident. If a lease as substantial as that of "hundreds of thousands of acres" of the Wichita-Caddo Reservation existed, no hint of it appeared in contemporary issues of the *Texas Live Stock Journal.* Yet Grayson not only recounted the story in his autobiography but twenty years later still delighted in having put one over on Wichita Agent Myers.[25]

In their public explanation at the time, Grayson and Perryman minimized the affair, presenting it as a rather tedious negotiation intended primarily to accommodate and reassure the concerned Indians. They insisted any documents involved "were read and reread and interpreted for about three days, it being our desire that there shall not be even a chance of a misunderstanding. There was no unfairness, misrepresentation or chicanery about this business and we feel satisfied that it was properly understood. Else why do not the delegates and head chiefs enter complaints?"[26]

Neither Sergeant Tom nor Arleecher claimed to be anything more than tribal members who, by Indian custom, had a right to speak their minds in council. Sergeant Tom admitted that he arrived after the talks were finished and the contract signed. He had not initially had misgivings about it but had told Grayson he wanted him to "fix us up in fine shape and enlarge our reservation." He asked Grayson to "put in a claim for us for as much as we had been promised, so that my descendants might have a home always." It was not until Sergeant Tom left and began thinking how the Creek National Council had recently agreed to the Oklahoma Cession that he had second thoughts about dealing with a Creek negotiator, concluding "he didn't value his land a great deal, [so] he didn't care for my land." Sergeant Tom said he was horrified when the agent interpreted the contract and his people found that they had agreed to "*sell*" [his emphasis] their land. Grayson, Sergeant Tom now charged, had bound them to "the main leaders in the effort being made to open up the Territory."[27]

One might well question how much Sergeant Tom and Arleecher understood about the contract if they feared, after talking to their agent, that they had sold rather than leased the land—land they did not own in fee simple and could not sell, a fact of which Grayson and the Wichitas were well aware. In that case, one might also question how accurately the flustered and angry agent interpreted the contract to them. On the other hand, if valid, a lease to Texas ranchers or a cattle syndicate might have interfered with the pending allotment of the reservation, a policy Grayson sincerely opposed. Or Grayson and Perryman might have leased the land, knowing that the transaction could establish its value prior to allotment. It seems much less likely that Grayson, whose sympathies were with these troubled tribesmen, who had conferred with them at many an international council, who had acted for them in Washington, and who valued their high regard for him, would defraud them of the only home they had left.

In an addendum to Sergeant Tom's letter to his Cherokee correspondents, Arleecher said that Grayson and Perryman were the main reason attendance at the International Council had been so slim that summer. But it is also interesting to note that in the midst of the Wichita affair the Iowas thought enough of Grayson to send Hay-wee-coo-raw as an envoy to him. They had objections to the recent agreement they had reached with the United States to allot their reservation and wanted to ask his advice.[28]

This, the most serious charge against Grayson's integrity, probably exacerbated conditions in a year of suspicion and accusation in the Creek Nation. While other territorial journals mentioned the affair, Union Agent Bennett's newspaper gave it the most coverage. As of September the *Muskogee Phoenix* professed disappointment that Grayson and Perryman still had not satisfied their critics. The editor implied that he had seen the contract and that it involved the cession of Indian land with a 10 percent fee for legal counsel. In the same edition appeared a letter over the pseudonym "Iste Maskoke" (Creek person). It reminded the public of the old $1,276 shortage in Grayson's accounts due to the burglary of his safe during his term as national treasurer. The writer recommended such "old defalcations" be investigated.[29] It is also worth noting that these innuendoes came at a time when *Muskogee Phoenix* owner Bennett perceived Grayson as a political enemy. One could suggest that Bennett used the affair to divert attention from a federal investigation of the Oklahoma Cession that embroiled him—the Union Agent—as well as several prominent Creek leaders.

If Grayson purposely distanced himself from the actual negotiations of the Oklahoma Cession, he acted wisely. In the weeks following the cession, Creeks and outsiders alike questioned the handling of the $2,280,000 payment. Prior to the cession, the Creek delegation—Porter, Hodge, and Spahecha—hired former Governor Crawford, something of an opportunist, to serve as their legal counsel for a 10 percent fee, even though the case involved a straight payment and not a suit requiring legal action. The Office of Indian Affairs deemed the fee exorbitant and refused to approve the contract. However, once the cession was final, the Creek delegation, still working with Crawford, withdrew $228,000 from Creek funds in the United States Treasury and paid him the fee.[30]

In June 1889, just about the time rumors of a Grayson-Perryman swindle began to appear in the territorial press, the delegation was called to present its report to a special session of the Creek National Council. Speculation about the fee for legal counsel was already circulating. Much of the objection originated in the Eufaula vicinity and in the pages of the *Indian Journal,* according to the *Muskogee Phoenix,* which defended the delegation. The editor, who had replaced Bennett in May after he became Union Agent, charged that the accusers were "broken down politicians who hope to ride into prominence by seeking the overthrow of abler men."[31] The rumors disturbed backcountry Creeks as well as townsmen. Conchaty Mekko (Concharty Micco), a National Council member, wrote that the *tvlwv* of Nuyaka, Apekochee, Okfuskee, and Fishpond had met to discuss the "woods talk" about the Oklahoma Cession. They had concluded that these could not be "true talks" and refused to accept them. Remembering that only a few years ago they had agreed to live in peace and accept the constitutional government, they judged that the "road of the true talk is plain to see." That road led to Okmulgee and the delegation's appearance before the council.[32]

When questions were raised at the June council session, Pleasant Porter defended the delegation's action in hiring Crawford by noting that time and time again the federal government refused to pay the Creeks the money it legitimately owed them until they employed attorneys to compel compliance. By a vote of sixty-seven to thirty the House of Warriors accepted the delegation's report but rejected the lawyer's fee because the Office of Indian Affairs had voided the contract with Crawford. After considerable discussion, the House of Kings refused to act. Creek records do not indicate how individuals voted, but subsequent accusations suggest strongly that Grayson was among those members of the House of Warriors who opposed the delegation's actions.[33]

The outcry over the funds continued throughout the summer, forcing Agent Bennett to consider holding an investigation that might have personal implications. At some point during the negotiations of the cession, both Grayson and G. W. Stidham, who was both Grayson's and Bennett's father-in-law, had been in Washington. Although Stidham insisted his visit was unrelated to the negotiations and Grayson had not arrived until the cession was ratified, Bennett, pleading his relationship by marriage to both sides in the controversy, finally disqualified himself and called in a federal special investigator. Bennett's self-disqualification did not satisfy the suspicious, among whom were Wash Grayson, Roley McIntosh, D. N. McIntosh, W. E. Gentry (vice president of the Indian Journal Printing Company), Creek ranchers E. H. Lerblance and Hence Posey, William Fisher, and Wallace McNac. They held that several "boodlers"—the Creek delegates, Crawford, and lobbyists in Washington— split the money. Conceivably, their suspicion extended to Bennett because of his delay in investigating the affair.[34]

Bennett defended himself by claiming without naming names that those who objected so strenuously to the attorney's fee were themselves "sharers in the attorneys fees heretofore paid by the Creeks." In this instance, though, they "were for once powerless to raise the percentage and pocket the differences, as they had done in former cases." He may well have been referring to Grayson, for the first time in years not a Creek delegate. The agitators, Bennett continued, clamored for "money or blood" and raised such a cry that only an investigation kept the peace.[35]

However, that investigation, conducted in July, left many questions unanswered, in part because Special Agent Robert S. Gardner took some of the most pertinent testimony behind closed doors. Publicly Porter and Hodge defended their actions and their disbursement of the money, including sixty thousand dollars that went to prominent white merchant and rancher Clarence W. Turner of Muskogee. In the end, Attorney General W. H. H. Miller vindicated the delegates. That the Creek National Council at the same special session resolved to withdraw four hundred thousand dollars from Creek funds for a per capita payment and entrusted the job to the same delegation was to the *Muskogee Phoenix* further evidence of public support.[36] Even so, Agent Bennett warned darkly and rather obscurely in September, "this craving for revenge may lead to assassination and other crimes, this having been for years their only method of obtaining their ends."[37]

According to the editor of the *Muskogee Phoenix*, such extravagance and shady dealing as were involved in the Oklahoma Cession were all too familiar in Creek finances. Again without naming names, he blamed the great monetary losses the Creeks had suffered over the years on the poor quality of past Creek treasurers. Echoing Bennett's charges of fraud in the delegates' paying out enormous fees for legal counsel, he pointedly asked his readers, "Why did one of the present agitators pay 50 percent to secure a claim of $32,000 only a year ago? We refer to the Watt Grayson claim."[38] The obvious allusion was to Wash Grayson, former Creek national treasurer and representative of the heirs of Watt Grayson in their claim against the federal government.

By December Bennett openly named Wash Grayson an enemy in reaction to complaints concerning his performance as Union Agent. His annual report also illustrated their differences: Bennett's official assessment of the status of the Creeks challenged several of the principles of self-government and land tenure Grayson espoused. Bennett called for the extension of original jurisdiction of the newly created federal district court at Muskogee over all criminal and most civil cases among the Five Civilized Tribes. While he stopped short of calling for the dissolution of the national governments, he believed the Union Agency should be abolished and the Constitution and laws of the United States imposed on the Indian Territory. Most Indians, he insisted, would approve allotment if it were offered to them by secret ballot. Most of those who opposed the idea, he declared, did so either out of custom, because they believed they could use the system to keep out the boomer and speculator, or because they thought the Indian was not ready for it. The most vocal opponents, he charged, were those with some "fat scheme" in mind.[39]

Bennett's recommendations were public record to which Grayson, a delegate and council member, ever vigilant where Creek affairs were concerned, had access. That he objected strenuously to Bennett's statements and took his objections to Bennett's superiors must be inferred from a heated letter the Union Agent addressed to the Commissioner of Indian Affairs. He charged that "certain Creek and Cherokee politicians under the leadership of G. W. Grayson and William Jackson with the advise [sic] of Messrs. Zack Taylor and T. A. Bland" were preparing to attack "my veracity and integrity." Bennett refused to retract his report and declared, "Grayson is a defeated candidate for the position I hold. Jackson is a white man who was the strongest worker for Capt. Hammer, another defeated candidate. . . . Taylor is an attorney from Tennessee who spent a month or so at Eufaula and Muskogee trying to bleed some one connected with the Creek Oklahoma Cession. He is the man whom the records of the Indian Office will show demanded my suspension from office because he alleged I *refused* [Bennett's emphasis] to investigate the Creek ten percent Council fee." Bennett concluded dramatically, "I have only to say that I am proud these men are *not* my friends, I cannot sink my manhood to desire their friendship, and the fact that such men fight me is an *honor* [Bennett's emphasis] which I highly appreciate."[40]

If Grayson and the others did indeed attack Bennett through higher levels of the Office of Indian Affairs, they did not succeed in having him removed as Union Agent. He remained in his position until former President Grover Cleveland's reelection swept out Republican office-holders in 1893. Bennett subsequently became a U.S. marshal, a prominent businessman, and mayor of Muskogee.[41]

While nothing concrete came of the rumors, accusations, and name-calling in either of these incidents, they give some indication of the multilayered working of Creek politics, the Gilded Age corruption that seeped into the Indian Territory, the facets of the delegate's role, and the anxieties that afflicted Indian peoples with changing federal Indian policy. More important than any personal, business, or even political feud between Leo Bennett and Wash Grayson were their different perspectives on the future of the Creek Nation and the Indian Territory—the boomer's view as opposed to the Creek nationalist's.

Bennett and Muskogee, the town he called home, represented the white and black incursion that Grayson worked so hard to forestall, the first wave of the "alien flood" that threatened Creek sovereignty. In 1890 Eufaula was still a small railroad town of about five hundred, an "Indian town"[42] that took pride in that designation. But it was quickly losing place to Muskogee, some thirty miles northeast up the Katy tracks. Muskogee had been established after the Civil War as freedmen squatted on abandoned plantations in the Three Forks area; given its strategic geographic location, it burgeoned in the following two decades. By 1890 its population of twelve hundred consisted of an aggregation of Indians, whites, and freedmen— some of whom were Indian citizens while others were "States" blacks.[43] But according to George W. Stidham, "The whole place is built up by non-citizens. They monopolize every kind of business carried on."[44]

Many of the whites at Muskogee originally came in as licensed traders. Too many, as far as Grayson and Stidham were concerned, expanded their commercial operations under the guise of "public necessity" to include hotels, bootshops, barbershops, restaurants, millinery stores, and, of course, ranches.[45] White merchant and noncitizen Clarence W. Turner was especially notorious for bringing in large herds of cattle, which he grazed in huge fenced pastures on Creek communal lands. These various enterprises all required additional labor and so contributed to the legal and illegal noncitizen population of the Creek Nation. Eufaula had its share of noncitizen entrepreneurs, too, but the town had so far maintained its Indian identification through its majority population of progressive Creek citizens. Muskogee, on the other hand, symbolized to Grayson and Stidham an alien beachhead on Creek soil.[46]

Muskogee's noncitizen residents, they believed, behaved as if the soil they occupied as tenants was theirs by law. They were also vocal about their lack of civil rights in the Creek Nation and vehemently demanded "home rule."[47] In the summer of 1889 a congressional delegation visited the Creek Nation and received an enthusiastic reception in Muskogee.[48] The party included members from neighboring Missouri and Kansas as well as W. M. Springer of Illinois, author of numerous bills aimed at opening the Indian Territory to non-Indian settlement. Grayson in an open letter to the *Muskogee Phoenix* asked, who were those who gave the congressional delegation such a welcome? They were not Indians, for "Muskogee is in no sense an Indian town" or even a town in which substantial numbers of Indians gathered. Grayson answered his own question: The enthusiastic audience included "those composing that non-citizen element found clustered around Muskogee which has no interest in our soil, institutions or welfare."[49]

The editor of the *Muskogee Phoenix*, in contrast, condemned Eufaula as a racist town in its hostility toward non-Indians, and he characterized the *Indian Journal* as the mouthpiece of destructive race prejudice.[50] Freedman George W. Bruner seconded the charge, disputing a recent quote from former editor S. B. Callahan that, "Both races [black and Indian] have a natural distrust and abhorrence for each other, consequently no advancement in civilization will ever be attained while the two races are mixed as they are at this time."[51]

The *Phoenix* found Eufaula's Indian self-consciousness and the *Indian Journal* ridiculous. "A certain class of persons have for years been harping upon the tune, 'Muskogee is a white man's town'" when, in fact, the editor claimed, Muskogee numbered the largest population of Indians-by-blood in the territory. But "do-as-our-forefathers-did" people always condemned any idea, no matter how progressive, if it first appeared in Muskogee. "Well what if it is a white man's move?" the editor demanded. Indians had a role to play; but, he continued, "if it were not for the whiteman . . . these very pull-backs would be clad in breech clouts and living in ignorance and heathenism"—sentiments not likely to endear him to Wash Grayson and other progressive Creek nationalists.[52] Some weeks later the editor remarked on the anniversary of the founding of the *Indian Journal*, perhaps in regard to associate editor Wash Grayson, "It is childish folly for one man or a whole army of men for that matter to try and clog the impetus which is moving the Indian people onward to a better and brighter civilization."[53]

In truth, by 1889 Grayson had reluctantly conceded that a change in the status quo was coming, but it was not the parallel development promoted by progressive nationalists. Commenting on the congressional visit, he wrote, "That individualization of lands and statehood is our ultimate good we can believe; but that we are ready now, or that we as a people will be ready the next year, or that congress can legislate our full blooded Indians into fitness for so radical a change, we do *not* believe [Grayson's emphasis]."[54] He could see that a major upheaval was imminent. While he was confident he could deal with life on the white man's terms, he knew that other Creeks, those he called "our full blooded Indians," could not. He was speaking not of genetics but of the tendency of some Creeks to cling to traditional ways. That would make them vulnerable to fraud and abuse if the Creek Nation and the protection it afforded them were abolished.

Further evidence of Grayson's recognition that times were changing appeared in letters to an *Indian Journal* stockholder in the spring of 1889, soon after the Oklahoma Cession and within days of the "run" into the Unassigned Lands. Grayson proposed that the newspaper modify its policy in view of recent congressional legislation.[55] He recalled that the founders of the newspaper intended it to stand for "certain cardinal principles."

Those principles had not changed, but *"policies, plans,* and *schemes"* [Grayson's emphasis] must change to suit present conditions.[56]

The principles Grayson believed the newspaper must defend were Creek self-government and communal ownership of the land. He knew that the boomer element so prominent in Muskogee and surrounding states demanded access to Indian land, formal territorialization, and statehood—the sooner the better. Intruders were boldly coming into the territory, squatting on Indian land, and exploiting Creek resources. They pastured cattle, cut valuable timber, harvested pecans, slaughtered game birds for export to Kansas City meat markets, and prospected for minerals. Then they had the audacity to demand the end of Creek government and "home rule."[57]

In January 1893 Grayson appealed directly to President Grover Cleveland, whom Indians understood to be somewhat sympathetic to their cause. He reminded Cleveland of the president's own recent condemnation of the attempt of American immigrants to overthrow the native government of Hawaii and to impose an American-dominated regime, drawing a clear analogy to the threatened Indian nations. Grayson suggested that the terms "boomer" and "intruder" covered the alien element in the Pacific island kingdom as well as the Creek Nation. He urged, "Remove and keep out of our country the intruder element as your government has solemnly promised it would do, and we will be a happy people without poorhouses, tramps, bomb throwing anarchists, houses of prostitution, whiskey and beer saloons but with a republican form of government quite as fairly administered as it is in Arkansas."[58]

Grayson also vigorously opposed allotment. Although the Five Civilized Tribes had avoided falling under the 1887 Dawes Act, the escape might be temporary, a point their delegates tried to make clear to all the *este Mvskoke*, the Muskogee people. In February 1893 delegates Pleasant Porter and A. P. McKellop composed and distributed a circular explaining the attitude of Congress and warning of its determination to abolish tribal government. About the same time, President Cleveland named Senator Henry L. Dawes head of a commission to visit the Indian Territory, test the attitude of citizens of the five Indian republics, and persuade them to accept allotment.[59]

On the commission of Chief Legus Perryman, Wash Grayson attended a meeting of the International Council, which convened in late February

1894 to hear the Dawes Commission present its case for allotment in severalty. At Lerblance Hall in Checotah, he interpreted for the Muskogee speakers as delegates of the Five Civilized Tribes, Osages, and Pawnees argued against allotment. Osage delegate Nickswashitonga told the representatives of the Five Civilized Tribes, "[W]e wish to hear what the commissioners have to say to you all, and as we count ourselves one of the red brothers . . . we do not care to be apart from you so whatever conclusions your people come to we are willing to abide by it. Anything that you do will be satisfactory to us."[60]

Spotted Horse, a Pawnee delegate, added, "[L]ike my brother Osages I am anxious to know what the five tribes are going to do. I have heard that we are in danger and I want to be prepared to tell our people what is going on. We once had commissioners to trouble us like those here yesterday and I am a little afraid. . . . I have come here to find out what the five civilized tribes are going to do about allotment. We want to be with you."[61]

The spokesmen for the Five Civilized Tribes presented the Dawes Commission a familiar defense against allotment. They pointed once again to the absence of almshouses and potter's fields in the Indian Territory, which they said demonstrated the benefits of their communal landholding system. They insisted that it protected the economically unsophisticated while it allowed the educated and ambitious citizen to prosper. They pointed to their thriving homes, farms, businesses, mines, and well-supported schools as evidence of their progress. The Five Civilized Tribes, they noted, spent more per capita for education than any state in the Union. So, how could they be accused, as they so often were, of standing in the way of progress?[62]

Unimpressed, the commissioners reminded the Indian representatives that with populous states now surrounding the territory, their way of life was bound to disappear and they would soon be crowded off the land by intruders. Allotment and individual landholding, they insisted, ignoring the laxity of the federal government in meeting its obligation to restrict noncitizen access, would at least solve the intruder problem. The commissioners also hinted that Congress might soon repeal their treaties without the Indians' consent just as it would any useless legislation. Moreover, they said, back in Washington the consensus was that the delegates to this convention were all large landholders, and that was the only true reason they objected to allotment. "Don't allow us to report that you do not want a change and that you believe that the treaties will be kept, and that you are able to take care of yourselves," they cautioned, or Congress might act that very session. "We believe we stand between you and a peril you do not see." They concluded that if the Indians knew their own best interests, they would accept allotment and eventual statehood.[63]

Neither side yielded to the arguments of the other, and the Dawes Commission moved in early April to Okmulgee. There they addressed an audience of two thousand, among them Wash Grayson. At the close of another round of admonitions and veiled threats, the commissioners asked the Creeks to step to the right if they opposed allotment and any change in their government. "The whole audience in a very orderly manner filed over to the right," the *Indian Journal* reported.[64] But the Dawes Commission refused to acknowledge that evidence of Creek public opinion. They listened instead, according to Grayson, "to only one side in this matter," that of "the outsiders [rather] than to the bona fide citizens."[65]

Among the outsiders was Union Agent Bennett, who repeatedly reported to his superiors in Washington that the majority of his charges were coming to favor allotment and would vote for it were the ballots secret. "The full-bloods are thinking for themselves. They are no longer blind followers of the half-breed and the adopted citizen," he wrote. "They are realizing who are decrying the taking of lands in severalty, yet lay out for themselves large farms in the richest bottoms, graze the free grass of the country, reap revenues from the coal interests, and keep their hands upon the national purse-strings." Bennett concluded, "The full-blood has been requited with the skim-milk after the rich cream of Indian politics has beeen [*sic*] skimmed for the benefit of those who run the machine."[66]

It is interesting to note that Wash Grayson—merchant, rancher, and farmer—was one of those Bennett could legitimately charge with skimming the "rich cream" in his exploitation of the Creek Nation's communal wealth. Grayson justified his entrepreneurship as leading the Creeks to a higher plane of civilization and defending their national sovereignty. Bennett condemned the enterprise of mixed-blood Indians such as Grayson as victimizing the poor full-bloods and white settlers, and he agitated for allotment and the end of tribal government as a way to restore just treatment for Indians as well as whites.

At the same time that Bennett served as Union Agent he owned a Muskogee newspaper, fenced pastures for his cattle on Creek land without Creek consent, and served as president of the Seminole and Muskogee Live Stock Association. He also established a real estate business while he calculated how much Creek allotments might be pared down to make improved townsite lots available to noncitizens as "surplus" lands.[67] Each of these men represented a vital contingent of the nineteenth-century Indian Territory population, and it might be argued that in advocating his design for the future of the Creek Nation, each claimed nationalistic goals and high ideals that also served his own interests. That the personal interests of individuals might be served by those goals and ideals did not negate their worth.

Grayson returned to Washington as a Creek delegate for the congressional sessions of 1893 and 1894. There he worked closely with his counterparts from the Five Civilized Tribes according to the method they had developed in the 1880s. Together they held the line against allotment, but they could not prevent legislation in 1895 that provided for the survey of their lands.[68]

It was not surprising, then, that by 1894 Grayson had reevaluated his position on allotment and found a way to accommodate it. Publicly he stated, "I believe the most intelligent portion of my people are in favor of allotment, but the masses are not, neither do I ever think they will be." But, he continued, "I am confident that our only safety lies in allotment among ourselves of all our land. Then we could hope to get rid of the intruders."[69] Allotment on a per capita basis might satisfy those determined to impose it on Indians as a way to undermine tribalism and prepare Indians for American citizenship. But by precluding the existence of any surplus lands, it would arrest the influx of noncitizens into the Creek Nation.

Although Grayson reluctantly came to support allotment, he continued to cling to the principle of Creek self-government. He was not willing to accept the dissolution of the Indian national governments or to view that development as the inevitable sequel to allotment. In the weeks after he explained his revised views to the press, the *Indian Journal*, of which he was a major stockholder, radically altered its policy of opposition to allotment and instead called for allotment per capita. At the same time, editor K. W. Whitmore advocated the creation of an organization in the Creek Nation to work against statehood.[70]

Grayson probably shared Whitmore's frustration that summer, as the editor noted that the average Creek citizen seemed unconcerned with the findings of the Dawes Commission and blind to the seriousness of its intent. Many, he wrote, reasoned that the federal government had sold them their land in fee simple and guaranteed them self-government within its boundaries in the treaties of 1832 and 1866. They held those treaties sacred and could not believe the federal government would not do the same. Therefore, they saw no reason to be concerned. When the Creek National Council met in October, Whitmore reported in disgust that the legislators spent so much time drinking, gambling, riding the carousel, and generally enjoying the attractions of the wide-open Creek capital that there was rarely a quorum present to conduct business. "Such scenes as were enacted at the last Creek Council cannot be re-enacted very many more times,"[71] he predicted, or the credibility of Creek self-government would be demolished. "Still," he finished sarcastically, "intelligent Indians [stand] back with a horrified look on their face and express astonishment at the change in sentiment that is being manifested at [Washington]."[72]

Grayson agreed with Whitmore that such irresponsible exhibitions worked against the Creek government's survival. Those who opposed the continuation of the Five Civilized Tribes as sovereign nations used this and any other shortcoming as an excuse to demand tribal dissolution. After visiting the Indian Territory the Dawes Commission reported to the Board of Indian Commissioners that the Indian courts and legislatures were corrupt, the schools primitive, crime unpunished, the lands engrossed by "a few enterprising half-breeds," and the whites without rights—all this among nations held up as models of Indian progress. Grayson and Whitmore knew that the cries of the white noncitizen for home rule, of the freedman against infringement of his civil rights, of the law-abiding citizen for protection against the outlaw—all redounded on the Creeks as evidence of their incompetence and backwardness. Opponents applied the vocabularies and demands of the contemporary populist and progressive reform movements to the Indian governments, so charges of chicanery in such affairs as the Wichita-Caddo contracts and the Oklahoma

Cession did substantial damage. But while Grayson might fend off charges of personal corruption, he was vulnerable to the charge of "monopolist."[73]

This charge originated in the growth of cattle ranching in the post–Civil War Creek Nation. As described earlier, ranching was a natural outgrowth of Creek agricultural and commercial enterprises and a logical exploitation of their prime bluestem prairies. The growing demand for beef in industrializing eastern cities encouraged Creeks to keep large herds of their own. In the early 1880s Creeks protested that the ever-growing herds of foreign cattle passing through the nation to Kansas consumed their grass and spread Texas fever. The Creek Nation attempted to tax transient cattle, but foreign drovers largely ignored the Creek law. In 1884 Wash Grayson took the Creek Nation's protest to the Department of the Interior, which he reported was sympathetic. However, an earlier decision by federal Judge Parker suggested the Creek tax interfered with interstate commerce and consequently was unconstitutional.[74]

Some white cattlemen circumvented the tax by setting up partnerships with Creek citizens, as did Clarence W. Turner and Pleasant Porter. In 1888 northwest of present-day Wagoner, Turner and Porter fenced the first of the pastures that enclosed many square miles of Creek grazing lands. Complaints to the Creek National Council led to a pasture law that limited cattlemen to three years occupation and charged them a modest five cents per acre per year.[75]

Other noncitizens simply ignored the Creek Nation boundaries and allowed their cattle to stray onto Creek lands from neighboring reservations. This became a major problem in 1890 when the Department of the Interior ruled that all foreign cattle must be removed from Indian lands, including the adjacent Cherokee Outlet. Some white cattlemen had apparently planned for this contingency by contracting with a few Creek citizens to pasture their herds. In October 1890 several petitions signed by Wash and Sam Grayson, Joseph M. Perryman, William McCombs, D. N. McIntosh, Moty Tiger, freedmen Snow Sells and Sugar George, and other prominent Creek citizens claimed that one hundred thousand head of white-owned cattle were illegally on Creek lands. Attempts by the Creek tax collector to seize the cattle were stymied by federal red tape, leaving the nation with little protection. The petitions were forwarded to Washington, where the department shrugged it off as an internal Creek problem. The petitions circulated back to Union Agent Bennett, who seemed skeptical of the complaint, and to Chief Legus Perryman, a cattleman with white tenant ranchers himself, who seemed uninformed and unconcerned.[76]

By that time, enterprising Creek cattlemen such as the Grayson brothers were taking advantage of the communal landholding system to expand their own ranching operations. As early as 1889, Chief Legus Perryman noted that some citizens had built pastures enclosing as much as fifty thousand acres. Protests by other citizens to the point of threatened bloodshed caused Perryman to ask the council to pass a new pasture law. It limited pastures to one square mile per head of family except on the borders of the nation, where enclosures might act as deterrents to intruding cattlemen. However, residents within the proposed pastures must first petition the district judge for permission to put up fences and must obtain a majority vote in open meetings. The proprietors of the pastures then paid five cents per animal per year for grazing rights.

In 1892 Wash Grayson, his father-in-law, and another partner obtained a permit to fence a large pasture on the southern boundary of the nation. Two years later Grayson fenced two pastures comprising a total of sixteen thousand acres. But these were relatively small compared to the standard thirty-two-thousand-acre pastures registered to the George Tiger Pasture Company, the John Buck Pasture Company, and the H. C. Reed Pasture Company. The Yuchee *tvlwv* held a contract for a pasture of 39,775 acres, while the A. P. McKellop Pasture Company and the Turner Pasture Company held more than fifty thousand acres each.[77]

Although some Creeks benefited from the large pastures, they also aroused much criticism from other citizens. The law required cattlemen to secure the permission of the people living inside a pasture before they erected a fence around it. Many Creeks were willing to put up with the inconveniences for a small payment, but others complained that the fences interfered with their freedom, hindered travel, and forced children to walk extra miles to school. They viewed cattlemen, such as Grayson's partner Hugh Henry, the McIntoshes, adopted Creek Frederick B. Severs, Porter, and Turner, as exploiting the resources of the nation at the public expense. Nor were the big cattlemen averse to tampering with Creek National Council proceedings to protect their interests. Eventually, the old war horse Spahecha emerged as a leader of the opposition. In 1890 he organized a party of four or five hundred Creeks who systematically destroyed the fence C. W. Turner had built to enclose two hundred fifty thousand acres. Turner's claims for compensation from the Creek Nation were rejected repeatedly, ending with a U.S. Supreme Court ruling in 1919.[78]

In the meantime critics, including the boomer press, found in the pastures a weapon to use against Creek sovereignty. With some logic, they construed the pastures as a monopoly of Creek lands imposed by a handful of mixed-blood Creeks. In so doing, they denounced those Creeks who demonstrated the enterprising individualism fostered by assimilationists, charging them with clinging to the communal landholding system for their own purposes.

Targeting the Creek cattlemen, the editor of the *Purcell Register*, a boomer periodical that sparred in print with the *Indian Journal*, charged in 1895 that the Creek newspaper belonged to "a corporation of Creek land monopolists devoted to the attempt to preserve their special interests from injuries threatened by impending changes."[79] The editor of the *Indian Journal* denied this, stating that the journal was owned by G. W. and Sam Grayson, "neither of whom derive an income of $10 from a monopoly of Creek lands. The gentlemen mentioned have from three to five hundred acres each of farming land in cultivation and any Indian in the Creek Nation not too lazy to fense [*sic*] it in can have just as good a farm." They also held an interest in some pastures for which they paid five cents per acre per year and from which they received no income. The Graysons' opposition to change in the landholding system, he continued, was "to protect the fruits of their industry from the rapacity of the boomer." If such monopolies existed as the *Register* charged, he asked, why did not more Creeks, especially the supposed full-blood victims of the practice, not join the demand for allotment?[80] Very few full-blood Creeks ever did.

As far as the Grayson brothers were concerned, the argument that they were profiting from the exploitation of their rights as Creek citizens, although once true, was rapidly losing validity. The days of their personal prosperity were running out as swiftly as those of the Creek Nation. In 1891 the Grayson Brothers listed assets totaling $71,150. These consisted of their homes in Eufaula, some rental properties, improvements on their acreage, fencing around pastures, several thousand head of livestock, and their shares in the Indian Journal Printing Company. But hard times set in following the Panic of 1893, when agricultural prices fell and the flush times of pasture leasing and cattle raising ended. Grayson Brothers Mercantile faced growing competition from other merchants, many of them white, in Eufaula and the proliferating market towns nearby. Wash Grayson spent many weeks each year in Washington on Creek business, and his own business probably suffered from neglect. True, he received compensation from the nation, particularly for his services as a delegate, but it was probably inadequate for the standard of living he maintained in Washington. Moreover, his salary was paid in Creek Nation warrants usually worth far less than their face value. Sam, his partner in business, also held time-consuming offices in the Creek government, including that of national treasurer. By the late 1890s the Grayson brothers were facing bankruptcy.[81]

So was the Creek Nation. Each year Grayson returned to Washington to continue the fight against allotment and the dissolution of the nation. But each year the fight grew harder and victory more ephemeral. In 1896 Congress authorized the Dawes Commission to begin preparing census rolls of the Five Civilized Tribes in preparation for allotment. Still the nations refused to treat with the commissioners. Opposition to allotment was perhaps the one issue on which all the parties fielding candidates in the Creek elections of the 1890s agreed.[82]

Continuing financial problems within the Creek government and resistance to allotment became the major issues of the decade. Chief Legus Perryman served two terms (1887–1895), representing the Union Party—the coalition of former Checote and Spahecha followers and Creek freedmen. Perryman's impeachment for financial irregularities and his refusal to step down in favor of Second Chief Hotulke Emathla late in his second term left the nation for a time with two chiefs. It also weakened the Union Party. As the election of 1895 drew near, political parties began rallying their supporters. In mid-March a caucus was called at the Green Leaf church ground, but few of "the full-blood element in Creek politics" turned out.[83] The *Indian Journal* commented favorably on John Tiger's idea that the full-blood, mixed-blood, and freedman subgroups within the nation should each present a slate of candidates. That, new editor John N. Thornton commented, would solve the race problem.[84]

As the election drew near, a number of names were put forward for the chieftaincy. Pleasant Porter headed one ticket with Conchaty Mekko for second chief. The *Indian Journal* tried to create support for Joseph M. Perryman, but the victorious candidate was Spahecha, who had "the confidence of a large following among the full-bloods." The *Indian Journal* knew him to be "a conscientious man" but expressed grave doubts whether he was "fitted at his advanced age and with his lack of knowledge concerning the affairs upon which the policy of the Creek Nation must soon so lightly touch, or be wrecked in the encounter."[85]

Spahecha's second chief was Roley McIntosh, the adopted son of the late Chief Roley McIntosh. Both Chief Spahecha and McIntosh intended to continue the fight, however quixotic, against allotment and against threats to Creek nationhood. Although McIntosh had little formal education, he had been admitted to the Creek bar and was known for his oratorical ability. A large-scale rancher, he was somewhat more fluent in English than the chief and possessed innate leadership abilities. Both represented the traditionalist perspective and relied on Wash Grayson for advice as well as interpretation. He served them well, interpreting both documents and policy in his role as a *yvtekv*.[86]

During Spahecha's term (1895–1899) Congress moved even more aggressively toward dissolution of the governments of the Five Civilized Tribes. As of 1895 the new white-style towns in the nation were allowed to set up municipal governments outside Creek jurisdiction. This greatly pleased the noncitizen element that dominated towns such as Wagoner and Muskogee. Congress also extended federal court jurisdiction over the Creek Nation and made all Creek legislation except negotiations with the Dawes Commission and resolutions of adjournment subject to presidential approval.

In 1898 Congressman Charles Curtis, a Kaw Indian of mixed descent from Kansas and a Republican Party wheelhorse, authored the Curtis Act. It was intended to place Indian national funds under the control of federal rather than tribal officers, provide for immediate abolition of the national governments, and require the citizens of the Five Civilized Tribes to submit to allotment without their consent. Thus the Indian Territory moved a long way toward the eventual alien control explicitly forbidden in the Removal treaties.[87]

The Creeks still had one avenue of escape left. Negotiation and ratification of an independent agreement with the federal government could prevent the imposition of the Curtis Act over the Creek Nation. To achieve such an agreement the council named a special commission—Pleasant Porter, Joseph Mingo, David M. Hodge, George Alexander, Roland Brown, William Sapulpa, and Conchaty Mekko—to negotiate with the Dawes Commission. Creeks were divided on the wisdom of such a step. Grayson, Porter, and a number of progressive Creek nationalists supported negotiation if it resulted in the continuation of their self-government. However, those who had the most influence with Spahecha preferred to end all negotiation and fight for the validation of their treaties in the U.S. Supreme Court. Some traditionalists stubbornly ignored the negotiations and clung to the guarantees of the old treaties. Chief Spahecha called a special session of the Creek National Council in August 1897 and asked for a voice vote by *tvlwv* on continuing the negotiations. Majority public opinion, according to some observers, was that the negotiations should end, but the council voted over Spahecha's objections to negotiate one last agreement.[88]

Debo has described the agreement that the Creek representatives drew up with the Dawes Commission as the worst of any of the Five Civilized Tribes. It left townsites open to the exploitation of the boomers, agreed to allotment with no restrictions to protect the allottees, and removed any weapon of defense from the Creek government. Spahecha turned the document over to the council with strong caveats and suggested that the Indian nations form a voluntary union in self-defense.[89] In August 1898 the *Indian Journal* noted that Spahecha did not want to call an election to ratify the agreement. But if no election were held to complete the process, the Creeks would lose any choice between the "Curtis monstrosity and the Creek agreement." The editor summed up the intransigent Spahecha as a sincere but conscientious lunatic whose cause was hopeless. The Creek-Dawes Agreement, on the other hand, he judged "a wise, just and satisfactory measure."[90]

Although he did not negotiate the Creek-Dawes Agreement, Wash Grayson knew its contents, having helped draft it and having been appointed with D. C. Watson to translate both it and the Curtis Act into Muskogee for the benefit of the Creek public. This accomplished, Grayson attended public meetings in outlying towns to explain the differences between the two documents to a Creek public confused by the alternatives offered them. Privately he harbored doubts as to the wisdom of the agreement.[91]

On November 1, 1898, the Creek people voted on ratification of the Creek-Dawes Agreement. Grayson's early impression was that the Creeks had accepted it, an outcome his associates greeted with jubilation. Later returns, though, showed their celebration to have been premature.[92] On Saturday morning, November 19, the Creeks convened in what Grayson considered a tragic landmark event. By joint resolution, the two houses gathered as was their custom on the north front of the capitol at Okmulgee so that ordinary Creek citizens could listen to the proceedings. The committee charged with counting the votes from the forty-seven *tvlwv* announced the defeat of the agreement by 152 votes. Then Chief Spahecha, Second Chief Roley McIntosh, and federal Inspector J. George Wright, acting for the Department of the Interior, addressed the assembly. Grayson translated the chiefs' remarks into English while David M. Hodge translated Wright's into Muskogee. Wright spoke at length, but only one thing was important to Grayson: Creek sovereignty had been abolished by the Curtis Act.[93]

The immediate imposition of the Curtis Act removed the power of the Creek national government while allowing it to continue to operate until the affairs of the nation, primarily the disposition of national property and the allotment of the tribal estate, were concluded. This meant that in 1899 the Creeks held an election for the positions of principal chief and second chief. It also offered Wash Grayson an opportunity to run for one of the primary offices.

Although political violence no longer wracked the nation after 1883, ephemeral coalitions and factions appeared and disappeared in this election and throughout the last third of the century. Adding to the dynamics were Creek freedmen and those claiming to have been Creek slaves, who formed a bloc hoping to swing elections to suit their interests. As a last resort, Grayson gravitated toward the faction favoring continuing self-government with allotment per capita. This put him at odds with the rising political star among progressive Creeks, Pleasant Porter.[94]

In 1899 Porter ran for principal chief on the National Party's platform of compromise with the Dawes Commission. On the ticket in the second position was Moty Tiger, a respected former lighthorse captain and school superintendent. Their major opponents ran on two tickets. One consisted of former chief Legus Perryman, a rancher and businessman from the Tulsey Town vicinity, who was now firmly identified with the boomer element, with William McCombs, a minister, for second chief. Perryman's second chief Roley McIntosh headed the third ticket with Wash Grayson running for second chief. The McIntosh-Grayson ticket finished third with only half as many votes as Porter and Tiger. The final disposition of national affairs, then, was in Pleasant Porter's hands.[95]

In spite of Grayson's defeat, he remained active in his nation's affairs. The Creeks had replaced their log post–Civil War capitol with a two-story cut sandstone building in 1878. Its simple rectangular shape, topped by a hipped roof, cupola, and spread-eagle weather vane, still dominates Capitol Square in Okmulgee. When the tolling bell announced the beginning of council sessions, Grayson climbed the narrow branching central stairway to take his place in the second-floor chamber of the House of Warriors, the Tvstvnvkkvlke, where he represented Koweta Town throughout the 1880s and 1890s. There he usually took his seat among the other *tvlwv* representatives, but periodically he acted as interpreter or sat on the raised dais as speaker pro tem. In addition, he served on the council's education and finance committees.[96]

In those days Okmulgee was a very small market town with several trading houses forming the beginning of a town square around the capitol. Behind them were scattered the log homes of Okmulgee's Creek and freedman population. There were few hotels in town in those days, so many council members brought their families by wagon and horseback to camp along the pleasant meanders of pecan-shaded Okmulgee Creek. But while he attended council sessions, Grayson boarded down the street from the capitol at the home of Police Chief Dick Farr. Farr recalled that however large the crowd in Okmulgee during council sessions, Wash Grayson's white beard set him apart among all the dark faces.[97]

George Reilley Hall, a white resident of the Creek Nation, editor of the *Henryetta Free-Lance*, and poet, retained an indelible image of those last days of the Creek Nation and the men who struggled to keep their nationhood alive. Looking back, he wrote in "The Old Council House":

> These time-stained walls have echoed back the shout
> Of native statesmen in profound sincere debate

The second Creek Council House at Okmulgee. Courtesy Western History Collections, University of Oklahoma Library.

When governmental treaties seemed to be in doubt
And vast uncertainties obscured the red man's fate.
These storied walls have heard the passioned cry
Of stately Grayson in his patriot appeal
That, though autonomy might fade away and die
Yet human destiny the red man's will should feel.
And here the stolid Spahecha stood in gloom,
Unsmiling, stern, implacable, erect and strong.
With sad, prophetic mind he seemed to sense the doom
That hovered over all the land when came the throng.
And pious Motey Tiger, with a smile for all,
Dispensed diminished powers in his realm of might.
He saw the pillars shaken—saw the structure fall
But never lost his faith in God and in the right.[98]

And so the battle continued. Chief Pleasant Porter, educated at Tulla-hassee Mission, bilingual, and an experienced politician, needed Grayson

less than had Spahecha. Still he welcomed his old companion-in-arms
from the Confederate Creek regiments to the first floor executive office,
calling on him frequently for advice and translation of public addresses.
Grayson continued to serve as a delegate to Washington and to the
International Council until the end of the decade. The Seminoles, who
also spoke Muskogee and stemmed from the same cultural roots, likewise
called on Grayson for his expertise, hiring him to translate their first
written laws and constitution.[99]

By 1899 Grayson found it increasingly necessary to take such odd jobs as
translation, for Grayson Brothers was sliding irretrievably toward financial
disaster. Wash and Sam searched for a way to minimize their losses and
found one. The laws of the Creek Nation stipulated that an individual's
improvements on communal land were exempt from bankruptcy. The
Grayson brothers knew their homes were safe as long as the land on which
Eufaula stood remained part of the Creek national estate. They also
understood that the allotment demanded by the Curtis Act, though still
pending, was inevitable and drawing ever closer. If they were to save
something from their enterprise, they must do it before the Creek National
Council and the Dawes Commission reached a formal agreement and made
the Eufaula townsite eligible for individual title. Consequently, in 1899 the
Grayson brothers filed bankruptcy. They lost their investment in four
thousand head of cattle. They probably lost their shares in the *Indian Journal*
at this time, too. But they kept their homes, perhaps one last coup against
the white greed they blamed for their personal and national losses.[100]

The long-dreaded allotment loomed over the Creeks for years, with the
survey of the land and the enrollment of Creek citizens proceeding into
the new century. Enrolling a family such as Wash and Annie Grayson's
was relatively simple; they understood when resistance became futile and
made the best accommodation they could. But many Creeks in the
backcountry were suspicious of the process if not actively hostile to it.
Individuals known by more than one name, deaths that occurred during
the allotment period, family relationships that were, from the white
perspective, convoluted, tribal intermarriages, and the sometimes dubious
claims of freedmen to Creek citizenship all complicated the enrollment
process carried out by the Dawes Commission, even when Muskogee-
speaking Creeks were employed to aid in the work.[101]

In at least one case, Sam and Wash Grayson were called to testify on the veracity of a claim of Creek citizenship. In a hearing before Dawes Commission Chairman Tams Bixby, Wash Grayson stated that "there is an Indian person by the name of Joe Grayson, but then there is a nigger by the name of Joe Grayson," as well as his young cousin Joe Grayson. The first was actually Joe Hutton, while the subject of the testimony, one of his grandmother Katy Grayson's former slaves, once lived in the Choctaw Nation and was only adopted as a Creek citizen by an act of the Creek National Council.[102] Such cases of duplicate or fraudulent enrollment and subsequent allotment became increasingly important as the values of Creek mineral rights escalated in the following decade.

A new Creek Agreement approved March 1, 1901, marked the nation's official, if reluctant, acceptance of tribal dissolution and allotment in severalty—another landmark in Creek history. The agreement designated March 4, 1906, as the date for the demise of the Creek government. Meanwhile, Creek land was to be allotted per capita with each citizen receiving an allotment valued at $1,040, that ideal figure based on 160 acres priced at the prime agricultural rate of $6.50 per acre. The proceeds from the sale of remaining lands and from national funds, once all national assets were liquidated, were to be used to offset any difference between the actual value of an individual's allotment and the $1,040 ideal valuation. Lands allotted to Creek citizens could not be encumbered by past debts; nor were they to be tied up in long-term leases. In each 160-acre allotment, the allottee was to choose 40 acres as his homestead. This nontaxable homestead was inalienable for twenty-one years; the remaining 120 acres could be sold five years after the allottee received his patent, or deed. Large pre-allotment landholders such as Wash Grayson were to vacate lands in excess of the acreage they could legitimately claim for all immediate family members. Townsites were to be surveyed and platted, with the lots and any improvements appraised. Creek citizens already occupying town lots might then purchase them at one-half their appraised value.[103]

The Wash Grayson family, though opposed to the policy of allotment, enrolled early and chose their lands well. Grayson selected adjoining allotments for himself, Annie, and his minor children—Washington, Eloise, and Tsianina—in the fertile bottomlands of the North Fork River near Fame, about five miles northwest of Eufaula, lands he had farmed for many years. This allowed the convenience of joint cultivation and oversight of the property. He chose an additional small acreage next to that of his adult son, Walter Clarence, and the latter's daughter, Lenore, just east of Hugh Henry's allotment outside Henryetta, an area coming into prominence for its coal deposits. Grayson also selected allotments for some of his fellow members of Koweta *tvlwv*. There is no evidence that he ever profited from these selections, as was too often the case during the heyday of the "grafters."[104]

Not all Creeks were so cooperative in the matter of choosing allotments. The most traditional Muskogees, unable to accept an alien landholding system that offended their spiritual values or a policy that had historically worked to their disadvantage, ignored the agreements between the Creek leadership and the Dawes Commission. Clinging to the old treaties guaranteeing them their land in fee simple as long as the waters ran and the grass grew, they refused to choose allotments or to accept the patents giving them individual title to the acreage they farmed. Most continued the simple agricultural "full-blood" life-style they preferred, but a few talked of moving voluntarily beyond the control of Anglo-Americans, perhaps to Mexico or Paraguay. Some repudiated Chief Porter and the entire constitutional government. Initially they turned to Spahecha for leadership, but, tired and in ill health, he withdrew to his home near present-day Beggs, leaving them to rally around Cheto Hacho (Chitto Harjo), or Crazy Snake.[105]

In 1900 at Hickory Ground six miles south of Henryetta, Cheto Hacho's "Snake" traditionalists set up a countergovernment based on the preconstitutional system. They organized a lighthorse company to enforce their laws and threatened corporal punishment for those who accepted allotment patents. It was even reported erroneously in the territorial press that Snake lighthorsemen had arrested Captain G. W. Grayson and former Second Chief Roley McIntosh, giving each man fifty lashes on his bare back for having employed white tenant farmers. Such rumors of Snake violence alarmed local white residents as did the fact that a number of blacks congregated with the Snakes at Hickory Ground. When the Snakes interfered seriously with the allotment process through intimidation of other Creek citizens, U.S. Marshal Leo Bennett and his men arrested and delivered them to Muskogee for trial. A sympathetic federal judge sentenced the Snakes to prison but then released them on the provision that they accept allotments.[106]

That was not the end of the so-called Crazy Snake Rebellion. Cheto Hacho continued to repudiate a government and a policy he believed was out of harmony with traditional ways. Repeatedly, even at an audience with President Theodore Roosevelt, he pleaded for restoration of traditional government and the treaties of 1832 and 1866. "Nor have I ever heard a human voice that carried more appeal or kindled greater sympathy than Chitto Harjo—Crazy Snake," wrote *Henryetta Free-Lance* editor George Reilley Hall.[107] The disturbance associated with Cheto Hacho flared periodically, reaching a climax in 1909 when a white posse, sheriff's deputies, and National Guardsmen converged on Hickory Ground in an incident two historians have deemed racially motivated and directed against Cheto Hacho's black, rather than Creek, followers. An attempt to arrest Cheto Hacho at his home near Pierce, Oklahoma, resulted in gunfire, and the Snake leader was wounded but escaped. He died in hiding in the Choctaw country two years later. Although they knew the cause of the Snakes was hopeless, progressive Creek nationalists such as Porter, Grayson, and writer Alexander Lawrence Posey sympathized with their distress. Indeed, Posey, who was gaining a reputation as a poet and humorist, wrote admiringly of Hotgun, one of the Snake leaders, and incorporated him into his satirical "Fus Fixico Letters."[108]

Over the objections of the Snakes, allotment and the dismantling of the Creek national government continued under the provisions of the Creek Agreement of 1901. Editor John N. Thornton of the *Indian Journal* recognized some defects in the agreement but judged them to be minor and optimistically hoped Congress would eventually correct them. Unfortunately, the defects and lax federal enforcement proved very damaging to vulnerable tribespeople. Already there were complaints that the more knowledgeable Creeks, usually characterized as "mixed-bloods," took the prime lands, leaving the poorer soil to the traditionalists who either did not understand the process or chose to ignore it.[109]

Lots in newly platted towns of the Creek Nation also became a divisive issue. Occupants could claim town lots for one-half their appraised value. Otherwise, they were to be sold at public auction to the highest bidder above the appraised value. Following the platting of Eufaula, the Grayson family claimed at least twenty-six lots in Eufaula for which they paid a total of $978. This was fairly modest compared to the acquisitions of town lots by Chief Porter, Clarence W. Turner, Frederick B. Severs, David M. Hodge, and William A. Sapulpa, who engrossed substantial areas. Turner and Porter, partners holding a large pasture within the city limits of Muskogee, acquired land either at face value, half-price, or by proxy. Porter owned nearly one hundred thousand dollars' worth of real estate at his death in 1906. According to Commissioner of Indian Affairs Robert G. Valentine, these conspiracies involving "dummies" who bought town lots at half-price for shadow purchasers defrauded the Creek Nation of substantial sums. By 1911, 231 lawsuits intended to recover the true value of about fifteen hundred lots had recovered eighty-six thousand dollars and ninety-four lots worth an estimated sixty thousand dollars for the Creek Nation.[110]

Creek allottees were supposedly protected under the Creek Agreement of 1901, but Creeks such as Grayson and Porter, who understood the vulnerability of many of their fellow citizens, doubted it was strong enough to stop grafters. White real estate dealers converged on the Creek Nation even before a gusher at Red Fork ushered in the great era of oil exploitation in the Indian Territory and transformed nearby Tulsey Town into the city of Tulsa. Thornton of the *Indian Journal* commented sardonically in June 1901, "God helps those who help themselves and the whiteman [*sic*] is certainly helping himself to Indian leases and options."[111]

In 1902 a Supplemental Agreement addressed some concerns for the more naive Creek citizen. Representatives of land companies opposed the agreement's requirement that each allottee's lease must have the signature of the Secretary of the Interior, but Grayson, Chief Porter, and others insisted that it was a necessary precaution against the exploitation of vulnerable Creeks. The Supplemental Agreement also provided for the appraisement of Creek lands in preparation for the equalization of allotments. The Appraisement Committee included three white members with Wash Grayson as the Creek representative. The committee traveled all over the Creek Nation that summer. Determined now to protect the individual Creek's ownership of his land, Grayson looked about him during his extensive travels and saw his worst fears of allotment realized.[112]

During the spring months of 1903 Wash Grayson placed his apprehensions before the Creek public in a series of open letters published in the *Indian Journal.* These letters demonstrated that he had now moved into a new phase as a cultural broker, bringing the abuses of allotment to public attention. In "A Chapter from Present Creek History," he described some of the exploitation he had witnessed as a member of the Appraisement Committee. Too often, he said, Creeks found themselves presented with allotments they had not chosen and did not want. When they complained, they were told the Dawes Commission did not make mistakes. Other Creeks and freedmen could not decipher the surveyor's marks or correctly locate their allotments from their patent descriptions. Sometimes they settled on the wrong plot, only to be evicted later by some "pale faced renter" with a lease from the real allottee. Grayson related how an impoverished young "full-blood" widow, her infant in her arms, appealed to him to help her evict white renters who had moved into her little cabin while she was away several weeks picking cotton to support herself. They refused to leave, and she told Grayson she was not yet ready to go to the new home in the "high city" the "praying people" told her awaited the faithful. Could he not help her? Grayson did the only thing he could do for her; he wrote a letter to the Dawes Commission. These calamities, he noted, were happening while the territorial newspapers lauded the grand work of the Dawes Commission. Grayson conceded that many errors were due to the fact that the Creek Nation was the first of the Five Civilized Tribes to be allotted and the system was still unrefined, but he could not accept the injustices he saw imposed on his fellow Creeks.[113]

Grayson also wrote an open letter to Assistant Secretary of the Interior Thomas Ryan, an old acquaintance, about the abuses he observed. He explained, "[M]any men, myself among the number, believing that it was the wiser course to align ourselves in harmony with the proposed change . . . and save what we may out of the approaching wreck," accepted allotment. They had insisted on the prohibition of alienation of title for five years to protect the ignorant. In spite of that stipulation, unscrupulous white grafters were bilking Creeks out of their lands. Every town in the nation now had its big land dealers, who maintained offices and boldly advertised in the newspapers. Elsewhere, Grayson wrote, "we find the small dealers panting and covered with perspiration and dust calling at the homes of our people and negotiating single handed with individual members who are needy and have more land than money."[114]

These grafters could not yet legally buy the lands, but they induced Creeks to lease their property for ridiculously low amounts of cash. No sooner did the naive Creek get his patent than he handed it over to a grafter, in violation of a law he did not understand and which the grafter ignored. Such manipulations tied up thousands of acres of Creek land in clouded titles. "One thing that is painfully certain," Grayson concluded, "is that [they] are unable to cope with the white land buyers now abroad in our land."[115]

Grayson concluded his open letter by calling for an investigation and action against the lease-buyers, although the flagrant participation of Office of Indian Affairs officials in the territorial real estate boom predestined such a probe to futility. Creek citizens of Muskogee, seconding Grayson's letter, agreed that many Indian allottees felt they had no recourse through the Department of the Interior when they discovered their mistakes in dealing with grafters.[116] In July the Creek National Council followed up Grayson's letter with a resolution calling on President Theodore Roosevelt for federal protection of allottees according to the Creek Agreement of 1901. Otherwise, the council warned, "these land companies plying their unrestricted vocation among our people will by fraud and dishonest dealing soon make homeless paupers of a large number of the citizenship of the Muskogee nation."[117] But the Office of Indian Affairs merely referred Grayson's letter to Indian Inspector Wright in Muskogee, who replied that he was well aware of what was going on but that there was no real penalty for making illegal leases except the expulsion of the leaseholders.[118]

Wright's failure to deal with the problems that resulted from poor enforcement of the agreements was typical of the behavior of federal officials in the Indian Territory in 1903. Revelations that Dawes Commission Chairman Tams Bixby, Commissioner Thomas B. Needles, Commissioner Clifton R. Breckinridge, Inspector Wright, Union Agent J. Blair Shoenfelt, and numerous lesser federal functionaries were at the same time officers and stockholders in territorial real estate, banking, and trust companies dealing in Indian lands caused a public outcry that eventually reached as far as Washington. Charles J. Bonaparte, a member of the Board of Indian Commissioners and later attorney general of the United States, was ordered to conduct an investigation that implicated even Creek Principal Chief Pleasant Porter. The Bonaparte Investigation resulted in the expected whitewash and some criticism but no dismissals of guilty officials.[119]

Grayson's work with the Appraisement Committee convinced him that federal officials were intent on stripping Creeks of their national estate. The committee went into the field with a schedule categorizing eighteen grades of land ranging from natural open bottomland, the top grade, valued at $6.50 per acre, to flint hills, valued at $.50 per acre.[120] This was in accordance with the understanding of the Creek National Council that the basis of evaluation was agricultural. But Grayson soon realized that the committee was using a different schedule, which classified land within two miles of a railroad at $6.50 per acre regardless of its worthlessness for agricultural purposes. At the same time, much of the hilly, rocky country of the western nation, now thought to lie atop valuable oil deposits, was not being graded at all. Grayson suspected little attempt at equalization of allotments would occur if most of the land were classified at the prime rate, while the unclassified western lands, held out of the process for later sale as "surplus," would create an irresistible temptation for the oil corporations and Congress. "To one in interest, & so well acquainted with the rapacity, the greed, and cunning of those who are after us on all sides as I am," Grayson wrote to Chief Porter, "it must be conceded that these fears & suspicions are natural as well as logical."[121]

He and writer Charles Gibson pleaded in the columns of the *Indian Journal* for the complete per capita distribution of the national lands to prevent any surplus that might pass into the hands of speculators. They also wanted a second supplemental agreement that would protect the right of Creek "newborn" children added to the census rolls by the Supplemental Agreement of June 30, 1902.[122]

Grayson's general pessimism concerning the results of allotment and his insistence that the Creek government continue to function as long as possible placed him at odds with Chief Pleasant Porter. At least in the beginning Porter, with a faction of progressive Indian Territory citizens, professed to expect great results from allotment. "It will be a good thing for us, for it will impose obligations on each member of the tribe which he has been relieved of heretofore," he told a newspaperman in early 1901. Sounding much like contemporary "friends of the Indian," he explained, "Every man must shift for himself, & the result will be that thrift & frugality will be practiced and the members of the tribe started on the road to financial success."[123]

Porter also looked forward to the end of federal control as stipulated in the Curtis Act, which had permitted federal officials to take over Creek affairs, finances, and schools. The Creeks had not always spent their money wisely, as Grayson was the first to admit, but they had taken pride in their schools and staffed them with Creek educators when possible. Although there was patronage involved in the process and some Creek appointees were blatantly incompetent, they felt their system was at least equal to educational systems in neighboring states. Creeks found federal control onerous and restrictive, federal spending of their school funds extravagant, and federal school administrators offensive in their open contempt for Creek education.[124] Porter was impatient for the end of the allotment process and federal control even though this would mean the formal end of the Creek Nation. He declared, "I tell you it will be a novel but glorious experience when we are at last ushered into the great highway of individual manhood. We will feel like people who are born and reared in prison and all at once are turned loose in the broad world to do as we pleased."[125]

Eventually Porter came around to Grayson's point of view. By the end of 1904 the chief saw allotment much more negatively. As he witnessed the land slipping out of the grasp of allottees, he urged Creeks not to sell so much as a foot of their land, even though some were too old or impoverished to work their allotments. One editor remarked that he hoped this indicated "the clouds roll[ing] away from the chief's mental horizon."[126] Under these circumstances, Wash Grayson believed he had something better to offer the Creeks in terms of leadership; he attempted to run against Porter for the chieftaincy in 1903. With formal national dissolution set for March 4, 1906, it was generally believed that the winning candidate would be the last chief the Creeks would ever elect.

Porter, the incumbent, got an unusually early start by declaring his intention to run for reelection as the accommodationist National Party candidate in December 1902. Eventually Moty Tiger was nominated for another term as second chief. The Snakes favored Cheto Hacho, but many also liked Charles Gibson of Eufaula, formerly a clerk for Grayson Brothers and now a merchant and popular columnist on Creek affairs. Observers believed the conservative Gibson could legitimately challenge Porter by pulling much of the traditionalist vote into the Independent Party. In June there was considerable support for Wash Grayson as the candidate of the Union Party. It advocated strict compliance with the treaties, just distribution of allotments according to surface agricultural value, and continuing support of Creek education for an informed electorate, while it opposed joint statehood with Oklahoma Territory—a fair summary of Wash Grayson's current political views.[127] The *Okmulgee Chieftain*, noting the upcoming caucus of the party, commented on Grayson's candidacy, "A great many friends in this vicinity . . . are pushing him for the place. He is probably more capable of looking after the interim of the Creek people than any other man in the nation. He has always shown himself thoughtful for their welfare. His many friends here hope he will be selected by the convention June 17."[128] It seemed as if 1903 would see a three-man race with Porter, Gibson, and Grayson the candidates.

But the situation changed abruptly at the Union Party caucus at Okmulgee. Observers believed Wash Grayson entered the hall the strongest candidate, but Legus Perryman seized control early and emerged with the nomination on the first ballot. Grayson and his friends were stunned.[129] Alexander Posey, a Gibson supporter who was by then editing the *Indian Journal*, wrote, "Our command of Creek is fluent and we are more or less familiar with English and Choctaw, to say nothing of our meager knowledge of stock quotations in Greek and Latin, but language fails us when we attempt to express our disapproval of the choice of the Union Party for the next chief of the Creek people."[130] Posey's disapproval was in part racially motivated: both Porter and Perryman were reputed to be of black decent.[131]

However, Posey also disliked seeing Perryman so neatly eliminate Grayson from the race. An Anglo-Creek reared near Eufaula and educated at Bacone College in Muskogee, Posey was a generation younger than Grayson. With some progressives, he favored allotment and immediate full United States citizenship as the best future for the Creek people. Even with this difference of opinion, he and Grayson were good friends and fellow intellectuals bound together by their love of literature and their deep concern for Creek affairs.[132] Posey was already known for his political satire in the "Fus Fixico Letters," conversations in dialect featuring full-bloods Fus Fixico (Posey's pen name), and characters Hotgun, Tookpafka Micco, Kono Harjo, and Wolf Warrior. The last, of course, was the English translation of Grayson's Creek name, Yaha Tustunuggee, and the name by which Posey often referred to Grayson in print. The major contribution of Kono Harjo and Wolf Warrior was to listen closely to the conversations of the others and spit into the weeds. But they all remembered "the ol' days when Checota was chief an' Injin Territory was a huntin' groun' for the Five Civilized Tribes 'stead of a paradise for Illinois politicians."[133]

So perhaps it was with considerable bias, that Posey in his "Fus Fixico Letters" left the only description of the caucus at which Grayson made his bid to be the last principal chief of the Creek Nation:

Well, so Legus Perryman was a sly old coon and was made Wolf Warrior hide out up to Okmulgee. Hotgun he say, "Well, so how he do it?"

And Tookpafka Micco he say, "Well, so they was had a big fight over the last bone."

Then Hotgun he say, "Well, so what Chief Porter do when they was get into it?"

And Tookpafka Micco he say, "Well, so he was just set off to one side and watch the wool fly and glad he was not had a hand in it."

. . . Then Hotgun he say, "Well, so what kind a bone Legus Perryman and Wolf Warrior was had a fight over?"

And Tookpafka Micco he say, "Well, so they was had a big caucus up to Okmulgee to see who be the last chief. They was get together in the council house and Marcey Harjo was called the roll and say, 'Well, so they was about thirty-one towns had delegates here.'

"This was sound like hombux che (make ready to eat) and Legus Perryman and Wolf Warrior was get ready to help they-selves. Then the chairman he say, 'Well, so who you was want for next chief?' and they was put near all hold up their hands for Legus Perryman, and it was made Wolf Warrior look like white folks that didn't get to the first table. Then the chairman he say, 'Well, so it's carried like a shack on a headrise in Oklahoma.' So this was bust up the powwow."

Then Hotgun he say, "Well, so I was mighty sorry old Legus got nominated, 'cause he ain't a fullblood Injin."

And Tookpafka Micco he say, "Well, so good men like Wolf Warrior don't all time get in office."

Then Hotgun he say, "Well, maybe so that's why it is old Legus was carried off the bone."[134]

How must Grayson have felt at having been cut out of the nomination? His entire adult life had been spent in the service of the Creek Nation, and elevation to the chieftaincy was the logical last step. That he wanted to be principal chief must be inferred from Fus Fixico's account. After Gibson dropped out of the race in mid-July, the only viable candidates were Pleasant Porter and Legus Perryman.[135] The Creeks once again chose Porter. Fus Fixico summarized the campaign: "Well, so I see in the newspapers they was lots a candidates for Creek Chief 'sides Pleas Porter and Charley Gibson and Legus Perryman and Yaha Tustunuggee. But I think it was laid between Yaha and Charley 'cause they get all the Injin votes and was left nothing for Pleas and Legus but niggers to vote for them and maybe so a few half breeds that was hungry for pie."[136]

So Pleasant Porter began a second term in 1903 with the general assumption that he would be the last Creek chief. Knowledgeable men understood that the dissolution of the nations and statehood must come soon. Looking toward these events, in 1904 Grayson, Porter, Ben Marshall, Roley McIntosh, and A. P. McKellop reportedly joined Cherokee Robert L. Owen in attempting to organize a political party limited to "Indians by blood." They explicitly excluded blacks. According to a newspaper, they intended to create a strong independent party they hoped could hold the balance of power after statehood, should the Indian Territory be joined to Oklahoma. They failed to rally enthusiasm among the Five Civilized Tribes, and the party died at birth, for no other mention of it appeared in territorial newspapers.[137] Perhaps the majority of Indians found politics beyond the tribal level irrelevant, while a few joined one of the two Anglo-American parties, as did Owen, who became a powerful three-term Democratic U.S. senator from Oklahoma.

To avoid the union of the two territories, Indian citizens made one last attempt to create a separate Indian state. Public sentiment in Oklahoma and Indian Territories differed over whether to work toward the union of both territories in a single state or to apply for statehood separately—single versus double statehood, respectively. In July 1905 Grayson served as interpreter as Creeks met to discuss the recent single statehood convention at Oklahoma City.[138] This meeting was the preliminary to a full-scale constitutional convention for an Indian state, organized primarily by Porter, Charles N. Haskell, and William H. "Alfalfa Bill" Murray (the latter two were white men married to Indian wives), at Muskogee beginning August 21. Grayson, a delegate from District 12 and one of 182 delegates from the Indian Territory, was appointed to the committee charged with drafting the preamble and declaration of rights and powers. In the preamble the delegates named the proposed state "Sequoyah." Had Grayson had his way, the state would have been called "Tecumseh" after the great Shawnee leader of resistance to Anglo-American expansion. The convention produced the Sequoyah Constitution, a document historians have since judged well-written, an example of Indian political ability, and a forerunner of the State Constitution of Oklahoma. Indian Territory citizens ratified it by a vote of more than five to one on November 7, 1905. But Congress, which had insisted on formal territorialization in the Reconstruction treaties, rejected the constitution and ended any hope of separate statehood for the Indian Territory.[139]

That Grayson said little about the convention, either publicly or privately, suggests that he ascribed no real importance to it in spite of his participation. Perhaps he saw too much white leadership in the convention in the persons of Murray, Haskell, and other intermarried or adopted citizens. Perhaps his intimate knowledge of Congress and the federal bureaucracy convinced him the cause was hopeless. The opinion of the Indian Territory's population to date had carried little weight in Washington. Grayson's mission as a delegate with Chief Porter in the winter of 1906 reinforced that conclusion: Even though they went at the express invitation of the Interior Department to help draft the final act dealing with their national dissolution, the congressional committee they were asked to aid virtually ignored them. Porter returned home and left Grayson keeping watch alone in Washington. Twelve days later on March

4, 1906, in compliance with the Creek Agreement of 1901, the Creek Nation ceased to exist even though its affairs were still far from finished.[140]

How bitter this time must have been for Wash Grayson, a progressive Creek nationalist who had defended his people's sovereignty and domain for four decades. No matter how hard they fought, no matter how sagaciously they organized and plotted strategies of unified resistance, no matter how convincingly they demonstrated their "progress" toward the Anglo-American ideal held up before them, they could not withstand the alien flood.

About 1912, Grayson summarized this latest period of Creek history in a passage in his autobiography that reverberated with his sense of injustice. He recalled that the Muskogees had governed themselves successfully for hundreds of years before the coming of the Europeans; yet they were forced to give up their sovereignty and accept a landholding system they believed much inferior to their own. The rationale for the change was not that they had violated treaties, or failed to keep the peace, or because any sizeable number of their people wanted it. It was because, Grayson wrote bitterly, "regardless of the plain dictates of justice and a christian conscience, the ruthless restless white man demanded it. Demanded it because in the general upheaval that would follow the change he, the white man, hoped and expected to obtain for a song, lands from ignorant Indians."[141]

CHAPTER SEVEN

Fallen to the Mercy of Other Power

According to Muskogee belief, a man passed through four stages of life. In the springtime of his existence he received his infant's name and his education from his elders. As a young man in the summer of his life, he provided for his people, defended them against enemies, and became a *tvsekiyv* as he acquired his war name. He served as a leader, an advisor, or perhaps a spokesman for his nation in the autumn of his life. Then he spent his winter years in his *tvlwv*, repeating the cycle of life by passing on to a new generation the wisdom and history of those who had gone before.[1]

Into his sixties Wash Grayson followed this customary pattern. As a child he was educated by his elders, according to Muskogee tradition as well as at the new Creek Nation schools and Arkansas College. As a young man he served with the Second Creek Mounted Volunteers, proved himself a man and a warrior according to Muskogee standards, and became a *tvstvnvkke*. In maturity he entered Creek politics, represented his *tvlwv*, and became an advisor to the chiefs, a *yvtekv*, and a representative of the Creek Nation. A dedicated scholar, in his old age he began to compose a history of the Muskogee people from their perspective and to write for his children an autobiography describing his role in that history. But the unfinished business of the Creek Nation, his detailed knowledge of what remained to be done, and his concern for the preservation of Creek lands prevented his laying aside his official work for the pleasures of his avocations. Rather than complete the traditional cycle, he continued to serve as a cultural broker, mediating between his people and the federal government during the infancy of the new state of Oklahoma.

The evening before the last Creek Council convened in March 1906, Chief Pleasant Porter meditated on the transient nature of all peoples. He compared the deterioration of the sovereign Creek Nation to that of its shabby capitol and told journalist Hamlin Garland, "My nation is about to disappear."[2] This was true to a certain extent. Federal bureaucrats now handled Creek finances and directed its schools along with those of the other former Indian republics. The Creek National Council met only with the consent of the Department of the Interior. The chieftaincy was void of any real authority, and the skeleton executive department, located in rented quarters in Muskogee, operated under the oversight of the Office of Indian Affairs.[3]

But in another way Chief Porter was wrong. The formal dissolution of the national government did not mean that the Creeks disappeared as a people. They became American citizens, but many, like Wash Grayson, retained their identity and continued to speak, live, and think of themselves as Muskogees. Moreover, the unfinished business associated with the dissolution of the nation—protecting the allottees, equalizing allotment values, and liquidating remaining Creek national assets—required the principal chief to retain his office and the council to convene as necessary. Because settling the affairs of the nation took several years and often involved negotiations in Washington, Wash Grayson continued to represent Creek interests. So at Chief Porter's request, rather than attend that presumed final session of the Creek National Council, he had remained on duty in Washington until the end of March 1906, once again the solitary rear guard watching the sun descend, this time on his nation.[4]

A number of issues concerned the Creeks, Chief Porter, and Wash Grayson, but Creek land ownership absorbed most of their attention. By 1906 allotment was nearly complete, and most allottees had received their patents, or deeds. The emphasis now was on protecting ownership of the individual's land and recovering fraudulent and duplicate allotments. The discovery of the rich Glenn Pool near Tulsa in 1905 stimulated oil exploration and increased pressure on Creek allottees to sell their acreage or lease mineral rights. According to the Creek agreements of 1901 and 1902, the Interior Department retained authority over leasing of allotments, causing oil men to complain loudly about the bureaucratic red tape that hindered their exploitation of Creek mineral wealth. Another provision allowed allottees to dispose of all except a forty-acre homestead after five years, or even earlier with the consent of the Secretary of the Interior. By 1906 long lists of Creek allottees who had just passed the five-year mark and were now eligible to dispose of their property appeared weekly in territorial newspapers. By then Chief Porter had come to agree with Grayson that the most naive of their people were rapidly losing their land and mineral wealth through unwise business transactions. In June 1907 he asked Grayson to join other Creek leaders at the capitol the following month. In the Muskogee way, they would express their thoughts on the problem and try to reach consensus as to what should be done.[5]

Grayson, an educated, mixed-blood Creek, had already taken advantage of the law that allowed him to apply for early lifting of the five-year restriction. A standardized form required the applicant to demonstrate his competence to manage property. As of July 14, 1905, Grayson, sixty-two years old and a Creek citizen of one-quarter blood, declared that having attended school for four years, he spoke and read Muskogee and English. Once one of the most prosperous men in his nation, he presently owned only a span of horses, twelve hogs, and no agricultural implements. He had eighty acres of his allotment under cultivation by sharecroppers with the approval of the Department of the Interior. As evidence of his competence, he noted his tenure as national treasurer for eight years and his career as a merchant in Eufaula for three years. In those positions he reported handling as much as ninety thousand dollars in cash. Grayson explained that he had no plans to sell but merely wanted his lands unencumbered by federal control should he care to dispose of them. Union Agent Dana H. Kelsey endorsed his application, noting that Grayson was a progressive businessman and prominent citizen of the Creek Nation.[6]

Grayson's claiming to be only one-quarter Creek is worth noting, considering his complex lineage and strong identity as a Muskogee. This was his attempt to take advantage of the federal government's perception of Indians and resulting restriction policy: The less Indian "blood," or ancestry, a person possessed, the more competent federal officials judged him or her to manage business affairs. Many observers, including some Indians, generally linked the adjectives *full-blood* and *ignorant*. But while Grayson meant by this that the traditional, somewhat isolated life-style preferred by the Creek majority often left them uninformed, white observers ascribed a childlike immaturity and naivete to them.

Many commentators, conversely, equated *mixed-blood* with *educated* and *acculturated*. The latter adjectives implied that the person described could understand the Anglo-American legal and economic systems and was able to conduct business matters accordingly. This was an overgeneralization to which columnist Charles Gibson, speaking for the literate and capable full-blood Creek, rightly took exception.[7] Restriction according to blood quantum was a well-intentioned policy meant to protect a people perceived as backward and gullible. The fact remained, however, that it did not reflect the broad spectrum of the Creek population accurately. Still, if Grayson wanted to hasten the lifting of the restrictions on his surplus lands, he knew the department was more likely to grant his request if he took advantage of his white "blood," or ancestry.

Although Grayson was quite competent to manage his own affairs, he recognized the vulnerability of many of his fellow Creeks to exploitation by grafters—oil prospectors, leasing agents, real estate dealers, attorneys, merchants, more than a few federal officials, and even some Creeks not averse to swindling other Creeks. The most helpless, of course, were the minor allottees, children suddenly endowed with potentially valuable property that neither they nor, in many cases, their elders were prepared to protect. By 1906 a territorial newspaper reported that fifty dollars would buy bootleg copies of the Dawes census rolls of the Creek and Seminole nations. Most real estate offices in the Indian Territory had up-to-date copies, which expedited identifying the Creek allottees nearing that important five-year deadline ending restrictions on their or their children's surplus lands. The situation was especially galling to the Creek executive staff, who complained that the Union Agency repeatedly ignored their requests for a copy of the Dawes census rolls from which to learn the addresses of allottees.[8]

To protect those Indians judged most likely to fall prey to the grafters, Grayson joined members of the Five Civilized Tribes in calling for an extension of the restrictions preventing the sale of Indian lands. Opposing them most vocally were the boomer element, oil men, and statehood proponents, who realized that the prolonged nontaxable status of restricted Indian land would hamper finances and economic development in a future state. While the 40-acre homestead of each allotment was inalienable and nontaxable for twenty-one years, they believed the remaining 120 acres should be unrestricted and made available on the real estate market as quickly as possible.[9]

An Okmulgee editor spoke for many of this persuasion when he stated flatly, "The interests of the state are paramount to the interests of individuals." Disparaging what he perceived as the hand-wringing of the Indian Rights Association on behalf of "Lo the Poor Indian," he shrugged off the harm that could be done to Indians through the loss of their allotted lands. "On the contrary, it would be better for the allotted Indians to be deprived of one half of their holdings without compensation, if need be, that they might benefit by the lesson in self-support and by the unearned increment to their remaining lands by reason of their juxtaposition [to non-Indian lands]."[10]

In November 1906 a senatorial investigating committee heard testimony in Muskogee on this and other topics. Witnesses aired a variety of views on restrictions. Cheto Hacho, ignoring the finality of allotment, called for a return to the old days: "O give us the land in common that we may hunt at will, hunting the wild deer, turkey, or gather the wary fish from the dancing streams." Equally unrealistically but at the other extreme, Cherokee citizen and Democratic politician Robert L. Owen supported lifting all restrictions, stating, "The wild Indian puts his child into swimming water and it swims. Individual responsibility, individual initiative, is absolutely essential to individual development." Former Creek Principal Chief Legus Perryman, now a Tulsa real estate dealer, echoed Owen's opinion. Perryman and Owen represented the majority of Indians of mixed descent, who wanted complete control of their lands now that allotment was forced on them. Like them, Grayson wanted his lands unencumbered, but in agreement with Creek National Attorney M. L. Mott and interpreter David M. Hodge, he favored restrictions to protect full-blood Indians, who he believed were most vulnerable to the grafters.[11]

Grayson, who did not testify at Muskogee, stated his views on allotment restrictions and other Creek affairs when in the winter of 1906–1907 he was called to interpret and testify at a Senate select committee hearing in Washington. Senators Clarence D. Clark of Wyoming, Chester I. Long of Kansas, Frank B. Brandegee of Connecticut, Henry M. Teller of Colorado, and William A. Clark of Montana queried Grayson about several matters: his objections to federal spending of Creek funds, the refusal of Creeks to participate in Anglo-American territorial politics, the mood of Creeks now that allotment was mostly accomplished, grafting, and what might be done to protect Creek allottees. After making it clear that he was not on this occasion a delegate speaking for the Creek people but only an interpreter giving his personal views, Grayson owned that he had little faith in some of the other witnesses, particularly the white lawyers and self-proclaimed authorities on Indian welfare. Rather, he said, it was men such as the "king of the grafters," who had testified shortly before, from whom the senators could glean the truth about Indian affairs. That man spoke unabashedly of his unscrupulous activities while presenting himself as a pioneer developing the Indian country.[12]

On the complex question of competency among Indians, Grayson stated that he believed restrictions should be removed from literate, acculturated mixed-bloods like himself. As far as full-blood Creeks were concerned, he testified that he knew many who were "good, smart businessmen . . . fully capable of taking care of their property and interests." To unencumber those men, Grayson suggested some sort of tribunal be set up in the soon-to-be-created state of Oklahoma "with some good, honest, and keen man who is not a politician at the head of it." This judge should not be a locally elected official, subject to local party pressures, but a court officer appointed for life or good behavior, similar to federal judges. A man in this position would be in office long enough to learn the Indian character but, having no concern for reelection, "he don't fear anybody or favor anybody." A full-blood Indian could present himself to this man to prove his competency; he could trust that he would receive a fair judgment. Unfortunately, as time would demonstrate, Grayson's plea for the naming of impartial judges free from local ties and pressures was not adopted.[13]

The following September, two months before Oklahoma was admitted to the Union as the forty-sixth state and with the issue of restrictions still unresolved, Chief Porter died unexpectedly. Second Chief Moty Tiger succeeded him with the approval of the Secretary of the Interior. Tiger, or Homvtika, had a sound reputation among his fellow Creeks based on long involvement in national affairs. About a year older than Grayson, he had fought alongside him in the Indian Brigade with Chilly McIntosh's Confederate regiment. A Methodist minister, he was a member of the House of Warriors from the traditionalist Tuckabachee *tvlwv* and had formerly served as a lighthorse captain, Creek attorney general, and superintendent of the Creek Orphan School. Observers described Tiger as kindly, good-natured, and devout. A territorial newspaper reported that a constant parade of visitors it characterized as "full-bloods" visited Tiger's office, hoping perhaps to rebuild conservative influence with a man they perceived as more sympathetic to their views than the late Pleasant Porter. A nationalist in his own way, Tiger had much in common with Grayson, including a realistic perception of Creek affairs.[14]

That Grayson respected Tiger's farsightedness and moral courage was evident in his recollection of the April 1894 visit of the Dawes Commission to Okmulgee. When the commissioners had finished their argument in favor of allotment and statehood, they asked all who opposed them to step to the right. The audience of three thousand Creeks took that step— except for one man. Moty Tiger, "true to his convictions, solitary and alone, deliberately crossed over the walk, the only one in that vast gathering of the Creeks who was favorable to the land policy outlined for the Indians by the government." Most Creeks regarded his action as treason, but as Grayson explained, Tiger saw the new policy as unavoidable and believed it his duty to say so; a "wave of white settlers would soon ruin [the] Indian Nations as independent; he maintained that the tribesmen needed what protection the U.S. could offer," even if the price was allotment.[15]

It was this protection that Chief Tiger sought in November 1907 from Congress and the Secretary of the Interior. Grayson, Creek businessman Samuel J. Haynes, and Johnson E. Tiger, Moty's son, accompanied him to Washington as delegates. With Creek National Attorney M. L. Mott, a white lawyer retained by the Creek Nation, they set up a temporary headquarters of the Creek Nation at the National Hotel. Chief Tiger was literate and spoke English well enough, but he took the position that as principal chief of a people whose native language was Muskogee, he would not conduct national business in any language except Muskogee.

A Creek delegation with Wash Grayson, seated far right, Johnson E. Tiger, standing right, and Moty Tiger, seated center. Courtesy Archives and Manuscripts Division of the Oklahoma Historical Society.

Therefore, Grayson served as his *yvtekv* more ceremonially than he had for past chiefs.[16]

Samuel Haynes had been educated at a small college in Jackson, Tennessee, and was now a businessman in Okmulgee. He was an experienced delegate, having testified at the Senate select committee hearings the winter before. But he doubted his ability to make himself clear in English and so asked Grayson to interpret for him, too. Haynes's selection to accompany Tiger perhaps demonstrated the traditionalist dominance of the Creek National Council that developed as the progressive Creeks focused their attention on their individual, rather than national, interests under the new regime. That Grayson accompanied the Tigers and Haynes was perhaps indicative of his own growing conservatism. If so, it put him at odds with those Creeks who now accepted the boomer attitude prevalent in Oklahoma.[17]

The delegation went to Washington with instructions from the Creek National Council to oppose the removal of restrictions, particularly from the forty-acre homesteads. Grayson realized that they faced opposition from two sources. A number of white men from the new state of Oklahoma were in the capital, and they strongly advocated the removal of all restrictions. At the same time, Cheto Hacho and a party of his followers were in the capital pleading their reactionary cause. While the former group could expect a warm welcome, the Snake delegates, Grayson supposed, would "push their claims for a restoration of our old laws under treaties now obsolete and dead" with "no possible show for success." Even so, Grayson was optimistic that the official Creek delegation would succeed in maintaining the restrictions. On December 3 they called on President Theodore Roosevelt, who listened sympathetically and assured them of his support. Grayson came away believing legislation on restrictions would pass in that session of Congress. "Whatever is done," he wrote, "we hope to exert such an influence as to prevent its provisions from swallowing up and rendering our citizens, freedmen as well as Indians, homeless."[18]

Two months later the delegates appeared before the House Committee on Indian Affairs as it considered legislation on allotment restrictions. Grayson interpreted as Chief Tiger reminded the congressmen that the federal government had set itself up as the protector of the Indian: "I look upon you very much as the Great Spirit, with his great power. If he were to withhold his power and mercy you would be destroyed."[19] So would the Creeks be destroyed if the protective restrictions were removed. Tiger, who was one-quarter white, explained that he understood that the sentiment for removal of restrictions on Indians of mixed descent was very strong, but he believed an infusion of white or other blood did not protect Indians from the rapacity of the white man. If the restrictions were removed, Tiger solemnly warned, "there are persons here in this city who will touch the wires all over this town, and the information will be down there in our country in a moment's time, and the people who are down there ready to rob our people, as it may be said, would have the lands already signed away to them in a few hours' time."[20]

The congressmen, including Bird S. McGuire of Oklahoma, questioned whether Tiger and the delegation represented the real sentiments of the Creek people. They reminded Tiger that he had not, after all, been elected chief but had merely succeeded the late Chief Porter. Tiger replied dryly that he was principal chief of the Creeks as surely as Roosevelt, who had succeeded the assassinated William McKinley, was president of the United States. Furthermore, he and the delegation reflected the majority opinion among Creeks because they spoke for the Creek National Council. It had thoroughly considered the matter in August 1907 and ordered the delegates to oppose the removal of restrictions. Tiger then had Grayson read a letter from Seminole Chief John S. Brown that seconded the Creek National Council's sentiments.[21]

To summarize their argument, the Creek delegation presented a letter very much in Grayson's prose style. It once again attempted to explain to the senators the Muskogee cultural and historical perspective. Creeks, the letter explained, viewed land the same as "the other cardinal elements of water, air, light, and sunshine, something spontaneous and ever existing, which has been beneficently provided by the Great Spirit for the free use and support of all His children and not a thing on which a money valuation may be placed." The government had forced allotment on them in spite of decades of resistance. "The Creeks have not forgotten their sad experience of a few generations ago in the States of Georgia and Alabama, their former homes, where were practiced almost identically the same things we see now occurring in the State of Oklahoma." The delegates explained how grafters used fraud, intimidation, extortion, and even abduction to gain control of the lands of naive Creeks who did not understand the Anglo-American legal and landholding system. Because so many lawyers were involved in grafting, Creeks were convinced they had no real recourse through the Oklahoma court system. In fact, the delegates asked that Indians be exempt from that system in any case dealing with land.[22]

Chief Tiger declared once again that "an infusion of white blood into the Creek does not always make him a good businessman." Many Creeks of mixed descent had little education and "were not able to take care of their property or their homesteads any better than I am or the people of the full blood."[23] The delegates requested that homesteads of all Creeks remain restricted except with the approval of the Department of the Interior. They concluded, "Once a great and noble people, friendly and hospitable to the visiting stranger, our race is run, our sun is set. You have no more great outlying west to which you may push us, as you formerly did, with the assurance that there we may live and prosper 'as long as grass grows and water flows,' and we beg of you to stamp out the practice of greed and avarice prevailing in our country until our citizens reach that advancement that will enable them with advantage to themselves to assume the full stature of American citizenship with all of its attendant advantages and responsibilities."[24]

The delegates were only partially successful in their attempt to conserve remaining Creek lands. In May 1908 Congress lifted restrictions on all intermarried whites, freedmen, and those less than one-half Indian by descent. Restrictions continued on the homesteads of those more than one-half Indian and on all the lands of full-blood Indians until April 26, 1931, except with departmental approval. This legislation did attempt to right wrongs by invalidating the deeds, contracts, mortgages, and powers of attorney made prior to the removal of restrictions. It provided funds for suits to recover the rights of the original allottees, and Creek National Attorney Mott vigorously set about filing those suits.[25]

But the act, which reformers called the "crime of 1908," threw nearly thirteen million acres of Five Civilized Tribes land, now taxable, onto the real estate market, prompting a week-long celebration in Muskogee. And each of the remaining restricted Indians and sixty thousand Indian minor children were declared incompetent, requiring guardians to oversee their property. These guardians were appointed by county courts subject to local political and economic pressures—exactly what Grayson had warned against at the Senate select committee hearing of 1906–1907. Immediately a lucrative, flourishing traffic in the sale of guardianships appeared, as attorneys and other individuals, some of them competent Indians, acquired wards whose estates they could tap for large fees for services rendered. Many Creeks and other Indians found themselves under the control of what one historian has termed a "vast criminal conspiracy" intent on looting their domain.[26]

Another concern of the Creek delegation was continuing the national government. In the absence of real power or election machinery to replace aging or deceased members, the legislatures of the former Indian nations gradually atrophied. But as it became clear that the affairs of the Creek Nation could not be concluded before March 4, 1906, the mandated dissolution date, the Creek National Council had petitioned the Secretary of the Interior for permission to continue its annual sessions. In January

1908 Wash Grayson forwarded another request to convene the council because it served as a clearinghouse for information now that the *Indian Journal,* under new ownership, no longer served as a native press. But occasional council sessions could not revitalize the Creek national government. It dwindled until it consisted of only the principal chief, the national attorney, and the executive office staff—an interpreter (generally Wash Grayson), a secretary, and two stenographers. The chief and his staff, except for the attorney, had little to do except distribute allotment patents and sign warrants while the federal government liquidated the few remaining national assets.[27]

The Creek executive office and delegation had good reason to fear for their national funds. According to the Curtis Act, the Department of the Interior now received and disbursed all Creek revenues. Grayson's old office of national treasurer had ceased to exist. Unfortunately, the federal officials who took over that function spent Creek funds freely with little attempt to keep accurate accounts. As early as 1905 Creeks questioned the handling of their money. Late that year Grayson asked for an official statement of the amount of Creek funds in the federal treasury, the royalties and income raised by the sale of town lots, taxes and names of taxpayers by quarter, and the disbursements of Creek money. It was a reasonable request that Creeks made often during the next several years as they anticipated funding needed to equalize allotment values, but it was one the federal bureaucracy generally ignored.[28]

On one occasion in 1906 Grayson lost his patience with the lack of information provided on the handling of Creek funds. He stiffly reminded the Commissioner of Indian Affairs that "Creeks do not class with that grade of their brothers designated as 'Blanket Indians'" needing constant federal oversight; they were, rather, "sufficiently advanced in civilization to intelligently negotiate important treaties and agreements with the United States and be held as a responsible party." To withhold information on "transactions involving large amounts of their moneys, without consulting them, [was], to say the least, irregular and not in accordance with the usages governing in ordinary civilized methods of business."[29]

Grayson questioned disbursements for roads, Indian depredations, guards, clerks, and office equipment, but especially the sum of $18,735 for suppression of smallpox. He denied that the Creeks had ever requested this type of aid. It was merely a pork-barrel project designed to provide lucrative employment for a few noncitizens who trumped up an epidemic and hoped to profit from the general alarm. Grayson demanded futilely that the Indian Office ask Congress for an appropriation of $83,725 to repay the Creeks for questionable expenditures.[30]

Even this amount was small compared to the extravagant sums spent yearly on Creek schools under federal administration. The education budget doubled the first year federal administrators took charge. Eventually, the Department of the Interior set a very generous annual limit of $105,493, well beyond the $76,468 the Creeks had spent in the last year they controlled their funds themselves. These expenditures, combined with losses on the mismanaged sale of town lots, oil royalties, unallotted lands, and other items, became increasingly important as Creeks contemplated the major residual problem, the equalization of allotment values. It was one to which Grayson, in his role as intermediary and Creek spokesman, gave much attention following the dissolution of his national government.[31]

According to the Creek Agreement of 1901, each citizen was to receive 160 acres. Ideally, if that acreage was prime agricultural land, it would have a maximum value of $1,040, based on the standard rate of $6.50 per acre. If the actual value of a Creek citizen's allotted lands was less than $1,040, the allottee was to receive the difference in cash once the allotment process and the liquidation of Creek national assets were complete. Thus, equalization was intended to assure that each Creek citizen's share of the national estate, whether in land or a combination of land or cash, amounted to $1,040. Toward that end the Dawes Commission prepared census rolls of all Creek citizens as of May 25, 1901, the date of the agreement, listing 15,784 citizens, including freedmen.[32]

In November 1904 the Creek National Council believed there would be a surplus of half a million acres once allotment was completed. Grayson with other Creeks feared this surplus would be made available to homesteaders, thus providing an opening for a further influx of noncitizen speculators. To prevent this, the council passed a resolution asking that all Creek children born up until March 4, 1906—the "newborns"—be added to the Dawes census rolls. Creek officials never formally forwarded the resolution; the delegates apparently passed the idea directly to Congress without going through the usual Creek and federal channels. The Department of the Interior eventually added 1,782 Creek newborns and 1,136 freedmen newborns to the rolls. Still, as of August 1907 J. George Wright, now the Commissioner to the Five Civilized Tribes, reported that 17,924 of the 18,698 Creeks on the rolls had received allotments valued on the average at $661.75. More than two hundred thousand acres remained to be allotted. When the process was complete, remaining Creek funds totaling $6.7 million should cover the equalization of allotments.[33] The process of allotting Creek lands equitably and equalizing the value of the allotments, however, was not to be accomplished so easily.

As early as 1907 the process seemed to the Creeks to be taking too long. Many, particularly the elderly, were land poor and needed the anticipated cash payment. In February 1907 Chief Porter, Grayson, and Samuel J. Haynes told the Commissioner of Indian Affairs they saw no reason why the equalization of allotments should not take place at once. Equalization would "provide nearly all adults . . . sufficient and ready means with which to improve their allotments, thus obviating the necessity of selling land." At the same time it would terminate the Creeks' position "as wards of the government, which under all circumstances is the most desirable thing to accomplish."[34]

But by summer the completion of equalization seemed as far away as ever. Creeks grew impatient, and that impatience turned to alarm as they realized the ease with which their national treasure was flowing through the fingers of federal administrators. In August 1907 the Creek National Council called on the federal government to settle its affairs as quickly as possible, to discard equalization, and instead to disburse the remaining Creek funds on a per capita basis. Commissioner Wright, however, rejected this as impractical because allotment was not yet complete, and the Commissioner of Indian Affairs agreed with him.[35]

In January 1908 Chief Tiger, Johnson E. Tiger, Grayson, and Haynes pursued the council's request in Washington. They told Secretary of the Interior James R. Garfield they were now aware that there would be a shortfall precluding equalization as stipulated in the Creek Agreement, and the passage of time would only increase the deficit. They admitted that a per capita distribution of remaining Creek funds would not be fair to all, but it would "for a considerable time remove from our people the temptations to yield to the blandishments of the unscrupulous land grafter, and quiet the voice of complaint now so rife throughout our country."[36] Grayson was disappointed when another spring session of Congress passed without per capita distribution being incorporated in the latest Indian Appropriations Bill. The federal government, it appeared, was determined to adhere to the policy of equalization even if it dragged on for several years to the detriment of the Creeks.[37]

Having now no control over the expenditure of their own funds, Creek officials tried to find ways to alleviate the shortfall in the meantime. In May 1908 Grayson asked for information concerning the survey of the Creek-Seminole boundary, pursuing possible compensation for seven thousand acres of Creek lands awarded to the Seminoles because of a survey error soon after the Civil War. Chief Tiger strove to cut the expenses of the executive office by dispensing with the usual delegations to Congress. Instead, he left communications with Washington to Mott, the Creek national attorney. In 1907, with the backing of the Creek National Council, Mott filed a number of suits to recover losses from the fraudulent sale of town lots, eventually winning back little more than the $101,000 the suits cost the Creeks. The most popular tactic was to charge that the Dawes Commission had inflated the Creek rolls by adding the "newborns" of the 1901–1906 period, as the Creek National Council did in a resolution on November 25, 1908. It asked that Congress appropriate $4 million to pay the resulting difference needed to equalize allotments as well as to compensate for land taken from the Creeks in the incorrect boundary survey.[38]

The Department of the Interior received this gambit coolly, while Congress continued to insist on equalization. On March 3, 1909, Congress passed an act to pay each Creek allottee $800 provided this settlement was final and conclusive. Chief Tiger called a special session of the Creek National Council to consider the act, but he made it quite clear that he opposed accepting anything less than $1,040 per allottee. The House of Kings unanimously rejected the act; the House of Warriors defeated it fifty to seven. Given his close association with Chief Tiger, Grayson probably supported the chief's hard line on the issue.[39]

The problem of equalization dragged on through the rest of 1909 and 1910. Tiger and Mott (undoubtedly with Grayson interpreting) appeared before Assistant Interior Secretary Frank Pierce in February 1910 to blame the shortfall on the Dawes Commission. Tiger claimed that federal bureaucrats repeatedly denied the principal chief and national attorney access to the Dawes census rolls. Consequently, they did not know until late 1907 that inclusion of the newborns exceeded the resources of the nation. Furthermore, Chief Porter had never signed the resolution whereby the newborns were added to the rolls; the unsigned document was found among his papers after his death in September 1907.[40]

Mott followed the same line of reasoning and suggested that the federal government had an ulterior motive for acquiescing to the addition of the newborns. He charged that Tams Bixby, chairman of the Dawes Commission, was "wholly responsible for this policy" and the department agreed to it on his recommendation. "The only result from it . . . was to give an opportunity for a select coterie of traders who had access to this information to speculate in Freedmen lands without any competition, which speculation included much lands with valuable mineral deposits." Mott was referring to revelations that had resulted in the 1903 Bonaparte Investigation of Bixby and other federal officials. As for the act of 1909 that offered each Creek allottee only eight hundred dollars from Creek funds, Mott concluded, "This Act of Congress . . . proposed to give the Indian what is already his on a condition that he relinquish something else which he is entitled to."[41]

Neither argument carried any weight with Congress or the Department of the Interior. Through 1911 and 1912 Senator Owen and Congressman James S. Davenport of Oklahoma submitted numerous bills (many "by request," or as a courtesy to a constituent) offering various amounts in equalization with optional referral to the federal Court of Claims. Lacking even their sponsors' genuine commitment, they all failed to pass. Meanwhile, Creeks became ever more restless and discontented. In an attempt to trim national expenses Chief Tiger refused from 1909 to 1912 to appropriate the twenty-five thousand dollars necessary to fund a session of the Creek National Council, but in doing so he eliminated the constitutional mechanism by which lines of communication were maintained and consensus established. It was not surprising, then, that some Creeks took matters in their own hands. According to their custom for making important decisions, they called together their leaders to consider all sides of the issues. What the newspapers called a "mass meeting" at Okmulgee that summer of 1912 was their traditional way of dealing with problems. The meeting generated a petition that complained that there was no National Council session at which Creeks could learn what Congress was doing, that they had a chief they had not elected, and that there was a lack of action in concluding their affairs.[42]

For all his economies, Chief Tiger refused to sacrifice one staff position, that of Wash Grayson as executive interpreter. Questioned as to the necessity of this expense, Tiger replied (through Grayson) that he had need of an interpreter "whose thorough competence and reliability is such as is not easily to be had except for liberal pay." Grayson served as his private secretary, ran the executive office when Tiger was ill, and translated his official correspondence because of Tiger's "very imperfect knowledge" of English, the last perhaps stretching the truth.[43] For this Grayson received $125 per month and paid his own expenses for board, lodging, and travel. Consequently, when Tiger went to Washington for the fall session of Congress in 1912, he took Grayson with him in the triple role of interpreter, private secretary, and unofficial delegate.[44]

The 1912 congressional term was no more productive than earlier sessions as far as the Creeks were concerned. Petitions came from dissident Creeks with the suggestion that Chief Tiger's lack of English kept him from fulfilling his responsibilities. They suggested that he be replaced.[45] There were also complaints against Creek National Attorney Mott, whose energetic campaign through the courts against grafters offended many influential people in eastern Oklahoma. By early 1914, when Commissioner of Indian Affairs Cato Sells visited Oklahoma to investigate grafting in the guardianships of Indian minors, Johnson E. Tiger and Samuel Haynes were vocal in their opposition to Mott on grounds ranging from his Republican affiliations to rumors that he had paid Chief Porter one thousand dollars for his initial appointment. Eventually Creek and white complaints resulted in the attorney's being called to Washington to show why his current contract should be renewed. In spite of Sells's and Chief Tiger's support, Mott's opponents won out, and Secretary of the Interior Franklin K. Lane refused to renew his contract, thus removing one of the Creeks' staunchest defenders.[46]

Although Grayson had supported Mott and accompanied Chief Tiger to Washington to stand by their attorney, he professed to see something positive emerging from the confrontation. He wrote from Washington that "thoroughly airing the frauds as practiced by bad men on helpless Indians, minors and others . . . advertised our state in a bad light." Grayson believed the revelations would be a caution to grafters who might think to try the same tactics in the future. Consequently, their new attorney, Richard C. Allen, would "not find it difficult to force people to do the right thing by our almost helpless Indians." If the result was a "benefit to our full-blood Indians," he concluded, "I shall be satisfied."[47]

In fact, Allen's appointment began a productive three-man working relationship involving the chief, his interpreter, and the new national attorney. Tiger and Grayson quickly made it clear to Allen that they gave the equalization issue top priority. At some point during the last several months, someone had suggested that by excluding the freedmen from equalization, enough money would remain to compensate other Creek citizens in full. This suggestion, as well as being a measure of expediency, reflected residual resentment among Indians, especially the Choctaws and Chickasaws, that they must share their national wealth with their former slaves. Tiger and Grayson wanted Allen to pursue this option and to insist that the federal government adhere to the unratified agreement of 1898 with the Dawes Commission. Section 24 of that agreement stated that each freedman should receive 160 acres but no equalization money. The Creeks, they told Allen, wanted to have a council session to discuss this option. Because there was no money to do so, the executive office mailed a ballot to each council member asking, "Do you want the freedmen members of the tribe to share in equalization money now in the treasury?" Whatever the result of the poll, federal officials quickly squelched it on the grounds that the Reconstruction Treaty of 1866 was quite clear on the equal rights of freedmen, later reinforced in a Supreme Court decision, *Whitmire, Trustee v. Cherokee Nation.*[48]

This was the Creeks' last ploy. In 1914 Congress finally attached a provision to the annual Indian Appropriations Act for the equalization of Creek allotments with $800, rather than $1,040, as the standard valuation. The Union Agent reckoned that eligible Creeks, mostly full-bloods and freedmen, were due a total of $1,824,284. Payment was to begin September 1. Allen recommended that federal officials pay only a small deposit to each individual, particularly to Creeks living outside Muskogee

County, site of the Union Agency, and hold the balance. Otherwise, he warned, people would probably spend the whole amount before they reached home.[49] The Department of the Interior attempted to protect restricted Creeks by ruling their equalization money exempt from attorneys' fees, creditors, and check-cashing fees. But it was now nearly a decade since the whole process had begun. Many recipients no longer lived at their Dawes rolls addresses and could not be located; others had died and were now beyond benefit of the payment.[50]

It was perhaps just as well that this last major issue of the national dissolution period was resolved, because by 1914 Chief Tiger's days of effective leadership were over. Like Wash Grayson, he was into his seventies. But while Grayson was still as mentally vigorous as ever, Tiger was, according to critics, "superannuated."[51] There were complaints in the spring of 1914, some politically inspired by disgruntled council members, that Chief Tiger was "inefficient, incapable, and remiss of duty." They sent a resolution to President Woodrow Wilson asking that he be replaced by a younger man fluent in both English and Muskogee, informed as to the wishes of the Creek people, and able to cope with their problems.[52] Former Creek Attorney Mott, a close associate of Chief Tiger's for years, testified, "In the matter of integrity and truth, I regard him as a man above reproach. He is of a gentle character, sympathetic, responsive to appeals; and he is timid in the matters of turmoil and strife, likes to avoid them."[53] This he said of the man willing to cast the single assenting vote on allotment in 1894. But by 1914 the elderly chief, always somewhat dependent on Wash Grayson as his interpreter and counselor, was overwhelmed by contending forces and demands beyond his present capacity.

Nothing was more indicative of this than the controversy swirling around Creek National Attorney Allen in 1915. Allen was typical of the ambitious young men who came to the Indian Territory at the turn of the century to make their fortunes. Originally from North Carolina, he began practicing law in 1902 in Coweta, Creek Nation. Eight years later the young Democrat was elected judge of the Third Judicial District of Oklahoma, comprised of booming Muskogee and Wagoner Counties. But Allen was also a member of the Coweta Realty Company and an acknowledged grafter said to have been named in seventy-three suits involving Creek lands. Among white residents in the territory, grafting was not necessarily regarded as an evil during that first tumultuous decade of statehood, but Allen's involvement in the Martha Verner McKinley incident was particularly scandalous. Knowing that restricted minors automatically received the patent to their surplus lands when they married, Allen allegedly supplied a groom and a marriage license for fifteen-year-old Martha Verner's elopement, provided a forged parental permission for the ceremony, and then promptly bought her eighty-acre surplus for a small fraction of its considerable value. Unfortunately, this case was typical of the times, and it was exactly what Wash Grayson had hoped to prevent in fighting to maintain restrictions.[54]

In spite of Allen's blemished past, Mott recommended him as his replacement as Creek national attorney, and the Department of the Interior and President Woodrow Wilson approved Allen's contract. Through the first year of his tenure he energetically worked through the county probate courts to correct some of the same sorts of abuses he had committed earlier. In doing so he, like Mott, made some powerful enemies in eastern Oklahoma. His contract came up for renewal in the spring of 1915 about the same time simmering discontent among Creeks intensified.[55]

While Creeks with the appearance, experience, and education of Wash Grayson were prepared to blend into white society and its institutions, the traditionalists, particularly full-blood Creeks, felt they had no access to Oklahoma's social and political structure. For nearly a decade federal Indian policy had also denied them the choice of their own leaders, the convening of their National Council, control over their affairs, and direct communication with Washington through their council-elected delegates. They were ripe for the manipulation of Allen's enemies.

According to Wash Grayson's account, he was in the Creek executive office in Muskogee, Oklahoma in April 1915 when Allen presented Chief Tiger the document renewing his contract. It was nearly three months early, but Allen said he wanted to adjust his work schedule according to whether he would be retained. Tiger hesitated and asked Grayson his opinion, but Grayson refused to advise the chief on the renewal. They dropped the matter for about ten days until Allen again presented Tiger his contract. Grayson and the chief then sat down privately, and Wash translated a few lines at a time until they had worked through the whole document. He noted Tiger's objections on a separate sheet, and when they were finished Tiger discussed and worked out his concerns with Allen. Still, Grayson insisted, he refused to comment on the contract even to former attorney Mott. "I told him I was not going to give any advice; that the Chief would have to do his own work."[56]

Grayson was stunned on his next visit to the Creek executive office in Muskogee to hear from Allen that Tiger had rejected the contract in a telegram and letter to the Department of the Interior. Tiger explained to Grayson that David M. Hodge and Samuel W. Brown had come to him with news of a proposed mass meeting at which Creeks planned to protest Allen's work and reappointment. Grayson knew both men well as fellow council members and Hodge as a fellow Creek delegate and interpreter. Both were Union veterans and representatives of the old Loyal Creek faction with its strong traditionalist ties. In addition, Brown, a merchant, rancher, and hereditary chief of the Yuchee Creeks, and his son Samuel W. "Billie" Brown, Jr., were heavily involved in Creek Nation real estate and oil leasing. Between them, they held powers of attorney or were guardians of a number of Creek, Seminole, and freedmen allottees, some of whom had lands with valuable mineral rights. Hodge and Brown had supplied Chief Tiger the letter and telegram by which he had rejected Allen's contract renewal.[57]

Now Allen, Tiger, and Grayson discussed this situation as well as the attorney's pending cases. They again reached agreement on the contract, and at Tiger's request Grayson wrote a second telegram and letter in Allen's favor and sent them off to Washington. Grayson thought the matter was finished, but two weeks later Chief Tiger again canceled the contract.[58]

While the chief vacillated, several peculiar telegrams arrived at the Department of the Interior. All contained basically the same wording, all were sent on April 28 or 29 in the early hours of the morning, and all carried the same message: that Chief Tiger was too hasty and Allen's reappointment should be delayed pending the arrival of further information from the sender. All the telegrams purported to be from full-blood Creeks. One was signed by Billie Bruner, a well-known former member of the House of Kings who was fluent and literate in English and Muskogee. Bruner subsequently inquired of Commissioner Cato Sells why the Washington office wired an acknowledgment of a telegram he never sent.[59]

Two weeks later with the Allen issue still unresolved, Saty (Sarty) Cowe, a Creek traditionalist, called a mass meeting for May 12 of those dissatisfied with the equalization settlement. However, the discussion focused not on equalization but on the Allen reappointment, criticism of Chief Tiger, and his possible replacement. A protest against Allen's reappointment and a petition demanding an investigation of his work circulated through the crowd. Later several signers, including Cowe, denied that they had ever endorsed more than a call for an investigation. In reaction, on May 21 letters from a number of leading Creeks and former council members— Timmie Fife, G. W. Stidham, Jr., Cheesie McIntosh, George M. Carr, William McCombs, Wash Grayson, and Billie Bruner—expressed complete confidence in Allen and his ability to withstand an investigation. They discounted the recent petition and suggested that the whole controversy was the work of oil men threatened by Allen's suits on behalf of the Creeks.[60]

At the end of May the understandably confused Office of Indian Affairs dispatched Chief Inspector E. B. Linnen to investigate the chaotic situation in the former Creek Nation. Linnen was less than objective. His findings on Allen's earlier career as a grafter probably led him to expect the worst from Allen supporters, including Wash Grayson. On May 27 he called together in Tulsa Chief Tiger, Hodge, Brown, Mott, and a handful of others. Notably absent was Tiger's usual interpreter, Wash Grayson. Hodge, an Allen opponent and author of the first rejection letter and telegram, presumably translated. Tiger told Linnen "he was induced and prevailed upon by Captain G. W. Grayson" to execute Allen's contract, but he revoked it after hearing that people objected to the attorney. He claimed that at a later meeting with Grayson and a number of other prominent Creeks in Muskogee, he was again "induced and prevailed upon by Captain G. W. Grayson principally" and by Allen to withdraw his rejection. Otherwise, they told him, the Department of the Interior would lose confidence in him and Allen would be appointed anyway. Tiger signed, he said, against his better judgment.[61]

Linnen also took testimony from Allen, who defended his early land deals as common practice in eastern Oklahoma. He attributed the resistance to his reappointment to several wealthy and influential men in the oil and gas business—Tulsa oil baron and philanthropist Charles Page and his March Oil Company partner R. A. Josey of Prague, Oklahoma, along with O. A. Morton, Will Morton, and Walter Morton, the last three being merchants and professional guardians of Creek minors.[62]

Others verified Allen's charges and elaborated on the roles of these men in the murky business climate of the former Creek country. One of Allen's defenders related how Page, who got his start in the oil business in the Glenn Pool in 1905, and Josey were involved in the Creeks' attempt to recover the Tommy Atkins allotment. Many believed the allotment to have been fraudulent because there was doubt that Tommy Atkins, supposedly a deceased minor, had ever existed. Page had more than a passing interest in the oil-rich allotment and employed Yuchee Creek Chief Samuel W. Brown as a "go-between" to negotiate drilling leases with several people claiming to be Tommy's "heirs." The Creeks lost their suit, but the implications of the litigation so embarrassed Page and Josey that the former stated before witnesses his intent "to get Allen's scalp." Josey declared he was willing to pay to see Allen ousted. According to the Allen defender, it was Josey and H. C. Walkley, a Page employee and "grafting Cherokee," who had circulated the questionable petition at the mass meeting of May 12.[63]

The former editor of an Okmulgee newspaper maintained that the Mortons, owners of a large store in the old Creek capital, were "guardians for hundreds of Indians, to whom they sell goods at their own price. . . . Allen was the first Creek attorney that had the nerve to tackle them." The Mortons' influence over traditionalist Creeks was such that they would "be able to get them to sign most any kind of document they wish."[64]

Allen was antagonizing the Mortons further, another witness wrote to Sells, by suing for the recovery of the Katie Fixico allotment. An impoverished, illiterate minor orphan, Katie had received an allotment in the Cushing Oil Field. O. A. Morton purchased it for $2,200. By 1915 it was producing eight thousand barrels a day and was worth half a million dollars. "Is it any wonder that Page, Josey, and the Mortons desire Allen's removal?" the Allen defender asked. If he were removed, who would replace him to continue the suits on behalf of victimized Creeks such as Katie Fixico?[65]

Billie Bruner (the "one and only William Bruner" as he described himself), a less biased observer, summarized the situation in a letter to

Commissioner Sells: Allen had incurred the anger of "the grafters and the land-grabbers who infest this country, among whom are many white men, some so-called prominent Indians, and in some instances, some of the courts, or Judges of Courts."[66]

But Inspector Linnen seemed less interested in these allegations than in exploring the relationship of Allen, Mott, and Grayson with Chief Moty Tiger. On May 31, before he even took testimony from Mott and Grayson, the federal investigator wired Sells that he had talked with Hodge, Brown, and Tiger, who told "of wrong influence used to send that telegram which Grayson wrote for Allen. I have the facts correctly on all these matters."[67]

A week later, on June 7, Linnen took affidavits from Grayson and former Creek Attorney Mott. The line of questioning made it quite clear that he believed these men and Allen exercised undue influence over the elderly Chief Tiger. While Linnen implied no purpose for that influence in the case of the two attorneys, he angled toward a motive for Grayson: Tiger's interpreter and counselor wished to be chief and needed Allen's support to win approval from the Department of the Interior.[68]

Mott testified that Tiger had told him the previous winter in Washington that he was considering retirement because of his fading vision. "The Chief and I both through my service have relied on Captain Grayson, especially the Chief, having more confidence in him than any other member of the Tribe, and I think properly so, have thought so," Mott stated, "but later he changed his mind about resigning I suppose. . . . I suggested . . . Captain Grayson would make a good chief for the tribe." Mott explained that he mentioned this to Allen, who also agreed that Grayson would be a good and deserving choice. But, Mott guessed, Tiger now favored his son Johnson as his successor if he intended to retire at all.[69]

Linnen took the same line of questioning with Grayson, pointing out that Tiger was old and feeble. He asked if Grayson had aspirations to succeed him. Grayson denied that ambition or that he had ever proposed himself to the chief as his successor. Although he had not discussed the matter with Allen, he supposed the attorney would support him should the topic of his becoming chief arise. Grayson admitted he had told Mott, "I would like it very well."[70]

On the second day of testimony, Linnen was more specific. "Is it not a fact that Mr. Mott told you that Attorney Allen had said that he, Allen, would hold up Chief Tiger's resignation and not present it to the Secretary of the Interior unless the Secretary was in favor of appointing you Chief?" Grayson answered no, although he agreed that Chief Tiger was easily influenced and that he could usually sway him. Grayson also denied knowledge of Allen's land deals or his present suits.[71]

Grayson did admit that he had expressed to Commissioner Sells his concern over the petitions circulating among the Creeks, saying these were typewritten papers containing statements naive Creeks accepted as facts. Outsiders also hired Indians to solicit signatures, and Creeks who knew no better signed petitions to oblige them. Grayson could name no names, he said, but he believed the grafters were after Allen. He concluded, "The air, it may be said, is almost saturated with a report; if that can be called gossip, why then this must be gossip."[72]

Again Linnen questioned Grayson about his ambition to be principal chief. Grayson insisted any discussion of his succeeding Tiger was quite casual. "There was something said that if the old gentleman would resign I might take his place. As I said before, that would be all right with me, but I have never done anything or had any extended conversation with anyone on the subject and never have thought much about it."[73]

If Linnen was attempting to prove that Grayson was manipulating the old chief in collusion with Mott and Allen, he failed to do so. All three denied it, and other witnesses, none of whom were strictly unbiased, contributed little of substance. Linnen's investigation was inconclusive, but it fueled the rumors circulating through the Creek country.[74]

Public and private speculation was that Chief Tiger would soon resign and that Grayson would become chief. This provoked mass meetings in Muskogee and Wetumka, Oklahoma, to reach consensus on what should be done. The Muskogee protesters, about half of them full-blood according to observers, called for Tiger's resignation but split over support of Allen.[75] The Wetumka meeting, organized by Saty Cowe and composed largely of traditionalist Creeks, produced a letter to Commissioner Sells redolent with their sense of helplessness and abandonment. They understood the agitation as the "Half Breed and Oil people Element" attempting to replace Tiger with Grayson. They wanted Tiger removed; but, Cowe wrote, "G. W. Grayson . . . has no real interest of the creek people and is some what too old in age. [We] wish to say that the Department is to day dealing with Full-Bloods as they have by legislature and rullings practicly has rulled [*sic*] out the Negroes and Half breeds but are still clinging to us Full Bloods and therefore we would like the privileges of nameing [*sic*] the best man who would have at heart the Full Bloods like us . . . we are fallen to the mercy of other power."[76]

The uproar attracted Commissioner Sells's personal interest. On June 25 he ordered Tiger to come to Washington immediately and insisted that Tiger bring Grayson as his interpreter. The problem was in locating Tiger. When Grayson arrived at the Muskogee office on June 23, he discovered Samuel Brown and Ben Grayson had taken the old man away and got him drunk. They had induced the chief to sign an attorney's contract with Allen's rival, Judge Thomas Leahy, and then spirited him away to Tulsa. According to Grayson, he followed them there and found the whole group, now including Hodge, intoxicated. He took Tiger away to prepare for the trip to Washington, but on June 29 Secretary Lane ordered Grayson and Tiger to wait in Oklahoma until summoned.[77]

Complicating matters further, telegrams in Tiger's name—sent on June 25 when the old chief was, according to his office, out of contact on his farm near Okmulgee—begged Senator Robert L. Owen and the Indian Rights Association to stop the Allen reappointment and to intercede with the Department of the Interior.[78] The Indian Rights Association in fact sent S. M. Brosius, a veteran of Creek country troubles, to investigate. He talked to Chief Tiger and found him "clear headed and sober [which] set at rest some of the stories I had heard regarding his conditions and habits."[79] But the interpreter during this visit was Samuel Haynes, a leader of the anti-Allen faction.[80] One might question whether Haynes, who had asked Grayson to translate for him in Washington in 1907, interpreted the conversation accurately and without bias.

By the end of June the affair reached the Oval Office when Tiger (or someone claiming to be Tiger) complained to President Wilson. Secretary Lane preferred to treat the matter lightly in response to Wilson's inquiry: "Moty Tiger . . . is not as anxious to see me as I am to see him. On Friday last I wired him to come here that we might consult, but he got drunk so that I have had to send a special officer to bring him here; expect him tomorrow unless the officer also gets drunk." Lane explained about the conflicting communications and put Tiger's erratic behavior down to senility. As for Allen, Lane wrote, "I think the chief trouble with him is that he has brilliant red hair and goes about things in a redheaded fashion, but I shall be careful in the matter."[81]

With Commissioner Sells out of town, Lane took over the investigation and summoned all parties concerned to Washington for a hearing on July 14. On the evening before their departure one of Allen's cronies overheard Hodge pressure Chief Tiger to use him rather than Grayson as his interpreter. Apparently Tiger agreed, for the next day Linnen, Tiger, Grayson, and Hodge left for Washington on the Katy Flyer, probably a very uncomfortable group of traveling companions.[82]

At the hearing Allen acquitted himself well enough to persuade Lane to renew his contract, and when Grayson returned home the document was on its way to President Wilson for his signature. Even then the intrigue continued, for as late as July 28, Moty Tiger denied supporting Allen. Tiger (supposedly) wrote to Lane, "Since my return from Washington, I have been told that Mr. Grayson, who interpreted for me before you, did not correctly state my remarks to you. At no time during our conference did I state that I favored R. C. Allen as Creek Attorney or desired his appointment."[83]

Out of this fog of charge, denial, countercharge, and retraction, one can draw some conclusions. Sadly, Chief Moty Tiger had lived beyond his usefulness to his people. His moral courage and judgment had weathered away with age and ill health, leaving a confused and vulnerable old man. Allen's enemies used his bewilderment to undermine the Creek attorney. But it is also probable that Inspector Linnen was correct: Mott, Allen, and Grayson were influencing the chief's decisions.

Those decisions, however, no longer carried the import they had even in Chief Porter's day. Tiger presided over the remaining Creek national estate, but as of 1916 this consisted of the Council House in Okmulgee, 2,495 acres of unallotted land, 168 town lots, and 4 boarding schools. Unfinished business included 450 undelivered allotment patents, continuing payment of equalization money, and cases of fraudulent or duplicate allotment that might yet yield revenue to the Creeks. The real work of the executive office fell to the attorney as he contended with these matters and with the grafters.[84] Although Wash Grayson had once aspired to be chief, the title was now more honorary than real. He did not covet Tiger's position in 1915 as he had Porter's in 1903, and at seventy-two he could not realistically expect to succeed him.

Tiger's growing incompetence was not a problem under normal circumstances. The federal government had assumed the major responsibilities of Creek government in 1906. Allen performed his work energetically if not always productively, with Mott still an informal advisor. Grayson was there to lead Tiger through the smaller tasks and to handle his official correspondence, out of the genuine respect he retained for the Moty Tiger he remembered. The shortcoming in this system was the failure of the principal chief to maintain effective contact with his scattered people and to reassure them that his office was still doing its best to guard their interests. Then again, perhaps these functions were beyond the power of any principal chief by 1915.

Problems arose when the machinations of Allen's enemies—the petitions, the protests, the forged telegrams, and the rumors—exacerbated the discontent of those who still had a stake in national affairs, the restricted Creeks. At the same time, the importunity of Allen's enemies and the attempts of Grayson, Mott, and Allen to keep the old man in line with the will of the federal government exposed Chief Tiger as gullible and ineffective. Had there been a real need for competency in the Creek executive office at this time, this controversy would surely have resulted in Tiger's removal from office.

But Moty Tiger, unfit or not, was allowed to keep his office for two more years. This suggests, first, that the chieftaincy was so empty of consequence that the Department of the Interior saw no reason to fill it with a more capable man. Secondly, although Allen's reappointment was important enough to some eastern Oklahomans to drive them to forgery and conspiracy, the Department of the Interior paid little real attention to their vehement protests or to the appeals of reliable Creeks for caution. In fact, the department never made public the findings of Inspector Linnen's investigation and refused to answer Oklahoma Congressman Davenport's inquiries concerning it. This may have been because Allen appeared to be satisfying the critics' demand for prosecution of the grafters. It may also have been because he was, after all, a loyal Democrat during Democrat Woodrow Wilson's administration. On the other hand, it demonstrated considerable official tolerance of a man of questionable integrity. Everyone involved, including Grayson, knew of Allen's earlier career as a grafter. Yet the Department of the Interior, over continuing Creek protests, approved his contract not only in 1915 but again in 1916. If nothing else, this demonstrates once again the federal government's decades-old lack of concern for the sincere opposition of the Creeks to its policies and actions.[85]

Lastly, the retention of Tiger as principal chief suggests that the department was well aware that it was not he but Wash Grayson who handled matters in the Muskogee executive office. Sells had insisted on June 25 that the chief and Grayson come to Washington, not that the chief come with an interpreter. And whatever Tiger's wish, it was Grayson rather than Hodge who interpreted for him at the Washington hearing. Wash Grayson had forty years of experience dealing with Washington, but Washington also had forty years of experience dealing with Wash Grayson. In his final report to President Wilson on the Allen affair, Secretary Lane indicated that it was "Captain Grayson, a member of the Creek Nation, and a very fine man," who served as intermediary between Tiger and the department.[86]

Evidence of official familiarity between the Office of Indian Affairs and Wash Grayson lay in the commissioner's defense of him in the face of criticism from Five Civilized Tribes Superintendent Gabe Parker in 1916. The interpreter's expense accounts, Parker noted, exceeded those not only of other tribal officers but also of Chief Tiger.[87] Sells replied, "Mr. Grayson is a man of quiet habits and . . . he is not given to incurring unusual or heavy expenses under ordinary circumstances."[88] More to the point, perhaps, Grayson was just the type of competent, progressive Indian Sells hoped to see emerging from the wardship of the federal government. It was not at all surprising that he was willing to allow the Creek interpreter extra latitude.[89]

Items listed in Grayson's expenses demonstrated that he was more than just the chief's interpreter—he was also an unofficial delegate. He received the standard per diem of four dollars for out-of-state travel and three dollars for in-state travel, as well as telephone service, postage, and trolley tickets. The only item that Sells disallowed was a two-month subscription to the *Congressional Record*, which Grayson, now in his seventies, read rather than attend each day's session.[90] In April 1915 Sells granted permission for Grayson to move his official headquarters from Muskogee to Eufaula in response to Allen's explanation that "a great many full blood Indians live in the vicinity of Eufaula, where Captain Grayson now lives and has lived all his life, and that it is necessary to use him at that point the greater part of the time."[91] People throughout the Creek country viewed Grayson as the "real chief" even though Moty Tiger still held the title.[92]

Grayson also came to see himself as the primary spokesperson for the Creeks in such affairs as remained. He and Tiger spent several weeks in Washington in the spring of 1916. Grayson wrote his son in early March that the chief would leave for home shortly to look after his private affairs. "So," Grayson concluded, "I presume I will soon be the only one here to watch our business, still his going away will not change any of the conditions here, as I have already been in effect the only one to watch our interests even though the old gentleman has been with me all the time."[93]

Grayson's duties allowed him to live in Eufaula and to commute by train on a regular basis to Muskogee for conferences with Chief Tiger and Allen. This allowed him to oversee his lawn, flower beds, tree plantings, garden, and chickens as well as attend to his remaining farmland. He could also indulge in his avocation, reading and writing history. Wash Grayson, the mediocre student at Asbury, had developed through the years into a self-educated scholar. On the east side of his home on Jefferson Avenue was a detached, one-room building that housed his library. A slanted writing surface ran along each wall, bisecting shelves for books from floor to ceiling. Most of his volumes were histories, and Grayson often lamented that he could not afford to buy as many rare old books as he wished.[94]

Here Wash Grayson found privacy to read and write. He had planned for some time to compose a history of the Muskogee people from their perspective to help preserve their culture and nationhood, but he completed another project first. At the urging of his children he wrote an autobiography between 1905 and 1912. It dealt primarily with his Civil War experiences, only sketching in his career as a Creek official. His writing was both a habit and pleasure. As early as 1889 Grayson had formed the habit of carrying a pocket diary in which he noted the details and impressions of his days. During twenty years he filled more than forty little volumes, scarcely missing a day and providing a very rare insight into the events affecting the Creek people from 1898 to 1917.[95]

The Grayson home on Jefferson Avenue in Eufaula. Note the detached library on the right. Courtesy Western History Collection, University of Oklahoma Library.

Grayson enjoyed discussing his views in the Informal Club, of which he, Alex Posey, John N. Thornton, and George Reilley Hall made up the total membership. They were all literary men; Posey and Thornton had been editors of the *Indian Journal,* Hall was editor of the *Henryetta Free-Lance,* and Posey and Hall were both poets. They met to discuss literature, Creek politics, and history whenever Hall came to town, but it was hardly a solemn gathering. They smoked cigars, joked, and perhaps had a drink or two, for on one occasion Thornton joked that Grayson had become "unduly intoxicated."[96]

Grayson conferred more seriously with linguist and missionary Anne Eliza Worcester Robertson on Muskogee orthography and linguistics and swapped Civil War reminiscences with Creek Union veteran and poet Judge James Roane Gregory. As early as the 1880s Grayson was interested in the work of anthropologists, particularly those at the Smithsonian Institution. While serving as a delegate to Washington, he provided information for Albert S. Gatschet's study of Creek migration.[97] On his visit to the Wichita Agency at Anadarko in 1889, Grayson took notes on his Kiowa and Wichita hosts for ethnologist Major John Wesley Powell. At the turn of the century, he contributed an article on Opothle Yahola to Frederick Webb Hodge's *Handbook of American Indians*. Beginning in 1911, anthropologist John R. Swanton came to the Eufaula area several times to study Creek culture. The Graysons opened their home to him, introduced him to other knowledgeable Creeks, and so facilitated his work that he labeled his "Social Organization and Social Usages of the Indians of the Creek Confederacy" a memorial to George Washington Grayson.[98]

The Grayson house was, in fact, rarely empty of visitors, whose sojourns lasted from a few days to several months. Besides Swanton, family tradition holds that Patrick Hurley, a Choctaw citizen and future ambassador to China, stayed with them. So did a number of aging relatives and young people on their own, such as Rosa Marshall Whitlow and Thomas Gilcrease, a Creek orphan whose allotment in the Glenn Pool helped make him a Tulsa oil tycoon and noted art collector. The Graysons maintained a proprietary and sentimental interest in Eufaula Boarding School, and on Sunday afternoons its young ladies regularly took over the Grayson parlor and kitchen to play the piano and bake treats. Annie usually served meals, including Anglo-American foods as well as *sofky* and the grandchildren's favorite blue dumplings, in a dining room that seated shifts of fifteen— the men first, the women next, and the children last. Official visitors, friends, relatives, children, and grandchildren were welcome at Wash and Annie Grayson's house. Rarely did Wash and Annie Grayson sit down to a meal alone, and such hospitality was occasionally wearing.[99]

All four of the Grayson children who survived into adulthood lived nearby in Eufaula. Lena Grayson Sanger died at age twenty-two, leaving two small children, but Walter Clarence became a Eufaula businessman. Washington, the Graysons' second son, pleased his father by graduating from West Texas Military Academy and rose from third lieutenant to captain in the Philippine Constabulary before returning to Eufaula. The Graysons supported education for women and provided the best they could for Eloise and Tsianina. After their marriages, Eloise Grayson Smock and Tsianina Grayson Fuller built homes on either side of their parents' house. Consequently, their children considered their grand-parents' home an extension of their own. They saw Grandfather Grayson as a stern-faced old gentleman who spoiled them, especially Walter Clarence's daughter Lenore (Nonie) and Tsianina's children Grayson (Gracie) and Mildred (Millie Mitiwohli) Fuller. One of Mildred's first memories was of holding onto her Grandfather Grayson's leg while he and Mr. Swanton strolled around the garden discussing Creek history.[100]

All of the Graysons took active roles in Eufaula's social life. Social occasions were typical of most small towns of the day: literary discussions, musical evenings, card parties, picnics, and garden parties, in addition to a traditional Creek event, the fishkilling. In her husband's absence, Annie Grayson made a full life for herself with her home, church work, sewing circles, and the Masonic ladies' auxiliary. Oddly enough, the only social organization in Eufaula Wash Grayson did not join was the Masonic Lodge founded by his father-in-law G. W. Stidham. Grayson was for many years Sunday school superintendent of the First Baptist Church but frequently walked out the dusty road to the West Eufaula Creek Baptist Church, where his friend Jackson Lewis was a deacon and the services were conducted in the traditional Muskogee way.[101]

In their life-style Wash and Annie Grayson and their children stood at one extreme of the spectrum of Creek culture, at first glance indistinguishable from their white neighbors. A census taker near the turn of the century noted that the "average Indian" had little property and desired little more than a few head of livestock, a few acres to grow corn for *sofky*, and a small log home. But he might well have been describing the Wash Grayson family when he wrote that the "educated Indians" lived according to their own tastes and means, "in good houses and enjoy the comforts of civilized life, are courteous, social, and hospitable in their intercourse with strangers." Then he added an important qualification to that seeming acculturation: "[B]eneath it all exists a pride of lineage and zealous admiration for the peculiar institutions of their people."[102]

The ability of this subgroup of Creeks to blend into the new order without losing their grasp on the old was particularly important as the new century brought statehood and an even greater in-migration of non-Creeks. Eufaula began to lose its character as an "Indian town" and became more typical of the rest of southeastern Oklahoma. While Wash Grayson, like most Creeks, did not take an active role in local politics after statehood, he retained an interest in the development of the town he helped found. In 1905, when Checotah ten miles up the Katy railroad tried to lure away the county seat, Wash joined Alex Posey, Jackson Lewis, and Charles Gibson in rallying the Indian vote through a Muskogee-language article in the *Indian Journal.* The county seat along with its economic benefits stayed in Eufaula. Having become a temperance man by 1910, Grayson protested against the lax enforcement of prohibition in the former Indian Territory that allowed three or four saloons to operate openly in Eufaula. His letter of protest to Governor Charles N. Haskell, an old acquaintance from Muskogee and the Sequoyah Constitutional Convention days, and the governor's concurring reply were, as usual, printed in the *Indian Journal.*[103]

The pattern as well as the character of the town also changed. White merchant C. E. Foley built a mansion on Chintz Mountain, and towns-people renamed it Foley's Mountain. Grayson Avenue was renamed for white entrepreneur J. C. Belt. Automobiles made their appearance about 1902, and the business district shifted a block west from the railroad to flank present U.S. Highway 69, which generally paralleled the old Texas Road. The McIntosh County Court House moved the center of gravity still another block west. Grayson Brothers' old store site on the east side of the tracks became a commercial backwater while imposing new brick and sandstone business buildings testified to the importance of newcomers to the town.[104]

These were Anglo-American families from Missouri, Arkansas, and Alabama, and they brought a distinctly southern flavor to Eufaula. Among other things, they organized a camp of the United Confederate Veterans and its various auxiliaries. Annie Grayson became a member of the United Daughters of the Confederacy and, using material gathered from her father and husband, wrote papers on the Indian nations' Civil War. Continuing to honor the warrior tradition, Wash joined the United Confederate Veterans and eventually rose to brigadier general of the Creek Brigade of the Indian Territory Division. He accompanied other Confederate veterans as they finally marched into Washington for their reunion in 1917. Thus, as the Muskogees always had, Wash and Annie Grayson built on Creek history and experiences to find middle ground with Eufaula's newcomers.[105]

Although the new character of Eufaula was increasingly southern and white, the Graysons, for all their association with their new neighbors, did not abandon their Creek identity. Annie encouraged Wash's ambition to write his history of the Creeks and helped him edit his work. So great was her contribution that Grayson dedicated his manuscript to her. Annie shared his sense of injustice as well as his pride in being Creek, and like him, she refused to be anything else. According to a family story, about 1918 some of her Stidham relatives who had moved to California invited her to come out for a visit. Annie packed her bags and was ready to leave when a note arrived. Her hosts advised her that because being Indian was not socially acceptable in California, she should not mention her Creek ancestry while visiting there. Annie, according to her granddaughter Mildred, tore up the letter, unpacked her bags, and refused to have any further contact with Stidhams who had forgotten they were Muskogees.[106]

Wash Grayson maintained his ties to his fellow Creeks publicly and privately. His official duties, of course, kept him in contact with traditional Creeks who did not speak English or understand white ways. For them he interpreted Anglo-American culture and law as well as language. He was at home on the ceremonial grounds, where he enthusiastically cheered his side in the stick ball games and washed his face with the black drink *vsse passv* at the Green Corn Festival still held each July. In participating in these ancient ceremonies, he differed from many Creek Christians, who shunned them as backsliding into heathenism. Federal officials, too, disliked the tribalism associated with such events, but Grayson defended them to Commissioner Sells. He respected the old ways enough to give each of his children a Muskogee name and to see that his son Washington received his war name, Katsa Tustunuggee, for his military service just as he had received his own for his Civil War experience.[107]

Whether in public documents, private correspondence, or in print, Wash Grayson lost no opportunity to recall the richness of the Muskogee heritage and to underscore the tragedy of Muskogee history. One of the most fitting occasions came in 1913 when the Rodman Wanamaker Expedition visited Oklahoma. Wanamaker, the son of retailer John Wanamaker, intended to preserve the culture and memorialize the history of the American Indian, a people he feared was fast vanishing. He financed three information-gathering expeditions led by Dr. Joseph K. Dixon. The expedition of 1913 made its way through the homelands of several Indian tribes, rallying support for the construction of a marble and bronze monument to be erected in New York Harbor. Accompanied by two photographers, two motion-picture cameramen, and a *New York World* reporter, Dixon traveled across Oklahoma in mid-June. Among the Creeks invited to join Dixon aboard his special train for the ride from Muskogee to Okmulgee was Wash Grayson.[108]

Dixon inquired if there was someone who could speak to him about Creek history. In describing the incident afterward for the *Indian Journal,* Grayson employed a literary device, introducing "an old Creek Yaha Tustunuggee by name," who had been chosen to select the one "great event, the most momentous, the superlatively conspicuous object, fact, or occurrence" in all Creek history. His speech was vintage Grayson. "The old native," as he described himself, began with the arrival of Hernando de Soto and his Spanish adventurers—"robbers thirsting for gold and gore"— among a Muskogee people "hospitable, honest, generous, and strictly truthful." There followed a chronology of unremitting white covetousness, deceit, and malice usually disguised as the imposition of a "better" civilization in place of traditional ways. Grayson recounted the conversion of many Creeks to Christianity, the adoption of a written constitution and laws, the establishment of schools to provide Creek young people with English education, the creation of homes, farms, and businesses—in short, all he had once supported as a progressive Creek nationalist.[109]

But these, Yaha Tustunuggee told Dixon, had not insured just treatment from Anglo-Americans, who rather had insisted the Creeks give up self-government and their traditional communal landholding system in spite of treaties guaranteeing their sovereignty. Whites who "by their acts taught the Creeks nothing good, but the exact reverse," helped destroy all the Creeks had accomplished and created among them "disrespect and disgust for civilized methods." Casting the Creeks in a heroic mold, he repudiated the idea that they were a vanishing people: "[T]ho' battered and bruised, we find them still in the ring, erect and in the midst of the struggle, and determined to win out despite all the sinister conditions and negative influences thrown athwart their pathway by misguided hands. . . . The present advancement of the Creeks in the ways of civilization," Yaha Tustunuggee concluded, was "the one stupendous monument standing out more gloriously conspicuous to their credit than any memorial of marble or bronze."[110]

Even at seventy-four, Wash Grayson was one of those "still in the ring." By 1917 there was little left of the Creek government; yet enough official business remained that when Moty Tiger left the chieftaincy Grayson was named his replacement. Federal records no longer shed light on the circumstances under which the transition occurred, but it is probable that the intrigues of 1914–1915 continued and Tiger was forced to resign. As of July, *Harlow's Weekly*, an Oklahoma City journal, reported that Richard C. Allen had been granted another year's contract as Creek national attorney over the opposition of Charles Page and "other big men of that section."[111] In a telegram dated October 5, 1917, Moty Tiger denied that he had either resigned or recommended Grayson as his successor, and he urged the Department of the Interior to delay any action on the Creek executive office. Yet Grayson received a presidential appointment on November 13 and signed the oath of office on November 27, 1917.[112]

Grayson found this latest development ironic; the principal chief of the Creek Nation was now just another federal employee. He carefully filled out a personnel form on which he noted his level of experience: "Do not recall any time since I have been of man's estate when some tribal responsibility did not rest upon me." As evidence of his qualifications for the position he wrote, "Having been born and reared among the Creeks of the full blood class, and been in intimate relations with them all these years, I believe I have an all-around knowledge of them that enables me to understand and manage them better than some others." While he claimed to be an expert linguist in Muskogee, he denied any skill as a clerk or typist. Quizzed about his musical ability, he answered tongue in cheek, "Can perform creditably well on the Jewsharp, but have not cultivated the art assiduously."[113]

Most of the major issues that so concerned Grayson early in the century were long since resolved. There were still many suits against grafters to be prosecuted, but that was the province of Allen and James C. Davis, Allen's assistant, who succeeded him as Creek national attorney. Of the 18,761 enrolled Creeks, 8,556 remained restricted, their homesteads inalienable and nontaxable until 1931. Many also had equalization funds held in trust by the federal government. Most agreed with Grayson that this state of affairs should continue for their protection; however, he dutifully forwarded the petitions of those who wanted their restrictions lifted. When the Competency Commission visited the Creek country in the summer of 1918, he explained its mission to his fellow Creeks to quiet their fears as he had explained the negotiations with the Dawes Commission to them twenty years earlier.[114]

Grayson also presided over the disposition of the Creek Council House in Okmulgee. No longer needed for council meetings, it housed Okmulgee County offices until a new court house was constructed in 1917 (financed through bonds bought by Katie Fixico's guardian with her money). Then Grayson leased it to the Red Cross during World War I. Evaluated by Sam Grayson and W. H. Aingell at sixty-five thousand dollars, the old sandstone building increased in market value, according to Wash Grayson and Field Clerk Eldon Lowe, to one hundred thousand dollars as the town boomed with exploitation of the Okmulgee Oil Field. While it was painful for Grayson to oversee the sale of the capitol to the City of Okmulgee in 1919, he was intent during his chieftaincy on seeing the Creeks realize the full value of their assets. The sale price would be distributed to those Creeks he felt had been shortchanged in the equalization of their allotments.[115]

More important to Grayson than either of these matters was the Creek-Seminole boundary issue. According to the Reconstruction Treaty of 1866, the Creeks ceded to the federal government the western half of their territory, a parcel of which the Seminoles bought to replace their forfeited reservation. In 1871 federal surveyor Frederick W. Bardwell established the north-south line marking the Creeks' western boundary with the Seminoles. One year later another federal surveyor, E. M. Darling, working in the Sac and Fox Reservation north of the Seminoles, placed his markers too far east for the length of the Bardwell line, encroaching into Creek territory. Another survey perpetuated this error, and it stood until the United States Geological Survey of 1895–1896 reestablished the Bardwell line as correct. In 1906 Commissioner W. A. Richards of the General Land Office said that the error in fact existed the length of the western Creek boundary from Township 11 North to 19 North, Range 6 East, embracing in all 5,575.57 acres in present Lincoln and Pottawatomie Counties (see map 4).[116]

From the time of the original survey, Grayson and other Creek officials periodically sought redress from the Seminoles or from the federal government. The matter had never been resolved even though Grayson conferred with the Seminoles as late as 1899 with the knowledge of Commissioner of Indian Affairs Ethan A. Hitchcock. That official so strongly supported the Creeks' case that he drafted a bill recognizing the error and asking thirty thousand dollars to compensate them. But J. George Wright, Commissioner to the Five Civilized Tribes at Union Agency, said his office had no knowledge of any such claim, and Congress failed to act. Grayson unsuccessfully revived the issue in 1908 while trying to replenish Creek funds before equalization of allotments took place. By then the error had created an intimidating legal tangle: Some of this Creek land had already been homesteaded in the earlier land runs while other parts had been allotted to Seminoles. The state had been taxing portions of it in error for years. Some of it overlay rich oil fields, increasing its value far beyond the original assessment.[117]

As principal chief, Grayson took the matter to Commissioner Sells in December 1918. Sells obliged Grayson by asking his office to investigate, but the information was so slow in coming that Grayson instructed Creek National Attorney James C. Davis to pursue it. The dilatory response of the departmental bureaucracy and Davis's own press of business prevented action for more than a year. Grayson grew impatient.[118] In January 1919 Davis tactfully urged Sells to immediate action as he wrote, "I think the Captain feels that this is an instance in which he can be of real service to the people of the Creek Nation, and he desires to take advantage of the opportunity thus afforded him . . . he has the matter very much at heart . . . because of a zealous desire upon his part to perform some active duty that will result beneficially to the members of his tribe."[119]

Nothing more happened before mid-May 1919. Grayson habitually traveled by train to Muskogee the first and fifteenth of each month to attend to business at the Creek executive office. This time he arrived a day early and found the entire staff away at a competency hearing. He spent the night in town but decided to return home the following morning because he felt ill. While waiting for his train at the Katy Depot he suffered a stroke. He insisted on going home to Eufaula, and by the time he arrived paralysis affected his right side. The stroke was so severe few expected him to recover, but four days later when Davis visited him, he found Grayson alert, cheerful, and optimistic, his speech only slightly impaired.[120]

During the weeks of his recovery, the Creek-Seminole boundary issue receded again into bureaucratic obscurity. However, Grayson showed the same determination to have it concluded that he demonstrated in his rehabilitation. He never completely recovered the use of his right arm and leg, and for the remaining eighteen months of his life he walked with a cane as he tended his garden and went about his affairs. But he refused to give up writing and taught himself to use a typewriter when wielding a pen proved too frustrating. By July he was able to resume his visits to the Muskogee office, and his most pressing concern remained the boundary claim. It was, Davis wrote repeatedly to the commissioner, the topic nearest his heart. Unfortunately, Sells's office insisted in February 1920 that the staff found no records of any such claim.[121]

But a new issue, that of Grayson's successor, soon supplanted it. In the summer of 1920 some Creeks foresaw in Grayson's recent illness the possibility of a vacancy in the office of principal chief. With that in mind, Grayson, in the traditional Muskogee way, called together Creek leaders to advise him regarding a successor in the contingency of his resignation or death. While executive duties involved little now except signing payroll warrants, the chief influenced the choice of national attorney. And as the Allen controversy demonstrated, the diligence and dedication of that attorney in prosecuting the suits of the nation or of individual Creeks were important to a number of prominent Oklahoma businessmen. At that moment Davis was continuing a suit begun by Allen to recover the suspected duplicate allotment of Hettie Lena, an oil property so valuable the nation had been offered seventy-five thousand dollars to settle out of court.[122]

Late in June 1920 Grayson decided to resign. He told his brother Sam that his inability to get around and visit his people frustrated him. Besides, there was so little to do he felt he was being paid for nothing. Grayson then tendered his resignation to President Woodrow Wilson and suggested Jefferson Canard or Louis Dunzy as his successor. They were, he believed, honest men, fluent in English and Muskogee, and satisfactory to their fellow Creeks.[123]

Grayson's action energized those with vested interests in the chieftaincy. Applications for the position arrived in Washington within days. Partisans backed a number of candidates and tarred opponents with charges of grafting. Superintendent Gabe Parker eliminated Dunzy. Eastern Oklahoma

Democrats led by powerful Senator Owen backed William Porter, son of the late Pleasant Porter. Republicans supported George W. Hill and, once Warren G. Harding won the presidential election that November, tried to prevent any further action until after he took office. Most of the controversy surrounded Grayson's candidate, Jefferson Canard. Former Creek National Attorney Allen objected to him because his brother Felix was a well-known grafter, while present National Attorney Davis upheld Canard and questioned the meddling of former national attorneys Mott and Allen. Once again the Creek people, with no sanctioned National Council session in which to seek consensus and with limited access to the federal bureaucracy that managed their affairs, resorted to mass meetings and petitions.[124]

The agitation over Grayson's successor startled the Department of the Interior. Unfortunately, among the complex and far-reaching affairs of the federal government, Creek views and problems were of negligible consequence. Sam Grayson spoke for many when he asked the department to delay any decision. Sam's interest was purely personal. He knew that his brother's main concern was bringing the affairs of the Creek people, particularly the Creek-Seminole boundary claim, to a successful conclusion. Speaking for the Grayson family, Sam asked that his brother retain his office until that problem was solved. For whatever reason, the department refused to accept Grayson's resignation, and the issue of his successor continued to agitate the Creeks.[125]

This latest affair demonstrated a development that Grayson recognized with regret. In addition to the pride he took in Creek "progressiveness," he had always esteemed the Creek people for their ancient traditions, beliefs, and values. He admired their bravery, patriotism, generosity, hospitality, integrity, and tolerance—qualities Anglo-Americans held up as the "civilized," Christian ideal but, in his opinion, failed to exhibit themselves. Now Wash Grayson, who subscribed to prevalent racist attitudes, believed this controversy illustrated that the mingling of the *este Mvskoke* with those of African and European descent—the "contamination resulting from association with other races and peoples," as he called it—had been detrimental to the Creeks.[126] Some, particularly mixed-blood Creeks, had become so like the whites in their acquisitiveness and materialism that they did not hesitate to victimize fellow Creeks through grafting. It was a bitter reality that traditional Muskogee values were no longer universal among the people. Those who clung to traditional ways felt alienated and power-less, abandoned by those who had learned to live in the white world. The result was more factionalism and acrimony as partisan groups struggled to control the vestigial Creek executive office for their own interests.[127]

With the problem unresolved, Wash Grayson died on the afternoon of December 2, 1920. As the news spread throughout the Creek country, Creek and white friends came to Eufaula to pay their respects. That many traditional Creeks came on foot and by horseback from miles away testified to their regard for Chief Grayson. By Saturday morning hundreds were encamped near the house on Jefferson Avenue. Annie set aside her private grief and, according to Muskogee custom, prepared food for them. Then the Creeks buried their chief among his family and friends at Greenwood Cemetery in Eufaula, on a pleasant cedar- and elm-shaded hillside overlooking the North Canadian River.[128]

Even as the funeral took place, mourners speculated as to who would replace Grayson as principal chief. It was indicative of the atmosphere that one of the tributes paid to him hinted at this issue. Richard C. Allen wrote to Commissioner Sells, "I have never known a man, white or red, in whom I had greater confidence than Capt. Grayson. If ever a man lived a godly life, he did. During his life time he held many offices in the Creek nation and for fifty years has been regarded as one of the most conscientious, devoted and learned members of the Tribe." Then Allen pressed his point—the nomination of his son Washington Grayson would "certainly be a credit to the Tribe, as well as a deserving recognition of the long and faithful service of his father."[129]

After several weeks of contention and controversy, of charge and countercharge by the candidates and their backers, the Department of the Interior made its own selection for its own reasons. Washington Grayson became principal chief of the Creek Nation. He had served honorably in the Philippine Constabulary for five years, had risen to the rank of captain, and had gained experience in the civil and military administration of several large Philippine provinces. On his return to Eufaula he had served as secretary to Chief Moty Tiger until 1917. He volunteered for duty during World War I, served with distinction in France, and on his promotion to major became one of the two highest ranking Indian officers overseas. In spite of the fact that Major Grayson did not speak Muskogee and had spent much of his adult life away from the Creek country, the administration presumably believed these experiences qualified him for the position.[130]

That he was not a part of the current factionalism perhaps worked in his favor as far as the federal government was concerned. The Office of Indian Affairs made its decision after conferring only with Superintendent Parker in Muskogee. What the Creeks wanted was not a prime consideration. However well or ill Washington Grayson performed in the office, he illustrated the distance of federal officialdom from the Creek people and their powerlessness to change it.

Wash Grayson had understood that distance and, through his role as a cultural broker motivated by Creek nationalism, had done all he could to secure Creek interests and rights in spite of it. First he fought to maintain the integrity of the Indian Territory until the barriers fell in 1889. He fought to sustain Creek sovereignty until the formal dissolution of the nation in 1906 and then carried on from within the vestigial executive office. He fought for the communal Creek landholding system until allotment replaced it, and then he fought to help individual Creeks keep their lands under the new system. He fought for the maximum equalization of allotments, and when Creek funds proved insufficient, he fought for ways to make up the difference. With so many battles lost and hopes destroyed, no wonder he was bitter when he reflected on his life as a Creek Indian in a white man's world.

Writing his history during World War I and near the end of his life, Grayson, still a Creek nationalist, pointed to the hypocrisy he saw in the Anglo-American's treatment of Indians: While they condemned Germany for trampling on the rights of weaker nations, white Americans behaved just as savagely toward "the poor and the weak" Indian. He concluded, "[W]ithout some general awakening of the public conscience of the people of the United States in the interest of common justice toward the red man, there appears to be little prospect of his ever coming into his own." Then, perhaps, he summarized his own life: "Like true patriots and true men, we battled long and well in the unequal contest finally losing out."[131] For Wash Grayson, who was also Yaha Tustunuggee, the long struggle was finally over.

CHAPTER EIGHT

Nevertheless Intensely Indian

In *Between Indian and White Worlds* (1994), Margaret Connell Szasz and other historians describe the importance of the individuals who emerged as intermediaries during five centuries of contact between American Indians and Euro-Americans. These intermediaries, often interpreters, traders, teachers, or diplomats by occupation, served both sides as cultural brokers. They traversed and illuminated frontiers of language, custom, and belief, shaping and being shaped by cross-cultural tensions.[1] George Washington Grayson belonged to that category of American Indians. He shared most of their traits and added a unique twist to one.

First, he was of mixed descent, a trait common to cultural brokers and one which facilitated the exposure to different cultures needed to generate understanding. In his case, dual cultural exposure began with his traditional Muskogee education and continued during his English education in the missionary schools of the Creek Nation. Then as a sixteen-year-old he was eager to go on to Arkansas College and gained much from his stay there, exhibiting two of the American Indian cultural broker's characteristics: curiosity about Anglo-American culture and the diligence needed to learn to function within it.

Cultural brokers, according to Szasz, must have the trust of both peoples. Wash Grayson's long political career demonstrated the trust placed in him by the Creek people. They repeatedly elected him to the Creek National

Council, while they also sent him to Washington, D.C., as a delegate, named him a member of the Committee of Prosecution in the Payne trial, and designated him their representative to the Okmulgee and Sequoyah Constitutional Conventions. In the chaotic post–Civil War period, the Creek Constitutional Party selected him to negotiate with Spahecha's faction. Later, he became a close friend and confidante of Spahecha, his former political enemy. In the late nineteenth century other tribes asked him to represent their interests in Washington and to do for them what he did for his own people. On the other side, the federal government learned to value Grayson in the 1800s and relied on him to manage Creek affairs in the 1900s after the dissolution of the Creek national government. In a time of increasing political corruption, only rarely was his integrity called into question by either side. Over six decades, he earned the reward of the cultural broker, honor for his service and respect for his knowledge.

Wash Grayson found many ways to mediate between the *este cate*, or "red people," as he called his people in the Muskogee language, and the *este hvtke*, the Anglo-Americans. As a young Confederate Creek officer he kept records and translated orders and saw them executed, oiling the machinery of a multilingual, multiethnic army. In his first political position as clerk to Principal Chief Samuel Checote, he handled the chief's correspondence and drafted diplomatic documents with other nations. As national treasurer of the Creek Nation, he was responsible for managing and disbursing funds for a people in transition from the barter system to a metal currency–supported market economy. As a member of the *Tvstvnvk-kvlke*, the House of Warriors, for many terms, he represented his *tvlwv*, at the same time he helped Creeks create and operate their version of republican constitutional government. Most importantly, through his leadership in the Indian Journal Printing Company, he led Creeks in using a new form of mass communication to understand and shape their world and the wider world beyond their borders.

From the House of Warriors, of course, Wash Grayson went on to other services, most importantly that of delegate to Washington. There it was his responsibility to be familiar with all federal legislation affecting the Creeks and to present the Creek perspective on that legislation to congressmen, the Department of the Interior, the president, and anyone else who would listen in order to maintain the status quo of the Indian Territory.

Not only did he work with federal officials, he also rallied the "friends of the Indian." Through personal contacts and the written word, he lobbied for Anglo-American public support of the Creek Nation. That done, at the end of each congressional session he went home to the Creek country to explain legislative developments in far-off Tvlwv Hvtke and the possible ramifications for the Creek Nation. If his service began with the interpretation of language, it continued through the interpretation of manners, behavior, beliefs, history, and policy.

Unlike some cultural brokers, Wash Grayson experienced no crisis of identity in spite of his mixed descent. From his birth, his membership in Koweta *tvlwv* and the Tiger clan established his place in the Creek community, a place reinforced by his service with the Confederate Second Creek Mounted Volunteers. His English education, rather than alienating him from the Creek community, drew him closer because it enhanced his value to the constitutional government dominated by progressive Creeks. They knew the worth of one of their own who could explain their perspective and defend their rights in the halls of Congress. And fighting beside and working with representatives of other Indian peoples on occasions such as the Okmulgee Convention and the Payne trial also fortified his sense of being Indian. He came to understand that the Indian nations had common interests and faced a common threat. Consequently, he shared the dual identity—Indian as well as national—that emerged in the face of Anglo-American aggression in the post–Civil War Indian Territory.

While these factors reinforced his bonds with the Creek and broader Indian communities, what he knew of the white man repelled him. History was a useful tool to the Creeks, part of every child's education and a tool that would later be employed in decision making and attaining consensus. From the stories his grandfather told him of Andrew Jackson and Horseshoe Bend to his own study of the laws and treaties affecting Indians, Wash Grayson found little to admire in the white man's behavior. That his own hair was red-brown and his skin fair was an embarrassment rather than a source of pride, though he was not above making use of his "white" appearance and ancestry to gain advantage.

When comparing Wash Grayson to other American Indian cultural brokers, it becomes obvious that he placed his own twist on one trait they had in common. Like them, he was receptive to some aspects of the alien culture and strongly advocated the adaptation of those he found useful. In his case, though, this was not simply an attempt to find common ground between different peoples. He identified himself with the "progressive" Creeks politically and philosophically in his support of constitutional government, English education, Christianity, and economic advancement, but he aimed toward parallel rather than convergent development. His motivation was nationalistic. He was genuinely devoted to the Creek Nation and saw pursuing these changes as the best way to strengthen and preserve Creek sovereignty.

Even though Wash Grayson chose a life-style that incorporated many aspects of white culture, he did not place himself outside the bounds of the Creek community by doing so. He knew that Creek culture was not a narrow stream; it was a broad river, constantly shaping and being shaped by the terrain over which it flowed. Creeks traditionally borrowed from other Indian cultures and from Euro-Americans—not only food, clothing, tools, and livestock, but also language, music, and religious beliefs. What they borrowed, they made their own by recasting, overlaying, and incorporating it into their Muskogee world. Wash Grayson's adaptation of white educational, economic, and political forms was as traditional as it was nationalistic. By demonstrating their "progressive" nature, or as Chief Joseph Perryman termed it, their ability to achieve a "higher civilization," Creeks stood a better chance of maintaining their sovereign status. It was Wash Grayson's role as a cultural broker not only to explain to Anglo-Americans the transition that was taking place in the Creek Nation of the late nineteenth century, but also to exemplify it. At the same time, he pointed his fellow Creeks in the direction he believed they must go. Only by changing could they continue to be Creek.

If nothing else, Wash Grayson's life demonstrates the breadth of Creek culture and the strength of Creek identity. He lived in a time of accelerating transition that saw the Muskogee culture expand to incorporate printing presses, gold watches, cotton gins, railroads, telephones, overalls, political barbecues, camp meetings, and graduation exercises. By Statehood Day, Creeks were real estate brokers, newspaper editors, teachers, lawyers, and Christian ministers as well as subsistence farmers tilling *sofky* patches and hunting game in the backcountry. In 1908 Creeks understood columnist Charles Gibson's joke when he said that Muskogees must truly be a vanishing race: there were only three hundred Graysons left. Although Wash Grayson saw the dissolution of the Creek Nation, he knew he did not witness the disappearance of the Creeks as a people. Like him, they simply went on being Creek while they learned to function as citizens of the new state of Oklahoma.

Nearly a century later the Creeks have dual citizenship, and the Muscogee (Creek) Nation operates under the Constitution of 1979 from its new capitol complex in Okmulgee, Oklahoma.[2] Today university administrators with terminal degrees participate in ancient square ground ceremonials. Nurses, accountants, and social workers may shun the same ceremonials but travel many miles on Sundays to worship in traditional Creek Christian churches where the songs, sermons, family ties, and community are Muskogee.

The observer looking for the "wigwams, robes, feathers, and vermillion" that Wash Grayson considered obsolete in 1877 may fail to recognize these modern Creeks, just as observers at the turn of the century failed to see past his gold-rimmed glasses, starched collar, and white beard to the Creek nationalist underneath. American Indian novelist Louis Owens notes that Americans have a "strangely concrete sense of what a 'real' Indian should be. . . . [W]oe to him or her who identifies as Indian or mixedblood but does not bear a recognizably 'Indian' name or physiognomy or lifestyle."[3] Owens goes on to quote Karen I. Blu, who has pointed out that same tendency of Americans to believe that "it takes a lot of Indian blood to make a person a 'real' Indian."[4]

Wash Grayson is a classic refutation of that misconception, a major reason he is worth remembering today, when the question "Who is an Indian?" still generates so much debate. Along with demonstrating the role of the cultural broker, Wash Grayson exemplifies the strength and flexibility of Creek identity that allowed a mixed-blood like him to think of himself as an *este cate*—a "red man"—and to assume the leadership of the Creek Nation. Creeks of his day accepted without question the Wash Grayson they knew—merchant, rancher, newspaper publisher, and scholar as well as Tiger clan, Koweta *tvlwv*, and *tvsekiyv*. And they knew he spoke from the heart when he said, "While fortune and circumstances have placed me in some respects in advance of some of my fellow-countrymen, I am nevertheless intensely Indian."[5]

Abbreviations

ADC   Angie Debo Collection, Special Collections, Edmon Low Library, Oklahoma State University, Stillwater, Oklahoma

AR CIA   *Annual Report,* Commissioner of Indian Affairs, Department of the Interior

AR DI   *Annual Reports of the Department of the Interior for the Fiscal Year Ended June 30, 1901,* U.S. House of Representatives. Department of the Interior. Indian Affairs. 55th Cong., 3rd sess., 1898.

ARP   Alice M. Robertson Papers, Special Collections, McFarlin Library, Tulsa University, Tulsa, Oklahoma.

CCF   Central Classified File, Part 1, Indian Office, Department of the Interior, National Archives, Washington, D.C.

CNR   Cherokee National Records, Oklahoma Historical Society, Oklahoma City, Oklahoma

CRN   Creek National Records, Oklahoma Historical Society, Oklahoma City, Oklahoma

FCT   Five Civilized Tribes, National Archives, Department of the Interior, Office of the Secretary, Indian Office, Record Group 75, file 5-1

GFC WHC   Grayson Family Collection, Western History Collection, University of Oklahoma, Norman, Oklahoma

GFC GI   Grant Foreman Collection, Gilcrease Institute of American History and Art, Tulsa, Oklahoma

GFC OHS   Grant Foreman Collection (collection number 83-229), Oklahoma Historical Society, Oklahoma City, Oklahoma

GI   Gilcrease Institute of American History and Art, Tulsa, Oklahoma

I-PH   "Indian-Pioneer History," Works Progress Administration, Western History Collection, University of Oklahoma, Norman, Oklahoma

ITD   Indian Territory Division, Department of the Interior, Record Group 48, National Archives, Washington, D.C.

LR OIA   Letters Received by the Office of Indian Affairs, 1824–1881, U.S. Bureau of Indian Affairs, Record Group 75, microfilm

LR WS   Letters Received by the Western Superintendency, Records of the Southern Superintendency of Indian Affairs, U.S. Bureau of Indian Affairs, 1832–1870, Record Group 75

NA   National Archives, Washington, D.C.

OHS   Oklahoma Historical Society, Oklahoma City, Oklahoma

PC   Phillips Collection, Western History Collection, University of Oklahoma, Norman, Oklahoma

SBMC   Samuel Bell Maxey Collection, Gilcrease Institute of American History and Art, Tulsa, Oklahoma

SFC   Stephen Foreman Collection, Western History Collection, University of Oklahoma, Norman, Oklahoma

WHC   Western History Collection, University of Oklahoma, Norman, Oklahoma

Notes

CHAPTER 1. DRIVEN UP THE RED WATERS

1. George Washington Grayson, untitled manuscript.

2. Photograph number 1116, Smithsonian Anthropological Archives, Museum of Natural History, Washington, D.C.

3. Interview of Eloise Grayson Smock, "Indian-Pioneer History," Works Progress Administration, Western History Collection, University of Oklahoma, Norman, Oklahoma, microfiche (hereafter cited as I-PH, 85:369).

4. G. W. Grayson, untitled manuscript.

5. Ibid.; W. David Baird, *A Creek Warrior for the Confederacy: The Autobiography of Chief G. W. Grayson*, 8–9.

6. John R. Swanton, "Social Organization and Social Usages of the Indians of the Creek Confederacy," 307; Morris Edward Opler, "The Creek 'Town' and the Problem of Creek Indian Political Organization," 171.

7. Opler, "The Creek 'Town'," 165–171; Angie Debo, *The Road to Disappearance: A History of the Creek Indians*, 4–5.

8. Opler, "The Creek 'Town,'" 171; Joel W. Martin, *Sacred Revolt: The Muskogees' Struggle for a New World*, 49–50. The *tvlwv* were divided into "red" and "white" towns, each group having special ceremonial responsibilities. Historians debate the importance of this division, its impact on Creek politics, and whether their powers continued after the Creeks were removed to the Indian Territory. Grayson certainly knew of the division and probably discussed it with anthropologists, but he never referred to it in any of his known writings. See particularly Duane Champagne, *Social Order and Political Change: Constitutional Governments among the Cherokee, the Choctaw, and the Creek*, 20–25.

9. Swanton, "Social Organization," 297–298; Champagne, *Social Order and Political Change*, 20–25; Linda Alexander, interview by author, Stillwater, Oklahoma, October 9, 1996; Ted Isham, interview by author, Stillwater, Oklahoma, October 9, 1996.

10. Patricia Galloway, *Choctaw Genesis, 1500–1700*, 322–323; Michael D. Green, *The Politics of Indian Removal: Creek Government and Society in Crisis*, 7–8. See also Richard Allen Sattler, "Seminoli Italwa: Socio-Political Change Among the Oklahoma Seminoles Between Removal and Allotment, 1836–1905," 44–60.

11. Opler, "The Creek 'Town'," 174–175; Martin, *Sacred Revolt*, 49–50; Swanton, "Social Organization," 67, 168–169, 228, 306; Debo, *The Road to Disappearance*, 14; *The Indian Journal* (Eufaula, Oklahoma), December 15, 1911.

12. Swanton, "Social Organization," 323; John R. Swanton, *The Indian of the Southeastern United States*, 652–653; J. Leitch Wright, *Creeks and Seminoles: The Destruction and Regeneration of the Muscogulgee People*, 101–127; Champagne, *Social Order and Political Change*, 37–38.

13. Vernor Crane, "The Origin of the Name of the Creek Indians." In Grayson's day, general opinion was that the Creeks were so named because they lived along the water courses. Grayson disputed this theory, pointing out with some logic that most Indians found it convenient to live near water. Grayson, untitled manuscript. Swanton, "Social Organization," 323–327; Green, *Indian Removal*, 11–13.

14. Green, *Indian Removal*, 17–20. A good account of the Creeks' transformation to commercial hunting and its impact on their society is Kathryn E. Holland Braund, *Deerskins and Duffels: Creek Indian Trade with Anglo-America, 1685–1815*.

15. See James H. Merrell, *The Indians' New World: Catawbas and Their Neighbors from European Contact through the Era of Removal*.

16. Louis W. Ballard, "Cultural Differences: A Major Theme in Cultural Enrichment," 6.

17. Wright, *Creeks and Seminoles*, 60–61; William C. Sturtevant, ed., "Commentary," 40–47.

18. Galloway, *Choctaw Genesis*, 322–323; Michael D. Green, "Alexander McGillivray," 42–43; Braund, *Deerskins and Duffels*, 147.

19. See also Jacqueline Louise Peterson, "The People in Between: Indian-White Marriage and the Genesis of a Metis Society and Culture in the Great Lakes Region, 1680–1830," and Jennifer S. H. Brown and Jacqueline Louise Peterson, eds., *The New People: Being and Becoming Metis in North America.* Peterson, Brown, and others, building on the foundation laid by Marcel Giraud in *Le Metis canadien: son role dans l'histoirie des provinces de l'Ouest* (1945), held that children of French and Native American parents became a "new people," a hybrid of the two races. They based their conclusions on the language, livelihood, settlement patterns, religion, kinship patterns, and art forms which differentiate the parents from the metis descendants. The main institution around which the metis

culture developed was the fur trade, usually dominated by the Hudson's Bay Company or another such monopoly. Canadians considered these metis neither white nor Native American, contributing to their sense of isolation and political discrimination. This, in turn, strengthened their sense of racial identity and political self-awareness.

20. Martha Condray Searcy, "The Introduction of African Slavery into the Creek Indian Nation"; Daniel H. Usner, Jr., "American Indians on the Cotton Frontier: Changing Economic Relations with Citizens and Slaves in the Mississippi Territory," 305–306.

21. Green, *The Politics of Indian Removal,* 54.

22. Ibid.

23. Don Martini, *Southeastern Indian Notebook: A Biographical-Genealogical Guide to the Five Civilized Tribes,* 61. Hawkins did not list Katy among Grierson's children, so one must assume that she was born after his initial visit. C. L. Grant, ed., *Letters, Journals and Writings of Benjamin Hawkins,* 1:15, 17–18; Baird, *A Creek Warrior,* 17.

24. Grant, *Writings of Benjamin Hawkins,* 1:13–15, 234–235, 301.

25. R. David Edmunds, *Tecumseh and the Quest for Indian Leadership,* 151–152.

26. Champagne, *Social Order and Political Change,* 116–117. See Martin, *Sacred Revolt.*

27. Debo, *The Road to Disappearance,* 78–80.

28. Grant, *Writings of Benjamin Hawkins,* 2:651–653; Interview of Mildred McIntosh Childers, I-PH, 17:414.

29. Grant, *Writings of Benjamin Hawkins,* 2:651–652.

30. Ibid.; Martin, *Sacred Revolt,* 142; Baird, *A Creek Warrior,* 17.

31. Debo, *The Road to Disappearance,* 80–81; G. W. Grayson, untitled manuscript; Baird, *A Creek Warrior,* 23–24.

32. Debo, *The Road to Disappearance,* 82–83; Green, *Indian Removal,* 43; Daniel F. Littlefield, *Africans and Creeks: From the Colonial Period to the Civil War,* 90–91.

33. Green, *The Politics of Indian Removal,* 76–78.

34. Ibid., 54–55, 81–91; Benjamin W. Griffith, Jr., *McIntosh and Weatherford, Creek Indian Leaders,* 46–47, 86–87.

35. William McIntosh married three times. His daughter Jane by Eliza Grierson married Samuel Hawkins, Eliza's nephew. McIntosh's daughter Rebecca by Susannah Rowe married Samuel's brother, Benjamin Hawkins. Samuel and Benjamin were sons of Sarah Grierson Hawkins, older sister of Eliza Grierson McIntosh. Harriet Turner Porter Corbin, *A History and Genealogy of Chief William McIntosh Jr. and His Known Descendants,* 84–86, 91. This book was endorsed by Creek Principal Chief Dode (Waldo Emerson) McIntosh. Debo, *The Road to Disappearance,* 88–90; Green, *Indian Removal,* 87–88.

36. Baird, *A Creek Warrior,* 26; Interview of George McIntosh, I-PH, 58:319–338; Interview of Richard Lewis Berryhill, I-PH, 7:434–440; Green, *Indian Removal,* 96–97, 122–125, 138–139, 148–153.

37. Charles J. Kappler, ed. *Indian Affairs: Laws and Treaties*, vol. 2, *Treaties*, 341–343; Green, *Indian Removal*, 171–173.

38. Kappler, *Laws and Treaties*, 2:343.

39. Debo, *The Road to Disappearance*, 99, 102–103; Green, *Indian Removal*, 174–186.

40. Debo, *The Road to Disappearance*, 104.

41. Ibid., 102, 105–106.

42. Ibid., 109–110; Kappler, *Laws and Treaties*, 2:388–391.

43. John W. Morris, Charles R. Goins, and Edwin C. McReynolds, "Indian Territory, 1830–1855," Map 23 in *Historical Atlas of Oklahoma.*

44. Debo, *The Road to Disappearance*, 109–111.

45. Ibid., 100–103; Depositions of Artus-Micco, Chewastie Yohola, and George Shirley in Colonel Ethan Allen Hitchcock, "Report on Frauds on Immigrant Indians," 528–530.

46. Debo, *The Road to Disappearance*, 84–85.

47. See the Catawba example of traditional education and the importance of history in the formation of an individual's identity in Merrell, *The Indians' New World*, 261–265.

48. G. W. Grayson, untitled manuscript.

CHAPTER 2. THE GRASS ON THE ISLAND

1. North Fork Town and its low-lying environs were submerged under Lake Eufaula in the early 1960s. As will be discussed in chapter 4, present-day Eufaula, Oklahoma, about a mile further west, replaced North Fork Town in the 1870s as the population center for the area surrounding the confluence of the Canadian and North Fork rivers.

Sam Grayson died in 1925. Pilot Grayson, a teacher and businessman, died in 1895. Malone, a Vanderbilt University alumnus, physician, and rancher, died in 1881. Louisa married Charles S. Smith; she died in 1928. James, Jr., died during the Civil War. Mildred Fuller Ewens, interview by author, Eufaula, Oklahoma, March 13, 1990; Inscriptions, Greenwood Cemetery, Eufaula, Oklahoma; W. David Baird, *A Creek Warrior for the Confederacy: The Autobiography of Chief G. W. Grayson*, 32.

2. Daniel Newnan McIntosh did not emigrate until 1830. Harriet Turner Porter Corbin, *A History and Genealogy of Chief William McIntosh Jr. and His Known Descendants*, 91; Interview of Joe Grayson, "Indian-Pioneer History," microfiche (hereafter cited as I-PH), Works Progress Administration, Western History Collection (hereafter cited as WHC), 33:445.

3. The Kowetas lived in the vicinity of Koweta Mission, located in the northwest quarter of Section 18, Township 17 North, Range 16 East of the Indian

Meridian. Chief Roley McIntosh also lived in this neighborhood. Muriel H. Wright and LeRoy H. Fischer, "Civil War Sites in Oklahoma," 212. John R. Swanton, "Social Organization and Social Usages of the Indians of the Creek Confederacy," 105; Baird, *A Creek Warrior*, 28–29.

4. U.S. Senate, Statement of G. W. Grayson, "Report of the Select Committee to Investigate Matters Connected with Affairs in the Indian Territory with Hearings, November 11, 1906–January 9, 1907," 59th Cong., 2nd sess., 1906–1907, *Senate Reports*, vol. 4, Indian Territory Affairs, 682.

5. Baird, *A Confederate Warrior*, 30.

6. It was not unusual for citizens of the Five Civilized Tribes to occupy land within the boundaries of a neighboring nation, although it sometimes created jurisdictional problems. In 1857 Katy Grayson was listed on the roll of "Various Towns of Creeks in the Cherokee Nation." Roll of Lower Creek Towns, 1857 Self-Immigrant Census, box 48, R5, Grant Foreman Collection, Gilcrease Institute of American History and Art, Tulsa, Oklahoma (hereafter cited as GFC GI). Harold O. Hoppe, "The Family of Robert Grierson and Sinoegee" (genealogical chart); Baird, *A Creek Warrior*, 32–33.

7. Emathla Hutke as a child was called Un-ah-yoh-ky; Johnnie in childhood was called Tsah-nu-tsee or "Little John." An untitled genealogical chart of the descendants of In-fak-faph-ky and Mary Benson (Enola Shumate Collection, WHC) contains some generational inaccuracies but agrees with Grayson's names for his great-uncles. Baird, *A Creek Warrior*, 21–22, 25; *The Indian Journal* (Eufaula and Muskogee, Creek Nation), February 27, 1878.

8. George Washington Grayson, untitled manuscript.

9. Muriel H. Wright, *A Guide to the Indian Tribes of Oklahoma*, 54–55.

10. Quoted in James H. Merrell, *The Indians' New World: Catawbas and Their Neighbors from European Contact through the Era of Removal*, 261.

11. Ibid., 261–264. See also David Michael Lambeth, *The World and Way of the Creek People*.

12. Baird, *A Creek Warrior*, 33; U.S. Senate, Statement of G. W. Grayson, "Report of the Select Committee," 682.

13. Baird, *A Creek Warrior*, 34.

14. Mildred Fuller Ewens, interview by author, Eufaula, Oklahoma, October 9–10, 1989. Several references to the "camp-hunts" appear in issues of *The Indian Journal* (Eufaula and Muskogee, Creek Nation) in the 1880s and 1890s.

15. See chapter 4. According to local historian James E. Carey, of Eufaula, Oklahoma (telephone interview, March 17, 1991), one of Grayson's childhood homes, much altered, stood until 1990 in the northeast quarter of Section 6, Township 9 North, Range 16 East of the Indian Meridian. Baird, *A Creek Warrior*, 33–34, 36.

16. Angie Debo, *The Road to Disappearance: A History of the Creek Indians*, 88; Baird, *A Creek Warrior*, 32–33.

17. Agent James Logan to Commissioner of Indian Affairs William Armstrong, September 20, 1845, Department of the Interior, Commissioner of Indian Affairs, *Annual Report, 1845*, 516 (hereafter cited as AR CIA and year); "Retrospect of the Life and Character of Napoleon Bonaparte Moore," *The Muskogee Nation*, Oklahoma Historical Society, Oklahoma City, Oklahoma (hereafter cited as OHS); Henry R. Schoolcraft, *Information Respecting the History, Condition, and Prospects of the Indian Tribes of the United States: Collected and Prepared under the Bureau of Indian Affairs*, 1:265–280; Stephen Foreman, diary entry of April 20, 1863, Stephen Foreman Collection (hereafter cited as SFC), WHC.

18. Logan to Armstrong, September 20, 1845, AR CIA 1845, 516–517; Creek Agent J. L. Dawson to Commissioner of Indian Affairs T. Hartley Crawford, September 5, 1843, Letters Received by the Office of Indian Affairs, 1824–1881, U.S. Bureau of Indian Affairs, Record Group 75, microfilm (hereafter cited as LR OIA) M234, reel 227.

19. At the turn of the twentieth century, Creek humorist Alexander Posey frequently used the term "sofky patch" in his "Fus Fixico Letters." *Sofky* is a traditional Creek drink made from corn; *sofky patch* implies a small subsistence farm. Baird, *A Creek Warrior*, 34, 55.

20. Morris Edward Opler found much evidence of the continuation of *tvlwv* traditions among the Creeks of the 1930s, but it must be remembered that he was researching during Commissioner of Indian Affairs John Collier's crusade to reinstitute self-government among American Indians. The *tvlwv* offered a convenient organizational base. See Opler's article, "The Creek 'Town' and the Problem of Creek Indian Political Organization." Interview of Joe Grayson, I-PH, 35:445–446; Baird, *A Confederate Warrior*, 60.

21. Augustus W. Loomis, *Scenes in the Indian Country*, quoted in Grant Foreman, *The Five Civilized Tribes: Cherokee, Chickasaw, Choctaw, Creek, Seminole*, 199.

22. Echo Harjo to Commissioner of Indian Affairs William Brewer, September 25, 1857, LR OIA, M234, reel 226.

23. Logan to Armstrong, September 20, 1845, *Senate Executive Documents*, vol. 1, 29th Cong., 1st sess., 1845, no. 17, 514.

24. Agent William Garrett to Superintendent Elias Rector, September 21, 1857, AR CIA 1857, 223; Garrett to Rector, September 12, 1859, AR CIA 1859, 179.

25. John W. Morris, Charles R. Goins, and Edwin C. McReynolds, "Geographic Regions of Oklahoma," Map 3, "Landforms of Oklahoma," Map 5, "Generalized Natural-Vegetation Map of Oklahoma," Map 9, in *Historical Atlas of Oklahoma*; Schoolcraft, *History, Condition and Prospects*, 269–270.

26. Morris, Goins, and McReynolds, Maps 3, 5, 9 in *Historical Atlas*.

27. Dawson to Armstrong, September 5, 1843, AR CIA 1843, 424–425; Logan to Armstrong, August 20, 1845, AR CIA 1844–1845, 169–170; *The Ft. Smith (Arkansas) Herald*, November 22, 1850, GFC GI, box 24, vol. 54; Logan to

Commissioner of Indian Affairs W. Medill, November 19, 1847, 30th Cong., 1st sess., *Senate Executive Documents*, vol. 1, no. 19 1/2, 887.

28. Michael F. Doran, "Negro Slaves of the Five Civilized Tribes," 335–350; Kathryn E. Holland Braund, "The Creek Indians, Blacks, and Slavery," 601–636; J. W. Abert, "Journal of Lieutenant J. W. Abert, from Bent's Fort to St. Louis in 1845."

29. Baird, *A Creek Warrior*, 26, 34.

30. G. W. Grayson quoted in J. Leitch Wright, *Creeks and Seminoles: The Destruction and Regeneration of the Muscogulgee People*, 78.

31. Logan to Armstrong, September 20, 1845, *Senate Executive Documents*, vol. 1, 29th Cong., 1st sess, no. 17, 517–518; Agent Phillip H. Raiford to Commissioner of Indian Affairs Luke Lea, July 2, 1852, G. W. Stidham to Raiford, June 3, 1852, LR OIA, M234, reel 228; James Roane Gregory, "Early History of the Creek Nation," *The Indian Journal* (Eufaula, Creek Nation), March 8, 1901.

The Pawnees and Skidi Pawnees from present-day Nebraska and the Osages from Missouri and Kansas regarded the Indian Territory as their traditional range. The Wichitas and Caddos lived in the Red River Valley or in the vicinity of the Wichita Mountains in present-day southwestern Oklahoma. Delawares, Shawnees, Kickapoos, and other Ohio Valley immigrants drifted into the Indian Territory near the turn of the nineteenth century. From 1700 until the 1870s, the Comanches considered themselves to have dominion over the Southern Plains, a claim few cared to challenge.

32. *The Indian Journal* (Eufaula and Muskogee, Creek Nation), March 8, 1901; Stan Hoig, *Tribal Wars of the Southern Plains*, 129.

33. Grant Foreman, *Indians & Pioneers: The Story of the American Southwest before 1830*, 27–29; Debo, *The Road to Disappearance*, 131–132.

34. Logan to Armstrong, September 20, 1845, AR CIA 1845, 518.

35. *To Keep the Drum, To Tend the Fire: History and Legends of Thlopthlocco*, 9, 11; Interview of Mildred McIntosh Childers, I-PH, 17:420; Interview of Mary Grayson, I-PH, 35:461–462; Interview of Sarah Fife, I-PH, 30:16–18; Logan to Armstrong, August 20, 1844, AR CIA 1844–1845, 169–170.

36. Logan to Acting Superintendent, Western Territory, Samuel L. Rutherford, September 11, 1848, AR CIA 1848, 520.

37. Interview of Scott Waldo McIntosh, I-PH, 58:373; Logan to Armstrong, September 20, 1845, AR CIA 1845, 516.

38. Logan to Rutherford, February 23, 1849, LROIA, M234, reel 228.

39. Logan to Armstrong, September 20, 1845, AR CIA 1845, 516; Debo, *The Road to Disappearance*, 114.

40. Abert, "Journal," October 15, 1845.

41. Baird, *A Creek Warrior*, 50, 53.

42. Abert, "Journal," October 15, 1845; Baird, *A Creek Warrior*, 41–42; T. H. Wolfe to G. W. Clark, February 17, 1848, LR OIA, M234, reel 228.

43. Edwards' Post was southeast of present-day Holdenville, Oklahoma; Shieldsville was on the north edge of present-day Okmulgee, Oklahoma. Honey Springs was about one mile northwest of present-day Rentiesville, Oklahoma near the Elk Creek Bridge on the Texas Road. The Creek Agency moved periodically during the antebellum period but was generally just west of Fort Gibson in the narrow angle between the Verdigris and Arkansas Rivers. Wright and Fischer, "Civil War Sites in Oklahoma," 193–194, 202; Morris, Goins, and McReynolds, Map 37, "Three Forks Area" in *Historical Atlas*; Schoolcraft, *History, Condition, and Prospects*, 269–270; Interview of Siegel McIntosh, I-PH, 58:392–393.

44. Baird, *A Creek Warrior*, 39–41; Grant Foreman, *The Five Civilized Tribes*, 196; Grant Foreman, *Down the Texas Road: Historic Places along Highway 69 through Oklahoma*, 41–42.

45. Carolyn Thomas Foreman, "North Fork Town," 79–111; Interview of M. G. Butler, "North Fork Town," Grant Foreman Collection, OHS, collection number 83-229, (hereafter cited as GFC OHS), box 13.

In 1846 Agent Logan enumerated white Americans living in the Creek Nation: two tailors, a cabinet-maker, five carpenters, a silversmith, a bricklayer, two masons, a shoemaker, a millwright, a miller, and a blacksmith. Presumably, several of them lived in relatively urban North Fork Town. Logan to Armstrong, October 1, 1846, AR CIA 1846, 61–63. Dr. Ward Howard Bailey lived in North Fork Town for ten years before being driven out at the beginning of the Civil War. Interview of Rowland S. Bailey, I-PH, 4:86–88.

46. Abert, "Journal," October 18, 1845; Interview of Andrew Jackson Berryhill, I-PH, 7:408–413; Debo, *The Road to Disappearance*, 155, 213, 286; Interview of M. G. Butler, "North Fork Town," GFC OHS; Logan to Armstrong, September 20, 1845, AR CIA 1845, 523.

47. Agent Philip H. Raiford to Superintendent John Drennen, September 15, 1851, AR CIA 1851, 122–125.

48. Logan to Medill, November 9, 1847, *Senate Executive Documents*, 30th Cong., 1st sess., no. 19 1/2, 886; Armstrong to Crawford, October 1, 1844, AR CIA 1844–1845, 155–156.

49. Logan to Medill, November 9, 1847, *Senate Executive Documents*, 30th Cong., 1st sess., no. 19 1/2, 886.

50. Ibid.; The Creek Council to Logan, November 20, 1847, LR OIA, M234, reel 228; Joel D. Boyd, "Creek Indian Agents, 1834–1874," 43–47.

51. Richard Allen Sattler, "Seminoli Italwa: Socio-Political Change Among the Oklahoma Seminoles Between Removal and Allotment, 1836–1905," 53–54.

52. Logan to Armstrong, September 20, 1845, AR CIA 1845, 515.

53. Debo, *The Road to Disappearance*, 85; Raiford to Drennan, November 15, 1851, AR CIA 1851, 122–125.

54. Arrell Morgan Gibson, *The American Indian: Prehistory to the Present*, 339–340.

55. Debo, *The Road to Disappearance*, 116–117; "Communications from the Missions: Creek Mission," *The Missionary Chronicle, Containing the Proceedings of the Board of Foreign Missions and the Board of Missions of the Presbyterian Church and a General View of Other Benevolent Operations* (June 1842):170–172, GFC OHS, box 6, file 10 "Missions and Missionaries."

56. Roley McIntosh, Ufaula Hadjo, Cowocooche Emarthla, Joseph Carr, Cussetah Micco, and others to the Secretary of War, July 9, 1845, LR OIA, M234, reel 227.

57. Ibid.

58. Ben Marshall to Armstrong, November 25, 1846, LR OIA, M234, reel. 227.

59. Charles Hudson, *The Southeastern Indians*, 122–128, 173.

60. Duane Champagne, *Social Order and Political Change: Constitutional Governments among the Cherokee, the Choctaw, the Chickasaw, and the Creek*, 20–25.

61. Debo, *The Road to Disappearance*, 117–118.

62. "Creek Mission," *The Missionary Chronicle*, 171.

63. Debo, *The Road to Disappearance*, 118–119.

64. Carolyn Thomas Foreman, "North Fork Town," 83; Interview of Sandy Fife, I-PH, 30:5; Interview of John D. (Cap) McIntosh, I-PH, 58:340–353; Interview of Maxie Bullet, I-PH, 13:132.

65. Debo, *The Road to Disappearance*, 119–122.

66. *The Fort Smith (Arkansas) Herald*, July 26, 1848.

67. *The Indian Advocate*, August, 1848, 2.

68. R. M. Loughridge and D. M. Hodge, *English and Muskogee Dictionary, Collected from Various Sources and Revised*; Debo, *The Road to Disappearance*, 120–121; Andre Paul DuChateau, "The Creek Nation on the Eve of the Civil War," 311.

69. *The Indian Advocate*, September, 1848, 3.

70. Baird, *A Creek Warrior*, 36.

71. *To Keep the Drum*, 1–2.

72. W. B. Morrison, "Father Murrow," *My Oklahoma* 1 (January 1928):41, Opothleyahola Collection, WHC; DuChateau, "The Creek Nation on the Eve of the Civil War," 313; Armstrong to Commissioner of Indian Affairs T. Hartley Crawford, October 1, 1844, AR CIA 1844–1845, 155–156.

73. John C. Brodnaxe to Armstrong, June 8, 1844, Letters Received by the Western Superintendency, Records of the Southern Superintendency of Indian Affairs, U.S. Bureau of Indian Affairs, 1832–1870, Record Group 75 (hereafter cited as LR WS), M640, reel 5; Debo, *The Road to Disappearance*, 121–122. Tullahassee Mission was one mile east of U.S. Highway 69 in the northeast quarter of Section 27, Township 16 North, Range 18 East of the Indian Meridian,

or about three miles east of present-day Tullahassee, Oklahoma. Wright and Fischer, "Civil War Sites in Oklahoma," 212.

74. Logan to Rutherford, September 11, 1848, AR CIA 1848, 520.

75. G. W. Grayson, untitled manuscript.

76. Baird, *A Creek Warrior*, 36.

77. Ibid., 32–37. This suggests James and Jennie Grayson had not yet moved into town to the house on the Texas Road.

78. *The Indian Advocate*, May, 1848.

79. Hay to Raiford, October 1, 1849, AR CIA 1849, 182–183; Baird, *A Creek Warrior*, 36–39.

80. Baird, *A Creek Warrior*, 41–44; Thomas B. Ruble to Logan, September 8, 1848, AR CIA 1848, 525–526; Ruble to Raiford, October 8, 1949, AR CIA 1849, 184–185.

Asbury stood in Township 9 North, Range 16 East of the Indian Meridian on a site presently inundated by Lake Eufaula. Several graves, cemetery markers, and a memorial from Asbury were relocated in Greenwood Cemetery at Eufaula, Oklahoma. Wright and Fischer, "Civil War Sites in Oklahoma," 193.

81. Ruble to Garrett, August 1, 1854, AR CIA 1854, 153–154; Ruble to Garrett, August 14, 1855, AR CIA 1855, 144–145.

82. John M. Jarner to Luke Lea, July 1, 1851, AR CIA 1851, 127.

83. J. Ross Ramsey to Raiford, August 25, 1851, AR CIA 1851, 127.

84. Baird, *A Creek Warrior*, 42.

85. Ibid., 43–44; Ruble to Garrett, August 1, 1854, AR CIA 1854, 153–154; Ruble to Garrett, September 24, 1858, AR CIA 1858, 147–148.

86. Ruble to Garrett, September 24, 1858, AR CIA 1858, 147–148.

87. Ruble to Garrett, August 14, 1855, AR CIA 1855, 144.

88. Baird, *A Creek Warrior*, 41–45. Unlike the federal/missionary boarding schools of the post–Civil War period, Tullahassee and Asbury did not attempt to eradicate all aspects of native culture from the students' lives. While holding up Anglo-European culture as the standard to be attained, they also worked diligently, particularly at Tullahassee, to provide bilingual instruction and educational materials. See particularly Althea Bass, *The Story of Tullahassee*.

89. Baird, *A Creek Warrior*, 44, 22–23.

90. George Bunney and Ted Isham, interview by author, October 30, 1996, Stillwater, Oklahoma; Hudson, *The Southeastern Indians*, 226–229; Lambeth, *Way of the Creek People*; Opler, "The Creek 'Town'," 173–174; Debo, *The Road to Disappearance*, 21–25.

91. Interview of Sandy Fife, I-PH, 30:12–13; Debo, *The Road to Disappearance*, 25; Georgianna Stidham Grayson, untitled manuscript (Mary Hansard Knight, Okmulgee, Oklahoma).

92. Debo, *The Road to Disappearance*, 118–119; Robert Graham to Garrett, September 8, 1855, AR CIA 1855, 139–141; Baird, *A Creek Warrior*, 46–48.

93. Baird, *A Creek Warrior*, 47–48.

94. Ibid.

95. Logan to Armstrong, September 20, 1845, AR CIA 1845, 520.

96. The Cherokees, for instance, in 1858 employed fifteen of their high school graduates as teachers for their common schools. Elias Rector to Charles E. Mix, October 26, 1858, AR CIA 1858, 128.

97. Baird, *A Creek Warrior*, 48, 49.

98. Ibid., 48–50.

99. Ibid., 50.

100. *The Arkansian* (Fayetteville, Arkansas), March 19, 1859 in W. J. Lemke, *Early Colleges and Academies of Washington County, Arkansas*, 68.

101. Lemke, *Early Colleges of Washington County, Arkansas*, 15–16, 61–62; Baird, *A Creek Warrior*, 50–51.

Robert Graham, an English immigrant, was a student of Alexander Campbell at Bethany College in West Virginia before coming to Fayetteville. Campbell's call for a return to simple New Testament Christianity during the Second Great Awakening contributed to the development of the Christian Church, Churches of Christ, and Disciples of Christ.

102. Baird, *A Creek Warrior*, 33, 52–53, 66–67.

103. Ibid., 52–53.

104. Ibid., 51.

105. Graham to Garrett, September 8, 1855, AR CIA 1855, 139.

106. Baird, *A Creek Warrior*, 46, 54.

107. Ibid., 53–54.

108. Ibid., 53–55.

109. "Treaty between the United States of America and the Creek and Seminole Tribes of Indians, Concluded January 4, 1845, Ratified March 6, 1845," LR WS, M640, reel 5; Commissioner of Indian Affairs G. W. Manypenny to Secretary of the Interior R. McClelland, November 26, 1855, AR CIA 1855; Manypenny to McClelland, November 22, 1856, AR CIA 1856.

110. Garrett to Rector, September 12, 1859, AR CIA 1859; Garrett to Rector, October 15, 1860, AR CIA 1860; Debo, *The Road to Disappearance*, 124–128.

111. Garrett to Elias Rector, September 12, 1859, AR CIA 1859, 179.

112. Ibid.; Baird, *A Creek Warrior*, 48.

113. Garrett to Rector, October 15, 1860, AR CIA 1860, 123–125; Richard C. Rohrs, "Fort Gibson: Forgotten Glory," 32–34.

114. Rector to A. B. Greenwood, September 20, 1859, AR CIA 1859, 159–160.

115. Rector to Commissioner of Indian Affairs J. W. Denver, September 12, 1857, LR OIA, M234, reel 230.

116. Ibid., 160.

117. Garrett to Rector, September 14, 1858, AR CIA 1858, 146; Garrett to Rector, September 12, 1859, AR CIA 1859, 179.

118. Baird, *A Creek Warrior*, 55–56.

268   NOTES TO PAGES 53-56

CHAPTER 3. THE SPIRIT OF OUR FATHERS

1. W. David Baird, *A Creek Warrior for the Confederacy: The Autobiography of Chief G. W. Grayson*, 56–57.

2. Newspapers were published in the Cherokee, Chickasaw and Choctaw nations in the antebellum years. See Grant Foreman, *The Five Civilized Tribes: Cherokee, Chickasaw, Choctaw, Creek, Seminole*. Angie Debo, *The Road to Disappearance: A History of the Creek Indians*, 126–127.

3. Elias Rector to Charles E. Mix, October 26, 1858, Commissioner of Indian Affairs, *Annual Report*, 1858, 127 (hereafter cited as AR CIA and year).

4. Ibid.

5. A. B. Greenwood to Rector, November 17, 1859, Samuel Checote's Book of Records, Creek National Records, microfilm (hereafter cited as CRN and reel number), Oklahoma Historical Society, Oklahoma City, Oklahoma (hereafter cited as OHS), 9.

6. Loughridge to Creek Agent William H. Garrett, September 13, 1859, AR CIA 1859, 180–182.

7. Motey Carnard (Kennard) and Echo Harjo to Garrett, January 19, 1860, CRN 9.

8. William Seward, quoted in Annie Heloise Abel, *The American Indian as Slaveholder and Secessionist: An Omitted Chapter in the Diplomatic History of the Southern Confederacy*, 58–59.

9. Arrell Morgan Gibson, *The American Indian: Prehistory to the Present*, 367; Debo, *The Road to Disappearance*, 142.

10. Mrs. G. W. Grayson, "Confederate Treaties," *The Indian Journal* (Eufaula, Oklahoma), May 9, 1914. It must be noted that this observer was Annie Stidham Grayson, daughter of a signer of the Creek-Confederate Treaty and wife of a former Confederate officer, and that her remarks were given in a speech to the Eufaula, Oklahoma chapter of the United Daughters of the Confederacy. Considering the sources of her information, referred to but not named in this article, she was probably relating the Confederate version of events.

11. Albert Pike to Robert Toombs, May 29, 1861, *War of the Rebellion: A Compilation of the Official Records of the Union and Confederate Armies. Published under the Direction of the Secretary of War*, (hereafter cited as *Official Records*), vol. 1, series 4, 359–361; Debo, *The Road to Disappearance*, 143–145.

12. Mrs. G. W. Grayson, "Why the Five Civilized Tribes Joined the Confederacy," *The Indian Journal* (Eufaula, Oklahoma), June 6, 1913; Debo, *The Road to Disappearance*, 143–145.

Fort Cobb, in present Caddo County, protected the Wichita Agency in the Leased District. Fort Arbuckle, in present Garvin County, and Fort Washita, in present Bryan County, defended Chickasaw, Choctaw, Creek, and Seminole settlers.

13. AR CIA 1861, 10.

14. *Official Records*, vol. 1, series 4, 426–443; H. F. Buckner to "Brother Robert," January 4, 1861, H. F. Buckner Collection, OHS, 96-47.03.

15. Mrs. G. W. Grayson, "Confederate Treaties."

16. Catlette J. Atkins and Robert G. Atkins were both North Fork Town merchants at the time. Carolyn Thomas Foreman, "North Fork Town," 8, 103.

17. Mrs. G. W. Grayson, "Confederate Treaties"; "G. W. Grayson," "Creek Biographies" file, Grant Foreman Collection, Oklahoma Historical Society, collection 83-229, (hereafter cited as GFC OHS), box 6; Charles Hudson, *The Southeastern Indians*, 224.

18. "G. W. Grayson," "Creek Biographies" file, GFC OHS, box 6.

19. Vertical File, Jim Lucas Memorial Library, Checotah, Oklahoma.

20. Debo, *The Road to Disappearance*, 144–145; Gibson, *The American Indian*, 367–368.

21. Duane Champagne, *Social Order and Political Change: Constitutional Government among the Cherokee, the Choctaw, the Chickasaws, and the Creek*, 203.

22. See Theda Perdue and Michael D. Green's introduction to Annie Heloise Abel, *The American Indian as Slaveholder and Secessionist*, 1–5. William G. McLoughlin viewed abolition as a by-product of the Unionist Keetoowah Society's emphasis on Cherokee traditional values and pointed to chattel slavery as the direct cause of its internal Civil War conflict with mixed-blood Cherokee planters. See his *After the Trail of Tears: The Cherokees' Struggle for Sovereignty, 1839–1880*, 120, 156–157.

23. *To Keep the Drum, To Tend the Fire: History and Legends of Thlopthlocco*, 2; Christine Schultz White and Benton R. White, *Now the Wolf Has Come: The Creek Nation in the Civil War*, 23.

24. Thomas F. Meagher Jr., "McGillivray Family Tree," "Creek Collection," Gilcrease Institute of American History and Art, Tulsa, Oklahoma (hereafter cited as GI); Interviews of Scott Waldo McIntosh, "Indian-Pioneer History," Works Progress Administration, microfiche, (hereafter cited as I-PH), Western History Collection, University of Oklahoma, Norman, Oklahoma (hereafter cited as WHC); 58:377; Interview of Joe M. Grayson, I-PH, 35:411–413; Interview of J. W. Stephens, I-PH, 87:194; Baird, *A Creek Warrior*, 120.

Una McIntosh may have been called "Union." The latter name appeared in post–Civil War documents.

25. Debo, *The Road to Disappearance*, 150.

26. Opothleyahola and Ouktahnaserharjo (Sands) to "the President our Great Father," August 15, 1861, quoted in Abel, *The American Indian as Slaveholder*, 245–246n.

27. D. N. McIntosh to Colonel John Drew, September 11, 1861, Grant Foreman Collection, GI (hereafter cited as GFC GI), box 43, vol. 97; Debo, *The Road to Disappearance*, 167; Interview of Jim Tomm, I-PH, 91:323; Interview of Malucy Bear, I-PH, 6:179–180.

The term "noncitizens" includes white and black Anglo-Americans as well as
a handful of Europeans and Syrian-Lebanese in the Creek Nation in the nineteenth century.

28. Colonel D. N. McIntosh to Drew, September 11, 1861, GFC GI, box 34,
vol. 97; Colonel Douglas H. Cooper to Drew, October 29, 1861, "Creek Civil War"
file, GFC OHS, box 6; Statement of Colonel D. H. Cooper, January 29, 1862,
statement of William P. Adair, R. Fields, J. A. Scales, D. N. McIntosh, James M. C.
Smith, Tim Barnett, March 19, 1868, OHS 84-19, "Opothleyahola," "Creek Civil
War," Section X.

29. Statement of Adair, et al., March 19, 1868, OHS, Section X, "Opothleyahola," "Creek Civil War," 84-19; Debo, *The Road to Disappearance*, 151–152.

30. AR CIA 1862, 27.

31. Agent George A. Cutler to Superintendent of Indian Affairs W. G.
Coffin, Southern Superintendency, September 30, 1862, AR CIA 1862, 139.

32. Coffin to Commissioner of Indian Affairs William P. Dole, September
24, 1863, AR CIA 1863, 176.

33. Murrow to "Bro Hornaday," January 11, 1862, GFC GI, box 34, vol. 97.

34. Interview of Richard Adkins, I-PH, 1:280–281; Stephen Foreman, diary
entry of April 20, 1863, Stephen Foreman Collection, Western History Collection
(hereafter cited as SFC); Georgianna Stidham Grayson, untitled manuscript
(Mary Hansard Knight, Okmulgee, Oklahoma).

Stidham apparently returned to his ranch near Creek Agency, where he stayed
until the Battle of Honey Springs in July 1863. The last two years of the war he
spent with other refugees in the Red River Valley. Interview of Jim Tomm, I-PH,
92:329.

35. Baird, *A Creek Warrior*, 58–59.

36. Ibid., 60.

37. Hudson, *The Southeastern Indians*, 267–268, 325–326; Richard Allen
Sattler, "Seminoli Italwa: Socio-Political Change Among the Oklahoma Seminoles
Between Removal and Allotment, 1836–1905," 57–58.

38. Baird, *A Creek Warrior*, 58–59.

39. Ibid., 59, 113–115; Hudson, *The Southeastern Indians*, 325.

40. Baird, *A Creek Warrior*, 59; Robert S. Boyd Collection, OHS, collection
number 82-059.

41. Baird, *A Creek Warrior*, 59–60.

42. Robert S. Boyd Collection, OHS; Application of G. W. Grayson to the
United Daughters of the Confederacy for the Southern Cross of Honor, January
1, 1905 (Mildred Fuller Ewens, Eufaula, Oklahoma); Baird, *A Creek Warrior*,
59–61; Monthly inspection report of the Second Creek Regiment of Mounted
Volunteers, October 31, 1863, reproduced in Abel, *The American Indian as
Participant in the Civil War*, facing 244.

43. Baird, *A Creek Warrior*, 61; Robert S. Boyd Collection, OHS; Stephen
Foreman, diary entries of January 26, March 7, April 11, 1863, SFC WHC.

44. Harold O. Hoppe, "The Family of Robert Grierson and Sinoegee," (genealogical chart); Untitled genealogical chart of the family of In-fak-faph-ky and Mary Benson, Enola Shumate Collection, WHC; Interview of Mrs. F. H. A. Ahrens, I-PH, 1:312–313; Monthly inspection report of the Second Creek Regiment of Mounted Volunteers, October 31, 1863, in Abel, *The American Indian as Participant*, facing 244; Betty Tiger Miller, "Motey Tiger," 1308.

45. Jerlena King, "Jackson Lewis of the Confederate Creek Regiment."

46. General Order No. ___ (unnumbered). June 23, 1862, *Official Records*, vol. 13, series 1, 839–840.

47. Report of Brigadier William Steele . . . of Operations in the Indian Territory in 1863, *Official Records*, part 1, vol. 22, series 1, 35.

48. Ibid.; Brigadier General Richard M. Gano to Brigadier General Samuel Bell Maxey, June 21, 1864, Samuel Bell Maxey Collection, GI (hereafter cited as SBMC).

49. Albert Pike, unaddressed correspondence, May 4, 1862, *Official Records*, vol. 13, series 1, 823.

50. Ibid., 820–823; Pike to Secretary of War George Randolph, June 27, 1862, *War of the Rebellion*, vol. 13, series 1, 847.

51. Baird, *A Creek Warrior*, 97.

52. Ibid., 109; A. G. Proctor to W. G. Coffin, Superintendent of Indian Affairs, November 23, 1863, AR CIA 1863, 224.

53. Ibid., 97–99.

54. "G. W. Grayson" file, GFC OHS, box 6; McIntosh to Pike, June 9, 1862, *Official Records*, vol. 13, series 1, 853.

55. Baird, *A Creek Warrior*, 79–81.

56. Pike, unaddressed correspondence, May 4, 1862, *Official Records*, vol. 13, series 1, 819; Interview of Bell Haney Labor Airington, I-PH, 1:350.

57. Agent Justin Harlan to Coffin, August 8, 1863, AR CIA 1863, 215.

58. John R. Swanton, "Social Origins and Social Usages of the Indians of the Creek Confederacy," 436; Baird, *A Creek Warrior*, 102–103.

59. Baird, *A Creek Warrior*, 85.

60. Baird, *A Creek Warrior*, 106–107. The military-political ranks earned in order were *haco*, *tvstvnvkke*, and *mekko*. Hudson, *The Southeastern Indians*, 325.

61. Federal troops had been withdrawn from Fort Gibson in 1857. Lary C. Rampp and Donald L. Rampp covered these events in *The Civil War in Indian Territory*, 1–29.

62. Stephen Foreman, diary entries of December 25, 1862, January 10, 1863, SFC WHC.

63. Ibid., January 14, 1863.

64. Ibid., January 15, 1863.

65. Ibid., April 19, 22, 1863.

66. LeRoy H. Fischer, *The Battle of Honey Springs*, 2.

67. Fischer, *The Battle of Honey Springs*, 2; Rampp and Rampp, *The Civil War in Indian Territory*, 21–22.

68. Baird, *A Creek Warrior*, 62–63.

69. Ibid., 61–63; Fischer, *The Battle of Honey Springs*, 3–7; Cooper to Steele, August 18, 1863, *Official Records*, vol. 22, series 1, 457–461.

70. Report of Brigadier General William Steele, February 14, 1864, *Official Records*, vol. 22, series 1, 33–34; "Second Re-enactment of the Battle of Honey Springs" (commentary by unidentified participant), July 15, 1990; Baird, *A Creek Warrior*, 61.

71. Fischer, *The Battle of Honey Springs*, 7; Rampp and Rampp, *The Civil War in Indian Territory*, 53.

72. Stephen Foreman, diary entries of July 18, 19, 29, 1863, SFC WHC.

73. Ibid., July 19, 1863; Baird, *A Creek Warrior*, 63n.

74. Stephen Foreman, diary entries of August 8, 12, 1863, SFC WHC.

75. Stand Watie, Principal Chief of the Cherokees, to His Excellency the Governor of the Creek Nation, August 9, 1863, *Official Records*, vol. 22, series 1, 1105–1106.

76. Ibid.

77. Stephen Foreman, diary entry of August 23, 1863, SFC WHC.

78. Baird, *A Creek Warrior*, 63–64.

79. Ibid., 64.

80. Ibid.

81. Interview of Jim Tomm, I-PH, 91:329–331; Interview of Bell Haney Labor Airington, I-PH, 1:338; Stephen Foreman, diary entry of August 26, 1863, SFC WHC.
   The Emancipation Proclamation affecting areas in rebellion legally if not actually freed Indian Territory slaves as of January 1, 1863.

82. Interview of Ella Coody Robinson, I-PH, 77:117.

83. Stephen Foreman, diary entry of September 5, 1863, SFC WHC.

84. Baird, *A Creek Warrior*, 112–113.

85. Baird, *A Creek Warrior*, 65–69; Report of Major General James G. Blunt, August 27, 1863, *War of the Rebellion*, vol. 22, series 1, 597–598.
   Perryville, an important commercial center at the junction of the Texas and California roads, was located four miles south of present-day McAlester, Oklahoma, in Pittsburg County. Muriel H. Wright and LeRoy H. Fischer, "Civil War Sites in Oklahoma," 203–204.

86. Rampp and Rampp, *The Civil War in Indian Territory*, 32–34.

87. Maxey to Colonel S. S. Scott, August 23, 1864, SBMC.

88. Ibid.; Arrell Morgan Gibson, *The Chickasaws*, 238.

89. Rampp and Rampp, *The Civil War in Indian Territory*, 85. Pleasant Bluff is on the north edge of present-day Tamaha, Oklahoma, in Haskell County. The action took place in Sections 11 and 12, Township 11 North, Range 22 East of the Indian Meridian. Wright and Fischer, "Civil War Sites in Oklahoma," 179–180.

90. Baird, *A Creek Warrior*, 81–82.

91. Ibid., 82–88; *Official Records*, vol. 34, series 1, 1012–1013.

92. Wright and Fischer, "Civil War Sites in Oklahoma," 181; Baird, *A Creek Warrior*, 83–84.

93. Baird, *A Creek Warrior*, 85–88.

94. Rampp and Rampp, *The Civil War in Indian Territory*, 90.

95. The hayfield fight took place in present-day Wagoner County about seven miles northeast of Wagoner, Oklahoma, in Section 19, Township 18 North, Range 19 East of the Indian Meridian. Wright and Fischer, "Civil War Sites in Oklahoma," 212.

96. Rampp and Ramp, *The Civil War in Indian Territory*, 104–106; Report of Captain E. A. Barker, September 20, 1864, *Official Records*, part 1, vol. 41, series 1, 771–772.

97. Baird, *A Creek Warrior*, 95–96.

98. Rampp and Rampp, *The Civil War in Indian Territory*, 106.

99. Baird, *A Creek Warrior*, 99–101. Both Battles of Cabin Creek took place in Mayes County in Section 12, Township 23 North, Range 20 East of the Indian Meridian, or about three miles north of Pensacola, Oklahoma, on the west bank of Cabin Creek. Wright and Fischer, "Civil War Sites in Oklahoma," 189; Rampp and Rampp, *The Civil War in Indian Territory*, 106–112.

100. Baird, *A Creek Warrior*, 101–103.

101. Ibid.

102. Rampp and Rampp, *The Civil War in Indian Territory*, 113–115.

103. Baird, *A Creek Warrior*, 102–104. Gano's Crossing was located near present Southwest 38th Street. Wright and Fischer, "Civil War Sites in Oklahoma," 210.

104. Maxey to Matilda Maxey, October 12, 1864, SBMC; Interview of Ella Coody Robinson, I-PH, 77:118.

105. Rampp and Rampp, *The Civil War in Indian Territory*, 115–116; Maxey to Choctaw Governor Peter Pitchlyn, January 10, 1865, Peter Pitchlyn Collection, WHC, file 16, box 4.

106. Barnett to Watie, March 3, 1865, Cherokee Nation Papers, Phillips Collection, WHC.

107. G. W. Grayson, quoted in Henry Cathey, ed., "Extracts from the Memoirs of William Franklin Avera," 213.

108. Baird, *A Creek Warrior*, 108. Wapanucka Academy, also known as Rock Academy, was a large three-story stone building with galleries on the first and second floors. It was built in 1852 by the Chickasaw National Council as a Presbyterian boarding school for girls. It stood about two miles southeast of present-day Bromide, Oklahoma, in Johnston County in Section 9, Township 2 South, Range 8 East of the Indian Meridian. It served as a military hospital and prison during the war. Wright and Fischer, "Civil War Sites in Oklahoma," 183–184.

109. Baird, *A Creek Warrior*, 111.

110. Ibid., 111–114.

111. Ibid., 109, 121, 123; Mary Alice Robertson, "Incidents of the Civil War," Alice Robertson Papers, OHS, box 1, 82–86; Debo, *The Road to Disappearance*, 163; *The Indian Journal* (Eufaula and Muskogee, Creek Nation), May 1, 1878.

112. Debo, *The Road to Disappearance*, 173–175.

113. Statement of I. B. Luce, September 6, 1884, Grayson Family Collection, Western History Collection (hereafter cited as GFC WHC), VI-18.

114. Debo, *The Road to Disappearance*, 174.

115. Ibid., 177.

116. Baird, *A Creek Warrior*, 122.

117. Watie to the Governor of the Creek Nation, August 9, 1863, *Official Records*, vol. 22, series 1, 1105–1106.

CHAPTER 4. INDIAN CAPITAL AND INDIAN BRAINS

1. W. David Baird, *A Creek Warrior for the Confederacy: The Autobiography of Chief G. W. Grayson*, 116.

2. Ibid., 121–123; Testimony of Sam Grayson, "In the Matter of Joe Grayson for Enrollment as a Creek Freedman," Applications for Enrollment of the Commission to the Five Civilized Tribes, 1898–1914, application number 92, Oklahoma Historical Society, Oklahoma City, Oklahoma (hereafter cited as OHS), microfilm, reel 327.

3. Angie Debo, *The Road to Disappearance: A History of the Creek Indians*, 170–171, 213.

4. Baird, *A Creek Warrior*, 126–127.

5. Georgianna Stidham Grayson, untitled manuscript (Mary Hansard Knight, Okmulgee, Oklahoma); "Stidham Family," Vertical File, OHS; Benjamin Marshall, David Barnett, G. W. Stidham, and Louis McIntosh, delegates, to Commissioner of Indian Affairs Orlando Brown, February 7, 1850, Letters Received by the Office of Indian Affairs, 1824–1881 (hereafter cited as LR OIA), U.S. Bureau of Indian Affairs, Record Group 75, Washington, D.C., M234, reel 228.

6. Baird, *A Creek Warrior*, 117–119; Georgianna Stidham Grayson, untitled manuscript.

7. Baird, *A Creek Warrior*, 117–118.

8. G. W. Stidham married Anna Herrod in 1838 and was widowed one year later. His second wife, name unknown, was the mother of Thomas W. Stidham (1841–1858). Stidham married Elizabeth Grace in 1843, mother of Celestia Stidham Foreman, born in 1846. Elizabeth died in 1846, and Stidham married Ariadna Carr in 1848. Her children were Georgianna, Phillip Raiford

Stidham (1852–1871), and Leonidas (Lee) G. Stidham (1855–1918). Ariadna died in 1855, and Stidham married Sarah Thornbury, a white Virginian. Sarah's children were Sarah Elizabeth Stidham (1857–1858), George Washington Stidham, Jr. (1859–1926), George Ella Stidham Bailey Tolleson (1861–1938), Albert Pike Stidham (born 1863), Lonie Stidham Bennett (1865–1894), Fernando Stidham (who died in infancy in 1868), and Theodore Stidham (1872–1927). Georgianna Stidham Grayson, untitled manuscript; "Stidham Family," Vertical File, OHS.

9. Georgianna Stidham Grayson, untitled manuscript.

10. Ibid.

11. Annie's sister Celestia, for example, married Evarts Foreman, the son of Cherokee missionary Stephen Foreman. "Stidham Family," Vertical File, OHS; Baird, *A Creek Warrior*, 127–129.

12. Georgianna Stidham Grayson, untitled manuscript.

13. Baird, *A Creek Warrior*, 109, 127–129.

14. Georgianna Stidham Grayson, untitled manuscript.

15. Baird, *A Creek Warrior*, 130–131. Watt Grayson lived at Sulphur Springs, about one and one-half miles west of Checotah, Oklahoma. *The Indian Journal*, (Eufaula and Muskogee, Creek Nation), September 1, 1877.

16. Baird, *A Creek Warrior*, 141; National Auditor Records, Third Quarter Reports, 1875, Creek Indian Memorial Association Records, OHS; List of Traders in Creek Nation—Indian, 1879-849, LR OIA, M234, reel 872; *The Indian Journal* (Eufaula and Muskogee, Creek Nation), January 9, May 15, 1878.

17. Charles Gibson, "What a Change," *The Indian Journal* (Eufaula and Muskogee, Creek Nation), February 21, 1902.

18. *The Indian Journal* (Eufaula and Muskogee, Creek Nation), August 10, 1876.

19. Ibid., April 26, 1877; Interview of Richard Young Audd, "Indian-Pioneer History," microfiche, (hereafter cited as I-PH), Works Progress Administration, Western History Collection, University of Oklahoma, Norman, Oklahoma (hereafter cited as WHC), 3:294.

20. *The Indian Journal* (Eufaula and Muskogee, Creek Nation), January 16, March 6, 1878; Debo, *The Road to Disappearance*, 367.

21. The best account of this type of enterprise and its impact on the Indian nations is found in H. Craig Miner, *The Corporation and the Indian: Tribal Sovereignty and Industrial Civilization in Indian Territory, 1865–1907*. Debo, *The Road to Disappearance*, 197–199; Acting Commissioner of Indian Affairs A. Buschard to T. J. Portis, General Solicitor, Missouri Pacific Railroad, June 18, 1888, Department of the Interior, Office of Indian Affairs, Land Division, Record Group 75, LB 174-106.

22. The *Indian Journal* (Eufaula and Muskogee, Creek Nation), April 26, 1877.

23. Union Agent S. W. Marston to Commissioner of Indian Affairs E. A. Hayt, May 30, 1878, LR OIA, M234, reel 870; *The Indian Journal* (Eufaula and Muskogee, Creek Nation), April 26, 1877.

24. "G. W. Grayson," Grant Foreman Collection, OHS, collection number 83-229, (hereafter cited as GFC OHS), box 6.

25. Interview of Richard Young Audd, I-PH, 3:292; Interview of Minnie Fryer Finigan, I-PH, 30:40. There were probably churches of other denominations, but they did not report their numbers for the edition from which this information was taken. *The Indian Journal* (Eufaula and Muskogee, Creek Nation), April 26, 1877.

26. *The Indian Journal* (Eufaula and Muskogee, Creek Nation), April 27, 1877; "North Fork Town," GFC OHS, box 13; Interview of W. E. Baker, I-PH, 4:269–270; Interview of Joe M. Grayson, I-PH, 35:435–436.

27. Interview of R. B. Buford, I-PH, 13:82–83.

28. Baird, *A Creek Warrior*, 141–143; *The Vindicator* (Atoka and New Boggy, Choctaw Nation), April 30, 1875.

29. *The Vindicator* (Atoka and New Boggy, Choctaw Nation), October 13, 1875; Baird, *A Creek Warrior*, 141–143.

30. The Grayson house has been razed, but some of the trees and shrubs Wash planted survive. Mildred Fuller Ewens, interview by author, Eufaula, Oklahoma, October 9–10, 1989.

31. Tsianina, mother of Mildred Fuller Ewens, was called "Dovie" because of her large grey eyes. Ibid.; "Creek Schools," GFC OHS, box 6. Washington Grayson was sometimes called erroneously "George Washington Grayson, Jr."

32. *The Indian Journal* (Eufaula and Muskogee, Creek Nation), January 23, 1878, February 13, 1878, January 29, 1880; "G. W. Grayson," GFC OHS, box 6.

33. Interview of Earnest Archer, I-PH, 3:6–7; Interview of Charles Augustus Berryhill, I-PH, 7:415–416; Interview of Andrew Jackson Berryhill, I-PH, 7:396; Clarence W. Turner, "Events Among the Muskogees During Sixty Years," 23–24.

34. *The Indian Journal* (Eufaula and Muskogee, Creek Nation), March 13, June 19, July 17, 1878. For the best study of Indian cattlemen, albeit somewhat short on Indian Territory ranching, see Peter Iverson, *When Indians Became Cowboys: Native Peoples and Cattle Ranching in the American West.*

35. "Henryetta-Hugh Henry," Vertical File, Henryetta Public Library, Henryetta, Oklahoma; Interview of Arminta Exon Henry, I-PH, 41:230–231; Interview of Texanner Guinn, I-PH, 36:369; Interview of John Likowski, I-PH, 54:86–104; *The Indian Journal* (Eufaula and Muskogee, Creek Nation), October 19, 1882.

36. Mildred Fuller Ewens, interview by author, October 12, 1989; *The Indian Journal* (Eufaula and Muskogee, Creek Nation), June 1, 1876, August 7, 1879.

37. *The Indian Journal* (Eufaula and Muskogee, Creek Nation), August 7, 1879.

38. Ibid.

39. Debo, *The Road to Disappearance*, 232; Tufts to Commissioner of Indian Affairs R. E. Trowbridge, July 31, 1880, LR OIA, 1880-967, M234, reel 877.

40. Tufts to Trowbridge, July 31, 1880, LR OIA, 1880-967, M234, reel 877.

41. Debo, *The Road to Disappearance*, 232.

42. *The Indian Journal* (Eufaula and Muskogee, Creek Nation), February 17, 1881.

43. Ibid., May 3, 1877; Althea Bass, *The Story of Tullahassee*, 241–245; Undated list of stockholders, Creek National Records, microfilm, OHS (hereafter cited as CRN with reel number), 40, 34100.

44. *The Indian Journal*, May 3, 1877.

45. Ibid.

46. "To the National Council, M[uskogee] N[ation]," November 2, 1877, CRN 40, 34080.

47. Ibid.; G. W. Stidham to Chief Samuel Checote, April 23, 1881, CRN 40, 34085.

48. Grayson to Chief Samuel Checote, November 19, 1881, CRN 40, 34086.

49. *The Indian Journal* (Eufaula and Muskogee, Creek Nation), January 3, 1888.

50. Ibid., November 14, 1889, June 8, 1895; *The Muskogee (Creek Nation) Phoenix*, November 28, 1889.

51. *The Indian Journal* (Eufaula and Muskogee, Creek Nation), various issues.

52. See, for example, the issues of November 9, 1876, May 8, 1877, February 20, 1878, April 8, 1880.

53. Debo, *The Road to Disappearance*, 260.

54. Daniel F. Littlefield, Jr., *Alex Posey: Creek Poet, Journalist & Humorist*, 137.

55. *The Indian Journal* (Eufaula and Muskogee, Creek Nation), May 5, 1887.

56. Ibid., November 14, 1889.

57. Ibid., (Eufaula and Muskogee, Creek Nation), January 2, 1902.

58. Grayson to N. B. Moore, February 21, 1890, Special Collections, McFarlin Library, Tulsa University, Tulsa, Oklahoma.

59. Sam Grayson, for example, served as clerk of the House of Kings for several years, a delegate to Washington, and National Treasurer in the 1890s. *The Vindicator* (New Boggy, Choctaw Nation), May 31, 1873; Debo, *The Road to Disappearance*, 354–359.

60. Interview of Samuel J. Haynes, I-PH, 40:315–316; Circular, Jefferson Davis to the Six Confederate Indian Nations, May 14, 1864, Samuel Bell Maxey Collection, Gilcrease Institute of American History and Art, Tulsa, Oklahoma, 5136.285; Debo, *The Road to Disappearance*, 179–181.

61. Duane Champagne, *Social Order and Political Change: Constitutional Government among the Cherokee, the Choctaw, the Chickasaw, and the Creek*, 203–204, 229–230. Champagne argues that the white towns—particularly Cusseta, Abeka,

Nuyaka, and Okmulgee—gradually replaced Tuckabachee and Coweta as the primary towns after the Civil War.

62. Checote was a member of the Hecheta white town of Sawokla, while Sands was from Abeka. Champagne, *Social Order and Political Change*, 230; Debo, *The Road to Disappearance*, 179–181.

63. Debo, *The Road to Disappearance*, 181–183; Richard Allen Sattler, "Seminoli Italwa: Socio-Political Change Among the Oklahoma Seminoles Between Removal and Allotment, 1836–1905," 59.

64. Debo, *The Road to Disappearance*, 181–183.

65. Interview of Samuel J. Haynes, I-PH, 40:320, 331–333.

66. Interview of Emma Bell Checote Canard, I-PH, 15:265; Daniel F. Littlefield, Jr., and James W. Parins, *A Bibliography of Native American Writers, 1772–1924*, 222; Baird, *A Creek Warrior*, 126. Grayson signed the reunification document as secretary on February 11, 1867. "Samuel Checote's Book of Records," CRN 9, 35–36.

67. Debo, *The Road to Disappearance*, 183, 185–186; Appropriations by the National Council of 1878, "Samuel Checote's Book of Records," CRN 9, 90–92.

68. Debo, *The Road to Disappearance*, 203–204; Annual Address of Samuel Checote to the National Council, October 4, 1881, Reports of Inspection of the Field Jurisdictions of the Office of Indian Affairs, 1873–1900, Department of the Interior, Records of the Office of Indian Affairs, Record Group 75, M1070, reel 55.

69. Debo, *The Road to Disappearance*, 265–268; "North Fork Town," GFC OHS, box 13; Interview of Will Robison, I-PH, 77:251–252.

For example, the federal government finally paid off the Creek Orphan Claim, which originated at the time of removal, fifty years later in 1882. Only about 25 of the 573 orphans were still living. The silver coins alone weighed 1,875 pounds. *The Indian Journal* (Eufaula and Muskogee, Creek Nation), January 25, 1883;

70. Debo, *The Road to Disappearance*, 375–376; Baird, *A Creek Warrior*, 132–134.

71. Baird, *A Creek Warrior*, 132–135.

72. Ibid., 136.

73. Debo, *The Road to Disappearance*, 229–231, 253.

74. Glenn Shirley, *Law West of Ft. Smith: A History of Frontier Justice in the Indian Territory, 1834–1896*, 86–91, 314; Charles Gibson in *The Indian Journal* (Eufaula and Muskogee, Creek Nation), September 12, 1902; Interview of Richard Young Audd, I-PH, 3:296; Contract between G. W. Grayson and J. B. Luce, July 10, 1876, LR OIA, 1886-26857.

75. Baird, *A Creek Warrior*, 138–140; Interview of Eloise Grayson Smock, I-PH, 85:370.

76. Baird, *A Creek Warrior*, 144–146; Grayson to Principal Chief Ward Coachman, August 8, 1877, Coachman to Grayson, February 14, 1878, CRN 21, 39329.

77. Coachman to the Houses of Kings and Warriors, August 1, 1878, CRN 21; Claim of Robert Sewell for Creek citizenship, (1904) 1065, Letters Received, Department of the Interior, Indian Territory Division, Record Group 48.

78. Debo, *The Road to Disappearance*, 244–245.

79. *The Indian Journal* (Eufaula and Muskogee, Creek Nation), August 7, 1879.

80. 45th Cong., 3rd sess., Senate Report 744, 709.

81. "Samuel Checote's Book of Records," CRN 9, 69–70.

82. Debo, *The Road to Disappearance*, 136–138; Superintendent C. W. Dean to Commissioner of Indian Affairs G. W. Manypenny, September 13, 1855, Department of the Interior, Commissioner of Indian Affairs, *Annual Report, 1855*, 121.

83. Debo, *The Road to Disappearance*, 144–145, 164–165.

84. Ibid., 205–207; "Journal of the General Council of the Indian Territory," 32–34.

85. Cotchochee was appointed a delegate, but illness forced him to send a substitute. Debo, *The Road to Disappearance*, 206; "Journal of the General Council of the Indian Territory," 36; "Samuel Cheocote's Book of Records," CRN 9, 39–40; Stan Hoig, *Jesse Chisholm: Ambassador of the Plains*, 164.

86. "Records of the General Council of the Indian Territory," September 27–30, 1870, Records of the Central Superintendency of Indian Affairs, 1813–1878, Office of Indian Affairs, Record Group 75, M856, reel 31; Debo, *The Road to Disappearance*, 205–206.

87. "Records of the General Council of the Indian Territory," September 27–30, 1870, M856, reel 31.

88. Ibid., December 6, 1870; Debo, *The Road to Disappearance*, 205–206.

89. Morton, "Reconstruction in the Creek Nation," 175–176; Debo, *The Road to Disappearance*, 206–207.

90. Ohland Morton, "Reconstruction in the Creek Nation," 176; William G. McLoughlin, *After the Trail of Tears: The Cherokees' Struggle for Sovereignty, 1839–1880*, 275–278; Debo, *The Road to Disappearance*, 207.

91. "Journal of the General Council of the Indian Territory," 35; McLoughlin, *After the Trail of Tears*, 274; Debo, *The Road to Disappearance*, 209–210. In the Cherokee Tobacco Case (1871), the U.S. Supreme Court ruled that Indian treaties were inferior to acts of Congress, in this case allowing a tax on tobacco products manufactured in the otherwise tax-free Indian nations.

92. Marston to Commissioner of Indian Affairs E. A. Hayt, March 22, 1878, LR OIA, M234, reel 870.

93. See, for example, CRN 37, 30845, 30847, 30851, 30862, and 30869; "Journal of the General Council of the Indian Territory," 35.

94. Union Agent G. W. Ingalls to Superintendent Enoch Hoag, December 7, 1875, Records of the Central Superintendency, U.S. Bureau of Indian Affairs,

1813–1878, M856, reel 37; Commission of G. W. Grayson as delegate to the International Council, Grayson Family Collection, WHC, V-26.

95. Baird, *A Creek Warrior*, 147–148.

96. *The Vindicator* (Atoka and New Boggy, Choctaw Nation), May 31, 1873.

97. Ibid., July 3, 1875.

98. G. W. Grayson, "An Apology," *The Indian Journal* (Eufaula and Muskogee, Creek Nation), July 7, 1881.

99. *The Indian Journal* (Eufaula and Muskogee, Creek Nation), October 17, 1902.

CHAPTER 5. ALL THAT IS LEFT FOR OUR CHILDREN

1. Portions of this chapter were first published in an article, "Fight for Survival: Indian Response to the Boomer Movement," *The Chronicles of Oklahoma* 67 (Spring 1989):30–51 and are reprinted here with the permission of the Oklahoma Historical Society.

2. Creek records indicate that Grayson represented Koweta Town in the House of Warriors from 1883 to 1891 and may have served in 1892 and 1897 as well. W. David Baird, ed., *A Creek Warrior for the Confederacy: The Autobiography of Chief G. W. Grayson*, 146.

3. The best general statement of the Indians' beliefs and fears about white designs on their territory and their rights may be found in the "Proceedings of the International Conference of the Tribes of the Indian Territory," Eufaula, Creek Nation, May 27, 1879, Creek National Records, microfilm (hereafter cited as CRN with reel number), Oklahoma Historical Society, Oklahoma City, Oklahoma (hereafter cited as OHS), 37, 30811-A.

4. *The St. Louis Globe-Democrat*, August 8, 1880.

5. Angie Debo, *The Road to Disappearance: A History of the Creek Indians*, 210. See also Thomas Burnell Colbert, "Prophet of Progress: The Life and Times of Elias Cornelius Boudinot."

6. *The New York Times*, December 18, 1880.

7. Ibid.; *The Cherokee Advocate* (Tahlequah, Cherokee Nation), July 13, 1878.

8. Stan Hoig, *The Oklahoma Land Rush of 1889*, 3.
The name Oklahoma, meaning "land of the red man," had been proposed by Choctaw delegate Allen Wright during the negotiations of the Reconstruction treaties. Arrell Morgan Gibson, *Oklahoma: A History of Five Centuries*, 129.

9. *The Indian Journal* (Eufaula and Muskogee, Creek Nation), October 9, 1879.

10. Bushyhead to Checote, January 30, 1880, "Indian Affairs" file, Cherokee National Records (hereafter cited as CNR), OHS, microfilm, reel 83, 1167.

11. "To the Delegates of the Several Tribes in Council Assembled," March 18, 1880, CRN 37, 30817.

12. Creek Principal Chief Ward Coachman to Cherokee Principal Chief Charles Thompson, March 16, 1879, Correspondence and Records of the Principal Chiefs, vol. 63, CRN 21, 245.

13. Chief We-qua-ho-ka to the Chief of the Creeks, May 4, 1881, CRN 37, 30822.

14. The two primary biographies of Payne are Carl Coke Rister, *Land Hunger* and Stan Hoig, *David L. Payne: The Oklahoma Boomer. The Indian Journal* (Eufaula and Muskogee, Creek Nation), May 15, 1879.

15. *The Cherokee Advocate* (Tahlequah, Cherokee Nation), October 13, 1880.

16. James E. Goodwin, ed., *The Federal Reporter: Cases Argued and Determined in the Circuit and District Courts of the United States, August–November, 1881*, vol. 8, 883–896.

17. Cherokee Principal Chief Dennis Wolfe Bushyhead to Chief Samuel Checote, September 10, 1880, CRN 37, 30765, October 5, 1880, CRN 37, 30767.

18. "Action of the International Convention held at Eufaula between the Five Nations in Reference to the Prosecution of David L. Payne before the District Court of the United States for the Western District of Oklahoma," October 20, 1880, CRN 37, 30768.

19. Ibid; Mary Jane Warde, "Fight for Survival: The Indian Response to the Boomer Movement," 42.

20. Grayson to Chief Checote, October 22, 1880, CRN 37, 30769.

21. Grayson to the National Council, October, 1881, CRN 37, 30780; *The Sumner County (Kansas) Press*, December 23, 1880.

22. Grayson to the National Council, October, 1881, CRN 37, 30780.

23. Duncan to Chief Bushyhead, December 17, 1880, Cherokee Nation Papers, Phillips Collection (hereafter cited as PC), Western History Collection, University of Oklahoma, Norman, Oklahoma (hereafter cited as WHC), box 1, "Intruders" file, F37.

24. Duncan, Grayson, Cloud, and Overton, "For the Advocate," *The Cherokee Advocate* (Tahlequah, Cherokee Nation), January 5, 1881.

25. Ibid.

26. Grayson to the National Council, October, 1881, CRN 37, 30780.

27. *The Sumner County (Kansas) Press*, December 23, 1880.

28. *The New York Times*, December 11, 1880; *The Chicago Evening Journal* reprinted in *The Indian Journal* (Eufaula and Muskogee, Creek Nation), December 23, 1880.

29. "Trouble Ahead," *The Indian Journal* (Eufaula and Muskogee, Creek Nation), July 15, 1880.

30. Grayson, "A Talk on the White Settler Question," *The Indian Journal* (Eufaula and Muskogee, Creek Nation), June 2, 1881.

31. Duncan, Grayson, Cloud, and Overton, "For the Advocate"; Grayson to the National Council, October, 1881, CRN 37, 30780.

32. *The Indian Journal* (Eufaula and Muskogee, Creek Nation), November 30, 1880; W. A. Phillips to Chief Bushyhead, November 30, 1880, Cherokee Nation Papers, PC, box 1, "Intruders" file, F33; *The New York Times*, December 18, 1880.

33. Chief Dennis Wolfe Bushyhead, Second Inaugural Address, *The Indian Journal* (Eufaula and Muskogee, Creek Nation), November 11, 1880.

34. Grayson to the National Council, October, 1881, CRN 37, 30780.

35. Parker to Bushyhead, September 14, 1880, Cherokee Nation Papers, PC, box 1, "Intruders" file, F20; Federal Prosecutor William H. H. Clayton to Chief Bushyhead, October 15, 1880, Cherokee Nation Papers, PC, box 1, "Intruders" file, F25.

36. Overton to Bushyhead, October 29, 1880, Cherokee Nation Papers, PC, box 1, "Intruders" file, F27.

37. *The Federal Reporter*, 8:883–896; Rister, *Land Hunger*, 96; Duncan to Chief Bushyhead, March 10, 1881, PC, "Intruders" file, M943-1-13, F42; Grayson to Chief Checote, March 17, 1881, CRN 37, 39772.

38. *The Federal Reporter*, 8:883–898; Hoig, *David L. Payne*, 110.

39. Grayson to the National Council, October, 1881, CRN 37, 30780. Grayson noted that he had worked twenty-six days and spent only $179.30 of the $500 and carte blanche the Creek Nation had given him for the prosecution. He returned the remaining $320.70. The Creek Nation further awarded D. W. C. Duncan $400 for his legal services in the case. Their total expenditures were $579.30. Historian Angie Debo has commented that if one considers the outrageous sums Creeks later spent on legal fees to secure their rights and dues from the federal government and the importance of the case, this was indeed a bargain. Debo, *The Road to Disappearance*, 258.

40. Wash Grayson and James Larney, "The Creek People," a letter to Commissioner of Indian Affairs H. Price, July 17, 1883, published in *The Indian Journal* (Eufaula and Muskogee, Creek Nation), July 26, 1883.

41. Debo, *The Road to Disappearance*, 226.

42. Duane Champagne, *Social Order and Political Change: Constitutional Governments among the Cherokee, the Choctaw, the Chickasaw, and the Creek*, 228–237.

43. *The Indian Journal* (Eufaula and Muskogee, Creek Nation), August 7, 1879.

44. 45th Cong., 3rd sess., Senate Report 744, 692.

45. C. W. Turner, "Events Among the Muskogees During Sixty Years," 33–34.

46. Hudson, *The Southeastern Indians*, 224; Interview of Samuel J. Haynes, "Indian-Pioneer History," Works Progress Administration, WHC, microfiche (hereafter cited as I-PH), 40:330.

47. See William G. McLoughlin, *After the Trail of Tears: The Cherokees' Struggle for Sovereignty, 1839–1880* for an account of this same type of struggle in the same period among the Creeks' neighbors.

48. Champagne, *Social Order and Political Change*, 230–233; Interview of Jimmie Barnett, I-PH, 5:381.

49. Champagne, *Social Order and Political Change*, 230–233.

50. Ibid.; Interview of Samuel J. Haynes, I-PH, 40:330–331.

51. Champagne, *Social Order and Political Change*, 231.

52. Union McIntosh may have been the "Una" McIntosh described as a supporter of Opothle Yahola in 1861. San[d]s to Central Superintendent Enoch Hoag, September 9, 1871, Letters Received, Office of Indian Affairs, Record Group 75 (hereafter cited as LR OIA), M856, reel 41.

53. Checote to Hoag, August 31, 1872, LR OIA, M856, reel 41.

54. Agent E. R. Roberts to Hoag, May 29, 1873, LR OIA, M856, reel 41; Roberts to Hoag, June 26, 1873, LR OIA, M856, reel 41.

55. Interview of Thomas Barnett, I-PH, 4:408.

56. Baird, *A Creek Warrior*, 133–134.

57. Interview of Polly Barnett, I-PH, 5:402–403; Debo, *The Road to Disappearance*, 202–203; Roberts to the Commissioner of Indian Affairs, July 21, 1873, Angie Debo Collection, Special Collections, Edmon Low Library, Oklahoma State University, Stillwater, Oklahoma (hereafter cited as ADC), microfilm, folder 20, box 38, OSU Debo 75.

58. Interview of Polly Barnett, I-PH, 5:402–403.

59. McLoughlin, *After the Trail of Tears*, 153ff; Interview of Timothy Barnett, Jr., I-PH, 5:412.

60. Roberts to Commissioner of Indian Affairs, July 21, 1873, ADC, folder 20, box 38, OSU Debo 75.

61. For a discussion of economic development on a territorial scale, see H. Craig Miner, *The Corporation and the Indian: Tribal Sovereignty and Industrial Civilization in Indian Territory, 1865–1907*.

62. R. M. Loughridge and David M. Hodge, *English and Muskogee Dictionary: Collected from Various Sources and Revised; To Keep the Drum, To Tend the Fire: History and Legends of Thlopthlocco*, 12.

63. McLoughlin, *After the Trail of Tears*, 75–76.

64. Champagne, *Social Order and Political Change*, 230–233; John Bartlett Meserve, "Chief Isparhechar," 54–56, 57.

65. Resolutions and Acts of Council, Creek Nation, 1873–1876, vol. 2, OHS, Section X, 84-42, microfilm, 121–122.

66. OHS, Section X, 84-42, microfilm, 119–124; Champagne, *Social Order and Political Change*, 233.

67. James McHenry, of Scots-Creek descent, earned the fifteen hundred dollar price on his head during the Creek War of 1836, but in the Indian Territory he was converted to Christianity and became an ordained Methodist minister. "James McHenry" file, Alice Robertson Papers, OHS, box 1, 82–86.

68. Petition to the Chief [Coachman], July 28, 1877, CRN 32555, 32557; *The Indian Journal* (Eufaula and Muskogee, Creek Nation), July 17, 1879.

69. *The Indian Journal* (Eufaula and Muskogee, Creek Nation), July 17, 1879.

70. *The Indian Journal* (Eufaula and Muskogee, Creek Nation), August 7, 1879.

71. Debo, *The Road to Disappearance*, 201–202, 213–227, 245–248. See Richard A. Sattler, "Seminoli Italwa," for a discussion of the roles of the *horre haponaya* (war speaker), *asimponaya* (speaker), and *yvtekv* (interpreter)—traditional positions reflected in the role of the nineteenth-century delegates.

72. John Bartlett Meserve, "Chief Isparhecher," 75–76; Interview of Samuel J. Haynes, I-PH, 40:316–317.

73. Grayson, Stidham, McCombs, and McIntosh to Itschas Harjo, August 27, 1881, CRN 28291.

74. Champagne, *Social Order and Political Change*, 234–235; Debo, *The Road to Disappearance*, 249, 251–253, 268–272, 274–278; Checote to Grayson and L. C. Perryman, January 16, 1883, Grayson Family Collection, Western History Collection (hereafter cited as GFC WHC), V-16; Interview of Will H. Robison, I-PH, 77:243–244; Interview of Alex Berryhill, I-PH, 7:388; Interview of Samuel J. Haynes, I-PH, 40:317–318.

75. "Battle Creek," Works Progress Administration Historic Sites and Federal Writers Project, WHC, folder 6, box 25; Meserve, "Chief Isparhecher," 62; Checote to G. W. Grayson and L. C. Perryman, January 2, 1883, GFC WHC, V-16.

76. *The Indian Journal* (Eufaula and Muskogee, Creek Nation), December 28, 1882, February 22, 1883; Checote to G. W. Grayson and L. C. Perryman, January 2, 1883, January 16, 1883, GFC WHC, V-16; Interview of Samuel J. Haynes, I-PH, 40:310; Interview of Lena Benson Tiger, I-PH, 91:67.

77. *The Indian Journal* (Eufaula and Muskogee, Creek Nation), December 28, 1882; Checote to G. W. Grayson and L. C. Perryman, January 2, 1883, January 16, 1883, GFC WHC, V-16; Alice M. Robertson, "The Last Christmas at Tulla-hassee," from "The Muskogee Nation," a manuscript at the OHS, Section X; Meserve, "Chief Isparhecher," 64–65.

78. *The Indian Journal* (Eufaula and Muskogee, Creek Nation), January 25, 1883; Turner, "Events Among the Muskogees," 29–30.

79. Turner, "Events Among the Muskogees," 29–30; Checote to Grayson and L. C. Perryman, February 2, 1883, GFC WHC, V-16.

80. Checote to Grayson and L. C. Perryman, February 2, 1883, GFC WHC, V-16; *The Indian Journal* (Eufaula and Muskogee, Creek Nation), February 22, April 5, 1883.

81. Checote to Grayson and Perryman, January 2, 16, February 2, 27, 1883, GFC WHC, V-16.

82. Baird, *A Creek Warrior*, 156.

83. Vore to Grayson, February 20, 1883, GFC WHC, V-9.

84. Grayson to Checote, February 17, 1883, quoted in Meserve, "Chief Isparhecher," 61n–62n.

85. *The Indian Journal* (Eufaula and Muskogee, Creek Nation), April 5, 1883; Debo, *The Road to Disappearance*, 275–277.

86. Grayson and Larney, "The Creek People," *The Indian Journal* (Eufaula and Muskogee, Creek Nation), July 26, 1883.

87. Report of Isparhechar to the Creek National Council, October 8, 1884, CRN 29934; Checote to Grayson and Larney, June 15, July 11, 1883, GFC WHC, VI-17.

88. Debo, *The Road to Disappearance*, 279–280; Chief Checote to Grayson and James Larney, June 15, 1883, GFC WHC, I-17.

89. Reports of Election Count of October 8, 1883, October 12 and December 4, 1883, Division of Manuscripts Collection, WHC, box 1.

90. [G.W.G.], "Manuscript Report of Election Count, Muskogee, Creek Nation, October 8, 1883," December 4, 1883, Division of Manuscripts Collection, WHC, box 1.

91. CRN 29907; Commission of G. W. Grayson to serve as a delegate, approved October 18, 1882, GFC WHC, V-34; Baird, *A Creek Warrior*, 159.

92. Baird, *A Creek Warrior*, 158–161.

93. Ibid., 161.

94. Teller to the Commissioner of Indian Affairs, February 27, 1884, CRN 23, 35506; Baird, *A Creek Warrior*, 161.

95. Perryman to Grayson, July 7, 1884, GFC WHC, VII-26.

96. Baird, *A Creek Warrior*, 161–162; Report of Isparhechar to the National Council, October 8, 1884, CRN 29934.

97. See various commissions, GFC WHC, IV-12, IV-13, IV-15, V-6.

98. See, for example, the following from Office of Indian Affairs, Letters Received, Department of the Interior, 1881–1907, National Archives, Washington, D.C.: Grayson to Commissioner of Indian Affairs H. Price, July 12, 1884, 1884-13146; Commission of the Creek Delegates, December 1, 1885, 1885-30524; Grayson and Porter to J. D. C. Atkins, January 5, 1887, 1887-868; Porter and Grayson to Atkins, January 21, 1887, 1887-2144; Grayson and Isparhechar to Atkins, February 14, 1888, 1888-4348; Grayson and Isparhechar to Atkins, March 29, 1888, 1888-8392.

99. Commission of Creek delegates, December 1, 1885, GFC WHC, IV-2.

100. See an article signed by Creek delegates G. W. Grayson, Coweta Micco, and Ward Coachman; Moses Keokuk and William Hurr for the Sac and Foxes; and G. W. Harkins and H. F. Murray for the Chickasaws reprinted from *The Evening Post* (New York?) in the *Atoka Independent* (Atoka, Choctaw Nation), June 5, 1886; Grayson to Alice Robertson, February 17, 1883, Alice M. Robertson Papers, Special Collections, McFarlin Library, Tulsa University, Tulsa, Oklahoma (hereafter cited as ARP), folder 592, box 12. The delegates of the Five Civilized Tribes in 1888 included George W. Harkins, W. P. Boudinot, L. B. "Hooley" Bell, Spahecha, B. W. Carter, George Sanders, and Stan W. Gray in addition to Grayson. "Indian Delegation," *The Cherokee Advocate* (Tahlequah, Cherokee Nation), May 23, 1888.

101. The Cherokee Advocate (Tahlequah, Cherokee Nation), April 4, 1888.

102. Ibid.

103. The commissions of the delegates in 1885 stated that the four had been chosen owing "to the peculiar interest of a portion of our citizens growing out of their allegiance to the United States during the last rebellion." LR OIA, 1885-30524. Debo, *The Road to Disappearance*, 312; "Indian Delegation," *The Cherokee Advocate* (Tahlequah, Cherokee Nation), May 23, 1888; Meserve, "Chief Isparhecher," 71, 75.

104. Baird, *A Creek Warrior*, 154–155.

105. Ibid., 156; Mildred Fuller Ewens, interview by author, Eufaula, Oklahoma, October 9–10, 1989. Grayson's correspondence from Washington often bore the letterheads of these hotels.

106. G. W. Grayson, untitled manuscript.

107. Interview of Eloise Grayson Smock, I-PH, 85:369.

108. Mrs. G. W. Grayson to Alice Robertson, January 22, 1923, ARP, number 1851, box 20.

109. Contract between the heirs of Walter Grayson and J. W. Smith and R. A. Burton, April 25, 1884, LR OIA, 1884-13480.

110. J. W. White and R. A. Burton to Commissioner of Indian Affairs J. D. C. Adkins, July 22, 1886, LR OIA, 1888-19456.

111. Contract between G. W. Grayson and J. B. Luce, July 10, 1886, LR OIA, 1886-26857.

112. Telegram from Captain [Richard] Pratt to the Commissioner of Indian Affairs, January 25, 1888, LR OIA, 1888-2287.

113. Baird, *A Creek Warrior*, 149, 151; *The Cherokee Advocate* (Tahlequah, Cherokee Nation), May 23, 1888.

114. Baird, *A Creek Warrior*, 151.

115. Grayson to the National Council, October, 1881, CRN 37, 30780.

116. The terminology, "alien flood," frequently occurred in Indian correspondence of the day. Hoig, *David L. Payne*, 216–217; Debo, *The Road to Disappearance*, 330–331. Full-length studies of the humanitarian reformers include Francis Paul Prucha, *American Indian Policy in Crisis: Christian Reformers and the Indian, 1865–1900* and Robert Keller, *American Protestantism and United States Indian Policy, 1869–1882.*

117. Baird, *A Creek Warrior*, 163–164.

118. Choctaw Governor Isaac L. Garvin, inaugural address, October 8, 1878, Records of the Principal Chiefs, Choctaw National Records, OHS, M235, reel 53.

119. G. W. Stidham, "What G. W. Stidham Thinks of Vest's Oklahoma Bill," *The Indian Journal* (Eufaula and Muskogee, Creek Nation), January 8, 1880.

120. Debo, *The Road to Disappearance*, 235–239.

121. Testimony before the Senate Investigating Committee, CRN 35, 18E.

122. Ibid., 27E–32E.

123. Debo, *The Road to Disappearance*, 239.

124. Testimony of G. W. Grayson, *Senate Reports*, vol. 4, *Indian Territory Affairs*, SR 1278, 190.

125. *The Indian Journal* (Eufaula and Muskogee, Creek Nation), March 19, 1885.

126. Ibid.

127. *The Indian Journal* (Eufaula and Muskogee, Creek Nation), January 28, February 25, March 12, 1886.

128. *Atoka (Choctaw Nation) Independent*, June 5, 1886.

129. "Compact between the Several Tribes of the Indian Territory," CRN 37, 30844. Jeffrey Burton called this compact the first formal instrument of diplomacy associating the Five Civilized Tribes with each other and some of the Plains tribes. See Jeffrey Burton, *Indian Territory and the United States, 1866–1906: Courts, Government, and the Movement for Oklahoma Statehood*, 102.

130. *The Indian Journal* (Eufaula and Muskogee, Creek Nation), July 8, 1886.

131. Ibid., January 5, 1887.

132. Ibid., January 12, May 5, 1887.

133. Ibid., May 5, June 9, June 23, July 28, 1887.

134. Debo, *The Road to Disappearance*, 321–322; *The Indian Journal* (Eufaula and Muskogee, Creek Nation), June 9, 1887.

135. *The Indian Journal* (Eufaula and Muskogee, Creek Nation), June 9, 1887.

136. Debo, *The Road to Disappearance*, 322.

137. *The Indian Journal* (Eufaula and Muskogee, Creek Nation), January 12, 1888.

138. "Protest of Creek Delegation against the Passage of H. R. 1277," January 27, 1888, ARP.

139. Debo, *The Road to Disappearance*, 314–315; Commissioner of Indian Affairs, *Annual Report to the Secretary of the Interior for the Year 1887* (hereafter cited as AR CIA and year), 104.

140. AR CIA 1887, 104.

141. Ibid.

142. Ibid., 105; *The Indian Journal* (Eufaula and Muskogee, Creek Nation), July 7, 21, 1887.

143. *The Muskogee (Creek Nation) Phoenix*, October 11, 18, 1888; Debo, *The Road to Disappearance*, 344.

144. *The Muskogee (Creek Nation) Phoenix*, March 1, April 19, May 10, August 2, August 16, September 13, November 1, 1888.

145. Pleasant Porter to "Friend Grayson," January 1, 1889, GFC WHC, I-17.

146. *The Muskogee (Creek Nation) Phoenix*, October 25, December 27, 1888, February 14, 1889; Baird, *A Creek Warrior*, 160–161; Porter to Grayson, February 2, 1889, GFC WHC, I-17.

147. Unfortunately, the only surviving documents in this exchange are those Porter addressed to Grayson. Porter to Grayson, January 1, January 23, February 2, 1889, GFC WHC, I-17.

148. Ibid., January 23, 1889.

149. Message of Chief Perryman, 1889, CRN, 23.

150. Porter to Grayson, January 23, 1889, GFC WHC, I-17.

151. *The Muskogee (Creek Nation) Phoenix,* February 28, 1889; Porter to Grayson, February 2, 1889, GFC WHC, I-17.

152. Porter to Grayson, February 2, 1889, GFC WHC, I-17.

153. *The Indian Arrow* (Vinita, Cherokee Nation), November 1, 1888.

154. *The Atoka (Choctaw Nation) Independent,* January 8, 1887.

155. *The Indian Chieftain* (Vinita, Cherokee Nation), March 14, 1889.

156. John W. Morris, Charles R. Goins, and Edwin C. McReynolds, *Historical Atlas of Oklahoma,* Map 48.

157. An unsigned, undated partial document suggests that this was Grayson's aim. GFC WHC, VII-16; *The Muskogee (Creek Nation) Phoenix,* November 22, December 6, 1888, February 14, 1889.

CHAPTER 6. SAVE WHAT WE MAY
OUT OF THE APPROACHING WRECK

1. Owen had immigrated to the Cherokee Nation in 1879. See Kenny L. Brown, "A Progressive from Oklahoma: Senator Robert Latham Owen, Jr." A third candidate was a Captain Hamar or Hammer of Fort Smith, Arkansas. *The Indian Chieftain* (Vinita, Cherokee Nation), January 17, January 31, 1889.

2. Existing documentation provides no evidence of who these "Businessmen of Texas" were, nor does Grayson's personnel file in federal records include any letters of recommendation. Grayson to Parker, April 1, 1889, Office of Indian Affairs, Letters Received, Department of the Interior (hereafter cited LR OIA), National Archives, Washington, D.C. (hereafter cited as NA), 1889-8812.

3. Parker to the Commissioner of Indian Affairs, April 5, 1889, ibid.

4. *The Muskogee (Creek Nation) Phoenix,* April 11, 1889.

5. James T. Grady, ed., *The State of Oklahoma: Its Men and Institutions,* 98; H. F. O'Beirne and E. S. O'Beirne, *The Indian Territory: Its Chiefs, Legislators, and Leading Men,* 122–124; *The Indian Journal* (Eufaula and Muskogee, Creek Nation), May 5, 1887, January 12, 1888; *The Indian Missionary* (Atoka, Choctaw Nation), January, 1888.

6. Lonie died in 1894. Anna was the "Indian maiden" in the symbolic wedding of the Indian and Oklahoma territories enacted on statehood day, 1907. "The Stidham Family," Vertical File, Oklahoma Historical Society, Oklahoma City, Oklahoma (hereafter cited as OHS); *The Daily Oklahoman* (Oklahoma City, Oklahoma), November 17, 1957; Mildred Fuller Ewens, interview by author, Eufaula, Oklahoma, October 9–10, 1989.

7. "Sour Grapes," *The Muskogee (Creek Nation) Phoenix,* November 1, 1888.

8. Ibid; *The Muskogee (Creek Nation) Phoenix*, October 25, 1888.

9. Perryman to the National Council, October 17, 1889, Creek National Records, OHS, microfilm (hereafter cited as CRN and reel number), 40, 34093; "Sour Grapes," *The Muskogee (Creek Nation) Phoenix*, November 1, 1888.

10. "Sour Grapes," *The Muskogee (Creek Nation) Phoenix*, November 18, 1888.

11. *The Muskogee (Creek Nation) Phoenix*, November 15, 29, 1888.

12. *The Indian Journal* (Eufaula and Muskogee, Creek Nation), January 3, 1889; *The Muskogee (Creek Nation) Phoenix*, December 20, 1888; *The Indian Chieftain* (Vinita, Cherokee Nation), December 22, 1888.

13. *The Indian Arrow* (Vinita, Cherokee Nation), January 10, 1889.

14. *The Indian Journal* (Eufaula and Muskogee, Creek Nation), November 14, 1889.

15. *The Muskogee (Creek Nation) Phoenix*, May 9, 1889. Bennett owned the *Muskogee Phoenix* until 1893. "Leo E. Bennett," in Grady, *The State of Oklahoma*, 98. See H. Craig Miner, *The Corporation and the Indian: Tribal Sovereignty and Industrial Civilization in Indian Territory, 1865–1907* for a discussion of the range cattle industry.

16. Agent W. D. Myers to the Commissioner of Indian Affairs, May 13, 1889, LR OIA, 1889-13332.

17. Owen to Whom It May Concern, April 23, 1889, LR OIA, 1889-13332.

18. The Dawes Commission visited the tribes to whom the Dawes Act applied to persuade them to accept and choose allotments as the preliminary steps to opening their reservations. Myers to the Commissioner of Indian Affairs, May 13, 1889, ibid.

19. Ibid.; *The Indian Arrow* (Vinita, Cherokee Nation), July 25, 1889; *The Muskogee (Creek Nation) Phoenix*, July 25, August 1, 1889.

20. *The Muskogee (Creek Nation) Phoenix*, August 22, 1889.

21. W. David Baird, ed., *A Creek Warrior for the Confederacy: The Autobiography of Chief G. W. Grayson*, 150.

22. *The Muskogee (Creek Nation) Phoenix*, August 22, 1889.

23. Baird, *A Creek Warrior*, 150.

24. Myers to the Commissioner of Indian Affairs, August 17, 1889, LR OIA, 1889-23707.

25. Ibid. Only a wrapper referring to a contract has survived among documents at the National Archives. Grayson had worked with Crawford in 1884 when the latter was hired as Creek attorney by the Creek delegates. Grayson to Chief J. M. Perryman, July 18, 1884, CRN 50, 39223; Baird, *A Creek Warrior*, 149–150.

26. *The Muskogee (Creek Nation) Phoenix*, August 22, 1889.

27. Ibid., August 1, 1889.

28. Ibid.; *The Indian Journal* (Eufaula and Muskogee, Creek Nation), July 3, 1889.

29. *The Indian Journal* (Eufaula and Muskogee Creek Nation), September 12, 1889. See chapter 4.

30. Ibid., June 27, 1889; *The Indian Arrow* (Vinita, Cherokee Nation), April 25, August 8, 1889.

31. *The Muskogee (Creek Nation) Phoenix*, May 16, 1889.

32. Ibid., June 6, 1889.

33. *The Indian Arrow* (Vinita, Cherokee Nation), August 8, 1889; *The Muskogee (Creek Nation) Phoenix*, August 22, 1889; Special Session, June 19–22, 1889, Journal of the House of Kings, CRN 8, 23–28.

34. *The Muskogee (Creek Nation) Phoenix*, August 1, August 29, 1889; Acting Commissioner of Indian Affairs R. V. Beer to United States Special Indian Agent Robert S. Gardner, June 24, 1889, Letter Book, Correspondence, Land Division, Office of Indian Affairs, Record Group 75, NA, LB 186/223, vol. 65; *The Indian Arrow* (Vinita, Cherokee Nation), June 6, July 25, August 29, 1889.

35. Bennett to the Commissioner of Indian Affairs, September 21, 1889, Commissioner of Indian Affairs, *Annual Report, 1890*, 209 (hereafter cited as AR CIA and year).

36. *The Indian Arrow* (Vinita, Cherokee Nation), August 8, 1889; *The Muskogee (Creek Nation) Phoenix*, June 27, September 19, 1889.

37. Bennett to the Commissioner of Indian Affairs, September 21, 1889, AR CIA 1889, 209.

38. *The Muskogee (Creek Nation) Phoenix*, September 12, 1889.

39. Bennett to the Commissioner of Indian Affairs, September 21, 1889, AR CIA 1889, 203–204.

40. Bennett to the Commissioner of Indian Affairs, December 5, 1889, LR OIA, 1890-9993. Ex-Congressman Zack Taylor of Tennessee reportedly conferred with Secretary of the Interior Noble about his employment as the special investigator. *The Indian Arrow* (Vinita, Cherokee Nation), July 25, 1889.

41. "Leo E. Bennett," in Grady, *The State of Oklahoma*, 98.

42. *The Muskogee (Creek Nation) Phoenix*, April 25, 1889.

43. *Special Census Bulletin*, Angie Debo Collection, Special Collections, Oklahoma State University, Stillwater, Oklahoma (hereafter cited as ADC), 10, folder 31, box 39, R77.

44. Stidham to Col. [Samuel] Chekote Dear Relative," June 2, 1881, CRN 43, 35725.

45. Grayson and D. M. Hodge to Commissioner of Indian Affairs Hiram Price, March 22, 1884, Grayson Family Collection, Western History Collection, University of Oklahoma, Norman, Oklahoma (hereafter cited as GFC WHC), VI-12.

46. The Creek delegates [George W. Grayson, Samuel Checote, D. M. Hodge, and Spahecha] to Commissioner of Indian Affairs H. Price, February 18, 1884, CRN 50, 39191, and March 1, 1884, CRN 50 39198; Grayson and Hodge to Price, March 22, 1884, CRN 50, 39208.

47. *The Muskogee (Creek Nation) Phoenix*, April 11, 1889.

48. Ibid., September 26, 1889.

49. Ibid., October 3, 1889.

50. Ibid., April 25, 1889.

51. Samuel Callahan, quoted ibid., June 14, 1888.

52. Ibid.

53. Ibid., November 28, 1889.

54. G. W. Grayson, quoted ibid., October 3, 1889.

55. Grayson to N. B. Moore, April 26, 1890, Special Collections, McFarlin Library, Tulsa University, Tulsa, Oklahoma, number 847, box 14.

56. Grayson to N. B. Moore, May 9, 1890, Special Collections, McFarlin Library, number 850, box 14.

57. See particularly ADC, file 36, box 39, R79.

58. Grayson to President Cleveland, January 15, 1893, LR OIA, 1894-4321.

59. Porter and McKellop, circular, February 9, 1893, CRN 35, 29991.

60. The other Osage representatives were Black Dog, Peter BigHeart, and James BigHeart. *The Indian Journal* (Eufaula and Muskogee, Creek Nation), February 22, 1894.

61. Ibid.

62. Ibid., February 22, 1894.

63. Ibid.

64. Ibid., April 12, 1894.

65. Ibid., March 1, 1894.

66. Bennett in the "Report of Union Agency," September 10, 1890, AR CIA 1890, 89.

67. *The Indian Journal* (Eufaula and Muskogee, Creek Nation), January 30, 1890; Judge E. R. Lerblance to J. P. Davison, January 3, 1890, CRN 30, 26581; Lerblance to Legus Perryman, January 11, 1890, CRN 30, 26582; AR CIA 1892, 251; "Leo E. Bennett," in Grady, *The State of Oklahoma*, 98.

68. Debo, *The Road to Disappearance*, 346, 348.

69. *The Vinita (Cherokee Nation) Chieftain*, quoted in *The Indian Journal* (Eufaula and Muskogee, Creek Nation), March 1, 1894.

70. *The Indian Journal* (Eufaula and Muskogee, Creek Nation), March 8, April 5, 1894.

71. Ibid., October 12, 1894.

72. Ibid., November 16, 1894.

73. Ibid., December 21, 1894, February 15, 1895. During this period, Grayson's brother Sam, Creek national treasurer, was impeached and forced to resign in connection with the unauthorized issuance of warrants. Debo concludes that his wrongdoing was "irregular, but not necessarily dishonest." Debo, *The Road to Disappearance*, 326–327, 358–359.

74. Delegates Grayson and Spahecha to Commissioner H. Price, June 13, 1884, CRN 42, 34792; "Wash" to "Friend Fisher," June 21, 1884, CRN 35, 29927; Wash Grayson to Chief [Joseph] Perryman, June 25, 1884, CRN 35, 29928.

75. Clarence W. Turner, "Events Among the Muskogees During Sixty Years," 31–32.

76. "Cattle 1890," ADC, R79, folder 39, box 17.

77. Message of Chief Legus Perryman, October 1, 1889, Mile Square Pasture Act, October 26, 1889, ADC, folder 36, box 39, R79. See permits of Pleasant Porter, S. B. Callahan, E. H. Lerblance, and William E. Gentry, CRN 42, 36960, 35002, 35003. See also CRN 42, 34912, 34913, 34918, 39775, 34905, and 34908.

78. Debo, *The Road to Disappearance*, 336–343; Interview of Mrs. R. M. Tiger, "Indian-Pioneer History," Works Progress Administration, University of Oklahoma, Norman, Oklahoma, microfiche (hereafter cited as I-PH), 91:83–85; *The Muskogee (Creek Nation) Phoenix*, May 16, 1889; Turner, "Events among the Muskogees During Sixty Years," 31–32.

79. *The Indian Journal* (Eufaula and Muskogee, Creek Nation), June 8, 1895.

80. Ibid.

81. Bond for Sam Grayson for $80,000 as Creek National Treasurer, December 5, 1891, CRN 51, 39350; Harold Grayson Hoppe, "In Re Grayson: A Critical View from a Native American Perspective."

82. Arrell M. Gibson, *The American Indian: Prehistory to the Present*, 502; Debo, *The Road to Disappearance*, 361.

83. *The Indian Journal* (Eufaula and Muskogee, Creek Nation), March 15, 29, 1895.

84. Ibid., April 5, 1895.

85. Ibid., June 8, 1895.

86. Duane Champagne, *Social Order and Political Change: Constitutional Government among the Cherokee, the Choctaw, the Chickasaw, and the Creek*, 235; John Bartlett Meserve, "Chief Isparhecher," 72–75; *The Muskogee (Creek Nation) Phoenix*, May 20, 1897; Harriet Turner Porter Corbin, *A History and Genealogy of Chief William McIntosh Jr. and His Known Descendants*, 85; Interview of Mildred McIntosh Childers, I-PH, 17:414–415.

87. Debo, *The Road to Disappearance*, 364–365, 371; William E. Unrau, *Mixedbloods and Tribal Dissolution: Charles Curtis and the Quest for Indian Identity*, 119–124.

88. House, "Creek-Dawes Agreement," Document Number 5, 55th Cong., 3rd sess., Indian Affairs, Department of the Interior, *Annual Report for the Fiscal Year Ended June 30, 1898*, 448; Address of Spahecha to the National Council, August 24, 1897, GFC WHC, VII-29.

89. Debo, *The Road to Disappearance*, 372.

90. *The Indian Journal* (Eufaula and Muskogee, Creek Nation), August 26, 1898.

91. Ibid., August 18, 1898.

92. Grayson to Commissioner of Indian Affairs William A. Jones, November 4, 1898, LR OIA, 1898-50457.

93. Harold O. Hoppe, "The Dissolution of a Nation: A Muscogee Retrospective," 26.

94. Debo, *The Road to Disappearance*, 324–325, 361; Election returns of September 3, 1895, CRN 34, 29586.

95. Election returns of 1899, CRN 23, 35654; Champagne, *Social Order and Political Change*, 236–237.

96. Election returns for the House of Warriors, September 20, 1897, GFC WHC, V-31; "James McHenry" file, Alice Robertson Papers, OHS, box 1, 82–86; Documents of October 14, November 24, November 25, December 1, 1899, Creek Indian Memorial Association Collection, OHS; Carselowey Collection, I-PH, 103:156.

97. "Okmulgee, Indian Territory," 1898, 1901, Fire Insurance Maps, OHS; *The Okmulgee (Oklahoma) Daily News*, December 3, 1920.

98. George Reilley Hall, "The Old Council House," *Oklahoma City Times*, May 13, 1935. Copyright 1935, Oklahoma Publishing Company. Used by permission.

99. Delegates to the International Council at Okmulgee, July 8, 1896, CRN 37, 30869; Statement of expenses of the Executive Office, December 5, 1901, CRN 23, 35671; Laws and Constitution of the Seminole Nation, Seminole National Records, OHS, microfilm, reel 1, 109.

100. Harold Grayson Hoppe, "In Re Grayson," 15–16.

101. Interview of Samuel Jefferson Checote I-PH, 17:320–321.

102. Applications for Enrollment of the Commission to the Five Civilized Tribes, 1898–1914, OHS, microfilm, reel 327, number 92.

103. 31 Stat. L, 361, included in Charles J. Kappler, *Indian Affairs: Laws and Treaties*, 1:730–731, 733, 739.

104. These allotments lay in sections 5, 8, and 17, Range 16 East, Township 10 North. Grayson's land near Henryetta lay in Sections 8 and 16, Range 13 east, Township 11 North. Abstract of the Annual Report of the Commissioner to the Five Civilized Tribes for the fiscal year ended June 30, 1911, Central Classified File, Part 1, Indian Office, Department of the Interior, NA (hereafter cited as CCF), 5-1; E. H. Hastain, *Township Plats of the Creek Nation*, 168–169, 236–237; Census Roll, Coweta Town, Muskogee Nation, Division of Manuscripts Collections, WHC, box 1.

105. James R. Gregory to Chief Isparhechar, July 28, 1899, CRN 23, 32453; Porter to J. Blair Schoenfelt, June 29, 1900, Executive Office Records, CRN 22, 152–156; Daniel F. Littlefield, Jr., *Alex Posey: Creek Poet, Journalist, and Humorist*, 143–147; Champagne, *Social Order and Political Change*, 235–236.

106. *The Daily Chieftain* (Vinita, Cherokee Nation), January 24, 1901; Daniel F. Littlefield, Jr., and Lonnie E. Underhill, "The 'Crazy Snake Uprising' of 1909: A Red, Black, or White Affair?" 307–324; Porter to J. Blair Schoenfelt, June 29, 1900, Executive Office Records, CRN 22, 152–156.

107. "A Pioneer Pays Tribute to the Old Council House," *The Daily Oklahoman* (Oklahoma City, Oklahoma), May 13, 1935.

108. Littlefield and Underhill, "The 'Crazy Snake Uprising'," 307–324; *The Tahlequah (Cherokee Nation) Arrow*, November 21, 1903; *The Indian Journal* (Eufaula and Muskogee, Creek Nation) April 24, 1908; Littlefield, *Alex Posey*, 143–147, 167–168.

109. *The Indian Journal* (Eufaula and Muskogee, Creek Nation), March 8, 1901.

110. Conveyances by the Principal Chief in the Town of Eufaula, November 6, 1903 through August 31, 1907, Indian Territory Division, Department of the Interior, Record Group 48, NA (hereafter cited as ITD), box 12, (1903) 8296, (1905) 1177, (1906) 17762, (1906) 81804, box 12; Ralph William Goodwin, "Pleasant Porter, Tribal Statesman," 46–47, 141–143; AR CIA 1911, 395.

111. *The Indian Journal* (Eufaula and Muskogee, Creek Nation), June 18, 1901.

112. 32 Stat. L, 500, in Kappler, *Laws and Treaties*, 2:762; Department of the Interior, Commission to the Five Civilized Tribes, *Annual Report*, Part II, Annual Reports of the Department of the Interior, 11; Littlefield, *Alex Posey*, 174; Grayson to Ryan, July 4, 1902, ITD, (1902) 4382.

113. *The Indian Journal* (Eufaula and Muskogee, Creek Nation), April 9, 1903.

114. Grayson to Ryan, July 4, 1902, ITD, (1902) 4382.

115. Ibid.

116. *The Indian Journal* (Eufaula and Muskogee, Creek Nation), July 18, 1902.

117. Ibid., July 25, 1902.

118. Wright to the Secretary of the Interior, July 31, 1902, ITD, (1902) 45887.

119. Littlefield, *Alex Posey*, 175–185; Angie Debo, *And Still the Waters Run: The Betrayal of the Five Civilized Tribes*, 118–119.

120. Instructions to the Creek Appraisement Committee, September 20, 1902, ITD, (1902) 7102.

121. Grayson to Porter, November 5, 1902, CRN 37, 31200.

122. Littlefield, *Alex Posey*, 174–175.

123. *The Muskogee (Creek Nation) Phoenix*, January 17, 1901. See also Baird, "Are There 'Real' Indians in Oklahoma?", 12.

124. A particularly interesting and sympathetic refutation of the criticisms of the Creek school system was written by Supervisor Alice Robertson, daughter of two generations of missionaries to the Indian Territory. "Report of Creek School Supervisor," Commission to the Five Civilized Tribes, *Annual Report, 1901*, 306–313.

125. *The Muskogee (Creek Nation) Phoenix*, January 1, 1901.

126. *The Okemah (Creek Nation) Independent*, October 14, 1904.

127. *The Indian Journal* (Eufaula and Muskogee, Creek Nation), December 12, 1902, April 17, 1903; *The Muskogee (Creek Nation) Daily Phoenix*, June 19, 1903.

128. The *Okmulgee Chieftan*, quoted in *The Indian Journal* (Eufaula and Muskogee, Creek Nation), June 5, 1903.

129. *The Indian Chieftain* (Vinita, Cherokee Nation), June 29, 1903.

130. Ibid., June 16, 1903.

131. Littlefield, *Alex Posey*, 154–157.

132. Their relationship was close enough that the Graysons permitted Posey to bury his son Pachina in the Grayson family plot in Greenwood Cemetery, Eufaula, Oklahoma. Mildred Fuller Ewens, interview by author, Eufaula, Oklahoma, October 9–10, 1989; Littlefield, *Alex Posey*, 6.

133. Minnie H. Posey, ed., *Poems of Alexander Lawrence Posey, Creek Indian Bard*, 17–33.

134. *The Indian Journal* (Eufaula and Muskogee, Creek Nation), June 26, 1903.

135. Goodwin, "Pleasant Porter, Tribal Statesman," 162–163; *The Cherokee Advocate* (Tahlequah, Cherokee Nation), July 18, 1903.

136. *The Indian Journal* (Eufaula and Muskogee, Creek Nation), June 29, 1903, quoted in Goodwin, "Pleasant Porter, Tribal Statesman," 164.

137. *The Chelsea (Cherokee Nation) Commercial*, March 14, 1905.

138. *The Holdenville (Creek Nation) Times*, July 20, 1905.

139. The primary work on the Sequoyah Constitutional Convention is by Amos D. Maxwell, *The Sequoyah Constitutional Convention*.

140. "To the Muskogee People," an open letter by Grayson and Porter, February 20, 1906, GFC WHC, VI-16.

141. Baird, *A Creek Warrior*, 163–164.

CHAPTER 7. FALLEN TO THE MERCY OF OTHER POWER

1. J. Leitch Wright, Jr., *Creeks and Seminoles: The Destruction and Regeneration of the Muscogulge People*, 33.

2. Hamlin Garland, "The Final Council of the Creek Nation," 190.

3. The offices of the Union Agent, Indian inspector for the territory, the supervisor and superintendent of schools, revenue inspector for the Creeks and Cherokees, and supervising engineer of the townsite survey were located in the Masonic Building in Muskogee, owned by C. W. Turner and his associates. Turner, of course, was the same white man who made his fortune in the Creek Nation as a merchant, rancher, and close associate of Chief Pleasant Porter. Report for the Agent for Union Agency, Indian Affairs, Part 1, Report of the Commissioner, *Annual Reports of the Department of the Interior for the Fiscal Year Ended June 30, 1901*, (hereafter cited as AR DI), (1902) 220.

4. The original delegation included Grayson, Porter, and Roley McIntosh. Inspector J. George Wright to the Secretary of the Interior, April 13, 1906, Office of Indian Affairs, Letters Received, Department of the Interior, Record Group 75, National Archives, Washington, D.C. (hereafter cited as LR OIA), 1906-34274; *The Indian Journal* (Eufaula and Muskogee, Creek Nation), March 2, 1906.

5. 31 Stat., 861; Angie Debo, *And Still the Waters Run: The Betrayal of the Five Civilized Tribes*, 86–91; Porter to Grayson, June 22, 1907, Grayson Family Collection, Western History Collection, University of Oklahoma, Norman, Oklahoma (hereafter cited as GFC WHC), V-13.

6. In claiming only four years' schooling, Grayson may have been overlooking his relatively unproductive years in Creek neighborhood schools. In noting only three years as a merchant, he was perhaps indicating that he viewed himself as something of a silent partner in Grayson Brothers Mercantile with Sam actually managing it after Wash's political career began in the late 1870s. On, the other hand, he may merely have been mistaken in the time elapsed on both counts. Application Number 2291, Western District of Indian Territory, July 14, 1905, LR OIA, 1905-63909.

7. See Gibson's "Rifle Shots" column, *The Indian Journal* (Eufaula and Muskogee, Creek Nation), March 9, 1906.

8. *The New-State Tribune* (Muskogee, Indian Territory), April 5, 1906; Creek National Attorney M. L. Mott, Presentation to the Commissioner of Indian Affairs, received June 30, 1910, Equalization of Allotments, Central Classified Files, Record Group 75, Bureau of Indian Affairs, NA (hereafter cited as CCF), 33359-1909-Creek-313, Part 1.

William T. Martin, Jr., an employee of the Dawes Commission, was convicted of the theft of the Creek census roll. *The Tulsa (Creek Nation) Daily World*, January 26, 1907.

9. Indian Affairs, Part II, AR DI 1903, 175–176; *The Tulsa (Creek Nation) Daily World*, November 23, 24, 1906.

10. *The Capital News* (Okmulgee, Creek Nation), September 22, 1904.

11. *The Tulsa (Creek Nation) Daily World*, November 24, 1906; W. David Baird, "Are There 'Real Indians' in Oklahoma? Historical Perceptions of the Five Civilized Tribes," 10–12.

12. U.S. Senate, Statement of G. W. Grayson, "Report of the Select Committee to Investigate Matters Connected with Affairs in the Indian Territory with Hearings, November 11, 1906–January 9, 1907," 59th Cong., 2nd sess., 1906–1907, *Senate Reports*, vol. 4, Indian Territory Affairs, 674–682.

13. Ibid., 679–680.

14. *The Tahlequah (Cherokee Nation) Arrow*, September 28, 1907; Betty Tiger Miller, "Moty Tiger," 1307–1309.

15. G. W. Grayson, quoted in Miller, "Moty Tiger," 1308.

16. *The Tahlequah (Cherokee Nation) Arrow*, September 28, 1907.

17. Testimony of Samuel Haynes, Report of the Select Committee to Investigate Matters Connected with Affairs in the Indian Territory, 427–433; Richard Allen Sattler, "Seminoli Italwa: Socio-Political Change Among the Oklahoma Seminoles Between Removal and Allotment, 1836–1905," 51; Unaddressed and unsigned letter, December 3, 1907, GFC WHC, I-2.

18. Members of the Cheto Hacho delegation that winter were Silas Jefferson, Pompey Phillips, Robertson Starr, David Derrisaw, and a Seminole named Kunchar-to-chee. Unaddressed and unsigned letter, December 3, 1907, GFC WHC, I-1.

19. "Removal of Restrictions on Indian Lands in Oklahoma," Hearings Before the Committee on Indian Affairs, House of Representatives, 60th Cong., 1st sess., H.R. 15641, 59.

20. Ibid., 60.

21. Ibid., 60–61, 111.

22. Ibid., 164–165.

23. Ibid., 60.

24. Ibid., 165–166.

25. 35 Stat., 312.

26. Debo, *And Still the Waters Run*, 197. One of the best brief studies of these events is Arrell Morgan Gibson, "The Centennial Legacy of the General Allotment Act," 228–251.

27. Grayson and Johnson E. Tiger to Secretary James R. Garfield, January 13, 1908, I-2, GFC WHC; *The Tahlequah (Cherokee Nation) Arrow*, September 28, 1907; Debo, *And Still the Waters Run*, 64–65.

The Five Tribes Act, 34 Stat., 822, allowed the continuation of the tribal governments indefinitely. In 1904 the council considered creating a "bureau of information" to print the rules and regulations of the "new country." *The Capital News* (Okmulgee, Creek Nation), October 27, 1904.

Creek writer Alexander Posey bought the *Indian Journal* in 1907, but he drowned shortly thereafter in the floodwaters of the North Canadian River. The newspaper passed out of Creek hands but is still published in Eufaula, Oklahoma, and is the oldest continuously published journal in the state. Mary Hays Marable and Elaine Boylan, *A Handbook of Oklahoma Writers*, 77–80.

28. Grayson and Roley McIntosh to the Commissioner of Indian Affairs, December 28, 1905, LR OIA, 1905-104065. Debo notes that the Creeks were the only tribe ever to receive even a partial accounting. Debo, *And Still the Waters Run*, 65, 75, 84–85.

29. Grayson to the Commissioner of Indian Affairs, undated, LR OIA, 1906-17053.

30. Ibid.

31. Debo, *And Still the Waters Run*, 74–75, 84–85.

32. 31 Stat., 861; Wright to the Secretary of the Interior, August 23, 1907, November 25, 1908, CCF, 33359-1909-Creek-313, Part 1.

33. *The Indian Journal* (Eufaula and Muskogee, Creek Nation), February 20, 1903; Resolution of the Creek Council, November 3, 1904, CCF, 33359-1909-Creek-313, Part 1. A good synopsis of the process is Kent Carter, "Snakes and Scribes: The Dawes Commission and the Enrollment of the Creeks," 384–413.

34. Porter, Grayson, and Hodge to the Commissioner of Indian Affairs, February 1, 1907, CCF, 33359-1909-Creek, 313, Part 1.

35. Commissioner of Indian Affairs to the Secretary of the Interior, September 7, 1907, Department of the Interior, Office of the Secretary, Indian Office, Record Group 75, file 5-1, Five Civilized Tribes, NA (hereafter cited as FCT), Acts and Resolutions.

36. Chief Tiger and the Creek delegates to Secretary Garfield, January 13, 1908, FCT, Creek, Tribal Officials, Part 1.

37. Grayson to Secretary Garfield, May 20, 1908, GFC WHC, I-17.

38. Grayson to Garfield, May 25, 1908, Resolution of the Creek National Council, November 5, 1908, CCF, 33359-1909-Creek-313, Part 1; Wright to the Secretary of the Interior, December 1, 1911, FCT, Creek, Tribal Officials, Part 1; Debo, *And Still the Waters Run*, 203–205.

39. Memorandum, Department of the Interior, January, 1909, Acting Commissioner of Indian Affairs R. G. Valentine to the Secretary of the Interior, March 24, 1909, CCF, 33359-1909-Creek-313, Part 1; *The Muskogee (Oklahoma) Phoenix*, April 18, April 19, April 23, 1909; Chief Tiger to Wright, November 24, 1908, Creek National Records, Oklahoma Historical Society, Oklahoma City, Oklahoma, microfilm (hereafter cited as CRN and reel number), 23, 35697.

40. Chief Tiger to the Secretary of the Interior, February 1, 1910, CCF, 33359-1909-Creek-313, Part 2.

41. M. L. Mott's Presentation to the Committee on Indian Affairs, April 30, 1909, Mott to Assistant Secretary Samuel Adams, July 21, 1911, CCF, 33359-1909-Creek-313, Part 2.

42. See various Senate and House bills, CCF, 33359-1909-Creek-313, Part 1; Wright to the Secretary of the Interior, December 1, 1911, Petition from H. M. Harjo to the Secretary of the Interior, July 30, 1912, FCT, Creek, Tribal Officials, Part 1.

43. It is highly likely that Grayson wrote this letter describing his services. Tiger to Wright, November 24, 1908, CRN 23, 35697.

44. Ibid.; F.H.A. to the Secretary of the Interior, November 11, 1912, FCT, Creek, Tribal Officials, Part 1.

45. Petition to the Secretary of the Interior, May 1, 1913, FCT, Creek, Tribal Officials.

46. *The Indian Journal* (Eufaula, Oklahoma), November 14, 1913; *Harlow's Weekly* (Oklahoma City, Oklahoma), January 10, February 14, 1914; Debo, *And Still the Waters Run*, 250–252.

47. *The Indian Journal* (Eufaula, Oklahoma), February 20, 1914.

48. Allen to Commissioner of the Interior Cato Sells, February 20, 1914; blank ballot form, February 19, 1914; First Assistant Secretary A. A. Jones to Chairman John H. Stephens, House Committee on Indian Affairs, April 4, 1914—all in CCF, 33359-1909-Creek-313, Part 2; *Harlow's Weekly* (Oklahoma City, (Oklahoma), February 28, 1914.

49. 38 Stat., 599; Page identified only "Muskogee, Oklahoma, August, 1914," Allen to Sells, August 6, 1914.

50. Wright to the Commissioner of Indian Affairs, August 19, 1914; Official notice from Wright to Field Clerk J. F. Farrar, August 29, 1914; Wright to Sells, August 29, 1914—all in CCF, 3339 (1909) Creek-313, Part 3.

51. *The Muskogee (Oklahoma) Phoenix,* July 11, 1915.

52. *The Indian Journal* (Eufaula, Oklahoma), April 10, 1914.

53. Exhibits in Re Allen Investigation, CCF, 83406-1915-Creek-154, Probate 1, Part 1.

54. The best study of grafting remains Angie Debo's 1940 volume *And Still the Waters Run.* "Richard Clyde Allen," 489–491; Chief Inspector E. B. Linnen to Sells, June 7, 1915, CCF, 83406-1915-Creek-154, Part 1, 1–8, 15–16.

55. Debo, *And Still the Waters Run,* 252–253, 259.

56. The date of the renewal was July, 1914. Affidavit of G. W. Grayson, Exhibits in Re Allen Investigation, June 7, 1915, CCF, 83406-1915-Creek-154, Part 1.

57. Ibid.; Samuel W. Brown Collection, unaccessioned, OHS.

58. Affidavit of G. W. Grayson; Secretary Lane to President Wilson, June 28, 1915; Exhibits in Re Allen Investigation, June 7, 1915—all in CCF, 83406-1915-Creek-154, Part 1.

59. Various telegrams, April 28, April 29, 1915, Billie Bruner to Sells, May 7, 1915, Sells to Bruner, May 10, 1815, CCF, 83406-1915-Creek-154, Part 2.

60. Statement of Sarty Cowe to Special Indian Agent Fred S. Cook, CCF, 83406-1915-Creek-154, Part I; Various letters, May 21, 1915, CCF, 83406-1915-Creek-154, Part 2.

61. Linnen to Sells, June 7, 1915, CCF, 83406-1915-Creek-154, Probate I, Part I, 38–39.

62. Ibid., 47–52; "Unto the Least of These: A Sketch of the Life of the Late Charles Page, Sand Springs, Oklahoma," a pamphlet in the "Oklahoma Biographies—Charles Page" file, Oklahoma Vertical File, Tulsa City-County Library, Tulsa, Oklahoma.

63. R. C. Armstrong to Sells, June 8, 1915, CCF, 83406-1915-Creek-154, Part 3. See also the Samuel W. Brown Collection, OHS.

64. George C. Morgenstern to Sells, May 27, 1915, CCF, 83406-1914-Creek-154, Probate 1, Part 3.

65. R. C. Armstrong to Sells, June 8, 1915, CCF, 83406-1914-Creek-154, Probate 1, Part 3.

66. Bruner to Sells, May 10, 1915, CCF, 83406-1914-Creek-154, Probate 1, Part 3.

67. Linnen to Sells, May 31, 1915, CCF, 83406-1915-Creek-154, Part 3.

68. Exhibits in Re Allen Investigation, June 7, 1915, CCF, 83406-1915-Creek-154, Part 1.

69. Ibid.

70. Affidavit of G. W. Grayson, June 7, 1915, CCF, 83406-1915-Creek-154, Part 1.

71. Ibid.

72. Ibid.

73. Ibid.

74. Ibid., testimony of Frank L. Montgomery, testimony of R. C. Allen.

75. *The Indian Journal* (Eufaula, Oklahoma), July 16, 23, 1915; *The Muskogee (Oklahoma) Phoenix*, July 11, 1915.

76. Sarty Cowe to Sells, June 28, 1915, CCF, 83406-1915-Creek-154, Part 2.

77. Sells to Grayson, June 25, 1915; Sells to Tiger, June 25, 1915; C. W. Lumpkin to Allen, June 23, 1915; Maude Roberts to Sells, June 27, 1915; Lane to Tiger, June 29, 1915—all in CCF, 83406-1915-Creek-154, Part 3.

78. Tiger to the Indian Rights Association, June 25, 1915; Tiger to Owen, June 25, 1915; Roberts to Sells, June 25, 1915—all in CCF, 83406-1915-Creek-154, Part 3.

79. Brosius had come to the Creek Nation in 1903 to investigate allegations of land dealing among federal officials some time before the Bonaparte Investigation. Brosius to Lane, July 9, 1915, CCF, 83406-1915-Creek-154, Part 3.

80. Ibid.

81. Lane to Wilson, June 28, 1915, CCF, 83406-1915-Creek-154, Part 3.

82. C. W. Lumpkin to Allen, July 12, 1915, CCF, 83406-1915-Creek-154, Part 3.

83. Tiger to Lane, July 28, 1915, CCF, 83406-1915-Creek-154, Part 3.

84. Abstract of the Annual Report of the Superintendent for the Five Civilized Tribes for the Fiscal Year Ended June 30, 1916, FCT, Part 3, Annual Reports, General, 8.

85. Congressman James Davenport to Wilson, July 3, 1916; Assistant Commissioner E. B. Merritt to Sells, July 14, 1916—both in CCF, 83406-1915-Creek-154, Part 3.

86. Lane to Wilson, July 19, 1915, Woodrow Wilson Papers, Library of Congress, Washington, D.C., reel 335, 2448.

87. Superintendent to the Five Civilized Tribes Gabe E. Parker to Sells, April 6, 1916, CCF, 25181-1914-Creek-162.

88. Sells to Parker, April 17, 1916, CCF, 25181-1914-Creek-162.

89. Lawrence C. Kelly, "Cato Sells, 1913–1921," 243–250.

90. Sells to Parker, April 17, 1916, CCF, 25181-1914-Creek-162.

91. Allen to Sells, April 30, 1915, CCF, 25181-1914-Creek-162.

92. *The Okmulgee (Oklahoma) Daily News*, December 3, 1920.

93. Grayson to Washington Grayson, March 8, 1916, GFC WHC, VIII-38.

94. Creek Attorney James C. Davis to Sells, October 2, 1920, CCF, 69442-1920-Creek-163; Mildred Fuller Ewens, interview by author, Eufaula, Oklahoma, October 12, 1989; G. W. Grayson, untitled manuscript.

95. Grayson, untitled manuscript; W. David Baird, ed., *A Creek Warrior for the Confederacy: The Autobiography of Chief G. W. Grayson*, 12–13; Grayson to Major John Wesley Powell, May 30, 1889, National Anthropological Archives, Smithsonian Institution, Washington, D.C., manuscript 568-a; Harold O. Hoppe, "The Dissolution of a Nation: A Muscogee Retrospective," ii.

96. John N. Thornton, quoted in Daniel F. Littlefield, Jr., *Alex Posey: Creek Poet, Journalist, and Humorist*, 114.

97. Grayson to Ann Eliza Worcester Robertson, June 9, 1899, Historical Manuscripts, Special Collections, McFarlin Library, Tulsa University, Tulsa, Oklahoma, 1899-992, box 15; "G. W. Grayson," Grant Foreman Collection, OHS, box 6; Albert S. Gatschet, *A Migration Legend of the Creek Indians*, v.

98. Grayson to Powell, May 30, 1889, National Anthropological Archives, manuscript 568-1; G. W. G[rayson], "Opothleyaholo," 141–142; John R. Swanton, "Social Organization and Social Usages of the Indian of the Creek Confederacy," 31–32.

99. Mildred Fuller Ewens, Marshall Foley, Dorothy Follansbee, interviews by author, Eufaula, Oklahoma, March 13, 1990.

100. The names *Tsianina* ("peeping") and *Mitiwohli* ("turning around") were two of Wash and Annie Grayson's contributions to Swanton's study of Creek naming customs. Swanton, "Social Organization," 100; Orlena Grayson Sanger monument, Greenwood Cemetery, Eufaula, Oklahoma; Parker to Sells, December 13, 1920, CCF, 69442-1920-Creek-163; Mildred Fuller Ewens, interview by author, Eufaula, Oklahoma, October 12, 1989, March 13, 1990.

101. At a fishkilling, Creeks pounded a plant called devil's shoestring in the water of a stream or pond. This produced a chemical that stunned the fish, which were then collected, dressed, and fried. The practice was later ruled illegal by the State of Oklahoma. Interview of Sarah Adams, I-PH, 1:222; *The Indian Journal* (Eufaula and Muskogee, Creek Nation), July 3, 1890, December 7, 1894, January 25, 1895, August 26, 1898; Mildred Fuller Ewens, interview by author, Eufaula, Oklahoma, October 12, 1989, March 13, 1990.

102. *Census Bulletin*, ADC, folder 39, box 17, R77, 63.

103. Littlefield, *Alex Posey*, 236–238; *The Indian Journal* (Eufaula, Oklahoma), August 26, 1910.

104. Dorothy Follansbee, interview by author, Eufaula, Oklahoma, March 13, 1990, October 2, 1990; Sanborn Fire Insurance Map, Eufaula, Indian Territory, January 1905, OHS.

105. Application of G. W. Grayson to the United Daughters of the Confederacy, January 1, 1905, Mildred Fuller Ewens, Eufaula, Oklahoma; Mrs. G. W. Grayson, "Why the Five Civilized Tribes Joined the Confederacy," *The Indian Journal* (Eufaula, Oklahoma), June 6, 1913; Mrs. G. W. Grayson, "Confederate Treaties," *The Indian Journal* (Eufaula, Oklahoma), May 9, 1914; *Confederate Veteran* 9 (August 1901): 357; *Confederate Veteran* 25 (September, 1917): 434.

106. Grayson's untitled history of the Creeks is redolent with his sense of the injustice and hypocrisy practiced by Euro-Americans. Mildred Fuller Ewens, interview by author, Eufaula, Oklahoma, March 13, 1990.

After Wash's death Annie continued to read works on Indian affairs and was an early member of the Society of Oklahoma Indians.

107. Washington Grayson probably received his name in 1908 after his first military service. Mildred Fuller Ewens, interview by author, Eufaula, Oklahoma, March 13, 1990; "Creek Dances," Grant Foreman Collection, OHS, box 6; Swanton, "Social Organization," 102, 509–510, 574–577; Grayson to Sells, September 26, 1913, CCF, 116759-13-Union Agency-047.

108. "Lewis Rodman Wanamaker," *Dictionary of American Biography*, ed. Dumas Malone, 19:409–410; *The Indian Journal* (Eufaula, Oklahoma), June 13, 1913.

109. G. W. Grayson, "America's Treatment of the Indians," *The Indian Journal* (Eufaula, Oklahoma), August 14, 1913.

110. Ibid.

111. *Harlow's Weekly* (Oklahoma City, Oklahoma), July 18, 1917.

112. The pertinent federal files are still closed. Tiger died in August 1921 and was buried in the Tiger family cemetery after a three-hour service conducted in the Muskogee language. Miller, "Moty Tiger," 1309. Tiger to the Commissioner of Indian Affairs, October 5, 1917, CCF, 94451, Status File; Presidential commission of George W. Grayson, November 13, 1917, Oath of Office, November 27, 1917, George W. Grayson file, United States Office of Personnel Management, St. Louis, Missouri.

113. George W. Grayson file, U.S. Office of Personnel Management.

114. This commission intended to identify and lift restrictions on competent Creeks so as to allow the Office of Indian Affairs to concentrate its attentions on the truly incompetent. Kelly, "Cato Sells," 248–249; James McLaughlin and J. R. Wise to Lane, January 10, 1918; Grayson to Lane, November 21, 1918; Grayson to Sells, November 7, 1918—all in CCF, 77840-1918-Creek-127, Creek Competency Commission, Part 1.

115. Sells to Lane, May 21, 1918; Acting Superintendent for the Five Civilized Tribes Joe H. Strain to Sells, July 21, 1919; Sells to Senator Robert L. Owen, March 11, 1918;—all in CCF, 16150-09-Creek-340, Creek Council House. The Old Creek Council House is currently a museum belonging to the Creek Indian Memorial Association.

116. Mott, Moty Tiger, Grayson, Haynes, and Johnson E. Tiger to Lane, February 21, 1908, CCF, 28476-1911-Creek-304, Creek-Seminole Boundary.

117. Hitchcock to the President, January 11, 1900, CRN 36, 39726-A; Hitchcock to the Chairman of the Committee on Indian Affairs, House of Representatives, April 9, 1906, CCF, 28476-1911-Creek-304.

118. Grayson to Sells, December 11, 1918, January 8, 1918; Davis to Sells, January 15, 1919, January 21, 1919—both in CCF, 28476-1911-Creek-304.

119. Davis to Sells, January 21, 1919, 28476-1911-Creek-304.

120. Davis to Sells, May 15, 1919, May 19, 1915, "George W. Grayson" file, U.S. Office of Personnel Management.

121. As of Grayson's death in December 1920 the Creek-Seminole boundary question was still unresolved. Davis to Sells, July 25, 1919; Sells to Davis, February 20, 1920—both in CCF, 28476-1911-Creek-304.

122. Davis to Sells, January 7, 1921, CCF, 69442-1920-Creek-163; Wright to the Secretary of the Interior, July 22, 1914; Allen to the Commissioner of Indian Affairs, October 30, 1914; Davis to Grayson, March 27, 1918; Grayson to Sells, March 12, 1919—all in CCF, 81252-1914-Creek-053, Hettie Lena-Emma Coker Case, Part 1.

123. Sam Grayson to Sells, July 7, 1920, CCF, 69442-1920-Creek-163; Grayson to President Wilson, June 28, 1920, "George W. Grayson" file, U.S. Office of Personnel Management.

124. Other contenders were Johnson E. Tiger, James H. Alexander, Samuel Logan, Peter R. Ewing, and William Sapulpa. Davis to Sells, July 21, 1920; Parker to Sells, July 21, 1920; Allen to Sells, January 7, 1921; Samuel B. Haynes and E. B. Childers to the Secretary of the Interior, August 17, 1920; petition of September 29, 1920—all in CF, 69442-1920-Creek-163; *Harlow's Weekly* 20 (February 25, 1921): 6–7.

125. Sam Grayson to Sells, July 17, 1920, CCF, 69442-1920-Creek-163.

126. Grayson, untitled manuscript.

127. Ibid.

128. *Okmulgee (Oklahoma) Daily News*, December 3, December 5, 1920; Mildred Fuller Ewens, interview by author, Eufaula, Oklahoma, March 13, 1990.

129. Allen to Sells, December 6, 1920, CCF, 69442-1920-Creek-163.

130. *The Daily Oklahoman* (Oklahoma City), March 22, 1919; Parker to Sells, December 13, 1920, CCF, 69442-1920-Creek-163.

131. Grayson, untitled manuscript.

CHAPTER 8. NEVERTHELESS INTENSELY INDIAN

1. Margaret Connell Szasz, ed., *Between Indian and White Worlds: The Cultural Broker*, 6, 294–300.

2. Sharon O'Brien, *American Indian Tribal Governments*, 132–135.

3. "Other Destinies, Other Plots: Louis Owens on Native American Novels," 1.

4. Karen I. Blu, *The Lumbee Problem: The Making of an American Indian People*, 25.

5. *The Indian Journal* (Eufaula and Muskogee, Creek Nation), July 7, 1881.

Bibliography

FEDERAL DOCUMENTS

Abert, J. W. *Journal of Lieutenant J. W. Abert, from Bent's Fort to St. Louis in 1845.* 29th Cong., 1st sess., 1845. Senate Executive Document No. 438.

"Applications for Enrollment of the Commission to the Five Civilized Tribes, 1898–1914." Microfilm, Reel 327. Oklahoma Historical Society. Oklahoma City, Oklahoma.

Commissioner to the Five Civilized Tribes. *Annual Report.* Part II. In *Annual Reports of the Department of the Interior,* 1901–1902. Washington, D.C.: Government Printing Office, 1901–1902.

Commissioner of Indian Affairs. *Annual Reports,* 1843–1901. Washington, D.C.: Government Printing Office, 1843–1901.

Department of the Interior. *Annual Reports for the Fiscal Year Ended June 30, 1901.* Washington, D.C.: Government Printing Office, 1902.

Department of the Interior. Indian Office. Five Civilized Tribes Files. National Archives, Washington, D.C.

Department of the Interior. Indian Territory Division. RG 48. National Archives, Washington, D.C.

Department of the Interior. Office of Indian Affairs. RG 75. National Archives, Washington, D.C.
> Central Classified Files.
> Five Civilized Tribes.
> Land Division.
> Letters Received.
> Letters Received, 1824–1881. Microfilm 234.

Records of the Central Superintendency, U. S. Bureau of Indian Affairs, 1813–1878. Microfilm 856.

Records of the Southern Superintendency, U. S. Bureau of Indian Affairs, 1832–1870. Microfilm 640.

Reports of Inspection of the Field Jurisdictions, Office of Indian Affairs. Microfilm 1070.

Goodwin, James E., ed. *The Federal Reporter: Cases Argued and Determined in the Circuit and District Courts of the United States, August–November, 1881*, vol. 8. St. Paul: Minnesota West Publishing Company, 1881.

Grayson, George W. File. United States Office of Personnel Management. St. Louis, Missouri.

Hitchcock, Ethan Allen. "Report on Frauds on Immigrant Indians." In *New American State Papers: Indian Affairs*, vol. 10, 528–530. Wilmington, Del.: Scholarly Resources Inc., 1972.

Kappler, Charles J., ed. *Indian Affairs: Laws and Treaties*. Vols. 1, 3–7, *Laws*, and vol. 2, *Treaties*. Washington, D.C.: Government Printing Office, 1904.

Library of Congress, Washington, D.C. Woodrow Wilson Papers. Microfilm.

National Anthropological Archives. Smithsonian Institution, Washington, D.C.

Swanton, John R. *Early History of the Creek Indians and Their Neighbors*. Bulletin 74. Bureau of American Ethnology. Smithsonian Institution. Washington, D.C.: Government Printing Office, 1922.

———. *The Indian of the Southeastern United States*. Bulletin 134. Bureau of American Ethnology. Smithsonian Institution. Washington, D.C.: Government Printing Office, 1946.

———. "Social Organization and Social Usages of the Indians of the Creek Confederacy." In *Forty-second Annual Report of the United States Bureau of American Ethnology (1924–1925)*. Washington, D.C.: Government Printing Office, 1928.

U.S. House of Representatives. *Annual Report for the Fiscal Year Ended June 30, 1898*. Indian Affairs. Department of the Interior. 55th Cong., 3rd session, 1898. Washington, D.C.: Government Printing Office, 1898.

U.S. House of Representatives. *Hearings before the Committee on Indian Affairs*. H.R. 15641. 60th Cong., 1st sess., 1908.

U.S. Office of Personnel Management, St. Louis, Missouri. George W. Grayson File.

U.S. Senate. "Report of the Select Committee to Investigate Matters Connected with Affairs in the Indian Territory with Hearings, November 11, 1906–January 9, 1907." 59th Cong., 2nd sess. 1906–1907. *Senate Reports*. Volume 4, *Indian Territory Affairs*.

U.S. Senate. *Senate Executive Documents*. Volume 1. 29th Cong., 1st sess., 1845. Washington, D.C.: Ritchie and Heise, 1846.

U.S. Senate. *Senate Executive Documents*. Volume 1. 30th Cong., 1st sess., 1847. Washington, D.C.: Wendell and Van Benthuysen, 1847.

War of the Rebellion: A Compilation of the Official Records of the Union and Confederate Armies. Published under the Direction of the Secretary of War. Series 1: vol. 13; vol. 22, part 1; vol. 34; vol. 41, part 1. Series 4: vol. 1. Washington, D.C.: Government Printing Office, 1880–1901.

Works Progress Administration. "Indian-Pioneer History." Microfiche. Western History Collection. University of Oklahoma, Norman, Oklahoma.

———. Historic Sites and Federal Writers Project. Western History Collection. University of Oklahoma, Norman, Oklahoma.

31 Stat., 861.

34 Stat., 822.

38 Stat., 599.

ARCHIVES AND RECORDS

Edmon Low Library. Oklahoma State University, Stillwater, Oklahoma. Angie Debo Collection.

Gilcrease Institute of American History and Art, Tulsa, Oklahoma.
    Creek Collection.
    Grant Foreman Collection.
    Samuel Bell Maxey Collection.

Jim Lucas Memorial Library, Checotah, Oklahoma. Vertical File.

Library of Congress, Washington, D.C. Woodrow Wilson Papers. Microfilm.

McFarlin Library. Tulsa University, Tulsa, Oklahoma. Special Collections.

Oklahoma Historical Society Archives, Oklahoma City, Oklahoma.
    Alice Robertson Collection.
    Applications for Enrollment of the Commission to the Five Civilized Tribes, 1898–1914.
    Carselowey Collection.
    Cherokee National Records.
    Choctaw National Records.
    Creek Indian Memorial Association Records.
    Creek National Records.
    Fire Insurance Maps.
    Grant Foreman Collection.
    H. F. Buckner Collection.
    Opothleyahola Collection.
    Robert S. Boyd Collection.
    Samuel W. Brown Collection.
    Section X.
    Seminole National Records.

Tulsa City-County Library, Tulsa, Oklahoma. Oklahoma Vertical File.

Western History Collection. University of Oklahoma, Norman, Oklahoma.
    Cherokee Nation Papers. Phillips Collection.
    Division of Manuscripts Collections.
    Enola Shumate Collection.
    Grayson Family Collection.
    Historic Sites and Federal Writers Project.
    Indian-Pioneer History.
    Opothleyahola Collection.
    Peter Pitchlyn Collection.
    Stephen Foreman Collection.

BOOKS AND ARTICLES

Abel, Annie Heloise. *The American Indian as Participant in the Civil War*. Cleveland: Arthur H. Clarke Company, 1919.
————. *The American Indian as Slaveholder and Secessionist: An Omitted Chapter in the Diplomatic History of the Southern Confederacy*. Cleveland: Arthur H. Clarke Company, 1915. Reprint edition, Lincoln: University of Nebraska Press, 1992 (page citations are to the reprint edition).
Baird, W. David. "Are There 'Real' Indians in Oklahoma? Historical Perceptions of the Five Civilized Tribes." *The Chronicles of Oklahoma* 68 (Spring 1990): 4–23.
Baird W. David, ed. *A Creek Warrior for the Confederacy: The Autobiography of Chief G. W. Grayson*. The Civilization of the American Indian Series, vol. 189. Norman: University of Oklahoma Press, 1988.
Ballard, Louis. "Cultural Differences: A Major Theme in Cultural Enrichment." *Indian Historian* 2 (spring 1969): 4–7.
Bass, Althea. *The Story of Tullahassee*. Oklahoma City: Semco Color Press, 1960.
Blu, Karen I. *The Lumbee Problem: The Making of an American Indian People*. New York: Cambridge University Press, 1980.
Boyd, Joel D. "Creek Indian Agents, 1834–1874." *The Chronicles of Oklahoma* 51 (Spring 1973): 37–58.
Braund, Kathryn E. Holland. "The Creek Indians, Blacks, and Slavery." *The Journal of Southern History* 57 (November 1991): 601–636.
————. *Deerskins and Duffels: Creek Indian Trade with Anglo-America, 1685–1815*. Lincoln: University of Nebraska Press, 1993.
Brown, Jennifer S. H., and Jacqueline Louise Peterson. *The New People: Being and Becoming Metis in North America*. Winnipeg: University of Manitoba Press, 1985.
Brown, Kenny L. "A Progressive from Oklahoma: Senator Robert Latham Owen, Jr." *The Chronicles of Oklahoma* 62 (Fall 1984): 232–265.

Burton, Jeffrey. *Indian Territory and the United States, 1866–1906: Courts, Government, and the Movement for Oklahoma Statehood.* Legal History of North American, vol. 1. Norman: University of Oklahoma Press, 1995.

Carter, Kent. "Snakes and Scribes: The Dawes Commission and the Enrollment of the Creeks." *The Chronicles of Oklahoma* 75 (Winter 1997-1998): 384–413.

Cathey, Henry, ed. "Extracts from the Memoirs of William Franklin Avera." *Arkansas Historical Quarterly* 22 (Summer 1963): 99–116.

Champagne, Duane. *Social Order and Political Change: Constitutional Government among the Cherokee, the Choctaw, and the Creek.* Stanford, Calif.: Stanford University Press, 1992.

Coleman, R. B. "Indian Tribes in the Confederate Service." *Confederate Veteran* 23 (February 1915): 73–74.

Confederate Veteran 9 (August 1901): 357.

Corbin, Harriet Turner Porter. *A History and Genealogy of Chief William McIntosh Jr. and His Known Descendants.* Long Beach, Calif.: n.p., 1967.

Crane, Vernor. "The Origin of the Name of the Creek Indians." *Mississippi Valley Historical Review* 5 (December 1918): 339–342.

Debo, Angie. *And Still the Waters Run: The Betrayal of the Five Civilized Tribes.* Paperback edition. Norman: University of Oklahoma, 1989.

———. *The Road to Disappearance: A History of the Creek Indians.* The Civilization of the American Indian Series. Norman: University of Oklahoma, 1941.

Doran, Michael F. "Negro Slaves of the Five Civilized Tribes." *Annals of the Association of American Geographers* 68 (September 1978): 335–350.

DuChateau, Andre Paul. "The Creek Nation of the Eve of the Civil War." *The Chronicles of Oklahoma* 52 (Fall 1974): 290–315.

Duncan, D. W. C., G. W. Grayson, Thomas Cloud, and B. F. Overton. "For the Advocate." *The Cherokee Advocate.* Tahlequah, Cherokee Nation. January 5, 1881.

Edmunds, R. David. *Tecumseh and the Quest for Indian Leadership.* Boston: Little, Brown and Company, 1984.

"Eufaula, Indian Territory, 1905." Sanborn Maps. Oklahoma Historical Society, Oklahoma City, Oklahoma.

Fischer, LeRoy H. *The Battle of Honey Springs.* Oklahoma City: Oklahoma Historical Society, 1988.

Foreman, Carolyn Thomas. "North Fork Town." *The Chronicles of Oklahoma* 29, no. 1 (1951): 79–111.

Foreman, Grant. *Down the Texas Road: Historic Places along Highway 69 through Oklahoma.* Norman: University of Oklahoma, 1936.

———. *The Five Civilized Tribes: Cherokee, Chickasaw, Choctaw, Creek, Seminole.* Norman: University of Oklahoma Press, 1934.

———. *Indians & Pioneers: The Story of the American Southwest before 1830.* The Civilization of the American Indian Series, vol. 14. Norman: University of Oklahoma Press, 1936.

Galloway, Patricia. *Choctaw Genesis, 1500–1700.* Indians of the Southeast Series. Lincoln: University of Nebraska Press, 1995.

Garland, Hamlin. "The Final Council of the Creek Nation." In *Hamlin Garland's Observations on the American Indian, 1895–1905,* edited by Lonnie E. Underhill and Daniel F. Littlefield, Jr. Tucson: University of Arizona Press, 1976.

Gatschet, Albert A. *A Migration Legend of the Creek Indians.* Brinton's Library of Aboriginal American Literature, no. 4. Philadelphia: D. G. Brinton, 1884.

Gibson, Arrell Morgan. *The American Indian: Prehistory to the Present.* Norman: University of Oklahoma, 1980.

———. "The Centennial Legacy of the General Allotment Act." *The Chronicles of Oklahoma* 65 (Fall 1987): 228–251.

———. *The Chickasaws.* Norman: University of Oklahoma Press, 1971.

———. "The Golden Years." In *Oklahoma: A History of Five Centuries.* 2nd ed. Norman: University of Oklahoma Press, 1981.

Gibson, Charles. "What a Change." *The Indian Journal.* Eufaula and Muskogee, Creek Nation. February 21, 1902.

Grady, James T., ed. *The State of Oklahoma: Its Men and Institutions.* Oklahoma City: The Daily Oklahoman, 1908.

Grant, C. L., ed. *Letters, Journals and Writings of Benjamin Hawkins,* 2 volumes. Savannah: The Beehive Press, 1980.

G[rayson], G. W. "Opothleyoholo." In *Handbook of American Indians North of Mexico,* edited by Frederick Webb Hodge. Vol. 2. New York: Pageant Books, 1959.

Grayson, G. W. "America's Treatment of the Indians." *The Indian Journal.* Eufaula, Oklahoma. August 14, 1913.

———. "An Apology." *The Indian Journal.* Eufaula and Muskogee, Creek Nation. July 7, 1881.

———. Application to the United Daughters of the Confederacy for the Southern Cross of Honor, January 1, 1905. Mildred Fuller Ewens. Eufaula, Oklahoma.

———. "A Talk on the White Settler Question." *The Indian Journal.* Eufaula and Muskogee, Creek Nation. June 2, 1881.

Grayson, Wash, and James Larney. "The Creek People." *The Indian Journal.* Eufaula and Muskogee, Creek Nation. July 26, 1883.

Grayson, Mrs. G. W. "Confederate Treaties." *The Indian Journal.* Eufaula, Oklahoma. May 9, 1914.

———. "Why the Five Civilized Tribes Joined the Confederacy." *The Indian Journal.* Eufaula, Oklahoma. June 6, 1913.

Green, Michael D. "Alexander McGillivray." In *American Indian Leaders: Studies in Diversity,* edited by R. David Edmunds. Lincoln: University of Nebraska Press, 1980.

————. *The Politics of Indian Removal: Creek Government and Society in Crisis.* Lincoln: University of Nebraska Press, 1982.

Griffith, Benjamin W., Jr. *McIntosh and Weatherford, Creek Indian Leaders.* Tuscaloosa: University of Alabama Press, 1988.

Hall, George Reilley. "The Old Council House." *The Oklahoma City Times.* Oklahoma City, Oklahoma. May 13, 1935.

Harring, Sidney L. "Crazy Snake and the Creek Struggle for Sovereignty: The Native American Legal Culture and American Law." *The American Journal of Legal History* 34 (October 1990): 365–380.

Hastain, E. H. *Township Plats of the Creek Nation.* Muskogee: n.p., 1908.

Hoig, Stan. *David L. Payne: The Oklahoma Boomer.* Oklahoma City: Western Heritage Books, 1980.

————. *Jesse Chisholm: Ambassador of the Plains.* Niwot, Colo.: University Press of Colorado, 1991.

————. *The Oklahoma Land Rush of 1889.* Oklahoma City: Oklahoma Historical Society, 1984.

————. *Tribal Wars of the Southern Plains.* Norman: University of Oklahoma Press, 1993.

Hudson, Charles. *The Southeastern Indians.* Knoxville: University of Tennessee Press, 1976.

Iverson, Peter. *When Indians Became Cowboys: Native Peoples and Cattle Ranching in the American West.* Norman: University of Oklahoma Press, 1994.

"Journal of the General Council of the Indian Territory." *The Chronicles of Oklahoma* 3 (April 1925): 32–44.

Keller, Robert. *American Protestantism and United States Indian Policy, 1869–1882.* Lincoln: University of Nebraska Press, 1985.

Kelly, Lawrence C. "Cato Sells, 1913–1921." In *The Commissioners of Indian Affairs, 1824–1977,* edited by Robert M. Kvasnicka and Herman J. Viola. Lincoln: University of Nebraska Press, 1979.

King, Jerlena. "Jackson Lewis of the Confederate Creek Regiment." *The Chronicles of Oklahoma* 41 (Spring 1963): 66–69.

Lambeth, David Michael. *The World and Way of the Creek People.* n.p., n.d.

Lemke, W. J. *Early Colleges and Academies of Washington County, Arkansas.* Bulletin Series, no. 6. Fayetteville, Ark.: Washington County Historical Society, 1954.

Littlefield, Daniel F. *Africans and Creeks: From the Colonial Period to the Civil War.* Contributions to Afro-American Studies, no. 47. Westport, Conn.: Greenwood Press, 1979.

————. *Alex Posey: Creek Poet, Journalist, and Humorist.* Lincoln: University of Nebraska Press, 1992.

Littlefield, Daniel F., and James W. Parins. *A Bibliography of Native American Writers, 1772–1924.* Native American Bibliography Series, no. 2. Metuchen, N.J.: The Scarecrow Press, 1981.

Littlefield, Daniel F., Jr., and Lonnie E. Underhill. "The 'Crazy Snake Uprising' of 1909: A Red, Black or White Affair?" *Arizona and the West* 20 (Winter 1978): 307–324.

Loughridge, R. M., and D. M. Hodge. *English and Muskogee Dictionary, Collected from Various Sources and Revised.* N.p., n.d. Reprinted by permission by B. Frank Belvin, General Missionary to Creek and Seminole Indians, Baptist Home Mission Board, Okmulgee, Oklahoma, 1964.

Malone, Dumas, ed. *Dictionary of American Biography.* Volume 19. New York: Charles Scribner's Sons, 1946.

Marable, Mary Hays, and Elaine Boylan. *A Handbook of Oklahoma Writers.* Norman: University of Oklahoma Press, 1939.

Martin, Joel W. *Sacred Revolt: The Muskogees' Struggle for a New World.* Boston: Beacon Press, 1991.

Martini, Don. *Southeastern Indian Notebook: A Biographical-Genealogical Guide to the Five Civilized Tribes.* Ripley, Miss.: Ripley Printing Company, 1986.

Maxwell, Amos D. *The Sequoyah Constitutional Convention.* Boston: Meador Publishing Company, 1953.

McLoughlin, William G. *After the Trail of Tears: The Cherokees' Struggle for Sovereignty, 1839–1880.* Chapel Hill: The University of North Carolina Press, 1993.

Merrell, James H. *The Indians' New World: Catawbas and Their Neighbors from European Contact through the Era of Removal.* Chapel Hill: The University of North Carolina Press, 1989.

Meserve, John Bartlett. "Chief Isparhechar." *The Chronicles of Oklahoma* 10 (March 1932): 50–76.

Miller, Betty Tiger. "Moty Tiger." In *History of Okmulgee County, Oklahoma,* compiled and edited by Okmulgee County Historical Society and the Heritage Society of America. Tulsa: Heritage Enterprises, 1985.

Miner, H. Craig. *The Corporation and the Indian: Tribal Sovereignty and Industrial Civilization in Indian Territory, 1865–1907.* Norman: University of Oklahoma Press, 1976.

Moore, William B., and Fred P. Branson. "Richard Clyde Allen." *The Chronicles of Oklahoma* 36 (Winter, 1958-1959): 489–491.

Morris, John W., Charles R. Goins, and Edwin C. McReynolds. *Historical Atlas of Oklahoma.* Rev. ed. Norman: University of Oklahoma, 1976.

Morton, Ohland. "Reconstruction in the Creek Nation." *The Chronicles of Oklahoma* 9 (June 1931): 171–179.

O'Beirne, H. F., and E. S. O'Beirne. *The Indian Territory: Its Chiefs, Legislators, and Leading Men.* 2 vols. St. Louis: C. B. Woodward, 1892.

O'Brien, Sharon. *American Indian Tribal Governments.* Norman: University of Oklahoma Press, 1989.

"Okmulgee Constitution." *The Chronicles of Oklahoma* 3 (September 1925): 218–228.

Opler, Morris Edward. "The Creek 'Town' and the Problem of Creek Indian Political Organization." In *Human Problems in Technological Change: A Casebook*, edited by Edward H. Spicer. New York: Russell Sage Foundation, 1952.

"Other Destinies, Other Plots: Louis Owens on Native American Novels." *Humanities Interview. A Publication of the Oklahoma Foundation for the Humanities*. 14 (Winter 1997): 1, 3, 10.

"A Pioneer Pays Tribute to the Old Council House." *The Daily Oklahoman*. Oklahoma City, Oklahoma. May 13, 1935.

Posey, Minnie H., ed. *Poems of Alexander Lawrence Posey, Creek Indian Bard*. Rev. ed. N.p.: Okmulgee Cultural Foundation and Five Civilized Tribes Heritage Foundation, 1969.

Prucha, Francis Paul. *American Indian Policy in Crisis: Christian Reformers and the Indian, 1865–1900*. Norman: University of Oklahoma Press, 1976.

Rampp, Lary C., and Donald L. Rampp. *The Civil War in Indian Territory*. Austin, Tex.: Presidial Press, 1975.

"Richard Clyde Allen." *The Chronicles of Oklahoma* 36 (Winter 1958–59):489–491.

Rister, Carl Coke. *Land Hunger*. Norman: University of Oklahoma Press, 1942.

Rohrs, Richard C. "Fort Gibson: Forgotten Glory." In *Early Military Forts and Posts in Oklahoma*, edited by Odie B. Faulk, Kenny A. Franks, and Paul J. Lambert. The Oklahoma Series, vol. 10. Oklahoma City: Oklahoma Historical Society, 1978.

Schoolcraft, Henry R. *Information Respecting the History, Condition, and Prospects of the Indian Tribes of the United States: Collected and Prepared under the Bureau of Indian Affairs*. Archives of Aboriginal Knowledge Series, vol. 1. Philadelphia: J. B. Lippincott, 1860.

Searcy, Martha Condray. "The Introduction of African Slavery into the Creek Indian Nation." *The Georgia Historical Quarterly* 66, no. 1 (1982): 21–32.

Shirley, Glenn. *Law West of Ft. Smith: A History of Frontier Justice in the Indian Territory, 1834–1896*. New York: Henry Holt and Company, 1954.

"Sour Grapes." *The Muskogee Phoenix*. Muskogee, Creek Nation. 1888.

Stidham, G. W. "What G. W. Stidham Thinks of the Vest Bill." *The Indian Journal*. Eufaula and Muskogee, Creek Nation. January 8, 1880.

Sturtevant, William C., ed. "Commentary." In *Eighteenth-Century Florida and Its Borderlands*. Gainesville: University of Florida Press, 1975.

Szasz, Margaret Connell, ed. *Between Indian and White Worlds: The Cultural Broker*. Norman: University of Oklahoma Press, 1994.

To Keep the Drum, To Tend the Fire: History and Legends of Thlopthlocco. Oklahoma City: Mvskoke Publishing Company, 1978.

"Trouble Ahead." *The Indian Journal*. Eufaula and Muskogee, Creek Nation. July 15, 1880.

Turner, Clarence W. "Events Among the Muskogees During Sixty Years." *The Chronicles of Oklahoma* 10 (March 1932): 16–34.

Unrau, William E. *Mixed-bloods and Tribal Dissolution: Charles Curtis and the Quest for Indian Identity.* Lawrence: University of Kansas Press, 1989.

Usner, Daniel H., Jr. "American Indians on the Cotton Frontier: Changing Economic Relations with Citizens and Slaves in the Mississippi Territory." *The Journal of American History* 72 (September 1985): 297–317.

"Wanamaker, Lewis Rodman." In *Dictionary of American Biography,* edited by Dumas Malone. Volume 19. New York: Charles Scribner's Sons, 1946.

Warde, Mary Jane. "Fight for Survival: The Indian Response to the Boomer Movement." *The Chronicles of Oklahoma* 67 (Spring 1989): 30-51.

White, Christine Schultz, and Benton R. White. *Now the Wolf Has Come: The Creek Nation in the Civil War.* College Station: Texas A & M Press, 1996.

Wright, J. Leitch. *Creeks and Seminoles: The Destruction and Regeneration of the Muscogulgee People.* Lincoln: University of Nebraska Press, 1986.

Wright, Muriel H., and LeRoy H. Fischer. "Civil War Sites in Oklahoma." *The Chronicles of Oklahoma* 44 (Summer 1966): 158–215.

NEWSPAPERS AND PERIODICALS

The Arkansian. Fayetteville, Arkansas. 1859.

The Atoka Independent. Atoka, Choctaw Nation. 1886–1887.

The Capital News. Okmulgee, Creek Nation. 1904.

The Chelsea Commercial. Chelsea, Indian Territory. 1905.

The Cherokee Advocate. Tahlequah, Cherokee Nation. 1878, 1880, 1888.

The Daily Oklahoman. Oklahoma City, Oklahoma. 1919, 1935, 1957.

The Fort Smith Herald. Fort Smith, Arkansas. 1848.

Harlow's Weekly. Oklahoma City, Oklahoma. 1914–1915, 1917, 1921.

The Holdenville Times. Holdenville, Indian Territory. 1905.

The Indian Advocate. 1848.

The Indian Arrow. Vinita, Cherokee Nation. 1888–1889.

The Indian Chieftain. Vinita, Cherokee Nation. 1888–1889.

The Indian Journal. Eufaula and Muskogee, Creek Nation; Eufaula, Oklahoma. 1877–1920.

The Indian Missionary. Atoka, Choctaw Nation. 1888.

The Muskogee Phoenix. Muskogee, Creek Nation, later Oklahoma. 1888–1915.

The New State Tribune. Muskogee, Indian Territory. 1906.

The New York Times. New York, New York. 1880.

The Okemah Independent. Okemah, Indian Territory. 1904.

The Okmulgee Daily News. Okmulgee, Oklahoma. 1920.

The Okmulgee Democrat. Okmulgee, Oklahoma. 1920.

The St. Louis Globe-Democrat. St. Louis, Missouri. 1880.

The Sumner County Press. Sumner County, Kansas. 1880.

The Tahlequah Arrow. Tahlequah, Indian Territory. 1903.
The Tulsa Daily World. Tulsa, Creek Nation. 1906.
The Vindicator. Atoka and New Boggy, Choctaw Nation. 1873–1875.

UNPUBLISHED MATERIALS

Colbert, Thomas Burnell. "Prophet of Progress: The Life and Times of Elias Cornelius Boudinot." Ph.D. diss., Oklahoma State University, 1982.

Goodwin, Ralph William. "Pleasant Porter, Tribal Statesman." Master's thesis, University of Oklahoma, 1953.

Grayson, George Washington. Untitled manuscript. David Grayson Hansard. Stewart, Tennessee.

Grayson, Georgianna Stidham. Untitled manuscript. Mary Hansard Knight. Okmulgee, Oklahoma.

Greenwood Cemetery. Inscriptions. Eufaula, Oklahoma.

"Henryetta-Hugh Henry." Henryetta Public Library, Henryetta, Oklahoma. Vertical File.

Hoppe, Harold Grayson. "In Re Grayson: A Critical View from a Native American Perspective." Harold O. Hoppe. Wichita, Kansas.

Hoppe, Harold O. "The Dissolution of a Nation: A Muscogee Retrospective." Harold O. Hoppe. Wichita, Kansas.

———. "The Family of Robert Grierson and Sinoegee." Genealogical chart. Harold O. Hoppe. Wichita, Kansas.

Peterson, Jacqueline Louise. "The People in Between: Indian-White Marriage and the Genesis of a Metis Society and Culture in the Great Lakes Region, 1680–1830." Ph.D. diss., University of Illinois at Chicago Circle, 1981.

"Retrospect of the Life and Character of Napoleon Bonaparte Moore." In *The Muskogee Nation.* Oklahoma Historical Society, Oklahoma City, Oklahoma. N.p., n.d.

Sattler, Richard Allen. "Seminoli Italwa: Socio-Political Change Among the Oklahoma Seminoles Between Removal and Allotment, 1836–1905." Ph.D. diss., University of Oklahoma, 1987.

"Stidham Family." Oklahoma Historical Society. Oklahoma City, Oklahoma. Vertical File.

INTERVIEWS

Alexander, Linda. Interview by author. Stillwater, Oklahoma. October 9, 1996.
Bunney, George. Interview by author. Stillwater, Oklahoma. October 30, 1996.
Carey, James E. Interview by author. Eufaula, Oklahoma. March 17, 1991.

Ewens, Mildred Fuller. Interview by author. Eufaula, Oklahoma. October 9–10, 1989, March 12–13, 1990.

Foley, Marshall. Interview by author. Eufaula, Oklahoma. March 13, 1990.

Follansbee, Dorothy. Interview by author. Eufaula, Oklahoma. March 13, 1990, October 2, 1990.

Isham, Ted. Interview by author. Stillwater, Oklahoma. October 9, 1996.

Index